Capturing the soul
The Vhavenda and the missionaries
1870–1900

Capturing the soul
The Vhavenda and the missionaries
Alan Kirkaldy

PROTEA BOOK HOUSE
PRETORIA
2005

For Albert Wirz
Mentor and Friend
I profoundly miss you, your sense of humour
and your deep commitment to academia and to life.

Capturing the soul
The Vhavenda and the missionaries
Alan Kirkaldy

First edition, first impression 2005
Protea Book House
PO Box 35110, Menlo Park, 0102
protea@intekom.co.za

Typography and design by Ada Radford
Cover design by Tienie du Plessis
Reproduction by PrePress Images, Pretoria
Printed and bound by Paarl Print

ISBN 1-86919-083-1

© 2005 Alan Kirkaldy
© All rights reserved.
No part of this book may be reproduced in any form,
without prior permission in writing from the publisher.

Acknowledgements

Professors Patrick Harries and Nigel Penn acted as supervisors for the Ph.D. thesis at the University of Cape Town from which this book grew. In addition, Professors Norman Duncan, Peter Geschiere and Christoph Marx read and commented on drafts of various sections. So too did Jean Marie Dederen, Murray Hofmeyr, Peta Jones, Premesh Lalu, Heike Schmidt and Virginia van der Vliet. They all influenced the final product. I hope that they are happy with at least some of the directions that I have taken using their ideas as my starting point (and will forgive me for cases where I have not taken their advice!).

Professor Elias Lukhaimane, Felix Malunga, Nkadimeng Mahosi and Rachidi Molapo, my colleagues in the Department of History at the University of Venda (UNIVEN), were extremely supportive. I thank them for the heated debates we have had about issues such as anthropophagy and *vhuloi* and hope that they feel that I have gone far enough in allowing their concerns and criticisms to inform my text.

My research in Germany was made possible by financial assistance from the Deutscher Akademischer Austauschdienst and the National Research Foundation. I thank them for their support. Conclusions reached in this work do not necessarily reflect the views of these institutions.

Thanks to funding organised by Phyllis Ferguson, I was able to present an earlier draft of my chapter on the Mphaphulis to the African Research Seminar at St Antony's. I would like to thank her and Professor Terrence Ranger for the trouble they took in giving detailed comments on my paper and in introducing me to the Oxford library system.

In Germany, I relied heavily on the expertise of the Berlin Mission Society librarians, Frau B. Golz and Frau D. Schmager, and the archivist, Frau B. Lück. They really went out of their way to help me and to make me feel welcome (and make the best coffee in the former GDR). My family and I have extremely fond memories of them and hope that we will be able to repay some of the assistance and hospitality one of these days. Mission-Director Hans Luther also made me extremely welcome. Jürgen Becher and Ulrich van der Heyden assisted me in finding my way around the archives and generally went out of their way to make my stay pleasant and memorable.

Professor Albert Wirz of the Institute for Asian and African Studies at Humboldt University at Berlin acted as my host Professor in Berlin. Beyond giving me office space and computer facilities in his Institute, he personally went out of his way to assist me in settling in and in learning how to use research facilities in Berlin. In regular meetings, we discussed the progress of my research and he bombarded me with fresh insights on how to approach my material. Those who know his ways of reasoning will find his presence clearly in this text. In him and his wife, Tina, I also had a ready hotline which was accessible at any time that I felt tempted to throw myself into the Spree. I thank them both for their assistance and their continuing friendship. I hope that I will find a way of getting a copy of this book to Albert on his long journey on the *African Queen*.

Tessa Kirkaldy read through the final draft, proof-reading and offering editorial suggestions. I thank her for this and for putting up with a husband involved in the final stages of writing. Nine times out of ten, she was more prepared than anybody could reasonably expect to discuss my work (and at least pretend to be interested) in the early hours of the morning with a full day of work ahead. I hereby promise her, Hannah and Benjamin that I will become human again now that this damn thing is finished.

Lastly, I would like to thank my editors, Jeanette Ferreira and Hanli Deysel, whose close reading, detailed comments and assistance made the task of meeting the requirements of a book, rather than a thesis, a relatively painless one.

Table of Contents

INTRODUCTION 11

CHAPTER 1: BACKGROUND AND CONTEXT 15
Dispelling some Persistent Myths 16
Sojourners and Settlers in Vendaland 19
Missionaries 24

CHAPTER 2: LOCAL BEGINNINGS 37
Johannes Mutshaeni and the Vendaland Conventicle 37
David Denga 48
The Arrival of the Missionaries 52

CHAPTER 3: THE MISSION AND ITS MISSIONARIES 79
The Mission 79
The Missionaries 83
The Training 92
Reinhold Wessmann and the Heart of Darkness 94
Klaas Koen – The Ideal Missionary 100

CHAPTER 4: THE LANDSCAPE 121
The Landscape of Vendaland 121

CHAPTER 5: MISSIONARY IMAGES 145
Constructing Vendaland and the Vhavenda 145
God's Gardens in the Heathen Wilderness 150
Fashioning the Colonial Subject 154
"Heathens" 157
Christians 161

CHAPTER 6: ETHNOGRAPHIES OF POWER 167
The Supreme Being and Other Supernatural Entities 168
The *Mahosi* 174
The Ancestors 179
The *Malombo* 182
"Witchery and Witchdoctors" – *Zauberei, Mahosi* and *Dzinanga* 186

CHAPTER 7: THE AFRICAN BODY 203
Vhutuka, *Murundu* and *Vhusha* 203
The *Thondo* 212
Twins 214
Burial Practices and Ritual Homicide 219
Tales of Cannibalism 223

CHAPTER 8: THE MPHAPHULIS 239
Before the Mission – Makwarela Mphaphuli 239
Hopes, Hostilities and Power 243
Makwarela – The Great Hope 249
Makwarela Breaks Free 266

GLOSSARY 281

BIBLIOGRAPHY 285

INDEX 311

TABLES
TABLE 1: Mission Estimates of the Number of Africans in Reach of Vendaland Mission Stations, 1874–1899 28
TABLE 2: Number of Congregants at Vendaland Mission Stations, 1874–1899 29

MAPS
MAP 1: Rulers and Mission Stations in Nineteenth-Century Vendaland
MAP 2: Nineteenth-Century Vendaland and Surrounds
MAP 3: The Zoutpansberg District

IMAGES
1. Reinhold Wessmann
2. Klaas Koen
3. "Missionary Schwellnus"
4. "Crossing a river in Bowenda"
5. Masthead of *Bawenda-Freund*
6. "The Missionary in the Palm-forest"
7. "Ha Tschewasse" (Ha-Tshivhase/Beuster/Maungani)
8. "Tchakoma" (Tshakhuma)
9. "Georgenholtz"
10. "Bawenda [Vhavenda] Children"

TABLE OF CONTENTS

11. "A Northern Transvaal Native Belle"
12. Warrior
13. "THEN: A Native Dance in Vendaland some years ago"
14. "Tshikona Dance in Ngovela at Ha Tschewasse [Ha-Tshivhase]"
15. "Dancing Heathens"
16. "Bawenda Huts"
17. "Out-Station Ha-Begwa"
18. Miryam, wife of Nathaniel, cooking
19. "The Village-Taylor of Beuster"
20. "The Helpers [Native Evangelists] at Tschakoma [Tshakhuma]"
21. "AND NOW: Converts to Civilization in the Zoutpansberg"
22. "Gertrudsburg, 1926, Candidates for Confirmation, Pentecost, 1925"
23. *Ndilo* [Divining bowl]
24. "Cannibal"
25. Audience with *Khosi* Makwarela Mphaphuli

Introduction

The structure that this work has finally assumed has been a product of negotiation – negotiation between myself and academic conventions, the nature of the sources and the voices of the long-dead missionaries and Africans which emerge from the diaries, reports, tractates and books of the Berlin Missionaries. The most strident voices, demanding to be heard, have been those of the missionaries. However, hidden behind this have been the quieter voices of local African rulers and their people. In working with the missionary voice, I have also set out to access the African voice – a voice not heard in this way in other nineteenth century sources. I do not claim to speak on behalf of, or for, anybody. I also do not claim to have recovered or captured the past. However, I believe that I have worked with a view into the past which engages perspectives not discernible in other contemporary sources. In doing so, I have deliberately begun the main body of the work (chapter 2) with African converts to Christianity and ended with an African ruler who attempted to engage with Christianity on his own terms but eventually chose to re-assert his power through the power of African religion.

The "Vendaland conventicle" of Johannes Mutshaeni, Totane (also known as Piet) and Solomon, together with individuals such as David Denga, was converted to Christianity while working as migrant labourers in Natal and the Cape Colony during the 1860s. While some abandoned their new faith, others managed to retain it. To varying degrees, the latter group blended Christianity with aspects of African Religion.

With the arrival of the missionaries, and their commitment to enforcing what they saw as conformity to doctrinally pure Christianity, new tensions were introduced. Those local Christians who transformed their religious beliefs to meet the local context faced censure or excommunication. In addition, with the presence of the new representatives of the Christian God, they suffered a diminution in status – they were now the assistants and interpreters (both cultural and linguistic) of the representatives, rather than the representatives themselves. While Johannes Mutshaeni and David Denga were able to handle this transformation and retain their faith, others – like Solomon – were not. Similarly, those – like Totane – who had managed to achieve power in local structures were not able to accept the subservient position to the missionaries which adherence to their brand of Christianity would have entailed. They either abandoned Christianity completely or formed their own blending of religious beliefs which, they hoped, would enable them to navigate in the local situation in which they found themselves. Christianity may mean different things to different people. It is possible that some previously-converted Christians managed to live a private religious life which successfully achieved a blending of Christianity and African religious beliefs. Similarly, it is likely that a number of those converted by the missionaries and their assistants managed to achieve this. However, at this stage, with the power of Mission Christianity and the power of African Religion challenging each other directly for supremacy, it was impossible to do this publicly. Looking at the situation rather cynically, while the wages of "sin" may have been death, both for the first Native Assistants and some missionaries, the price of serving God was the same.

Having begun in Africa, I move to Germany in an attempt to understand the making of the missionaries who became the recorders of what occurred in Vendaland. Starting with the history and nature of the Berlin Mission Society, I go on to look at the lower-middle and artisan class background and personal biographies of the candidate missionaries and the training that they received in the seminary. In so doing I argue that, on the whole, the Mission was successful in instilling the obedient, petite-bourgeois – and German – mindsets that they set out to develop in these prospective servants of the Lord and representatives of German culture and values. In their training of the missionaries who would serve in Vendaland, the mission authorities failed dramatically in two cases. Carl Stech and Reinhold Wessmann were both expelled from the mission for sexual misconduct. At the other end of the scale, in missionary terms, they succeeded dramatically in transforming the "rude matter" of Klaas Koen, a South African of mixed ancestry, into the ideal German missionary. Wessmann and Koen are the subjects of two case studies, the first revealing the "Heart of Darkness" which was in danger of being exposed when missionaries "went native" and the second just how far one could go in serving the Lord and sacrificing oneself for His greater glory.

Against this background, I return to Vendaland with the missionaries. Here, I look at the ways that they experienced, came to terms with and inscribed themselves on the environment. This leads to discussions of the ways that the missionaries portrayed the landscape textually and iconograpically for themselves, their superiors at home and the wider circle of friends of the mission back in Germany. Their relationship with the environment was a dynamic one and varied over time, depending on the perceived level of hardship and danger that they faced, with the fluctuating fortunes of missionary endeavour, and with their changing relationships with local rulers and their people. At times, they revelled in its beauty and splendour; comparing its natural features, bird and animal life to those of beauty spots in Germany. At other times, they felt threatened by its darkness and impenetrability, its serpents and devouring beasts, and the hidden menace of "fever". In addition to their use of texts and photographs, when "reality" was either not as "dark" or as "light" as the missionaries wished it to be, they called etchings into service to capture the moods and emotions that they wished to engender in their readers.

INTRODUCTION

Hostile as it sometimes was to them, the missionaries saw the inhabitants of Vendaland as being concealed and nurtured by the environment. They wrote of "the dark forests of Bawendaland and the dark hearts of the heathen Bawenda", saw their mission stations as "God's gardens in the heathen wilderness" and portrayed themselves as "pioneers of culture" in the area. However, in order to make converts – (re)fashioning them as Christians and as colonial subjects – they had to draw the local people out of the environment and understand them. In their terms, only by first understanding local ways could they hope to transform them. Examining their attempts to do this, I begin by looking at missionary attempts to transform the bodies, clothing, housing, economic life, and even the musical life of local people. Arising from this, I engage with missionary writings on local beliefs in the supernatural and their impressions and their analysis of the metaphysical and physical bases of the power of local rulers, the ancestors and medico-religious practitioners. I argue that missionary analysis of themes such as these focused around two opposing premises. On the one hand, they wrote about what they saw as the very real power of Satan operating in local engagements with the supernatural. On the other, they cynically described what they interpreted to be manipulation of local "superstitions" by local *mahosi* and *dzinanga* as a means of social control, maintaining and increasing power, and self-enrichment. For the missionaries, conversion thus became as much of a battle over secular power as over religious power – a battle over bodies as well as over souls. Despite the very obvious distorting effects of the missionary gaze here, I found useful material for comparison with other accounts. In addition, these texts provided a useful bridge away from missionaries and back to Africans.

Opposed as they were to these practices, the missionaries reserved their greatest opprobrium for social institutions through which membership of society, and the power of its rulers, was inscribed on, or reflected royal control over, the bodies of subjects. In particular, they focused their criticism on the male initiation schools of *vhutuka* and *murundu* and the female equivalent of *vhusha*. In all of these schools, the body was subjected to hardships and pain. In the latter two, social conformity and submission to authority was inscribed on the body by circumcision and lengthening of the *labia minora* respectively. At a less symbolic level, the power of the ruler was reflected in military conscription and the maintenance of the *thondo* – a military school which also served as a stage of initiation – at his capital.

Some of the missionary opposition to local practices was based on what they saw as purely humanitarian grounds. Thus, they fought against the practice of the killing of twins. In an important test case, they also managed to gain exemption from this practice at Ha-Tshivhase Mission station and, indirectly through this, at the other stations as well. I find it surprising that, during the nineteenth century, the missionaries do not appear to have contested the alleged killing of retainers to accompany members of the royal family in death and other forms of ritual homicide. This I ascribe to local secrecy surrounding such practices. Commoners, even converts to Christianity, either did not know about them or saw them as tabu topics of conversation. Members of the wider royal family may have known about them but would have felt disinclined to discuss them outside royal circles, especially with outsiders. The failure to discuss this certainly did not arise from missionary reticence to expose what they saw as the hidden "darkness" of local society. They were more than prepared to discuss the purported use of human body parts in iron smelting and give credence to the wildest tales of cannibalism. For the missionaries, "cannibalism" became an icon of the "darkness" that they were fighting. They also described in gory detail the fate of slain and captured enemies, which reportedly included the symbolic manipulation and consumption of severed body parts.

I draw all of these themes together in the case study of the interaction between the missionaries and the rulers of the Mphaphuli people which concludes the book. As with the opening chapter, it is here that the African voice again cries to be heard. Even through the distorting missionary ethnographic lens, and their failure to see deeper than his "bad language", *Khosi* Ranwedzi Mphaphuli is revealed as a skilled and shrewd ruler, attempting to negotiate both his own continued survival and independence and that of his people. On the other hand, even with their venom after what they saw as his fall, I find the missionaries' far more nuanced portrayal of *Khosi* Makwarela extremely moving. He refuses to fit into the moulds that they keep on fashioning for him and emerges from the pages of their records full of vitality and bursting with life, not as a cardboard cut-out of a "civilised" or "savage" ruler. Having lived with Makwarela for six years, I am going to miss him. (I suspect that my family may be more pleased at his departure than me.) I nevertheless believe that this work in general, and his story in particular, dramatically support my assertion that the window into the past opened by my reading of the Berlin Mission records makes a valuable contribution to our knowledge of the nineteenth-century history of Vendaland and of studies of missionary history in South Africa.

CHAPTER 1
Background and Context

The precolonial boundaries of the area which the Berlin missionaries called Vendaland are difficult to define. The borders of the territories of the various *mahosi* and their subordinates, and of Vendaland itself, varied over time, depending on the strength of the rulers. During the 1890s, the Boer authorities unsuccessfully attempted to fix these boundaries to confine the rulers and their people to the so-called locations. It was only after the colonial subjugation of the area after the Boer-Mphephu War of 1898 that this could be achieved, mainly by the new British rulers after the return of Makhado from exile in what was then called Rhodesia in 1904 and then by the so-called Location Commission of 1906. In addition, the Berlin missionaries found groups of Tshivenda-speakers living on the supposed Tsonga-Shangaan (XiTsonga-speaking) side of the Luvuvhu River and vice versa.[a] There were also a number of Sotho-speaking groups settled within the boundaries of areas claimed by Tshivenda-speaking *mahosi*. However, despite these difficulties, during the nineteenth century, the Venda heartland seems to have lain between the Limpopo and the Luvuvhu, mostly within latitude 22° to 23° [see Maps 1 and 2].[1]

Scholars used to think that the Vhavenda occupants of the area consisted of various unrelated clans that were united under the Singo about 250 years ago. The Singo were thus seen as the "original" or "real" Venda.[2] Despite having been challenged by Ralushai, this interpretation well-suited the needs of the apartheid and the Bantustan regimes.[3] For example, President P.R. Mphehpu assumed the apparently-invented title of *khosikhulu* ("chief of chiefs" or "paramount chief") and Bantustan political life was dominated by Singo

---

a. The fact that the Luvuvhu River did not form a rigid ethnic boundary became particularly clear once Swiss missionaries established themselves in the area from the mid-1870s. In consultation with missionaries from the Berlin Mission Society, the Swiss agreed to restrict their activities to the area south of the Luvuvhu River. They believed that, in doing so, they would mainly work among groups who would later be classified as Tsonga-Shangaan. This was meant to ensure that they would not compete with the Berlin missionaries, who were already operating among the predominantly Vhavenda groups to the north of the river, and the Pedi to the south of their area of operations. In fact, settlement of Tshivenda- and Xitsonga-speakers was far more mixed than they, or later apartheid planners, realised. Because of this, in order to implement its Bantustan policy, the apartheid state had to undertake major forced removals in Venda and Gazankulu in the late 1960s and 1970s (see especially P. Harries, "Exclusion, Classification and Internal Colonialism: The Emergence of Ethnicity Among the Tsonga-Speakers of South Africa", in L. Vail (ed.), *The Creation of Tribalism in Southern Africa*, London, James Currey, 1989, p. 86; Surplus People Project, *Forced Removals in South Africa, Vol. 5: The Transvaal*, Cape Town and Pietermaritzburg, Surplus People Project, 1983, numerous references).

mahosi and *magota*. Instead, recent research shows that many of the Tshivenda-speaking *mahosi* that the missionaries came into contact with in the 1870s ruled over people whose ancestors had been settled in the region since at least the Early Iron Age. Moreover, even the Singo rulers, and the Singo admixture to the population, were but the last major wave of immigrants to the area who merged with the Tshivenda-speaking majority. Lastly, not all of the rulers were Singo in origin.

DISPELLING SOME PERSISTENT MYTHS
People and Places

Early Iron Age archaeological sites in the far north of the Limpopo Province of today have been dated to the third and fourth centuries A.C.E. The people living here at that time were agro-pastoralists, who also possessed the ability to smelt and work metal, including iron and copper. Hunting remained an important source of food. Because their diet was deficient in salt, they needed to obtain this from an outside source. Salt flats, such as those in the Soutpansberg, became important meeting places and trading centres. So too did areas where copper and iron ore were mined and worked.[4]

The spatial layout of Early Iron Age settlements followed the Central Cattle Pattern. Cattle already seem to have been used as a means of reckoning wealth. To prevent their theft, the cattle kraal was placed in the centre of the village. The cattle were herded into this at night. Dwellings and living areas formed a roughly circular pattern around the cattle kraal. It would appear that Early Iron Age societies were reasonably egalitarian, with a relatively weakly-developed institution of chieftainship.[5]

Important changes took place among societies living in the Limpopo River valley from about 800. Although smaller villages continued to exist, larger centres began to emerge. The archaeological sites of Schroda (dated to between about 800 and 850) and K2 (dated to between about 950 and 1 150) show evidence of trade networks extending to the east coast and linking into the trade between this area and seaborne Arab traders from the northern hemisphere.[6] Huffman and Hanisch have argued that, accompanying the growth in trade, at K2 the central cattle pattern gradually began to give way to a situation where the cattle kraal was situated on the side of the town. This they ascribe largely to a decrease in the value of cattle in favour of a new form of wealth reckoning based on the trade goods acquired through the East Coast trade.[7] Taking this argument further, Hanisch has argued that the chief's growing role in controlling trade, and in settling disputes arising from this, led to his being increasingly secluded from his people.[b] In his opinion, this

---

b. Since we do not know what language was spoken at this time, I use the English terminology when referring to rulers of pre-Dzata social formations. I also refer to rulers of large formations as "kings".

reached its height with the shift from K2 to the Leopard's Kopje B kingdom based on Mapungubwe Hill, somewhere between about 1075 and the beginning of the twelfth century. Already before the occupation of Mapungubwe, the residences of headmen, chiefs or kings had commonly come to be situated so that commoners could not look down upon them. Excavations have shown that the hilltop area at Mapungubwe was occupied by the aristocracy. Below this lay a less rich though still important area, the south terrace. Livestock and the majority of the human population lived spread out in the town beneath, and surrounding, the hill. It is estimated that about 5000 people lived here at any given time. From here, the ruler controlled a trading kingdom which extended over much of the Limpopo Valley area and apparently also across the river into modern Zimbabwe.[8]

Mapungubwe appears to have been abandoned in about 1250. With this, the main centre of power and trade seems to have shifted to Great Zimbabwe. However, this did not mean that the Leopard's Kopje B kingdom disappeared without a trace. The culture persisted for at least a further 200 years in the Soutpansberg and the Matopos. In Zimbabwe, it evolved into Shona culture.[9]

Great Zimbabwe seems to have begun to decline towards the middle of the fifteenth century. There appear to have been several movements away from the capital. Communities moving southwards across the Limpopo at this time incorporated or annihilated people identified in oral tradition and later written accounts as the Vhangona, the VhaNgona or the BaNgona – the scattered descendants of earlier communities in the area. There was also a considerable degree of interaction and amalgamation between the Shona-speaking immigrants and early Sotho-speakers. Known archaeologically as the Moloko culture, the last-mentioned groups had settled in the Soutpansberg from about 1300, interacting and mixing with the remnants of the Mapungubwe people and others.[10] Traces of this interaction are found in the strong linguistic resemblance that Tshivenda, the Venda language, has with both Shona and Sesotho/Sotho-Tswana. There are also many other cultural elements in common between these groups. As part of this process of interaction and re-alignment, new settlements were founded and existing ones were further developed. Stone-walled villages built on the Zimbabwe pattern arose at Thula Mela and Makhahane on the banks of the Luvuvhu River in what is today the Kruger National Park; Tshitaka tsha Makoleni in the mountains above the present-day village of Mianzwi in the Mutale River Valley; Tshaluvhimbi across the Mutale River to the east of Mianzwi; Mutakolwe high up in the mountains near the present-day village of Netshiendeulu; as well as Matshema and Verdun along the Sand River in the western part of the Soutpansberg.[11] A number of Tshivenda-speaking groups, such as the Mbedzi, the Nyai and the Lembethu claim their ancestry from these ruins. Thus, there is clear evidence of occupation of the Soutpansberg by early Shona speakers long before the Singo occupation took place. In addition, as Huffman and Hanisch have pointed out, key elements of what would be called "Venda culture had evolved well before the arrival of the Singo". Far from being the "original" or "real" Venda who introduced political centralisation to the area for the first time the Singo had essentially the same political structure and cosmology as the people they conquered.[12]

The archaeological record suggests that the much-later Singo breakaway only occurred during the second half of the seventeenth century as a result of a succession dispute at Dhlo Dhlo. This was a successor state to the Khami empire which in turn had broken away from the declining Zimbabwe kingdom sometime after the 1450s.[13] According to oral tradition, on their movement southwards the Singo were protected by a drum with magical powers. This drum was known as the *Ngoma Lungundu*, the drum of the dead or the drum of Mwari/Mwali. It is said to have been given to the breakaway chief by his father/ancestor, the God/king Mwari. The chief and, through him, his people, were greatly feared because of the powers of the drum. Provided that it was continually beaten by the chief during times of threat, it would both protect the people against attack and cause them to defeat their enemies. The drum struck such fear into the souls of the enemies that they either fled in terror or fell to the ground in a swoon "as in death". This then enabled them to be defeated with ease. If the chief stopped beating the drum, or allowed it to touch the ground, the Singo would be vanquished. Indeed, it was the power of this drum that enabled the Singo to undertake their migration and occupy and hold land to the south of the Limpopo River. At times, the power of the drum was so great that it appeared to play itself. This was because the invisible Mwari himself was playing it.[14]

Eventually the Singo crossed the Limpopo river and settled at Dzata. Some accounts suggest that they entered the Nzhelele Valley immediately and settled at Dzata.[15] Others (which seem to be supported by ongoing archaeological research in the area) contradict this, stating that the Singo first settled on top of the mountains at Tshiendeulu (Dzata I).[16] Within these two broad interpretations, there is a considerable degree of disagreement about the genealogies of the rulers who led the occupation.

Dzata II seems to have been occupied in about 1700 A.C.E. and abandoned some fifty to sixty years later.[17] Hanisch has argued that, at the height of its power, the Dzata empire extended as far as the Olifants River near Phalaborwa in the south, the Blouberg in the far west, and northwards to across the Limpopo River.[18] I have found no evidence to contradict this assertion. However, based on my reading of the difference between idealised conceptions of royal power and the situation "on the ground" at a later date, I do have reservations about the degree of control that the centre would have been able to exert over peripheral areas or even some of the supposedly subordinate *mahosi* closer to the centre of power. Carolyn Hamilton has argued that, throughout his reign, even Shaka's position was by no means secure.[19] There is no reason to suspect that conditions in Vendaland were any different. Thus Huffman and Hanisch's assertion that the contribution of the Singo lay in their having unified "the mountainous country for the first and apparently the only time in pre-colonial history" may be true at an abstract level.[20] However, the way that this was reflected in the actual exercise of power may have been different, and varied over time.

This was certainly the case during the nineteenth century. Oral tradition concurs that after the death or disappearance of the Singo leader Thoho-ya-Ndou, civil war broke out. Dzata was abandoned and the nation fragmented into independent chiefdoms. Accounts vary as to who succeeded him but include various combinations of his sons and/or his nephews. During this time of upheaval, some of the subordinate *mahosi* and *magota* also managed to establish themselves as independent rulers in their respective areas.[21] The area came to be dominated by three great *mahosi* of Singo descent: *Khosi* Makhado (Ramabulana), *Khosi* Tshivhase and *Khosi* Mphaphuli[c] [see Maps 1 and 2]. There were also a considerable number of lesser *mahosi* and *magota*, who exhibited varying degrees of independence. Some of these, such as the Madzivhandila *mahosi* at Tshakhuma and the Maphuphe *mahosi* at Lwamondo were not of Singo descent. They nevertheless did have ties through marriage to the VhaSenzi (the descendants of Thoho-ya-Ndou).[22] By this stage, these rulers were also beginning to come into sustained contact with the first white hunters and pastoralists to enter the region.

SOJOURNERS AND SETTLERS IN VENDALAND

It is possible that Portuguese hunters and traders may have entered Vendaland during the eighteenth century. However, it was only during the nineteenth century that significant numbers of people of Western European origin began to enter the area. They were largely in search of hunting and grazing lands.[23]

At some time between 1810 and 1820, Coenraad de Buys, a hunter and adventurer from the Cape Colony, his black wife and their children were given land on the outer regions of Vhavenda-held territory by *Khosi* Ravele Mpofu.[d] His sons were also provided with wives from the royal settlement. After Coenraad's wife died, possibly of malaria, he moved on, leaving his sons behind. The sons subsequently settled at Tshikhovhokhovo (near the Blouberg Mountains and the Sand River) on stands allocated to them by Mpofu [see Map 3].[24]

---

c. The Berlin missionaries recorded Makhado as Makato; Tshivhase as Tschewasse or Schewasse; and Ranwedzi (Masindi) Mphaphuli as Pafuli or Pafudi.
d. According to the Ramabulana version of local history, *Khosi* Tshisevhe, also known as Ravele Mpofu, was the son of Thoho-ya-Ndou who succeeded him as ruler of Dzata II in the Nzhelele Valley. *Khosi* Mpofu was succeeded by *Khosi* Rasetuu Ramabulana, then by *Khosi* Makhado and then by *Khosi* Mphephu. They were all of the Mphephu/Ramabulana dynasty.

Following this, between 1836 and 1837, a number of Voortrekker groups temporarily established themselves in the general area. Their first main base was on the western side of the mountain at the salt-pan after which the Soutpansberg is named [see Map 3]. Later, they moved to the area surrounding what would become Schoemansdal and the present-day town of Makhado/ Louis Trichardt. They found that the area was abundantly stocked with game for hunting and provided ample pasturage for their cattle.

At about this time, the Voortrekker leaders Louis Tregardt (Trichardt) and Hendrik Andries Potgieter – together with the Buys brothers and BaTlokwa and Pedi combatants – assisted *Khosi* Rasetuu Ramabulana in his succession conflict with his brother, Ramavhoya. Having defeated and strangled Ramavhoya in late November or early December 1836, Rasetuu allegedly promised Tregardt and Potgieter access to land in the area should they desire it.[26]

After this early contact, the Voortrekker leader Andries Hendrik Potgieter and his followers settled in the Soutpansberg in 1848. First called Zoutpansbergdorp, the new settlement was later re-named Schoemansdal. Situated at the foot of the Soutpansberg mountains, this was overlooked by the capital village of *Khosi* Madzhie (known by the Boers as Katlachter), a Vhavenda ruler and "vassal" of the Ramabulanas [see Map 3]. These developments created the potential for conflict. Not only did the Vhavenda cede a part of their land to the newcomers, they were also forced either to provide them with labour (so-called *diensdoende* Africans) or to pay tax (so-called *opgaaf* Africans).[27]

Michael Buys, son of Coenraad, was placed in charge of the collection of *opgaaf* in 1855.[e] This was largely because he had the military power necessary to collect it – an estimated 15 000 to 20 000 Africans either recognised his leadership or, at the very least, were placed under his authority.[28] In 1859 he was joined by João Albasini, the Portuguese trader and adventurer, who was appointed as collector of *opgaaf* from Africans to the east, north-east and south-east of Schoemansdal. Known as "Juwawa" by the local Tsonga-Shangaan people, Albasini (who died in 1888) was considered by many to be the "white chief" of the "knobnoses".[f] He had started building a following of slaves and volunteers during his time as a trader (principally in slaves and ivory) in Portuguese East Africa during the 1830s. He continued strengthening this following after his move to the Lowveld in the 1840s and Schoemansdal (with the Voortrekkers) in 1848. In particular, he absorbed Tsonga-Shangaan groups fleeing from Mozambique as refugees from the

---

e. Gabriël Buys, Michael's brother had originally been appointed. With his death in the same year, Michael took over his position (see J. Boeyens, "Black Ivory", p. 210 n 52).

f. The Tsonga-Shangaan, also frequently referred to as the MaGwamba, especially in Swiss mission sources. The term "knobnoses" is thought to be derived from the nasal cicatrization practised by some of the immigrants (see especially *BMB*, 1867, p. 314; P. Harries, "Exclusion, Classification and Internal Colonialism", pp. 84–90).

wars of Soshangane and the later civil war between Mzila and Mawewe in the 1860s. Albasini based these followers on the farm Goedewensch at Piesangkop. He himself moved there from Schoemansdal in 1857. Goedewensch also boasted a fort, which could be used as a refuge in times of unrest. Appointed as *Superintendent van Kafferstammen* ("Superintendent of Kaffir-tribes") in 1863, Albasini's main task remained the collection of *opgaaf*. He also served as Portuguese Vice Consul to the South African Republic from about this time until 1866.[29] At the height of his power, he could reportedly "summon an estimated 4000 VaTsonga supporters by merely beating a drum". Indeed, as with Buys, it was because of this following, and the military power which it brought, that he was placed in charge of the collection of *opgaaf*.[30]

In marked contrast to the received orthodoxy of Boers as farmers, the hunting industry – especially the elephant hunting industry – was the greatest source of income for the Zoutpansbergers. For about nineteen years, Schoemansdal was the most important trade centre in the Northern Transvaal. Thousands of tons of wild animal meat, horns, whips, wood and salt were taken from there to Mozambique, the Cape Colony and Natal. White employers also illegally armed local Africans with firearms to hunt elephants for them.[g] The area became one of the major centres for the ivory trade in the interior of South Africa.[31]

Running alongside this "white ivory" trade, there was a brisk illegal trade in what was euphemistically referred to as "black ivory" or "apprentices". Even before the establishment of an official tax-collecting system, the early Boer settlers in the area – assisted by African auxiliaries, especially the armed bands of Buys and Albasini but also other Tsonga-Shangaan forces – were raiding for African stock and children. Many of these captured children were, in fact, slaves under a different name. Since the term "apprentices" is thus a misleading one, following the lead of Jan Boeyens, I will refer to such people as *inboekelinge* – their particulars were supposed to be recorded in a book by a landdrost or field-cornet of a district at the time that they were indentured.[32] As Boeyens has argued, it is impossible to determine the number of African children indentured in Zoutpansberg with any real degree of accuracy. However, according to the Berlin missionaries Heinrich Grützner and Alexander Merensky, the annual total was about 1000.[33] Coupled with the

---

g. The Hunting Act of 1858 specified that no black person was to be sent on an elephant hunt without the presence of a white; all black hunters had to be registered with the landdrost; black hunters separated from their white supervisors during the hunt had to be back with him by the same evening; and no white was allowed to take more than two black *skuts* (marksmen) into the field with him (R. Wagner, "Zoutpansberg", p. 31). For a discussion of hunting legislation in the South African Republic between 1858 and 1881, see E.J. Carruthers, *Game Protection in the Transvaal, 1846 to 1926*, Archives Year Book For South African History, Pretoria, Government Printer, 1995, pp. 25–44.

resistance over attempts at collecting taxes, this raiding provoked widespread resistance from the Vhavenda.

In these campaigns, it was often the black auxiliaries who bore the brunt of the fighting. To encourage their enlistment, re-enlistment and continued loyalty, they were given the women captured during the engagements. They were also given land formerly belonging to those who they defeated.[34]

In attempting to trace the fate of *inboekelinge*, Boeyens has argued that "racial and other differences precluded [them] ... from being fully incorporated into Boer society". However, they underwent a process of acculturation and, in many cases learned to speak Dutch. Since the majority were indentured at an early age and since they often married other *inboekelinge*, some of whom were of different "ethnic" origin, this process of acculturation was often comprehensive. For example, *inboekelinge* often lost the ability to speak their mother tongues and forgot the cultural practices of their youth. As a result, they "became estranged from their societies of origin". It is probable "that a new social stratum emerged from the ranks of the 'apprentices', and that many of the so-called 'oorlams' Africans referred to in nineteenth-century literature on the Transvaal could trace their roots to the 'apprenticeship' system".[35]

As different factions among the Boers became involved in succession struggles and conflicts within and between Vhavenda and Tsonga-Shangaan groups stretching into Mozambique, tensions rose. The different Boer factions were often at loggerheads with each other almost as much as with the Africans. Given the deteriorating strategic situation, the Zoutpansberg community was nevertheless forced to submerge its differences and remain in laager from April 1865. Various Tsonga-Shangaan and Vhavenda rulers closed the elephant-hunting grounds to the Boers. In addition, the Vhavenda were in possession of a large number of guns retained by the *skuts*. They were able to use them with deadly accuracy against their former masters.[36]

Periodic negotiations aimed at reaching a peaceful settlement failed. So too did a number of attempts to call up a commando from other districts to assist the Schoemansdal community. Many of those liable for commando duty were unwilling to respond. They feared the outbreak of conflicts in their home districts if they left them to fight in Schoemansdal, and worried that they would contract malaria in the Zoutpansberg in summer. There was also a widely-held feeling that the Zoutpansbergers had brought their fate upon themselves by giving firearms to blacks in contravention of the law. As was the case in other parts of the country, men were also resistant to periods of long, unpaid commando duty.[37]

It was only in June 1867 that a commando under Paul Kruger, commandant-general (and later President) of the ZAR, reached Schoemansdal. Hampered by a shortage of ammunition and the small number of people who had responded to the call, and facing a well-armed foe, they failed to dislodge

Madzhie from his stronghold above Schoemansdal. Shortly afterwards, in the face of the continued closure of the hunting fields by the Vhavenda, the unsatisfactory military situation, the depletion of local wildlife reserves through overhunting, and with the settlers suffering a high incidence of malaria, the decision was taken to withdraw and abandon Schoemansdal, retreating southwards. Schoemansdal was abandoned on 15 July 1867. Albasini remained in the district and his fort provided a focal point for the small group of remaining white families in the area. A new town, Marabastad, was established in the south of the Zoutpansberg district [see Map 3].[38]

In the aftermath of the retreat from Schoemansdal, a number of attempts were made to subjugate the Vhavenda. These included attacks by commandos supported by African auxiliaries and a disastrous Boer-sponsored campaign by Swazi forces.[39] Although these failed, the stresses of the campaigns were taking their toll. This pressurised a number of *mahosi* to approach the *Uitvoerende Raad* to open negotiations for peace. As a result, a commission headed by Paul Kruger succeeded in negotiating a fragile peace in November 1869. This did not mean that Makhado, *Khosi* Rassetuu Ramabulana's successor whom the Boers had opposed in the succession struggle after his father's death in 1864, accepted the authority of the Transvaal government. He ruled as an independent chief north of the Thorn River, a tributary of the Luvuvhu. The Transvaal government had lost effective control over a part of the Zoutpansberg District.[40] Attempts to subjugate the Venda were temporarily abandoned after this. Marabastad continued as the centre for administration until the founding of Pietersburg (present-day Polokwane) in 1885 [see Map 3].[41]

Officially, this brought to an end the capturing of women and children as war spoils in the Zoutpansberg area.[42] However, Boeyens has pointed out that slave trading may have continued in the area. Morrison Barlow, special commissioner for Waterberg during the first British administration of the Transvaal (which had begun in 1877), stated that he had been offered first two and then three children in exchange for a Martini Henry rifle by *Khosi* Mphaphuli. The *khosi* had reportedly taken them from the Tsonga-Shangaan ruler, Xikundu, whom he had beheaded. Commissioner Barlow also reported that "certain white traders, I regret to say, Englishmen, are carrying on a regular slave trade with some of the Chiefs in the Zoutpansberg Mountains". They were allegedly exchanging "guns, powder and lead" for young Africans provided by Mphaphuli, Makhado and Tshivhase.[43]

The northern part of the Zoutpansberg District was essentially cleared of white settlers until the conquest of the Vhavenda by the Boers in the Boer-Mphephu War of 1898. By then, the Boers had conquered the other African groups in the Transvaal. They were thus in a position to devote their full attention to the conquest of Vendaland. In common with other northern areas, this area had also been devastated by famine arising from a combination of the destruction of crops by locust swarms, drought and the decimation of livestock holdings by rinderpest in 1896 and 1897.[h] The Berlin missionaries estimated that a third of the population of Vendaland had died in this famine.[44] This seriously weakened the military might of the local *mahosi* and the ability of their people to withstand siege and the disruption caused by warfare. Against this background, Tshivhase and Mphaphuli seem to have concluded that the forces ranged against them were too powerful to defeat in open warfare. They also appear to have treated the war as a further campaign in the continuing battle for supremacy between the three great ruling houses. They rejected Mphephu's pleas for the formation of a united front against the invading Boers. Instead, they accepted the assurances of the Berlin missionaries working in their areas that their best hope of retaining at least some degree of power and independence lay in distancing themselves from the fray and negotiating with the Boers. With the fall of his mountain stronghold, and relentlessly hunted by the Boers who had put a price on his head, Mphephu was forced to flee into what was then called Rhodesia in December 1898. (He would only return in 1905, after the British victory in the South African War of 1899–1902.) The Vhavenda were thus the last of the African groups in the Transvaal to be subjugated by the Boers.[45]

These events clearly demonstrated that, despite their vaunted military strength, Boer claims of supremacy in the Zoutpansberg had never been unconditionally accepted by Africans. During "the third quarter of the nineteenth century the dominion of the South African Republic over black communities was by no means a foregone conclusion".[46] In addition, the Zoutpansberg Boers were often engaged in factional disputes and were not the united group that they have often been portrayed as. Similarly, the ZAR was not as powerful, or as capable of imposing its will on its inhabitants, as nationalist historiography would have us believe.[47]

It is against this background of conflict, labour-raiding, shifting alliances and mistrust, as well as the victory over the Boers at Schoemansdal, that missionaries came to operate in Vendaland.

MISSIONARIES

The first church at Schoemansdal had been built in 1851. Until the appointment of a full-time *Dominee*, the Rev. N.J. van Warmelo of the Nederduitsch Hervormde Church, services were held by community members and visiting

---

h. Mpahpuli's country was the worst hit in Vendaland and the famine only started easing off there at the end of 1897. In other parts of the region it lessened far earlier. From about March 1897, people began moving from Mphaphuli's area to Makhado's area, where conditions were better. From about this time onwards, parts of Tshivhase's country also had good harvests. In July, people were still moving out of Mphaphuli's country and into Makhado's lands in considerable numbers. So serious was the situation that people caught stealing any remaining food in other people's gardens and fields were put to death.

Ministers.⁴⁸ This church was intended for the exclusive use of the inhabitants of Schoemansdal and their visitors. The first mission station to be established in the immediate vicinity of Vendaland was the Dutch Reformed Church station of Goedgedacht, founded among the Buys people by the Rev. Alexander McKidd in 1863 [see Map 3]. The land to establish the station was given to him by the Brothers Lottering^i and was on the periphery of the lands claimed by Makhado. Sotho groups (particularly those under *Kgoši* Seakamela) and Tsonga-Shangaan groups also had some claims to authority in the area. On McKidd's death (from "fever") at the end of the same year, he was succeeded as missionary by Stéfanus Hofmeyr. Having abandoned Goedgedacht because of disturbances caused by the Boer–Mphephu War of 1865, Hofmeyr moved the mission station to the nearby farm of Kranspoort, which had been purchased from the Lotterings by McKidd.⁴⁹ Although the mission had African members, it remained largely Buys-centred. Because of its geographical situation (about 34 km to the west of Makhado/Louis Trichardt in lands that did not fall under the direct control of Vhavenda *mahosi*) and its membership, its activities remained largely peripheral to developments in Vendaland proper. Hofmeyr and the Berlin missionaries nevertheless maintained a cordial relationship.⁵⁰

In an interesting aside on the attitude of the Schoemansdalers to the mission, Hofmeyr would later record that, at the time of his arrival, the Boer attitude towards missionaries was distinctly unfavourable. His predecessor had been threatened with physical violence by two farmers armed with sjamboks. He himself had suffered ostracism because of his vocation. He had often to outspan in the market square of Schoemansdal, eating and sleeping alone in his wagon, since nobody would have him in their house.

It was missionaries from the Berlin Mission who would establish themselves in the heartland of Vendaland in areas under the direct control of local *mahosi*. They began to feel their way into the Zoutpansberg area and give tentative thought to establishing themselves in Vendaland from the mid-1860s. An article in the *Berliner Missionsberichte* for 1866 introduced readers to the area:

> The Sautpansberg district is in the northern part of the Transvaal Republic ... The mountain, which is named after the effervescent salt-pans at its foot, has also given its name to the entire district, which is bounded in the west and north by the Limpopo, in the east by the meeting of the Drakensberg and the upper reaches of the Lepalule, and in the south by the district of Pretoria. Many mountain ranges give the whole area the character of a mountainous landscape. There are also many springs.⁵²

---

i. Referred to in some sources as Lothering.

Turning to the inhabitants of this landscape, the article drew attention to the fact that the missionaries had "only recently ... managed to find out the names of some of the smaller tribes and their chiefs – some have not yet been identified".[53]

A visit to *Khosi* Madzhie – *khotsi-munene* and a sub-ruler of *Khosi* Makhado – by Mission-Inspector Charles Murray of the Dutch Reformed Church in mid-1865 had been followed by a journey of exploration by Brothers Merensky, Grützner, Trümpelmann and Köhler from the Berlin Mission Society in September 1869. Included in this journey was a meeting with Madzhie. Murray had incorrectly described Madzhie as "the paramount chief of all the Kaffir tribes in the Sautpansberg [Zoutpsansberg]" and his German Brothers accepted this.[55] By the time of the meeting of 1869, the Berlin Mission were noting that:

> The Batsoëtla or Batsoëta,[j] number about 40–50 000 heads; they are not proper Bassuto or Betscuana, because their language differs from Sutho [Sotho] as sharply as from Zulu, and shows a relationship with the languages of the tribes further north.[56]

In October 1870, Brother Beyer, at Blauberg mission station – the closest Berlin Mission station to the Soutpansberg – undertook an investigative journey to what he identified as "the Batschuetla [Vhavenda] in the east of the Zoutpansberg" [see Map 3]. His main aim was to meet with Tshivhase to sound him out about the possibility of starting a mission station in his lands. He nevertheless had to give up the attempt only about half a day's journey beyond Albasini's farm, as large areas were cut off by flooding as a result of extremely heavy rains.[57]

In May 1871, Missionaries Grützner, Beyer and Beuster visited Makhado to discuss opening a mission station in his lands. By now they had realized it was he, rather than Madzhie, who was one of the great *mahosi* of Vendaland. At this meeting, Makhado managed to keep their hopes that they would be given land for a mission station alive, without actually committing himself to anything.[58] Just under a year later, in March 1872, Missionaries Beyer (from Blauberg) and Baumbach (from Makgabêng) made a reconnaissance journey to *Khosi* Tshivhase.[k] At this meeting, the *khosi* made it very clear that "he had already for a long time wanted teachers to come, who could teach his people to read and write".[59]

Early in October 1872, Brothers Beuster and Stech started a mission station in the lands of *Kgoši* Mutle, a vassal of Sekhukhune. However, within a few days of its opening, and allegedly "much to Mutle's sincere regret", Sekhu-

---
j. The Sotho name for the Vhavenda.
k. At this stage, the missionaries wrote Makgabêng as Makchabêng. In this particular case, they recorded Tshivhase as Sebase. They also used the spellings Sebâse, Sewase and Shewasse.

khune "ordered that they stop work and leave his country". They returned to Botshabelo (the big mission station which Merenksy had established near Middelburg for the Christian refugees during the Sekhukhune wars) on 9 October. In the words of the *Berliner Missions-Berichte*: "Soon after that they made their way to Sebase [Tshivhase], who accommodated them and gave them permission to start a new station there."[60]

From 24 October to 4 November 1872, Grützner, as Vice-Superintendent of the Berlin Mission in the Transvaal, and Beyer accompanied Beuster and Stech to the lands of *Khosi* Tshivahse. In Grützner's words, they had gone "there to come to know the conditions there and to consider the feasibility of establishing a new mission station there". Beuster and Stech would be left behind at the newly-founded station.[61] First called Ga-Sebase, following the SeSotho orthography developed by the missionaries in Sekhukhuneland, this was also at first known as "Sebâse (pronounced Schwâhsse)"[l] [Tshivhase – see Maps 1 and 2].[62] Commenting on the people, Grützner noted that:

> Outwardly the people seem friendly; the language is very different from that of the Basutho or Matabele [Basotho or Ndebele]. Our mission will again be entering a new language area! and Brother Beuster, who has just learned to speak the language of the Basutho, has the work, as well as the pleasure, to start at the beginning for a second time.

The founding of the first station was followed by the establishment of Ga Matzebandela (later called Tshakhuma),[m] in the lands of *Khosi* Madzivhandila, by Br. Erdmann Schwellnus, in May 1874 [see Maps 1 and 2].[64] Although he was in fact an independent non-Singo ruler, the missionaries at first incorrectly identified him as a vassal of *Khosi* Makhado.[65] Three years after the foundation of this station, in July 1877, a third station, named Georgenholtz, was established in the lands of *Khosi* Makwarela Mhaphuli,[n] son and vassal of *Khosi* Ranwedzi Mphaphuli[66] [see Map 1]. The first missionary to be stationed there was Klaas Koen, a "born Hottentot", who had received some of his schooling and his theological training in Germany.[o]

---

l. Later, the correct Tshivenda orthrography of Ha-Tshivhase was used. After the death of Beuster, the area became known as Beuster. Today, it is either known as Beuster or by its Tshivenda name of Maungani.
m. Earlier spellings of Tshakhuma by the missionaries were Tschakoma, Tsakoma, Tshakuma and Tsakhuma. They referred to Madzivhandila as Matzebandela or Matzebandala.
n. Missionary sources from the nineteenth century refer to *Khosi* Makwarela Mphaphuli as Makoarele. While Makwarela eventually came to succeed his father as *khosi*, during the period when his father was still alive his actual position was that of a *gota*. However, in common usage, a *gota* is referred to as *khosi* by his subjects. To show respect to somebody, one makes them greater than they are. On the other hand, people in positions of power often make people under them in the hierarchy smaller than they are. Throughout this work, I refer to Makwarela as *khosi*.
o. Although mission sources noted that he himself spelt his name as Klaas Koen, in the writings of the Berlin Mission his name was usually "Germanised" to Klaus Kuhn or Klaas Kuhn.

One of the great difficulties faced by the missionaries in Vendaland was that of making, and keeping, a significant number of converts. Missionary estimates of the number of African people in reach of the mission stations in the area during the last three decades of the nineteenth century ranged between 5000 and 50 000 for Ha-Tshivhase, 6000 and 50 000 for Tshakhuma (with an apparent misprint of 80 000 for 30 000 for the year 1888) and 10 000 and 20 000 for Georgenholtz.[67] Based on the spread of these figures, over the period as a whole, I would estimate figures of 50 000 each for Ha-Tshivhase and Tshakhuma and 10 000 for Georgenholtz. This fits in well with Johannes Flygare's estimation of the population of Vendaland as being 100 000 people in 1899.[68] While these figures do not take into account population movements and the decrease in population occasioned by the famine of 1896/1897, they seem to be realistic enough for some conclusions on the successes and failures of mission work to be drawn.

Table 1: Mission Estimates of the Number of Africans in reach of Vendaland Mission Stations, (1874–1899)

	Ha-Tshivhase	Tshakhuma	Georgenholtz	Vendaland
1874	5 000	6 000		11 000
1875	10 000	6 000		16 000
1876	10 000	6 000		16 000
1877	10 000	6 000	11 000	27 000
1878	10 000	6 000	11 000	27 000
1879	10 000	6 000	11 000	27 000
1880				
1881	50 000	10 000	11 000	71 000
1882	50 000	15 000	11 000	76 000
1883	50 000	15 000	20 000	85 000
1884	50 000	25 000	20 000	95 000
1885	50 000	25 000	20 000	95 000
1886	50 000	30 000	20 000	100 000
1887	50 000	30 000	20 000	100 000
1888	50 000	80 000	20 000	150 000
1889	50 000	30 000	20 000	100 000
1890	50 000	40 000	20 000	110 000
1891	50 000	50 000	20 000	120 000
1892	50 000	50 000	20 000	120 000
1893	50 000	50 000	10 000	110 000
1894	50 000	50 000	10 000	110 000
1895	50 000	50 000	10 000	110 000
1896	50 000	50 000	10 000	110 000
1897	50 000	50 000	10 000	110 000
1898	50 000	50 000	10 000	110 000
1899	50 000	50 000	10 000	110 000

Over the same period, the maximum size of the congregation at Ha-Tshivhase was 147 people (1899). Corresponding figures for Tshakhuma and Georgenholtz were 190 (1897) and 62 (1892) congregants respectively. Considering all of the stations together, the maximum congregation size was that of 382 people in 1897.

Table 2: Number of Congregants at Vendaland Mission Stations, 1874–1899

	Ha-Tshivhase	Tshakhuma	Georgenholtz	Vendaland
1874	1			1
1875	6	1		7
1876	4	3		7
1877	4	19		23
1878	4	28		32
1879	8	31	4	43
1880				
1881	43	48	23	114
1882	57	57	28	142
1883	61	69	27	157
1884	69	87	28	184
1885	84	72	27	183
1886	102	94	29	225
1887	104	103	37	244
1888	107	114	44	265
1889	131	114	51	296
1890	132	122	55	309
1891	102	161	60	323
1892	121	165	62	348
1893	130	170	48	348
1894	130	150	46	326
1895	138	177	53	368
1896	126	182	55	363
1897	131	190	61	382
1898	134	159	48	341
1899	147	170		317

Working on my figure of a total of 110 000 people in reach of the various stations, even at their maximum sizes, the congregations of these stations represented only a small percentage of the number of inhabitants of the area. Thus, at best, only 0.29% of the people in the environs of Ha-Tshivhase had formally converted to Christianity and been baptised. Corresponding figures for the remaining two stations were 0.38% and 0.62% respectively. For Vendaland as a whole, the best figure was 0.35%.

In addition to making converts, missionaries were faced with the difficulties of keeping them. Despite fluctuations, it is clear that, during the period under review, the general tendency for Vendaland as a whole, and for individual stations, indicated an increase in the number of converts.

While several out-stations were established from these three stations, the main *mahosi* were resistant to allowing the founding of further main stations in their areas or those of their subordinate *mahosi* and *magota*.[69] My own reading is that what they were attempting to do was to give themselves access to missionaries through intermediaries without allowing them to establish themselves too close to the royal capitals or establish too great a presence in Vendaland. One of their aims in doing so was that they hoped in turn to be able to use the missionaries as intermediaries between themselves and the encroaching Boers but still keep them at a distance from the socio-political centre.[70] Indeed, it was only in 1899, after the defeat of *Khosi* Mphephu, Makhado's successor, and the seizure of large sections of his former lands, that a fourth Berlin station could be established. Named Gertrudsburg, this was situated at Makhado, near the new white settlement of Louis Trichardt, on lands given to the mission by the Boer authorities. The missionaries saw this as a high-point in the development of mission activity in the area.[71] In many ways, it was. It will nevertheless become increasingly clear that, despite the relatively small number of formal conversions during the nineteenth century, their role as potential intermediaries and as mediators of the new ways accorded the Berlin missionaries a power and influence which was far greater than that suggested by these figures.

Lastly, Swiss Missionaries first came to the northern part of what came to be called the Transvaal in 1873. Their first mission station and farm was established at Valdezia (Lwalani) in 1875. Elim mission station was established in 1879 [see Maps 1 and 2]. The mission farm of Kurulen was later established nearby. In continuation of their earlier medical work, the missionaries would establish Elim Hospital in 1899.[72] We have already seen that they came to an agreement with the Berlin Mission not to compete with them. They thus operated outside Vendaland. They nevertheless maintained a close collegial relationship with their German colleagues. In particular, they provided treatment for malaria and other medical care for the Vendaland missionaries and vaccines for them, their converts and local people whom they were able to persuade to be vaccinated against diseases such as smallpox.[73]

On a first reading, these events appear to follow the conventional pattern of popular consciousness whereby missionaries carry the Gospel to areas where its message has not been heard before. However, despite its apparent conventionality, this story has some surprising twists. When missionaries from the Berlin Mission Society arrived in the area, they found a small number of Christian converts already living there. It is to their activities that we now turn.

1. *Berliner Missions-Berichte* [*BMB*], 1881, p. 335; 1885, p. 74; 1891, p. 451; 1898, p. 7; C.J. Conerly, "The Surrendering of the Lands in the Northern Transvaal of Mahosi Davhana, Makhado, Mphephu and Sinthumule", BA Honours thesis, University of Cape Town, 1990, pp. 47, 55–56, 78–82; D. McDonald, "Vendaland", in *The Blythswood Review: A South African Journal of Religious, Social and Economic Work*, X (110), February 1933, p. 12; M.H. Nemudzivhadi, "The attempts by Makhado to revive the Venda kingdom 1864–1895", Ph.D. thesis, Potchefstroom University for Christian National Higher Education, Vaal Triangle Campus, 1998, pp. 2, 3, 6–7, 106, 148, 159, 239–248, 250, 266, 270–273; and R. Wagner, "Zoutpansberg: the dynamics of a hunting frontier, 1848–67", in S. Marks and A. Atmore, *Economy and Society in Pre-Industrial South Africa*, London, Longmans, 1980, pp. 322–323. Although I consulted first-language German-speakers on aspects of translations from the *BMB*, the final versions appearing in the text are my own. So too are translations from the other German texts, as well as those from Afrikaans and Dutch sources. Translations from French were performed by Pippa Davies.

2. S.M. Dzivhani, "The Chiefs of Venḓa", in N.J. van Warmelo (ed.), *The Copper Miners of Musina and the Early History of the Zoutpansberg*, Union Of South Africa, Department of Native Affairs, Ethnological Publications, Vol. VIII, Pretoria, Government Printer, 1940, pp. 33–50; E. Gottschling, "The Bawenda, A sketch of their history and customs", in *Addresses and Papers read at the Joint Meeting of the British and South African Associations for the Advancement of Science held in South Africa, 1905*, Volume III, Johannesburg, South African Association for the Advancement of Science, 1905, pp. 195–198; G.P. Lestrade (a) "Some notes on the political Organisation of the Venda-Speaking Tribes", in *Africa: Journal of the International Institute of African Languages and Cultures*, III(3), July 1930, pp. 306–307 & (b) "Some Notes on the Ethnic History of the Vhavenda and their Rhodesian Affinities", in N.J. van Warmelo (ed), *Contributions towards Venda History, Religion and Tribal Ritual*, Union of South Africa, Department of Native Affairs, Ethnological Publications, Volume III, Pretoria, Government Printer, 1932, pp. XX–XXVIII; E.K. Lukhaimane, "A short history of the Venda", unpublished manuscript held in the Special Collections section of the University of Venda Library, n.d.; M.M. Motenda, "History of the Western Venḓa and of the Lemba", in N.J. van Warmelo (ed.), *The Copper Miners of Musina*, pp. 51–70; E. Mudau, "Ngoma lungundu and the early invaders of Venḓa", in N.J. van Warmelo (ed.), *The Copper Miners of Musina*, pp. 10–32; H.A. Stayt, *The Bavenda*, London, Oxford University Press, 1931, pp. 9–19; and N.J. van Warmelo (ed.), *Contributions Towards Venda History*, pp. 5–36.

3. N.M.N. Ralushai, "Conflicting Accounts of Venda History with Particular Reference to the Role of Mutupo in Social Organization", Ph.D. thesis, Queen's University of Belfast, 1977.

4. W.S. Fish, "Cows and Kraals: The Early Iron Age, Nandoni and interaction", unpublished paper presented at the international conference "From the Zoutpansberg to the Sea" held at the University of Venda, 16–18 September 1995, p. 1; M. Hall, *The Changing Past: Farmers, Kings and Traders in Southern Africa, 200–1860*, Cape Town, David Philip, 1987, pp. 39–43, 66–68; E.O.M. Hanisch, "Legends, Oral Traditions and Archaeology: A look at early Venda history", in *Luvhone*, Department of Education and Culture, Venda, 3(4), April 1994, p. 69; T. Maggs, "The Early History of the Black People in Southern Africa", in T. Cameron and S.B. Spies (eds.), *A New Illustrated History of South Africa*, Second Edition, Johannesburg and Cape Town, Southern Book Publishers and Human & Rousseau, 1981, p. 37–39, 43; P. Maylam, *A History of the African People of South Africa: from the Early Iron Age to the 1970s*, Cape Town, David Philip, 1986, pp. 2–3, 5–7, 9; and S.M. Miller and J.W.N. Tempelhoff, "Die romantiek van 'n grensterrein", in *Fauna and Flora*, Transvaalse Direktoraat Natuur- en Omgewingsbewaring, 47, 1990, p. 34.

5. W.S. Fish, "Cows and Kraals", p. 1; E.O.M. Hanisch, "Legends, Oral Traditions and Archaeology", p. 70; T.N. Huffman, "Broederstroom and the Central Cattle Pattern", in *South African Journal of Science*, 89, 1993, pp. 220–226; M. Hall, *The Changing Past*, pp. 72, 73; T. Maggs, "The Early History of the Black People in Southern Africa", p. 39; and P. Maylam, *A History of the African People of South Africa*, pp. 11, 15.

6. M. Hall, *The Changing Past*, p. 77; E.O.M. Hanisch, "Legends, Oral Traditions and Archaeology", pp. 69–70.

7. E.O.M. Hanisch, "Legends, Oral Traditions and Archaeology", p. 70; T.N. Huffman, "Archeology and the ethnohistory of the African Iron Age", in *Annual Review of Anthropology*, 11, 1982, pp. 133–150.

8. E.O.M. Hanisch, "Legends, Oral Traditions and Archaeology", pp. 70–71. See also M. Hall, *The Changing Past*, p. 82; T. Maggs, "The Early History of the Black People in Southern Africa", p. 41.

9. M. Hall, *The Changing Past*, p. 88; E.O.M. Hanisch, "Legends, Oral Traditions and Archaeology", pp. 71–72; and T.N. Huffman, "The Rise and Fall of Zimbabwe", in *Journal of African History*, XIII(3), 1973, pp. 353–366.

10. E.O.M. Hanisch, "Legends, Oral Traditions and Archaeology", p. 74 (quotation); T.N. Huffman and E.O.M. Hanisch, "Settlement Hierachies in the Northern Transvaal: Zimbabwe Ruins and Venda History", in *African Studies Journal*, 46 (1), 1987, p. 79; G.P. Lestrade, "Some Notes on the Ethnic History of the Vhavenda", pp. XXI, XXII; and H.A. Stayt, *The Bavenda*, p. 9.

11. E.O.M. Hanisch, "Legends, Oral Traditions and Archaeology", p. 73; T.N. Huffman and E.O.M. Hanisch, "Settlement Hierachies in the Northern Transvaal", pp. 106–110; and N.V. Ralushai "A Preliminary Report on the Early History of Thulamela Archaeological Site", unpublished report, Kruger National Park/Thulamela Project, n.d. (1997).

12. E.O.M. Hanisch, "Legends, Oral Traditions and Archaeology", p. 73; T.N. Huffman and E.O.M. Hanisch, "Settlement Hierachies in the Northern Transvaal", especially pp. 79, 106, 112–114 (quotations, pp. 113, 114).

13. M. Hall, *The Changing Past*, pp. 119, 121–122, 133–134; E.O.M. Hanisch, "Legends, Oral Traditions and Archaeology", p. 74 (quotation).

14. E. Mudau, "Ngoma lungundu", see especially pp. 10–11, 13–14, 17, 28. See also S.M. Dzivhani, "The Chiefs of Venḓa", pp. 33–34.

15. S.M. Dzivhani, "The Chiefs of Venḓa", pp. 33–34; E.O.M. Hanisch, "Legends, Oral Traditions and Archaeology", p. 75; E.K. Lukhaimane, "A short history of the Venda", pp. 9–10; M.M. Motenda, "History of the Western Venḓa", p. 53; and N.J. van Warmelo (ed.), *Contributions Towards Venda History*, p. 6.

16. E.O.M. Hanisch, "Legends, Oral Traditions and Archaeology", p. 75; E. Mudau, "Ngoma lungundu", p. 23; L. Norden, "Die Heilige Tamboere van Tshiendeolo", in *Die Huisgenoot*, 6 November 1942, pp. 7, 31; H.A. Stayt, *The Bavenda*, p. 12; and J.W.N. Tempelhoff, *Townspeople of the Soutpansberg: A Centenary History*, Louis Trichardt, Greater Louis Trichardt Transitional Local Council, 1999, p. 17.

17. E.O.M. Hanisch, "Legends, Oral Traditions and Archaeology", p. 75; G. Liesegang, "New light on Venda traditions: Mahumane's account of 1730", in *History in Africa*, 4, 1977, pp. 163–181.

18. E.O.M. Hanisch, "Legends, Oral Traditions and Archaeology", p. 76. See also J.W.N. Tempelhoff, *Townspeople of the Soutpansberg*, p. 17.

19. C. Hamilton, *Terrific Majesty: The Powers of Shaka Zulu and the Limits of Historical Invention*, Cape Town, David Philip, 1998, pp. 49–50.

20. T.N. Huffman and E.O.M. Hanisch, "Settlement Hierachies in the Northern Transvaal", p. 114.

21. S.M. Dzivhani, "The Chiefs of Venḓa", pp. 39–40, 44; E. Gottschling, "The Bawenda", p. 196; E.O.M. Hanisch, "Legends, Oral Traditions and Archaeology", p. 76; T.N. Huffman and E.O.M. Hanisch, "Settlement Hierachies in the Northern Transvaal", p. 112; E.K. Lukhaimane, "A short history of the Venda", p. 10; M.M. Motenda, "History of the Western Venḓa", pp. 54–60; E. Mudau, "The Dau of Tshakhuma", in N.J. van Warmelo (ed.), *The Copper Miners of Musina*, pp. 76, 78, 79; H.A. Stayt, *The Bavenda*, p. 15; and N.J. van Warmelo (ed.), *Contributions Towards Venda History*, pp. 6, 12–24, 30–32, 36.

22. *Der Bawenda-Freund*, VI(23), 1888, p. 67 and 11(42), 1893, p. 161; BMB, 1878, p. 490; G.P. Lestrade, "Some Notes on the Ethnic History of the Vhavenda", p. XXVII; *Mitteilungen des Vereins "Heidenfreund"*, V(18), 1887, n.p. (p. 2); and R. Wessmann, *Philippus Thai, ein Treuer Nationalhelfer im Bawendalande*, Missionsschriften für Kinder Nr. 46, Berlin, Buchhandlung der Berliner evangelischen Missionsgesellschaft, n.d. [1902], p. 1.

23. J.W.N. Tempelhoff, *Townspeople of the Soutpansberg*, p. 18.

24. *BMB*, 1866, p. 69; C.J. Conerly, "The Surrendering of the Lands", p. 6; W.L. Maree, *Lig in die Soutpansberg: Die Sendingwerk van die Nederduitse Gereformeerde Kerk in Noord-Transvaal, 1863–1963*, Pretoria, Sinodale Sendingskommissies van die Nederduitse Gereformeerde Kerk, 1962, pp. 42–45; S.M. Miller and J.W.N. Tempelhoff, "Die romantiek van 'n grensterrein", p. 35;

and J.W.N. Tempelhoff, *Townspeople of the Soutpansberg*, pp. 18–19. See also D. Möller-Malan, *The Chair of the Ramabulanas*, South Africa, Central News Agency Ltd., 1953, pp. 39–41.

25. *BMB*, 1866, pp. 69–70; S.M. Miller and J.W.N. Tempelhoff, "Die romantiek van 'n grensterrein", p. 35; and J.W.N. Tempelhoff, *Townspeople of the Soutpansberg*, pp. 19–22.

26. J. Boeyens, "Louis Tregardt en die Opvolgingstryd tussen Ramabulana en Ramavhoya", in *South African Historical Journal/Suid-Afrikaanse Historiese Joernaal*, 23(1990), pp. 41–53; C.J. Conerly, "The Surrendering of the Lands", pp. 8–10; E. Gottschling, "The Bawenda", p. 197; M.M. Motenda, "History of the Western Venḓa", pp. 55–56; J. Tempelhoff and H. Nemudzivhadi, "Riding the storm of change: Makhado, Venda and the South African Republic (1864–1895), in *New Contree* (Department of History, Potchefstroom) (in 1999), 45 (September 1999), p. 104; and N.J. van Warmelo (ed.), *Contributions Towards Venda History*, pp. 6, 20–22.

27. J.C.A. Boeyens (a) *Die konflik tussen die Venda en die Blankes in Transvaal, 1864–1869*, Archives Year Book for South African History, Pretoria, Government Printer, 1990, Part I, p. 110 & (b) "'Black Ivory': The Indenture System and Slavery in Soutpansberg, 1848–1869", in E.A. Eldredge and F. Morton (eds.), *Slavery in South Africa: Captive Labour on the Dutch Frontier*, Boulder, San Fransisco and Oxford, Westview Press and Pietermaritzburg, University of Natal Press, 1994, p. 195; C.J. Conerly, "The Surrendering of the Lands", pp. 13–14; B.H. Dicke, *The Bush Speaks, Border Life in the Old Transvaal*, Second Edition, Pietermaritzburg, Shuter & Shooter, 1937, pp. 27–29; J.W.N. Tempelhoff, *Townspeople of the Soutpansberg*, p. 22; and R. Wagner, "Zoutpansberg", p. 333.

28. J. Boeyens, "Black Ivory", p. 196 (quotation); W.L. Maree, *Lig in die Soutpansberg*, p. 49; and R. Wagner, "Zoutpansberg", p. 321.

29. The standard biography of Albasini is J.B. de Vaal, *Die Rol van João Albasini in die Geskiedenis van die Transvaal*, Argiefjaarboek vir Suid-Afrikaanse Geskiedenis, Pretoria, Staatsdrukker, 1953, Deel I. See also especially *BMB*, 1880, p. 403; 1882, p. 422; 1885, pp. 71–72; J.C.A. Boeyens, *Die konflik tussen die Venda en die Blankes*, pp. 4–5; J.W.N. Tempelhoff, *Townspeople of the Soutpansberg*, p. 24; and T.A. van Ryneveld, "Remembering Albasini", MA thesis, University of Cape Town, 1998 (for Albasini's biography, see especially pp. 16–41). Many of Albasini's personal details are contested. Elizabeth Eldredge has suggested that Albasini may have fabricated his past, possibly to conceal mixed European and African ancestry (E. Eldredge, "Delagoa Bay and the Hinterland in the Early Nineteenth-Century: Politics, Trade, Slaves and Slave Raiding", in E.A. Eldredge and F. Morton (eds.), *Slavery in South Africa*, pp. 163–164). For uncritical acceptance of Albasini as a "chief", see especially J. Albasini III, "João Albasini, 1813–1888", pamphlet produced by the Albasini family and printed by Leach Printers, Louis Trichardt, n.d. (1988?); B.H. Dicke, *The Bush Speaks*, pp. 19–40, especially p. 24; and H. Klein, "Die Wit Opperhoof van die Sjangaans", in *Die Brandwag*, 8 July 1938, pp. 8, 9, 43. For a discussion of the whole question of what the title of "Chief of the Knobnoses" could have meant, see T.A. van Ryneveld, "Remembering Albasini", especially pp. 41, 60–64, 112–113, 132–133, 135, 138, 140–143, 148–150.

30. J. Boeyens, "Black Ivory", p. 196.

31. *BMB*, 1860, p. 63; 1863, p. 3; C.J. Conerly, "The Surrendering of the Lands", pp. 12–17; J.B. de Vaal, *Die Rol van João Albasini*, p. 15; J.W.N. Tempelhoff, *Townspeople of the Soutpansberg*, pp. 22–25; J. Tempelhoff and H. Nemudzivhadi, "Riding the storm of change", pp. 104–106; T.A. van Ryneveld, "Remembering Albasini", pp. 31, 33–34; and R. Wagner, "Zoutpansberg", especially pp. 315, 330–331, 333, 336, 337.

32. J.A.I. Agar-Hamilton, *The Native Policy of the Voortrekkers: An essay in the history of the interior of South Africa – 1836–1858*, Cape Town, Maskew Miller, 1928, pp. 187, 192–193; J. Boeyens (a) "'Zwart ivoor': Inboekelinge in Zoutpansberg, 1848–1869", in *South African Historical Journal/Suid-Afrikaanse Historiese Joernaal*, 24(1991), pp. 31–66 & (b) "Black Ivory", pp. 187–217; S. Hofmeyr, *Twintig Jaren in Zoutpansberg. Een Verhaal van Twintig Jarigen Arbeit onder de Heidenen in de Transvaal door den Eerw. Stéfanus Hofmeyr*, Kaapstad; J.H. Rose & Co., 1890, p. 27; T.A. van Ryneveld, "Remembering Albasini", pp. 34–35; and R. Wagner, "Zoutpansberg", pp. 332–333.

33. J. Boeyens (a) "Zwart ivoor", p. 32 & (b) "Black Ivory", p. 202.

34. J. Boeyens, "Black Ivory", pp. 196, 201. Note that reports invariably fail to mention what happened to the children.

35. J. Boeyens (a) "Zwart ivoor", p. 32 (quotations) & (b) "Black Ivory", pp. 206–207.
36. J.C.A. Boeyens, *Die konflik tussen die Venda en die Blankes*, pp. 4–5, 10–12, 18, 19, 110; P. Bonner, *Kings, Commoners and Concessionaires: The evolution and dissolution of the nineteenth-century Swazi state*, Johannesburg, Ravan Press, 1983, pp. 96–99; C.J. Conerly, "The Surrendering of the Lands", pp. 18–27; J.B. de Vaal, *Die Rol van João Albasini*, pp. 57–58, 75–76, 78–79, 82–83; T.A. van Ryneveld, "Remembering Albasini", pp. 35–37; and R. Wagner, "Zoutpansberg", pp. 326–329, 335–337.
37. T.A. van Ryneveld, "Remembering Albasini", pp. 37–38.
38. *BMB*, 1868, p. 102; J.C.A. Boeyens (a) *Die konflik tussen die Venda en die Blankes*, pp. 66–82, 110 & (b) "Black Ivory", pp. 200, 211 (note 69); C.J. Conerly, "The Surrendering of the Lands", pp. 23–28; J.B. de Vaal, *Die Rol van João Albasini*, pp. 90–104; S.M. Miller and J.W.N. Tempelhoff, "Die romantiek van 'n grensterrein", p. 36; and T.A. van Ryneveld, "Remembering Albasini", pp. 38, 50, 51–52, 84, 123.
39. J.C.A. Boeyens (a) *Die konflik tussen die Venda en die Blankes*, pp. 83–101 & (b) "Black Ivory", pp. 200–201; P. Bonner, *Kings, Commoners and Concessionaires*, p. 115; J.B. de Vaal, *Die Rol van João Albasini*, pp. 105–110; and T.A. van Ryneveld, "Remembering Albasini", pp. 38–39.
40. J.C.A. Boeyens, *Die konflik tussen die Venda en die Blankes*, p. 110; C.J. Conerly, "The Surrendering of the Lands", pp. 28–31; and T.A. van Ryneveld, "Remembering Albasini", p. 39.
41. J. Boeyens (a) "Zwart ivoor", p. 32 & (b) "Black Ivory", p. 193; J.B. de Vaal, *Die Rol van João Albasini*, pp. 142–143; T.A. van Ryneveld, "Remembering Albasini", p. 39; and R. Wagner, "Zoutpansberg", p. 316.
42. J. Boeyens (a) "Zwart ivoor", p. 32 & (b) "Black Ivory", p. 201.
43. J. Boeyens, "Black Ivory", pp. 208–209 n 30.
44. *Der Bawenda-Freund*, 14(56), 1896, pp. 328–330; 15(57), 1897, pp. 343–345; 15(58), 1897, p. 351; 15(59), 1897, pp. 358–363; and *BMB*, 1897, pp. 69, 108, 109, 110, 112, 274–275, 336–339, 531–532, 724–727, 732–733; 1898, pp. 5–11, 314–315, 318, 585.
45. C.J. Conerly, "The Surrendering of the Lands", p. 31; D. McDonald, "Vendaland", No. 110, p. 12; S.M. Miller and J.W. Tempelhoff, "Die romantiek van 'n grensterrein", p. 37; and U. der Heyden, "The Fighting Tradition of the Venda People", in *Sechaba: official organ of the African National Congress of South Africa*, January 1986, pp. 10–12.
46. T.A. van Ryneveld, "Remembering Albasini", p. 28 (quotation); R.Wagner, "Zoutpansberg", p. 318.
47. See especially J. Boeyens (a) "Zwart ivoor", p. 31 & (b) "Black Ivory", pp. 187, 194–195; T.A. van Ryneveld "Remembering Albasini", pp. 27–28, 121; and R. Wagner "Zoutpansberg", pp. 318–320.
48. J.B. de Vaal, *Die Rol van João Albasini*, p. 13; J.W.N. Tempelhoff, *Townspeople of the Soutpansberg*, p. 24.
49. *BMB*, 1866, p. 74; J.C.A. Boeyens, "Die Konflik tussen die Venda en die Blankes", p. 110; Bureau for Economic Research Co-operation and Development and the Institute for Development Studies, Rand Afrikaans University, *The Independent Venda*, Pretoria, Benso, 1979, pp. 20–21, 34; C.J. Conerly, "The Surrendering of the Lands", pp. 6, 27–31; S. Hofmeyr, *Twintig Jaren in Zoutpansberg*, especially pp. 35–42; W.F. Malunga, "A Century of Dutch Reformed Church Missionary Enterprise in the Soutpansberg Area – the story of Kranspoort", MA thesis, University of the North, 31 January 1986, pp. 1–7; W.L. Maree, *Lig in die Soutpansberg*, especially pp. 13, 36, 49–60; and S.M. Miller and J.W. Tempelhoff, "Die romantiek van 'n grensterrein", pp. 35–36.
50. *BMB*, 1866, pp. 74, 77, 88; 1872, p. 161; 1873, p. 133; 1874, pp. 70–71, 125, 136; 1881, pp. 335–336, 337, 340.
51. S. Hofmeyr, *Twintig Jaren in Zoutpansberg*, p. 26. See also J.A.I. Agar-Hamilton, *The Native Policy of the Voortrekkers*, pp. 117–118.
52. *BMB*, 1866, p. 69.
53. *Ibid*. pp. 71–72.

54. *Ibid.* pp. 74–76 (Murray visit); 1870, pp. 215–216.
55. *BMB*, 1866, p. 74.
56. *BMB*, 1870, p. 215.
57. *BMB*, 1872, p. 159; 1873, p. 133; 1874, p. 123 (quotation).
58. *BMB*, 1872, pp. 158–162.
59. *BMB*, 1873, pp. 132–137 (quotation p. 136); 1874, pp. 123–136.
60. *BMB*, 1873, p. 132.
61. Acta der Berliner Missionsgesellschaft betreffend Personalia: Beuster, Carl, Abt. II, Fach 3, Nr. 14, 1865–1902; *BMB*, 1874, pp. 67–69 (quotation p. 67), 130–134, 136–137 (note that the first report on the station is pp. 136–143).
62. *BMB*, 1874, pp. 123, 136. For the history of Ha-Tshivhase Mission station, see especially W. Gründler, *Geschichte der Bawenda-Mission in Nord-Transvaal*, Berlin, Buchhandlung der Berliner evangelischen Missionsgesellschaft, n.d. [1897], pp. 23–52; G. Sauberzweig-Schmidt, *Ha Schewasse, eine Hütte Gottes unter den Bawenda*, Zweite Auflage, Neue Missionsschriften Nr. 32, Berlin, Buchhandlung der Berliner evangelischen Missionsgesellschaft, n.d. [1896].
63. *BMB*, 1874, p. 68.
64. Acta der Berliner Missionsgesellschaft betreffend Personalia: Schwellnus, Erdmann, Abt. II, Fach 3, No. 25, n.d.; [Anon.] *75th Anniversary of the Berlin Mission Station Tshivhase, 8 November 1872–1947*, Pamphlet distributed for the celebration, No Publisher [Berlin Mission Society], n.d.[1947]; M.I. Bressani [Comp.], *Im Dienst der Mission: Ein Gedenkbüchlein der Berliner Missionsgesellschaft*, Berlin, Berliner Missionsgesellschaft, 1963, pp. 57–58. For the history of Tshakhuma Mission Station, see especially W. Gründler, *Geschichte der Bawenda-Mission in Nord-Transvaal*, pp. 52–68.
65. *BMB*, 1875, p. 364.
66. Stationschronik von Georgenholtz, p. 1 in Acta der Berliner Missionsgesellschaft betreffend Missions-Station Georgenholtz, Abt. IV, Fach IIE, Nr. 13, Stations-Synodalakte Band I von 1906 bis 1962, p. 125. Filed in Berlin Mission Archives, Berlin, Acta der Berliner Missionsgesellschaft betreffend Missionsstationen: Georgenholtz: NT von 1906 bis 1962, AUFB. FRIST a; ABGEL. IV, 2E, 13, Bd.1; Tagebuch der Station bei Ha Makoarela (Nicolaus Koen), 26. Juli 1877, in Berlin Mission Archives, Berlin, Acta der Berliner Missionsgesellschaft betreffend Missionsstationen: Tagebücher der Missionare auf Makoarela (Georgenholtz), Abt. III, Fach 5, No. 16, (I); *Bawenda-Freund*, 14(54), 1896, pp. 292–293; *BMB*, 1876, p. 400; 1878, pp. 256, 490–492; *Mitteilungen des Vereins "Heidenfreund"*, V(18), 1887, n.p. (pp. 2–3); V(19), 1887, n.p. (p. 2–3); and G. Sauberzweig-Schmidt, *Klaas Kuhn, ein Missionar aus den Hottentotten*, 4. Auflage, Dornen und Ähren vom Missionsfelde Nr. V, Berlin, Buchhandlung der Berliner evangelischen Missions-Gesellschaft, n.d. pp. 11, 12, 14. For the history of Georgenholtz Mission Station, see especially W. Gründler, *Geschichte der Bawenda-Mission in Nord-Transvaal*, pp. 69–91; G. Sauberzweig-Schmidt, *Georgenholtz im Lande der Bawenda,* Neue Missionsschriften Nr. 33, Berlin, Buchhandlung der Berliner evangelischen Missions-Gesellschaft, 1891. For New Geogrenholtz, established after the station was moved for health reasons, see P. Heimbach, *Neu-Georgenholtz im Wenda-Lande*, Neue Missionsschriften [Neue Folge] Nr. 25, Berlin, Berliner Missiongesellschaft, n.d. [1909].
67. Jahresbericht 1873–1899 in *BMB*, 1874–1900. Note that no figures at all were supplied for any of the stations for the year 1880 and 1900 and no figures except for the number of African people in reach of the station were provided for Georgenholtz for 1899.
68. J. Flygare, *De Zoutpansbergen en de Bawenda Natie*, Pretoria, The State Library Reprints, No. 86, 1979 (originally published at Pretoria, De Volksstem Drukkerij, 1899, p. 6).
69. *Der Bawenda-Freund*, 11(42), 1883, p. 161; VI(23), 1888, p. 67; 14(54), 1896, p. 292; 14(55), 1896, p. 310; 31(2), 1914, p. 22; 33(4), 1916, p. 11; 35(2), 1918, p. 5; *BMB,* 1873, pp. 132–137, 213; 1874, pp. 123–143; 1875, pp. 231, 368; and *Mitteilungen des Vereins "Heidenfreund"*, V(16), 1887, n.p. (pp. 2–3).
70. See, for example, A. Kirkaldy (a) "'Digging in the Archives': *Khosi* Masindi Mphaphuli, *Khosi* Makwarela Mphaphuli and the Berlin Missionaries in Vendaland, c.1876–1897", unpublished paper presented to the Biennial Conference of the South African Association of Archaeologists, Thohoyandou, 6 July 1998, pp. 18, 37, 43 & (b) "Makoarele's return to 'the darkness of hea-

thenism': *Khosi* Makwarela and the Berlin Missionaries", in U. van der Heyden and J. Becher (eds.), *Mission und Moderne Beiträge zur Geschichte der Christlichen Missionen in Afrika anläßlich der Jahrestagung der VAD und des 12. Afrikanistentages vom 3–6. Oktober 1996 in Berlin*, especially pp. 122, 128.

71. *BMB*, 1899, pp. 94, 326, 643, 696; 1900, pp. 259, 304, 306, 308, 680, 694, 696, 706; G. Sauberzweig-Schmidt, *Klaas Kuhn*, pp. 31–32; and Stationschronik von Georgenholtz, p. 2.

72. *BMB,* 1876, p. 394; 1881, p. 335; C.J. Conerly, "The Surrendering of the Lands", p. 35; and Alexandre Jaques, "Les coutumes funéraires des meurt dans l'eau", in *Bulletin de la Mission Suisse Romande*, XXXVI (475), March–April 1927, p. 256. See also [Anon.], "Das Missionshospital der Mission Romande in Elim", in *Mitteilungen des Berliner Vereins für Ärtzliche Mission und seiner Zweigvereine*, Nr. 2, Berlin, März 1910, pp. 49–56; Nr. 3, Mai 1910, pp. 73–83; and Nr. 4, Juli 1910, pp. 101–107; M. Dreyer, "'Welche Gleichgültigkeit! Welch Widerstand!' – Elim Hospital 1899–1906", student seminar paper, University of Basel, 1999; and T.N. Thavhiwa, "Elim Hospital: Pure, Medical and Political Administration, 1899–1997", BA Honours thesis, University of Venda, 1998.

73. See especially *BMB*, 1877, p. 485; 1878, pp. 251, 489; 1879, p. 410; 1886, p. 78.

CHAPTER 2
Local Beginnings

Extremely surprised at finding a group of Christians in Vendaland whose conversion pre-dated the arrival of missionaries there in 1872, the Berlin Missionary Carl Beuster referred to them as having formed "a kind of conventicle".[1] Sundkler and Steed have pointed out that in doing so, he was using "a classic Pietist term, in vogue at the same time in nineteenth-century Germany and Sweden" to describe this early local group of believers.[2] Their core members had originally been Johannes Mutshaeni, Piet (who would assume the name and title of Totane) and Solomon.[a] Basing their arguments on cases such as these, Sundkler and Steed have also argued that the first few years of Vhavenda, Pedi and Lobedu "Church history elucidate in sharp relief an important theme in the South African development: the extent to which the spread of Christianity depended on local African initiative".[3] In attempting to explain this for the Pedi, Delius has argued that, for some, their first encounter with Christianity had come through their having been *inboekelinge* of the Boers. Others had sold their labour to eastern Transvaal farmers, or had taken part in hunting parties organised by the Boers and other white hunters. With the developing importance of migrant labour, increasing numbers of men had also been exposed to the Christian message though their having worked as migrant labourers in the Cape Colony (particularly Port Elizabeth and Uitenhage) and Natal.[4] These themes also recur in the life histories of converts from Vendaland who adopted Christianity prior to the arrival of the missionaries. Interestingly, they also contradict Delius' assertion that, while significant numbers of Pedi, Sotho, Tsonga-Shangaan and Lobedu migrant workers were tied into providing labour to the Cape Colony and Natal in the 1860s and 1870s, "the Venda do not appear to have been involved".[5]

JOHANNES MUTSHAENI AND THE VENDALAND CONVENTICLE

In presenting his life history to Beuster, who would later publish it in the Berlin Mission's *Neue Missionsschriften* series, Johannes Mutshaeni fondly

---

a. Piet's father was a *gota* of Tshivhase's whose throne-name was Totane. I have been unable to trace the son's name prior to his baptism. Piet was his baptismal name. After succeeding to his father's throne, he adopted his throne-name, Totane. I use the name Totane both before he was baptised as "Piet" and after his accession to his late father's throne as *gota*. For the period when he was part of a Christian fellowship, I refer to him as Piet. Note that mission sources consistently refer to him as *Häuptling* (*khosi* or chief). Since he was a *gota*, and not in the line of succession of one of the great houses, I describe him as such unless in quotation. Thus far, all efforts to trace Totane and his father in sources other than Berlin Mission sources have proved to be unsuccessful. I have also been unable to trace Solomon's family name.

recalled both the hardships and the joys of his childhood. On the whole, his description focused on the peaceful rhythms of a "traditional" rural lifestyle. Mutshaeni portrayed himself very much as an ordinary Muvenda, having grown up in a way which did not differ from that of his contemporaries. The obvious sub-text here was that just as he had been reborn as a new man in Christ, so they too could experience the same wondrous transformation.[6]

Mutshaeni stated that he was born about 1840 in the Province of Tshiheni, ruled by a *gota* of Tshivhase's.[b] His mother died when he was very young but he was well looked after by his father's two remaining wives. It will be seen that the missionaries were vehemently opposed to the practice of polygyny and could see no good in it. The irony of one of their greatest converts having benefited from this practice in his childhood seems to have escaped them.

When Mutshaeni was a young man, Albasini's forces and the Boers began to raid for *inboekelinge*, and impose taxes, in the areas surrounding Tshiheni. Only the protection offered by its inaccessible position high in the mountains saved the village from the "savage atrocities of the Knopneusen". It was only with the fall of Schoemansdal that some kind of more widespread peace was secured.[7]

Mutshaeni informed Beuster that, at first, local people had been very suspicious of voluntarily going to work for these people who forcibly carried off their compatriots. In addition, during the time of his youth, the idea of working for wages had not yet taken root in the area. However, after several years people who had some experience of the Boers began to return to Vendaland. Presumably they were either *inboekelinge* who had been freed by or escaped from their former masters, or the first returning voluntary migrant labourers. They stated that the Boers badly needed labour and paid a cow for a year's work. This was reportedly

> something unheard of for the Bawenda [Vhavenda]. The prospect of obtaining cattle – and thereby acquiring the means to buy wives and so gain the honour and respect of their people – even overcame their fear and aversion of the unknown foreign regions. And when this one, and then that one, returned hale and hearty, driving the well-earned cow proudly before him, the wanderlust took hold of more and more of the young people around there. It was soon regarded as a disgrace if one had not been to foreign lands.[8]

Thus, the idea of going away to work gradually became an important rite of passage on the road to manhood. Apparently in the late 1850s or early 1860s, Mutshaeni and several of his companions left and successfully found work

---

b. In present-day terms, this is the village on the north-west boundary of the Tate Vondo forest, at the lookout tower which overlooks Lake Fundudzi [see Map 2].

with a Boer. As with his fellows, he was reportedly "harsh and demanded hard work". Mutshaeni nevertheless rose to the challenge and proved to be a hard worker.

Apparently reflecting both Mutshaeni's testimony and Beuster's impressions of the Boers, and in direct contradiction to the commonly-held impression in South Africa that the Boers used to have their servants attend home prayers, Mutshaeni reportedly

> did not get a good understanding of Christianity from what he saw in the home of the Boer. The Black people [*farbigen Leute*] were not allowed to participate in the morning and evening prayers, and no-one in the home thought of worrying about the well-being of the souls of the Black people. After all, they were just *skepsels* i.e. creatures, like the animals of the fields, good enough to be used and then to be cast aside.[9]

Moreover, according to Mutshaeni's testimony, undisputed by Beuster, these Boers were not to be trusted:

> The closer it came to the end of the year, the harder the work became, and the harsher and hostile the treatment was. This was the usual way which many Boers regularly applied, to get their Black labourers – who were by then tired of the drudgery – to run away. The labourers had then broken the contract, and their master was the no longer obliged to pay them the cow for the work done. Motscheni however had a tough nature, and he persevered.[10]

In addition to this portrayal of the Boers as hypocritical, exploitative, devious and cunning, the account characterized them as being cruel as well. Mutshaeni continued his tale by stating that there were still many lions in the area where the Boers lived. One day, he went hunting, taking Johannes with him to carry his gun. Seeing a lion, the Boer instructed Johannes to give him the gun and to carry on walking towards the lion, presumably to attract its attention, while he shot. "But Baas, the lion will bite me!"

"Be quiet Boy," commanded the Boer, "and walk. I will shoot it."

Mutshaeni tremblingly followed his master's order. The Boer fired but missed. Again the Boer loaded and told Johannes to walk towards the lion. Terrified out of his wits, Mutshaeni attempted to climb a tree. The Boer threatened to shoot him if he refused to come down and approach the lion. Climbing down, he begged for a knife so that he could at least attempt to defend himself. His master refused to supply him with this but Johannes was as scared of him as of the lion and continued walking. The Boer fired for a second time, again missing the lion. Wheeling his horse around, he fled from the scene, leaving Mutshaeni at the mercy of the lion. In what he would later interpret as a sign of divine protection, the enormous lion calmly turned its back and walked away.[11]

As the account continues, it becomes clear that Mutshaeni and Beuster were strongly implying that there could have been more to the flight of the Boer than mere cowardice. Were his labourer to disappear or die in his service, there would be no need to pay him his wage of a cow at the end of his contract. To this end, the Boer reportedly once more exposed Mutshaeni to an attack by lions during the closing part of the contract period.[12]

In the light of Mutshaeni's later consciousness, and in an interpretation shared (and possibly partly shaped) by Beuster, God was clearly protecting Mutshaeni and leading him to the point where he would have to make a decision about conversion and salvation – the gradual turning to God so characteristic of Pietistic thinking. In line with this cosmology, the hardships and disappointments that he was experiencing were also helping to strengthen and shape his character and lead him to the point where he would turn to God. However, before he could reach this position, he would need to learn that, without the grace of God, all human endeavour and all human strength were bound to fail. While he would reach the first stage of this new consciousness in continuing labour for a Transvaal Boer, later developments would have to await his move to Natal as a migrant labourer.

From a less theological perspective, Johannes' elder brother wanted to get married. The negotiations with his prospective bride's family had already taken place but he did not have enough cattle to hand over to them. As the younger brother, Johannes therefore agreed to go and work for another year. He would then give his cattle to his brother so that he could get married. At a later date, his brother would help him to obtain a wife.[13] This arrangement was (and still is) the expected one in terms of the local cosmology. In ideal terms, there was a strong pecking order and the younger was expected to be submissive to the elder. To balance this, the older one was expected to take care of the younger one. It was therefore normal for the older brother to marry first. Also, what one had earned did not belong to one alone, but belonged to the family or clan. It was therefore natural for the cow to be used for the elder brother's marriage. In this particular case, the father was still alive and was the head of an extended polygamous family. Under such conditions, the eldest son could not be expected to go away to work, leaving the family alone, as he was expected to assist his aged father in managing the family. So the younger ones could be sent out to work, while he remained at home helping his father, the head of the family.

Since he was still young, strong and a hard worker, Mutshaeni soon found work again. At the end of his year's contract, "he had had more than enough of his work for this Boer and his heart beat impatiently for home, which he did not intend to leave again. But man proposes and God disposes". On his way home, in the vicinity of Waterberg Mission Station, near present-day Kranspoort, he met some people from home. They informed him that his eldest brother had died of smallpox. All that he had been looking forward to reportedly evaporated. "The joy in the cow as well as the return to his home all disappeared and turned to disgust, and he reached Tschehene [Tshiheni] in a state of gloom and depression."[14]

Having spent some months at home, Mutshaeni came into contact with some local people who had returned home from labour contracts in Natal. They reportedly

> told him that far, far beyond the land of the Boers, there lived another people, called the Muinglisman [*Vha-Isimane*] i.e. Englishmen. They are said to be as rich as kings, but they have better customs and treat their labourers more gently than the Boers. And the main thing was, that one could there buy precious guns for the easily earned money – the possession of a gun was the essence of the longing of all black people. Motscheni [Mutshaeni] did not take long to make up his mind. This time he did not have to go alone. Some of his earlier comrades – amongst whom was Totane, the son and heir of the Chief – accompanied him, hoping to also procure guns in this far away land.[15]

Although guns were freely available to Africans in the Cape Colony, especially on the Kimberley diamond fields, laws against the possession of firearms by Africans were much more vigorously enforced in Natal. This did not prevent a lively trade in illegal weapons from developing to cater for the demands of African migrant workers. A number of authors have commented on the crucial importance attached to firearms both for use in the defence of home communities against settler intrusion or in other local battles, and as an essential symbol of manhood.[16]

After a long and difficult walk, Mutshaeni and his travelling companions reached Pietermaritzburg. Some of their fellow countrymen had reached the area earlier, found jobs, married and no longer wished to return home. A number of these had already been baptised, or were attending baptism classes. They made it their special concern to take care of the new arrivals. They helped them to find work and encouraged them to attend Christian meetings with them during the evenings and on Sundays. Neither Mutshaeni nor any of his travelling companions "had the least idea about what these meetings were about". However, out of "mere curiosity", on the Sunday after his arrival, he attended the Methodist chapel, hearing the sermon of the Rev. James Allison, "who proclaimed the Gospel to the Black people [*Farbigen*] with holy zeal". Since the preaching was in Zulu, Mutshaeni "could not understand very much. But the service itself made a deep impression on him.

On the next Sunday, he went again and never missed a single church meeting after that".[17]

In true Pietistic mould: "The more he began to understand the sermons, the more a new light began to shine over his whole previous life. Suddenly he realised that he was a terrible sinner, and a big turmoil took hold of him." In his time of trouble, he turned to his Christian friends for advice. They informed him that the only way to quieten his heart again was to "go to the teacher and learn about the Word". Accepting their advice, he began attending baptism classes. He was joined in this by some of his friends, including Totane. It was reportedly

> no easy matter for the men to practice the difficult art of reading by the sweat of their brows, in the evening, after they had worked hard for the whole day. Sometimes the curly signs would just not stick in Motscheni's [Mutshaeni's] head. Where the natural aptitude of the others put them ahead of Motscheni, he had to make up for it with faithful and hard work, so that his teacher came to have a special soft spot for him.[18]

Having received the name Johannes on his baptism, he and his fellow Vhavenda baptismal mates, Piet (Totane), Jacob, Jesaias and Solomon "promised each other that they would faithfully keep contact with one another and mutually strengthen each other in the new-found faith". They also decided to return to Vendaland "to preach the Good News to their relatives and friends there".

Leaving Pietermaritzburg, the party formed "a considerable caravan". Not only had they used their wages to buy firearms and "other desirable goods", they had also bought several horses to carry their purchases. "Accompanied by the best wishes of the small congregation, they started off on their journey, and walked along proudly, with heads held high, next to their pack-animals."[19]

Alas, their joy was short-lived. Upon reaching Boer territory, they were stopped. It was forbidden for Africans to import guns, gun-powder, bullets or horses into the ZAR. Thus, the most valuable parts of their possessions were confiscated – it was left to them to carry the remainder on their backs. Solomon wrote to Allison, requesting him to assist them in reclaiming the confiscated goods. The missionary replied that there was nothing that he could do as the officials had been acting in terms of the law. "He could only advise his pupils to rather look for the treasures which neither moths nor rust could destroy; the things which thieves will not dig up or steal." Despite "being very sad himself", Mutshaeni took this test in his stride and used it to build the faith of the group. He comforted his companions as best as he could, telling them that the Word which they had learnt was better than all that they had lost. He also insisted that they regularly pray and read God's Word throughout the journey.[20]

As the converts neared their homeland, they heard of a "white teacher" living at Blauberg. Deciding to visit him immediately, they were well received by Missionary Beyer. He promised to visit them at some stage after they had reached home and to ask *Khosi* Tshivhase whether he would allow white teachers to live in his realm. Johannes' eyes reportedly "lit up with sheer joy" at this prospect. Hardly had they returned home when he persuaded his companions to accompany him to Tshivhase to tell him about all that had befallen them.

As was customary "on special occasions", Tshivhase took the Christians aside and listened to their tale:

> Without any reservations, they confessed that they were now Men of the Book. On his insistence, they read to him out of the Book, during which Tschewase [Tshivhase] was most amazed by the turning of the pages. When Johannes then turned the conversation to the teacher, he [Tshivhase] declared: "Listen, you people, if this teacher feels like you are saying he does – that, if I wish it, a White teacher would probably come here – then find one for me. I will give you the region of Tschimbone [Tshimbone]. You can live there with your teacher, and I myself will go there and learn."[21]

After they had taken their leave from Tshivhase, this small group separated, each returning to his own family. Soon thereafter, Jacob and Jesaias abandoned Christianity as a result of "the enticements of their heathen relatives".[22] For a time, Johannes Mutshaeni, Piet and Solomon formed the core of the "conventicle" whose existence had so surprised Beuster. Both Piet and Solomon were married and their wives joined the praying and the singing.[23] Having been a particularly bright student, Solomon had received extra training as a so-called "Native Teacher" from Allison, who had also appointed him as teacher for the Vendaland area. He began by teaching his eldest son "most earnestly, and also witnessed in other ways".[24] Having failed in their attempts to proselytize adult members of the community, Piet and Johannes turned their attention to the children, teaching them all the songs and stories which they knew.[25] In Mutshaeni's words, Piet's wife "used to cheer up us men". On the occasions when the three Christians and the two wives come together to pray and offer each other mutual support, they "had great pleasure" together.[26]

Because he lived reasonably far away from Mutshaeni and Piet, Solomon gradually began to drift away from them. Despite his lack of regular contact with his fellow believers, he nevertheless seems to have still considered himself to be a Christian.[27] This left Mutshaeni and Piet in contact with each other. Due to his noble birth, Piet faced pressures and temptations which commoners like Mutshaeni and outsiders like the missionaries could presumably not have understood or related to. Similarly, even today, we can only attempt to unravel and understand some of these complexities but cannot claim anything approaching a full insight into them.

While Piet managed to resist these pressures for some time, they began immediately after his return. His father having died while he was away in Natal, with Piet's return home, *Khosi* Tshivhase appointed him as *gota* [*Kraalkapitain*] of the area formerly ruled by his father. With this, he started to use, or reverted to using, the name Totane. To me, this strongly suggests a rejection of missionary-interpreted Christianity by assuming his deceased father's throne name, which may or may not also have been his name prior to baptism.[28] The changeover is marked in mission reports by an entry referring to the *gota* as "Chief Totane (who was called Piet in previous Mission Reports)".[29] From here onwards, he is only referred to by the name of Totane.

Despite these changes, Totane "for a long time, continued to pray and remained faithful" after his return from Natal. Beuster would later record that the *gota* had at first used his position "to spread the Word amongst his people. He did not drink any intoxicating beer, observed the Sunday and gathered the children of his village around him to teach them how to pray and sing". On Sundays, Johannes Mutshaeni would come through with a children's choir which he was training. They would then celebrate the Day of the Lord together. However, in Beuster's interpretation, "soon the enthusiasm of the young chief cooled down. The strength of his faith was not up to resisting the temptations – a man in his position had to face double the usual temptations". Gradually, he began to evade "Johannes' serious and penetrating warnings, or he would interrupt Johannes abruptly with: 'You have now spoken enough good words; so you can go.'"[30]

In my interpretation, Totane had retained some of the Christian teachings that he had been exposed to in Natal but was gradually becoming less orthodox in terms of the then-current western definitions of Christian belief and practice. As with many other local people at the time, he would later raise the issues of polygyny and power as his main reason for turning aside from Christianity and argue that:

> The traditions of his country and the constant nagging of his relatives, as well as the king [Tshivhase], finally got the better of him – they had often wondered why he, who had enough cattle to buy other wives, only had one wife.[31]

Polygyny was frequently used as a symbol of problems with accepting Christianity, or as a reason for rejecting Christianity, especially by male members of the local elite. They frequently expressed concern about what would happen to their other wives if they had to select just one. Even male commoners used a similar argument, either worrying about sending wives away or about closing off the possibility of marrying more than one wife.[32]

On the one hand, this perhaps shows how deeply-rooted was the idea that one had to have more than one wife if possible. On the other, the elite had the most to lose through conversion. Bearing in mind the status that they had to uphold, and the social and economic role that they were expected to perform, it is unlikely that they could have succeeded with only one wife.

In spite of difficulties and concerns such as these,

> For a long time he had persevered: It is God's wish that he only has one [wife] and he wants every man to have only one wife. And, oh, he bore this with pain, as his wife was without child for a long time. This caused his own people to despise him even more. They said to him: He can now see how God punishes him, because he did not keep to the customs of the land; he had to have another wife because he had to provide the descendants.[33]

This was a matter of no trivial concern. It would appear that, according to local belief structures, a man who had not fathered children had not fulfilled one of his primary missions (if not his primary mission) in life.[34] Without descendants, the family line, and hence its ancestors, would die out. Some idea of the seriousness with which this was viewed locally may be gleaned by the discussion of rites surrounding the death of a young man who had not yet given birth to children in the chapter on missionary photography.[35]

In spite of this extremely difficult situation, Totane managed to resist the pressure to take a second wife until his brother died, without any descendants. In terms of local Levirate practices, he was expected to take his brother's widow into his home and provide her with children. These would continue his deceased brother's lineage. The *Berliner Missions-Berichte* reported: "Again he refused for a long time, until his resistance was finally worn down by all the threats and nagging, and he took her as his wife."[36]

What the missionaries did not explain was that the *gota* had little option but to act in the way that he did. Refusal to do so would have represented a complete dereliction of his social duty to ensure the continuation of the lineage and to care and provide for his brother's widow. It was only acceptable to refuse to do this in cases where the woman was suspected of witchcraft or was "of doubtful worth in other respects".[37]

Having broken with Christian practice by taking a second wife, Totane was faced with a further serious challenge to his faith. Again, this was a situation where refusal to follow existing practices would have placed him beyond the pale of local society, placing not only him but the whole society in danger:

> But then a strange thing happened: His own wife gave birth to twins. Now, according to the custom here, only the first-born child is allowed to live. The second child is automatically, as if

> it was the most natural thing to do, immediately strangled at birth. In this case, the first-born child was still-born and he naturally let the last child live. But this caused a new fight. Through all impossible means, they tried to force this poor person to strangle his last-born child. Again he refused to do so, for a long time. At first it looked like he would win, in that he declared: The first child did not have life. It therefore was not a child. Only the second child was a child. That is why not two, but only one child was brought into the world. And that child is staying alive. But the Power of Darkness here is still an almighty Power and its king is even mightier. Again his soul became weary and he permitted his child to be murdered.[38]

Given that there was no mission station in Vendaland at the time, I do not see that the future *gota* had any option other than to bow down to societal pressure in these two major cases. Perhaps he could have gone to one of the mission stations in the Sotho-speaking areas, but this would have represented a complete break with his people. Even if he had been accepted at the Dutch Reformed Mission to the Buyse, this would have represented an equally dramatic break. There is also the possibility that, despite his assertions to the contrary, he had not rejected his upbringing and believed that the actions that he was forced to take in terms of local ways were, to varying degrees, "correct" or "just".

Such tensions and subtleties had no place in missionary thinking. Once they established themselves in the area, they would attempt to make sense of these events for themselves. For Beuster, it was Totane's decision to allow the surviving twin to be killed that marked "his real defection from the faith". The missionary also reported that Mutshaeni had been greatly saddened by these events as "he knew very well that the defection of the chief would also close the ears of his people to the Word of God".[39] He would later inform the *gota* that: "Totane, you are like the leader of a wagon. If the leader takes a wrong turn, the whole wagon will have an accident. You are now walking on the wrong path and you will destroy your whole nation."[40]

With Solomon too far away for any kind of sustained contact and Totane increasingly moving away from orthodox mission-style Christianity, Mutshaeni became isolated. Since the adults in his area generally turned a deaf ear to him, his main contact was with the children. He taught them all of the Bible stories and Christian songs and hymns that he knew.[41] He also continued to read his Bible on his own and prayed all the more. In conformity with local practice, he married Mufanatsho, the woman who had been promised to his deceased brother as a bride. The big difference between his action and that of Totane was that he resolved to take her as his only wife. Also, although she was not a Christian, "he presented his marriage to the Lord through God's

Word and prayer, and he did everything he could to also win over the heart of his wife for the Lord."[c]

Soon after his marriage, at his father's wish, Johannes moved to Tshakhuma with his father and their extended family. On his arrival there, he heard that "white teachers" [Beyer and Baumbach] had passed through the area on their way to Tshivhase. Seeing this as a fulfilment of Beyer's earlier promise to him and his fellow converts:

> A happy and excited Johannes rushed after them. But he was too late. They had already returned to Blauberg along a different route. A disappointed and dejected Johannes returned home to Tschakoma [Tshakhuma]. His longing to hear God's Word regularly intensified all the time, and he contemplated leaving his homeland and friends, and moving to Blauberg. But his plans were wrecked by opposition from his wife and the constant pleas from his grey-haired father. So he remained in Tschakoma and in quiet hope, continued to sow the seed of the Word.[42]

Thus, by the time that the Berlin missionaries began to enter Vendaland, the so-called conventicle of Christians who had been baptised by Allison were suffering the effects of their isolation from a wider established Christian community. A sense of group identity would not only have been much more cohesive in a larger group but, as relatively new converts, they would also have had the support and guidance of more experienced Christians whose faith had been forged and strengthened over time. Coupling this with pressures to resume local ways and local indifference towards, or hostility to, their teachings, their group identity was very much weaker than it had been on their first return from Natal. Mutshaeni (Johannes) and Solomon were basically the only two out of the original five who maintained a commitment to their new religion. It will also become clear that Mutshaeni remained much more orthodox than Solomon. In order to illustrate that these experiences were not confined to this small group alone, I will now examine the story of David Denga. The unfolding story will also demonstrate that the situation of previously-baptised Christians in Vendaland became even more complex after the arrival of the missionaries.

---

c. Despite the fact that his brother had died before his wife had moved to his home, the negotiations for the marriage had already taken place. Mufanatsho (recorded as "Mofanatso") had thus already been promised to the Mutshaeni family, and they had promised to receive her. So they were responsible for her welfare. Since Johannes was a Christian, and could only have one wife, he took her as his one and only wife, even though she was not a Christian. Mufanatsho would finally be baptised on the First Sunday after Trinity of 1877, in the year after her husband's death. At her baptism, she took the name Johanna to commemorate Johannes. Soon after this, the late Mutshaeni's brothers followed her example (*BMB*, 1878, p. 486; C. Beuster, *Johannes Motscheni*, p. 22).

DAVID DENGA

As with Mutshaeni, Denga was portrayed as being very much of the people. It will become clear in discussing Makwarela Mphaphuli's life history that even heirs to the throne grew up in a similar way to their peers.[43] Despite the fact that his mother was of royal blood, "David's youth was spent in a similar way as that of other heathen boys – herding the cattle, guarding the mealie [*corn*] fields against baboons and birds, working in the gardens [fields], etc."[44]

Memories of hardships suffered at the hand of the encroaching Boers, and their raids for *inboekelinge* played a more significant role in Denga's recollections than in those of Mutshaeni. Interestingly, while some of these appear to be direct memories, others have a folkloristic element. In dealing with these invaders, personal experience could be integrated with the collective experience and the collective claimed as the individual. In this situation, where much of the "truth" was bizarre, even the bizarre could be accepted, and claimed, as "true". Thus:

> When he [Denga] had grown into a youth [teenager?], he also came to feel the pressure under which the whole country groaned at that time, viz. the strong hand of the Boers [*Bauern*]. The Boers, with the terrible gun in their hands, intimidated the Black man into slavery. David still remembered well how the Boers, sjambok (riding crop) in hand, entered his village and demanded to see the chief, and how he appeared trembling, and had to supply food and people – as much as they demanded. As the poor Blacks cannot return force with force, they try to protect themselves against total domination with cunning trickery. While the Black servants appear to willingly follow the Boers to the hunting fields, they scheme to escape as soon as possible under cover of the darkness of night. But the Boers soon became experienced; they tied their servants, just like their oxen, to the wagon every evening. This also happened to our David several times. It is said here that the Bakalanga[d] use another form of trickery to escape from the Boers. When they are surprised by the Boers in the plains, and it is not possible to hide, they stand on their heads with their legs stretched straight up into the air. The Boers then take them to be poles and go past them [?].[45]

The *inboekeling* system was extremely harsh. Thus, despite the polemical and exaggerated style of the account, the descriptions of the ruthlessness of the Boers in demanding food and labourers and their treatment of their workers

---

d. Karanga (or VhaKaranga) – the people living in eastern Zimbabwe, who are closely related to the Vhavenda.

seem plausible. Whether, in commenting on this, Denga was recounting his own experiences or whether these were influenced by a common experience is unclear but, I would argue, irrelevant. It certainly seems that he was either coerced into accompanying, or willingly accompanied, the Schoemansdal Boers on hunting trips. This suggests the possibility that he originally came from, or settled for a time in, Makhado's area, the western Soutpansberg. Alternatively, he may have been captured elsewhere and taken there by force. There is also the strong possibility that, like many others, he went there to earn some money. Since, at the time that the missionaries arrived in Vendaland, he, his mother and the rest of the family were living in Mphaphuli's area, this seems to be the most likely explanation.[46] However he came to be there, it would seem that he got very little in return for his labour.

The statement about Karanga methods of hiding from the Boers is more complicated. As indicated by the question mark appearing in the original text, even the missionaries had problems in accepting local assertions about people disguising themselves as poles. I am convinced that it is a folkloristic element. It is nevertheless difficult to know what to make of it. On the one hand, it may symbolise the fear that the Boer raiding parties engendered by showing that people were prepared to try anything to escape from them. On the other, Denga and other local people may have been attempting to show how ingenious or cunning Africans were in comparison to what they saw as the rather slow-witted Boers. More cynically, in telling Beuster what they thought that he wanted to hear, perhaps his informants were attempting to find the boundaries of what the missionary was prepared to believe.

At a more metaphorical level, Denga and others could have been saying to Beuster that the Boers could not differentiate between people and "things" – a commentary on their relations with African people. Alternatively, it could have been a metaphorical way of saying "we have ways and means of avoiding capture by these Boers". Thus, David Denga and his compatriots were apparently using their statements about disguising oneself as a pole as a way of commenting on fear of capture by, and forced labour for, the Boers, on power relations and on African ingenuity.

As with Mutshaeni, Denga's life story reveals that, in addition to the horrors of war and labour raids, he had also tasted what he interpreted to be the hardships and dangers of working for the Boers:

> While on these hunting trips with the Boers [*Bauern*], it often meant doing long journeys. And it was not seldom that David was put in danger and was tired to the point of exhaustion. "Tobacco revives the dead," he once said and when I expressed my doubt about this, he told me how, on such a trip he used tobacco to bring back to life one of his comrades who already appeared to be dead. He did this by pourisng a good dose of snuff into the mouth of his dying friend. After that, totally

exhausted as he was, he still managed to get his companion to the water. They regained some of their strength there. And when they then craftily managed to catch a badger [*Dachs*], and had eaten the meat raw, they could again walk on slowly ...ᵉ Once David accompanied a Boer [*Bauer*] far into the hunting-field. All the Boer's oxen died after being bitten by tsetse-flies. The Boer had to leave his wagon behind in the veld. They had to walk back on foot.⁴⁷

Again in conformity with his later world view, which corresponded with that of Beuster, Denga still had to be tempered more by disappointment and suffering before he could become a fine tool in the service of the Lord. According to what he later told the missionary, once he became a man, "he was also drawn to Natal, the country of guns".⁴⁸ At this stage, labour opportunities in Natal included work in the port or work in agriculture, either on the sugar cane plantations or other farms. Taking up these opportunities involved a long journey, which was usually completed on foot. Working so far away from home, to obtain the cash to purchase a gun, a sign of manhood, was obviously something which had to await the assumption of the status of manhood through attending (depending on the time period) a so-called "bush school" or circumcision lodge.⁴⁹

Denga was reportedly "a hard worker [who] ... knew how to satisfy his master". It did not take him long to earn enough to obtain a gun and return home. However, in a similar experience to that suffered by Mutshaeni and his party, he "was not destined to reach home with his treasure". Discovered in possession of the firearm, it was taken from him "and after that his beautiful gun decorated the bare room of a Boer [*Bauer*]".⁵⁰

Denga's sense of honour did not allow him to return home without the gun he had worked so hard for. Thus, without even reaching his home, he reportedly turned back to work to obtain another gun. Enlisting for a second period of labour on the same farm where he had worked before, he was determined to be more careful when smuggling the gun home this time.⁵¹

A number of his fellow workers on this farm were Christians. They attempted to persuade him to "recognise God's ways and become a believer". However, he mocked them, telling them: "You are foolish boys. I am a man; what can you teach me." After having earned enough to buy a second gun, he again left for home, ignoring the pleadings of the believers. Unfortunately for him, he was just as unsuccessful this time:

> Once again his gun ended up in the house of a Boer – another cunning farmer had outsmarted David. It was of no use feeling

---

e. The Afrikaans word "dassie" is derived from the Dutch "*das*" (badger). Both words are similar to the German "*Dachs*". I suspect that they ate a dassie or rock rabbit, rather than a badger.

angry, or sorry for oneself; it was impossible to take revenge. But to appear at home without a gun was too sad to bear thinking about. After all, the thing that mattered was not so much how long he stayed away from home, but much rather on what he gained from it. For this reason David once again turned his foot-steps to the Land of Guns – and that was not nearby.[52]

This third trip was destined to change his whole life. In Beuster's interpretation, "David had mellowed; his pride was broken." Having been foiled in his smuggling attempts, he began to listen to the believers and to believe that he could achieve nothing in his own strength. Although he again worked hard and earned another gun, "this time he did not only think about the work – the Hand of the Lord had become too powerful for him". He started attending Christian instruction with the believers.[53]

In keeping with the Pietistic idea of a conversion experience, his acceptance of God was not only the product of a gradual process. He also experienced what he (and Beuster) interpreted as the power of God at first hand:

> One day, a crowd of workers stood in front of the house of the teacher, Mr Allison, and asked for passes so that they could return home. They had worked in the town for a while and were carrying many goods [home with them]. The teacher drew their attention to the fact that they should have rather stayed so that they could still learn about God's Word; after that they could return home with this additional most precious treasure. Some of the people heeded to the teacher's words and stayed. But others, ten in number, hit together the metal bracelets on their wrists so that they clattered and said: "We are *Makarapa* [*Magaraba*] i.e. well travelled men who are experienced in the ways of the world. We do not need this." and they left. After a short while, the newspapers brought news that ten Black men [*Kaffern*], on their way back from Natal, had been attacked and murdered by Mapoch's people.[f] Those were the world-wise men. A beneficial shock-wave passed through all members of that congregation and even through the heathens, when the teacher publicly related this tale during the church service. It made a huge impression on David. The works of the Christians were also powerful testimony of the truth of their teachings. He had always despised them, but they had always been prepared to accept him lovingly.[54]

---

f. The Pedi ruler who stayed in Sekhukhuneland, just east of the Steelpoort River, on the western slopes of the Steenkamps Berg (see also P. Harries, *Work, Culture and Identity*, p. 66).

Having accepted the Lord, Denga would remain firm in his faith. Although he managed to take his third gun home, this did not bring him the kind of pleasure that it would have previously. At the time that he returned home, he was the only Christian convert returning to Vendaland. While there were converts such as Mutshaeni living in other areas, there were no Christians living in or near Denga's parents' village at the time:

> He had to walk a solitary road back home – no fellow-Christian stood by his side ... David declared to his mother and his family: "Only my body is here; my heart is not here, it is with the teacher." His whole family insisted that David often had attacks of madness. David told his people of other people who are just as he is – he could not show them these people because of the great distances.[55]

Like Mutshaeni and Solomon, Denga was awaiting the arrival of missionaries. Their wishes would soon be granted. The question remains as to whether or not they got what they were longing for. In my reading, Solomon was sadly disappointed when the reality did not meet up with his expectations. In contrast, Mutshaeni and Denga made themselves indispensable to the missionaries and managed to win their respect and support. They gladly gave their lives in the service of the new God.

THE ARRIVAL OF THE MISSIONARIES

In commenting on the role played by previously-converted Christians after the arrival of the missionaries in Pedi areas, Delius has argued that they "provided a number of ready adherents for the missionaries when they arrived, and ... continued to play an active role in the spread of Christianity within Pedi society". Lacking the necessary linguistic, political and social skills to engage with the local community in any meaningful way, the missionaries were "heavily dependent" on the assistance of this group. In Delius' reading, most souls won for the Lamb were won through the efforts of other converts. Far from leading the way, certainly in the early days, "the missionaries were constantly attempting to keep pace with these converts".[56] Similar patterns are revealed by the continuing case studies of the converts in Vendaland.

Solomon was the first of the Vendaland conventicle to come into contact with the Berlin missionaries. He would do so at the urging of Samuel, another Christian who had been converted earlier while working as a migrant labourer.[g] This came about when Missionaries Beyer and Baumbach stopped at Makhado's village on the way to *Khosi* Tshivhase for their March 1872 meet-

---

g. Since Samuel does not seem to have become involved with the missionaries to any significant degree after this first meeting, I have been unable to reconstruct his life history.

ing.⁵⁷ Reportedly "very happy to hear that [they] ... were going to his father-in-law", Makhado provided them with Samuel as a guide.⁵⁸

The missionaries were extremely pleased with Makhado's choice. On their journey, Samuel proved to be "the best guide" as he pointed out or named every "mountain or village or other obvious significant fact".⁵⁹ He must have spoken Northern-Sotho, English, Dutch or a combination of these as, at this stage, the missionaries could speak no Tshivenda. However, his use to them would have gone much deeper than this. In common with the other previously converted Christians, at the most obvious level, Samuel was an "insider" – one of "us", rather than one of "them". It is safe to argue that Beyer and Baumbach would have felt that they had more in common with a Christian than with the mass of the population. Already having received the Christian message, Samuel would have grasped what they were saying and been able to translate it for others, much more easily and accurately than a non-Christian.

From the perspective of the local people, Samuel was also an insider. He knew his way around the area and around local ways of doing things. They would presumably have trusted him far more than any Native Assistant from Northern-Sotho or Tswana speaking areas who may have accompanied the missionaries. Moreover, it is likely that Makhado saw him as an ideal informant and intermediary. Not only would he have been more trusted by Beyer and Baumbach than non-Christian local people, he would also have had non-Christian relatives in the area and had to continue to live there after the departure of the missionaries. This would have ensured that any loyalty that he may have had to the new God and his representatives did not cancel out the duty to keep his ruler informed of anything he should know about the missionaries. Moreover, as with other former migrant labourers, since he knew both local ways and the ways of the whites, he would have made the best possible intermediary between the *khosi* and the missionaries.

Since one of the stated aims of the trip had been that of making contact with previously-converted Christians, Beyer and Baumbach were extremely pleased when Samuel put them in touch with Solomon. Beyer wrote that, after the meeting with Tshivhase, just before they were about to leave:

> Solomon appeared; he had not heard about our arrival earlier, until Samuel had come to him to fetch him. We went to a remote hut with these two Christians, Samuel and Solomon. There we reminded them, through God's Word, to remain firm in their faith and to love Christ; we advised them to come to one of our stations every now and again, to strengthen themselves through contact with other Christians and through partaking in Holy Communion; finally we prayed with them and for them. Both Samuel and Solomon gave us the impression that they were still Christians, albeit very weak ones.⁶⁰

Samuel would again prove his worth on the trip back from Tshivhase. As he and the missionaries approached a mountain village, they received a message that Makhado was visiting there and wished to speak to them. Unsaddling at the foot of the mountain, Baumbach waited with the horses while Beyer and Samuel climbed up, to hear what the *khosi* wanted. Invited to stay and take part in the feasting, drinking and dancing which was about to begin, the missionary was clearly unimpressed. Moreover, in his interpretation, the real reason why Makhado had invited him then became apparent, for he "immediately" began to ask him for his saddle. This made Beyer even more grumpy:

> I did not feel like using this given opportunity to preach the Word of God to such a crowd of heathens with their empty chatter. I therefore asked Makchato [Makhado], and those around him, to pay attention to me for a short time only, because I have an important message for them. At this hour, the Lord gave me much joy and enthusiasm, to speak about him in front of this crowd of heathens; to my amazement they listened to what I had to say. An added joy was having the king listening to me – had he known that I would speak so freely and that I would attack his superstitions and idol-worshipping with the word of God, he would surely not have called us to him.[61]

Acting as both a cultural interpreter and a mediator, Samuel clearly felt that the missionary had gone too far. On the way back, he said: "Teacher you spoke harshly. The words will give Makchato sleepless nights." He also attempted to ameliorate the missionary's impression of his *khosi* by informing him that "Makchato would like teachers but his people constantly talk against it".[62]

After this, it would be some time before the missionaries would again have contact with the previously-converted Christians of Vendaland. It would be Johannes, rather than Solomon, who would first come into contact with them this time. The initiative would also come from him, rather than the missionaries. This was because they had to neglect the interests of the previously-converted Christians while they began establishing a base from which they could operate. They were simply too busy with essential building and clearing work to undertake journeys in search of the Christians and evangelisation journeys. After about two months of hard work in heavy summer rains, on Boxing Day 1872, Beuster and Stech sat in front of their candlelit Christmas tree in the small home which they had constructed. As they did so, they reportedly reflected on:

> What a sad Christmas it was! Not one of the Christians, whom they had so hoped to find here, had made an appearance. The heathens shyly stood back and looked at the White men with distaste and suspicion. So it was no wonder that the faces of

both missionaries were troubled when they sat opposite one another on the second day of Christmas, and that all sorts of fearful thoughts moved their hearts.[63]

As the missionaries sat contemplating their misery:

That is when a young, strong man walked into the house. He wore a leather loin-cloth like all the men of his tribe do [see Illustration 12]; a leather apron hung across his back; and his head was covered with the leather helmet of a soldier. He wore not a single item of European clothing. The man looked all around the house, and as he did this his face became more and more pleased and satisfied. He then sat down and explained in broken Dutch: "My name is Johannes. I am a Christian. Some teachers already know me. You can ask Brother Beyer about me."[64]

The association of western clothing with civilisation or a civilised veneer in missionary writing forms a recurring theme in this work. Skin clothing, on the other hand, was associated with the "forest" and the "darkness of heathenism".[65] In the person of Mutshaeni, these opposites were presented in inverted form.

Commenting on the arrival of Mutshaeni, Beuster recorded that: "You can imagine with what joy the missionaries greeted this first Christian amongst the Bawenda [Vhavenda]." He and Stech had indeed heard a great deal about his "dedication and enthusiasm" when they were still at Blauberg. They had also been informed that it had been he who had first asked Tshivhase to allow missionaries to stay in his kingdom.[66]

When asked why he had not come earlier, Mutshaeni answered that, because of the move to Tshakhuma, his extended family had not been able to prepare their fields in time. Their supplies had soon been exhausted. So, he had taken a goat, hoping to exchange it for maize. At Lwamondo, the prices had been too high. He also could not agree on a price in the neighbouring area. So, he had "moved on further and further" until he had finally reached Tshimbone in Tshivhase's country:

That is when I heard that Boers had settled here. When I heard that these Boers are called "Mynheer", I had a premonition which I had to investigate. I looked around in your house; I saw you and the books, and immediately knew that these are the teachers whom I had asked God to send for so long already. It is God the Lord who has led me to you.[67]

They spent some hours talking "with each other about that which lay closest to their heart". After this Johannes left, promising to come to Sunday services regularly after this. In a continuation of the inversion of missionary ideas about forms of dress and the recurring theme of the interplay between the outer and the inner personality, Beuster's descriptions of Mutshaeni would also reverse the usual trope of a "bright" or "pleasant" exterior masking a hidden "dark" core. Mission sources would record that:

> [Mutshaeni's] visit had miraculously comforted the missionaries. And yet, at that time they had no idea what a Christmas gift God had presented to them in the form of this man – the man of whom Missionary Beuster was to later testify: that his outward appearance may have been coarse and harsh, like John [the Baptist], but his inner self had been kind and gentle, like that of Jesus' favourite apostle.[68]

Undeterred by the four-hour walk, Mutshaeni appeared again on the following day. He soon "found all sorts of ways of making himself useful to the missionaries". He showed them what sorts of wood to use to build their houses and ensured that the children supplied them with good thatching grass, rather than merely collecting the grass found nearby, which easily rotted. He also intervened to ensure that the local people did not cheat the missionaries in trading.[69]

In February 1863, Beuster received a message that he should immediately leave for Natal to be married, a round trip which was expected to take between four and five months.[h] Johannes was reportedly "overjoyed" when he heard about this: "That is good Mynheer. You will then have a totally different standing in the eyes of my people."[70] Mutshaeni was the natural choice to accompany Beuster to Natal as his guide as he had travelled to Natal on foot before and was experienced in handling oxen. It was on this journey that Beuster really began to appreciate the worth of the man who would become his assistant. Just after they left, as a result of a serious cold, Beuster suffered an attack of rheumatism. This was soon exacerbated by gout. For days on the way down to Natal, he was in too much pain to get off the wagon. During this time, Mutshaeni, the "outwardly coarse man nursed him with true motherly care". He prepared Beuster's "food for him, made his bed, and knew how to anticipate the patient's every wish before the words had even been properly uttered". When they reached Pietermaritzburg, "he was rewarded with the

---

h. The missionaries were forced to get established at their mission stations before their brides or wives were sent out to join them. In some cases, as with Beuster and Koen, they married women whom they had already met while in Germany. For others, as with Stech and Baumbach, brides were chosen for them by the Director of the *Missionshaus* in Berlin – usually from girls who had declared themselves willing to do mission work. In those days, women were not sent out as mission workers, instead they were prepared for the mission field as wives of missionaries. They would be sent out to the Transvaal via Port Natal (Durban). If the man had come out unmarried, they would be married at Christianenburg Mission Station, just outside Port Natal. If they were already married, they would meet up again at Port Natal or Christianenburg.

joy of having his beloved teacher walk towards his bride, supported by a stick".[71]

The journey was also a symbolic turning point for Mutshaeni. Not only his mind was being transformed but also his body. The whole time that they were travelling, he had worn the skin loincloth and cape described at his first meeting with Beuster and Stech. Entering Pietermaritzburg with Beuster,

> he now found that in the whole town, not a single Black person appeared on the street without European clothing. A strange feeling of shame came over him, when he noticed that the passers-by stared at him in amazement and with disapproval. As soon as he had out-spanned the oxen, he crept into the back of the wagon, pulled down the flap and only stuck his head out to see around him. Missionary Beuster gave him a shirt, to help him overcome part of the problem. But how amazed he was when Johannes came towards him that evening, fully clothed. With a beaming face he told Beuster that his Christian friends had heard of his arrival and had brought him all these things. So he was able to participate in his master's day of celebration, dressed in wedding clothing.[72]

While Beuster was away, Stech was left in charge of the embryonic station at Ha-Tshivhase. By this stage, the missionaries had managed to make contact with Solomon. In the absence of Mutshaeni, Stech had to completely rely on Solomon in his efforts to continue mission work in the area. He described the rather long-winded process of translation that this involved:

> With much trouble I got Solomon to translate the Holy Our Father and also a small short prayer which I had already written down when I was at Lekalekale [Lekgalekgale].[i] For every Sunday, I chose a passage which suited me out of the books of the New Testament and asked Solomon to come very early on a Sunday. Then I would read the relevant text to him, in Sesutho [SeSotho][j] and he translated it for me, word for word and sentence for sentence into Setzuetla [Tshivenda]. Then I would read it to him several times, until he was satisfied and I became more fluent in it. This then covered the first half of the church service. During the second half of the service, I read to them out

---

i. Also sometimes spelt "Legalegale" in mission sources. This was the mission station at the old Makapanspoort – just north of the first town of Potgietersrust. The town was later moved to its present place and the mission station was also moved in 1891, as it served the people working in the town as well as Mankopane's (Makapan's) people.
j. In this context, Northern Sotho. There are three variants of SeSotho, namely that spoken in Lesotho, that spoken in the Limpopo Province (Northern-Sotho), of which Sepedi is a dialect, and Tswana (spoken in the Blauberg area).

of the Catechism and Solomon interpreted it to the people – sentence for sentence or paragraph for paragraph, depending on what I thought best. At my request, he added what he himself knew and what he had learnt from the text he had just interpreted.[73]

Stech obviously thought that this situation was unsatisfactory. While he could not stop Solomon completely from extempore speaking, he seems to have worried about what he, as a Christian who had been without pastoral supervision for some time, said when speaking on his own behalf. Beyond the fact that he was attempting to learn Tshivenda, this would seem to be one of the reasons why he went to so much trouble to speak for himself, working out detailed Tshivenda translations with Solomon and then speaking them himself. It would have been much simpler to speak in Northern Sotho and get Solomon to translate for him, as he would later do with Joseph of Matlala. In addition, Stech was no linguist. Despite having spent time at Ga-Matlala and Lekgalekgale learning the basics of Northern Sotho, this helped him little in mastering the tonal language of Tshivenda as the two languages are very different. Commenting on the Easter services on 13 April 1873, three days after his colleague, Beyer, had arrived from Blauberg, Stech noted that this was

> one of the specially blessed Sundays for me and the people, because Brother Beyer preached here with gusto and vigour, in Sesutho [SeSotho], which almost all the men here understand fairly well. Solomon interpreted his four short parts excellently. But I was very despondent when I saw how the words of this dear faithful Witness of God just flowed out of his mouth.[k] What a bungler am I? Oh, how much one has got to complain, to tell and ask the Lord about things which one cannot express in words. Yes, the language is truly a mountain, which has to be crossed; especially this new language of our people [Tshivenda].[74]

Beyer had come in response to an urgent plea from Stech. Shortly after his arrival in Vendaland, Stech had suffered heat exhaustion. After this, he had suffered from a variety of debilitating bouts of illness.[75] Diagnosing Stech's condition just under 130 years later, and basing this diagnosis on my translations of the missionary's descriptions of his symptoms, a local general practitioner with long and varied experience in the area argued that he almost definitely had typhoid. Cholera is also a possibility but it was not yet common in the area, so typhoid is far more likely. He also possibly either had

---

k. Beyer had come to South Africa as a missionary in 1864 and had worked amongst Sotho-speakers since 1865. By 1873 he could speak SeSotho fluently.

amoebic dysentery or a number of bouts of food poisoning (salmonellosis). On top of this, he also contracted malaria.[76] At what he thought was the height of his illness, Stech had written a letter of farewell to his Brothers. On 16 March 1873, he had managed to get a messenger to carry this to Beyer.[77] "In his fright", Beyer had immediately sent this "farewell letter" to Grützner at Matlala. After this, he had left for Ha-Tshivhase, taking two Christians from Blauberg with him, to see what he could do to help Stech. The three had arrived there on 8 April 1873. Two days later, they had been joined by Joseph of Matlala. In response to Grützner having presented Stech's "distressing situation" to his congregation, Joseph had immediately offered to go and help him until Beuster returned from Natal.[78]

With the arrival of Joseph of Matlala, Stech was liberated from the worst of his linguistic difficulties. He reported that Joseph soon became his "mouth and interpreter, which was urgently needed for my sake and especially for Sundays".[79] Stech also cut back drastically on using Solomon, replacing him with the thoroughly Christianised Joseph, whom he trusted much more. Not only had Joseph translated for him when he was at Ga-Matlala during his period of acclimatisation and language studies, he had also for long felt the guiding hand of a white Lutheran pastor. In addition, Joseph's presence enabled Stech to expand his potential target group by freeing him to preach his sermons into the so-called *Oorlamstaal* – the simplified form of Dutch used by people who had worked for whites for so long, either as *inboekelinge* taken in childhood or as the children of workers, that they no longer spoke their native languages. This would form one of the strands of the language which would become known as Afrikaans.[80]

Stech seems to have been too blind to see that his joyful adoption of Joseph had alienated Solomon, who obviously felt that he had been cast aside. On 20 April, Stech recorded that: "Solomon was not here. It was a sad service; at least, I felt a great sadness in my heart. Otherwise, many people came."[81] With the benefit of hindsight, this was the first real sign that he was beginning to separate himself from the mission, a sadly disillusioned man.

One can well imagine Solomon's hurt and bitterness. A common theme running through the life histories of converts discussed in mission sources is the opprobrium they faced from their non-Christian family members and the wider community. On the one hand, this took the form of subtle (or not so subtle) pressure to conform to societal norms, such as polygyny and participation in circumcision and religious rituals, which conflicted with missionary interpretations of Christianity. On the other, it was frequently expressed in hostility or physical violence against the persons of the converts, or prospective converts.[82] Keeping his faith before the arrival of the missionaries in the face of societal disapproval, and while his fellow converts (with the exception of Mutshaeni) were abandoning or transforming theirs, must have taken considerable courage and fortitude on Solomon's part. In many ways, he must have become an outcast from society. With the arrival of the missionaries, and the central role that he played under Stech, he must have felt vindicated. Not only had his choices not been in vain but he must have acquired a new status as the right-hand of the missionary. With Joseph's arrival, he must have felt all his faith, courage and fortitude had been for nothing and that he was now being cast down and humiliated. Even Beuster's return from Natal with his wife, Ida, on 27 June 1873, did not improve matters for Solomon. Beuster, who was in charge of the station, used his own assistant, Johannes Mutshaeni. Basically from April, Solomon had again been cast aside.

Shortly after Joseph's arrival, Stech had recorded that

> it was especially painful to hear that even Solomon, who almost always attends our church service, and who has always helped me so well as an interpreter, also has two wives. And that, although he does not practice witchcraft [*Zauberei*] himself, he accompanies his father [a traditional healer] when he goes out to do witchcraft, and they are earning many goats through this.[83]

While I have no direct evidence of this, I am convinced that these actions were signs of an attempt by Solomon to rebuild a sense of identity for himself in the wake of Stech's cooling towards him. In doing so, he further alienated himself from the missionary. Stech appears to have had nothing (or extremely little) more to do with him before being transferred to Blauberg to replace Beyer, who had had a nervous breakdown, in November 1843.[84] Beuster nevertheless attempted to re-establish the connection, albeit completely on terms dictated by the missionaries.

In November 1873, Beuster recorded, in a way that revealed his stereotypes about the untrustworthiness of the local people, that they "had informed me in their way, i.e. they had lied, that Solomon had gone to Natal to work". The missionary was reportedly surprised by this, because Solomon had not informed him of his intention or asked him for a travel document.[1] He nevertheless abandoned a planned visit to the convert, at which he had intended to discuss his failure to attend church services, his polygyny and the fact that he was beginning to practice as a traditional healer.[85]

Again, I see these as signs that Solomon was attempting to rebuild a meaningful life outside of the mission setting. Despite this, the fact that he had been close to, and needed by, the missionaries obviously continued to exert a pull over him. A short while later, Solomon sent a messenger to Beuster to

---

1. According to the provisions of the pass law of 1866, it was an offence for any black person to be found outside his residential district without a pass from his employer, "paramount chief", a missionary, magistrate or field-cornet. He could be detained by any citizen and handed over to the nearest field-cornet for punishment. Subsequent legislation differentiated between employed and unemployed blacks (D.H. Heydenrych, "The Boer Republics, 1852–1881", in T. Cameron and S.B. Spies (eds.), *A New Illustrated History of South Africa*, p. 153).

convey his greetings and inform the missionary that he was sick. Since he had not been seen at the mission station "for a long time, and [since] it would most probably be a long time till there was an opportunity to speak to him", Beuster went to visit him on 7 November. Accompanied by Johannes Mutshaeni, he found that

> Solomon seemed somewhat frightened; his illness does not seem to be too serious, at least not serious enough to prevent him from attending church services. His child was seriously ill. Solomon's father is a very prominent doctor who has acquired a multitude of wives with his noble craft. His son has also started – he already has two wives and many goats are at his disposal. Solomon did not lie that he had sinned greatly: "I am not feeling happy; my heart is sick," he said, "I have no peace." I said to him what I had also already said to Totane: that I would pray to God that He should never let them have peace.[m] I reminded him of his responsibility which he would have towards his wife and children. I said: "Can you be happy about your children if you know that they will burn in hell?" Solomon reckoned: "It is not good, it is not good. But there is no power."[n] We spoke about Him, who is mighty in the weak ones. He promised to come to the church service next Sunday.[86]

Beuster claimed that the person that he felt the most sorry for was Solomon's first wife, who found herself

> in a similar situation as Totane's wife. She was inclined towards the Word, but now that the leader has become blind, she will also fall into the pit.[o] But whose fault will be the greater? This woman has remained faithful to her husband during the seven years of his absence, in spite of all the encouragement from others that she should take another man as Solomon would not be returning again. Solomon rewarded her faithfulness by taking a second wife.[87]

By this stage, Beuster was becoming exceedingly concerned about the defected Christians in Vendaland. Beyond any concern that the missionaries may have had for the souls of these men, and their wives, it is clear that they were becoming extremely embarrassing to the mission. Widely identified as "People of the Book" by both commoners and royalty alike, the missionaries felt that what they saw as their failings and shortcomings were broadcast

---

m. Totane's story will be discussed next.
n. In other words, "I do not have the power to resist temptation."
o. Matthew 15:14 – "If a blind man leads a blind man, both will fall into a pit."

about, and relished, as reflecting on all Christians, including their "teachers".[88] Winning them again for Jesus was thus as crucial for the standing and prestige of the mission as for the state of their souls. However, they were destined to fail spectacularly in the task they had set themselves.

This was not a new issue for the missionaries. They saw it as being symptomatic of a much deeper problem, arising from the different attitude towards mission work held by Lutherans and the Methodist missionaries who were working in Natal. They believed that the difficulties arising from this deep-seated difference were serious enough to threaten their entire credibility in Vendaland. Earlier in the year, Stech had already commented that the most serious difficulty faced by the "young station" in Tshivhase's area was "the trouble caused by the so-called Christians who were converted and baptised by the Methodists, years ago, in Natal".[89]

The way that Stech described these Christians cannot be translated directly. He referred to them as "methodistisch Angehauchten und Getauften".[p] Allison and his colleagues in Natal seem to have believed in the power of the Holy Spirit through baptism. In the interpretation of the Berlin Missionaries, they concentrated more on the baptism than on the Christian principles. That is why Stech called them *Angehauchten* – he believed that they had not heard the full words of the Gospel but only got a breath of it (and, through it, the Holy Spirit), before being baptised. He and his colleagues believed that, as such, these converts did not have the resilience to withstand pressures to conform to what they saw as the snares of "heathen" practices, such as polygyny and local religious beliefs. For Lutherans, this was unacceptable – the Spirit could only be seen in the way that people lived. Only once it was apparent that they had welcomed the Holy Spirit into their hearts could they be baptised. Put simply, the conflict was between the Methodist attitude of "baptise first and the Spirit will heal you" and the Lutheran insistence on "show me that you have the Spirit before I accept you into the body of Christ".

Thus, the missionaries worried about more than the souls of the earlier converts – they were equally concerned with the way that their behaviour would impact on the credibility and standing of the mission as a whole. Beuster's concern about the situation clearly underlies his accounts of his interaction with them. Thus, on Sunday 16 November 1873, the missionary recorded that

> neither Solomon, nor any other Christians appeared today. That makes me very sad. When, through Johannes, I asked for an explanation, Solomon excused himself by saying that he had gone to hunt with the others. For some time now there had been lions in the area; three were killed, one escaped. For the time being, I accepted the excuse.[90]

---

p. In other words, the Methodists had given them a breath (of Christianity) and then baptised them.

On the next Sunday, 23 November, "neither Solomon nor any other Christians appeared again". This time, it was Totane who offered an excuse. During the following week, he stated that he had been ill.[91] Totane had re-entered missionary consciousness in April 1873, after having been contacted by the two Christians who had accompanied Beyer on his visit to Stech. He had reportedly been "just as surprised as he was happy, when he suddenly saw the Christians whom he had known from so long ago". He had nevertheless told them that he was "afraid" to go to the mission station because he had "given up his faith and [had] ... big sins on his conscience". As with many others, he raised the issues of polygyny and power as his main reason for turning aside from Christianity.[92] Although the Christians had encouraged him to visit the station, Totane had not done so. Stech had also meant to visit him but had not managed to do this by the time that Beuster got back.[93] After his return from Natal, Beuster had paid a number of visits to Totane. Each time, he had promised to visit the mission station soon but had failed to do so.[94]

These visits to Totane demonstrated that missionary perceptions that he and other previously-baptised Christians were topics of conversation in Vendaland were not unrealistic. For example, when Beuster and Mutshaeni were on their way to visit the *gota* for the first time, in September 1873, they had stopped at Tshivhase's capital on the way. On their departure, the *khosi* had "mockingly" said to Johannes: "Tell Totane (who is a defected Believer), he must pray hard."[95] Moreover, and more interestingly for me, Totane's replies to Beuster and Mutshaeni raise questions both about the state of his relationship with the Christian God and the motivations behind his repeated promises to visit the mission station and attend a service there when, with the benefit of hindsight, it is clear that he had no intention of doing so.

This apparent evasiveness stands in marked contrast to what Beuster had seen as Totane's forthright and honest answers to questions about the state of his soul. Even the missionary had been taken aback by Totane's statement that: "Mynheer, you have come to look for me so I will not run away. I wish to tell you that I have sinned; I have deserted my faith." As recorded by Beuster, for the *gota*, the core of this desertion had lain in his having "taken two wives". In his own words, in response to a question by Beuster: "Yes, I have two wives; I have sinned."[96]

Beuster thought that the *gota*'s broken promises stemmed from "fear of people and earthly possessions". In other words, the fear of what people would say or do and the love of earthly possessions and power acting as obstacles to Totane's return to the fold of Christians. For Beuster, this boiled down to the fact that Totane was unprepared to give up his second wife and was unwilling to risk losing his position and power as a ruler. Thus, his conscience caused him to agree to come to services while the missionary was present. However, once he was gone, the *gota*'s baser instincts could take over and he could forget about his good intentions.[97]

Based on this premise, Beuster made it very clear to Totane that there was nothing that he could do to make the choice any easier for him. In response to a question from the *gota* about what he should do, he stated that:

> As long as you have two wives, I cannot regard you as a Christian; as long as this is so, you cannot partake in Holy Communion – only the Christians receive that. Through it they receive forgiveness of their sins. Therefore, as long as you cannot come to Holy Communion, your sins are not forgiven, and you cannot be blessed. You must therefore leave your second wife.[98]

In response, without expressing it directly, Totane implied that leaving one of his wives and returning to the fold would result in his losing the support of his people and, through this, his status and power. He told Beuster: "That is difficult. They will despise me." In his, and his mission's, interpretation, Beuster had no choice but to reply:

> Yes, it might be difficult for both of you, but I cannot make it easier for you. God's Word says so and I know no other way. And even if it will be difficult, it is certainly not too difficult. God is mighty. He will give you the strength. Earnestly pray, then you will be able to overcome all things.[99]

In my reading, fear of losing his position may have played some role in Totane's actions. However, the situation seems more complex than this. Caught between old and new ways, it is impossible to know with certainty whether or not he was seriously thinking of turning back to orthodox mission-interpreted Christianity. My own feeling is that he was not – not only did he seem to view the prohibition on marrying more than one wife as nonsensical but, as a ruler, he had far more to lose by "repenting" and "turning back" than in continuing as he was. However, the *gota* did not want to alienate the missionaries completely in case he needed them, or their religion, in the future. Under these circumstances, the best course was to fob them off with excuses and what they wanted to hear about his visiting the mission station and coming to attend church services for as long as possible.[q] By these means, he managed to buy time so that the missionaries would leave him in peace between visits and also managed to avoid serious confrontation with the mission for a considerable period.

---

q. These methods of operating fit in well with local etiquette. If one requests something that the other person cannot, or does not want to, do, it is very rare that one will receive an outright refusal. To do so would be extremely rude. Instead, there are ways of saying "yes" that actually mean "no". If one is unable to see through these, the other person will continue to find excuses about why s/he has not performed the desired action and will promise to do it soon until the message finally sinks in. Read in this way, Totane was continually politely trying to tell Beuster to keep out of his business.

Support for the idea that Totane did not yet want to sever ties completely from the mission or from Christianity is provided by a description of a meeting with Beuster on 3 November 1873. Here Isaiah was also present. Beuster argued that the defected Christians were hindering others from finding "the Way of Life". He then continued by asserting that people were saying: "Where is Totane? Where is Isaiah? They have thrown away their faith. So there is nothing in this faith." He and the other Christians had nothing to say to counter this kind of assertion. While they did not want to put Totane and Isaiah "to shame", what were they supposed to say?

Totane reportedly replied that: "You must not tell the people that we have thrown away our faith, we have defected. You must tell them: 'God's Word is still with them; they are still praying; they can turn around again.'" He then "promised to count the days and come to the church service in two weeks time". With this, Beuster and his delegation left. Totane had managed to win himself a respite of more than seven months (until May 1874) without missionary interference.[100] During this time, Beuster and Mutshaeni first concerned themselves with the state of Solomon's soul.

Solomon failed to attend any services during November. As a result, Beuster and Mutshaeni visited him on Monday 8 December. At this meeting, they did everything in their power to persuade him to leave his second wife and return to the Lord. They also managed to get an opportunity to speak to his elderly father, berating him for his polygyny, his practising as a *nanga* and (as they saw it) having tempted Solomon away from the Christian path by helping him to marry a second wife. "You are having such an evil time with your many wives, now you want your son to have the same experience, you have no sympathy for him," they accused.[101] Little did they realise that this was the last time that they would see Solomon alive.

In January 1874, Beuster started to hear rumours that Solomon had died. This unexpected news reportedly came as a "real shock" to him. He also recorded that:

> Although I did not want to believe the rumour at first, I soon noticed that there could be some truth in this matter because it was spoken of everywhere. As Solomon acted as the interpreter here when we first came, he is generally known as a "Person of the Book". That is how the news of his death was passed on everywhere. "What is the use," it was said, "when we learn, when we read; here we see that the People of the Book also die, just like all people. Yes, if it could make us live!"[102]

On 27 January, Schwellnus and Beuster were due to visit Tshivhase. Taking a detour on their way to the capital, they set out to discover for themselves whether or not the rumours were really true. In Beuster's words, on arrival at Solomon's place: "we soon noticed that he had really died. Unnecessarily, I still asked: 'Where is Solomon?' 'He is not here,' was the reply."[103]

What at first sight seems to be the evasive reply that Solomon was not there flows directly from local customs. Even today, many local people will not immediately say that a person has "passed away". The death of a person leaves a weakness in the family, especially if it is a man, and even more so if it is the head of the family or the eldest son. For this reason, they say he is away, he has gone to visit, and so on, so that the enemy should not know that the family is vulnerable now.

Despite his concern for the family, Beuster was more concerned with the state of Solomon's soul and with admonishing his father than with expressing condolences. One gets the idea that the missionaries would have found a deathbed recantation far more useful for propaganda purposes locally and at home in Germany than with the way that things had occured. Solomon had decisively and finally turned his back on the mission:

> I would have liked to speak longer there than I could have on that day; to the wife, who was receptive; to the mother, who was dead sick; to the father, the great doctor [*Doktor*]; to the children, who had already had lessons from Solomon. Oh, how sad everything looked. On all the faces one could see the hopeless misery. I tried to find out whether, in his last hours, Solomon had maybe shown signs of repentance and done penance; whether he had maybe still looked for the Lord. But no, there was nothing to be found of that. Twice he allowed the magic dice [bones] to be thrown out over him. After this he had taken medicine of the doctors. He then spat blood. "Leave me," he had said, "the women are killing me." After they had gone away a short while, they found him dead.[104]

With Solomon beyond the reach of salvation, as they saw it, the missionaries again turned their attention to Totane. They saw this as being particularly urgent as, by May 1874, he was apparently looking for a third wife. He had also reportedly committed adultery with a woman from Isaiah's extended family. Sentenced to a fine of two beasts by Tshivhase, "he refused it and asked to fight it out with weapons". In Beuster's opinion, "these erstwhile Christians" were setting a "deplorable" example to the unconverted. People were "pointing at them with their fingers" and saying that: "They have spat out the medicine which was poured into them in Natal. They are now behaving worse than the others. That is why it is not good to become a Christian."[105]

Beuster recorded that, from time to time, he received reports of Totane's doings. As the *gota* occupied "no insignificant position", having about twelve villages under his supervision, his actions were "not unknown in the land". In Beuster's opinion, he had "become a public nuisance". As far as the missionary could discern, his visits to Totane had produced no beneficial result. While the *gota* had always promised to visit Ha-Tshivhase, he had not yet done so. So Beuster came to the conclusion that "it was now time to serve him with the last labour of love which I can still do for him, in that I solemnly exclude him from the congregation".[106] It seems that Beuster hoped that, by doing this, he would shock him into mending his ways, set an example to other Christians that deviations from mission-interpreted Christianity would not be tolerated and send a message to the "heathens" that the Christians were as determined to maintain order among their subjects as the *mahosi* were among theirs. He seems also to have hoped that this would replace discussion about the bad examples set by Christian converts with positive comments on what they were achieving.

Arriving at Totane's village on the evening of 6 August, Beuster became even more convinced that he was taking the correct course of action. The *gota*'s brother was taking advantage of the tension between him and Tshivhase to attempt to usurp Totane's throne. Beuster recorded that, as he approached the village:

> Next to the road I saw a baboon's head as a protective remedy against the enemy, his brother; then a bone and then an old basket. I have never seen so many devices at any heathens. Even on Totane's body I noticed many amulets.[107]

Revealing the kind of power that the missionaries saw it as their right to wield even over royal Christian converts, on the very evening that he arrived, "without any frills", Beuster told the *gota*'s, councillors, his wife and others who were in Totane's presence:

> "Your Chief has strayed from God's ways. He is causing you to also stray. You must not follow him! Everyone is accountable for his own soul. If he wants to be ruined, let him. Everyone of you has to take care of his own soul. Save yourselves!"[108]

This may be read as a dramatic representation of the fact that any ruler who converted to Christianity was automatically ceding a significant part of his power to the missionaries. Berating a ruler in these terms in front of his family, his councillors and his subjects was a complete breach of etiquette and a sign of complete lack of respect for his person and his office. The missionaries clearly saw a Christian *khosi* or *gota* as subservient to them and their rules. Were he to remain a Christian, he would essentially rule through their grace.[r] The alternative was to court excommunication. On the following day, 7 August, with Mutshaeni as his witness, Beuster solemnly excommunicated Totane from the congregation of the Lord and officially handed him over to Satan, to whom, in the interpretation of the missionary, the *gota* had until then "confessed allegiance".[109]

---

r. This is one of the main themes running through the discussion of *Khosi* Makwarela Mphaphuli in chapter 8.

This marked the end of the road for Totane and the missionaries. In his report on conditions at Ha-Tshivhase during the second semester of 1875, based on reports sent to Berlin by Beuster, Mission Director Wangemann recorded that:

> Totane, the unfortunate defector ... has opposed the warnings of the missionary with growing defiance, so that the missionary had to excommunicate him ... After this, things went down-hill for the unfortunate one; to such an extent that he annoyed his subjects worse than any heathen chief. He gave himself such a name amongst his subjects, that he had to flee from the country. The books which he had left behind created a big problem to his relatives – their superstitious fear prevented them from keeping or destroying them. Finally it was decided to hand them over to the safe keeping of the teacher.[110]

Finally, a report on events at Tshakuma during the course of the year 1878 recorded that Totane had "stated plainly that he would stay a heathen from now onwards".[111] This was the last reference to him in missionary sources.

These events left only Johannes Mutshaeni from the original Vendaland conventicle as a practising Christian. In the time that the relationship between the other Christians was deteriorating, Beuster had increasingly come to depend on him. During the course of their journey to Natal and on their return, it was Mutshaeni who assisted the missionary to learn Tshivenda. As they progressed, Mutshaeni became "inordinately proud of the advances and achievements of his pupil". One day, after Beuster had preached, Mutshaeni said to him: "It cannot be said that the people do not believe because they do not understand. They understood very well. Today I did not hear you make even one mistake. Everything was correct."[112]

As evidenced by frequent references to Mutshaeni accompanying Beuster to visit the defected Christians and to various local rulers, and undertaking evangelisation journeys on his own or in the company of other so-called Native Assistants, he became increasingly indispensable to Beuster in what the latter called "the real mission work".[113] For example, commenting on his and Mutshaeni's journey back from a visit to Totane on 8 and 9 September 1873, Beuster wrote that:

> On the way back, we still had some time over to proclaim God's Word. Johannes helps bravely to talk. He translates that which he hears me say, in his own words and his own special style. [With my limited command of Tshivenda,] I do not always see the connection [between what I say and his translation], but what does that matter! ... He [also] takes note of that which he finds specially interesting in my sermons and uses it at every opportunity. Even if I have not up to now had much success

> here, I have had much pleasure in him; that he has learnt so much from me already, and that he has obtained new courage and enthusiasm for the work through the teacher. He is very receptive to the Word.[114]

Khosi Tshivhase himself reportedly

> enjoyed listening to Johannes and his teacher. He often called them, and then took them aside, to listen to what they had to say with amazement. But he was not ashamed to later use what he had heard, and joke about it with his councillors, while sitting around the fire. There was no sign in him of a serious yearning for salvation. In spite of this, the two confidently continued their work, hoping for blessings in the end.[115]

In summing up his feelings for Mutshaeni, in June 1874, Beuster wrote that: "The love and consideration which this old boy extends is really touching."[116] He was also particularly moved when, at the same time, Mutshaeni informed him that he had finally decided that he would "resettle at Ha-Tshivhase – if necessary against the will of his family".[117]

By being so closely associated with the missionary, Mutshaeni cut himself off from many of the local people. Beuster ascribed much of this "hatred" to the "envy [at] the better clothing which he now wore" and what he described as "scapegoating".[118] By this, he meant that, since they could not get rid of him, those who opposed a missionary presence in Vendaland would get at him through Mutshaeni. For example, on 31 October 1874, Beuster recorded that:

> As they cannot get at me, Johannes will become my scapegoat. They try to make him the instigator of all my undertakings. It is generally said that he will not be able to escape the poison of the witch-doctor [*Zauberer*] for much longer. So-called friends continually advise him to take care and to keep quiet. The poor man even has to bear the guilt of my being able to speak the language; he is being scolded for teaching me the language. "When we are with the Boers [*Bauern*]," they say, "we can scold and swear at them in our own language as much as we wish. Here we cannot do it. *Mynheer* understands everything. That is all your fault!"[119]

While there may have been some truth in Beuster's assertion of "scapegoating", it is clear that the causes of this clash went much deeper than this. In modern political parlance, Mutshaeni would be described as an *impimpi* or a sell-out. Not only by his actions but also by his core beliefs, he had rejected and set himself against local people and local ways. One of the accusations levelled against him was that: "You have deserted us, and have turned your love towards a foreign nation."[120] Tshivhase's senior wife was allegedly even "more hostile". She clearly regarded him as *persona non grata*. On more than one occasion, she reportedly "sent out her messengers to kill Johannes on the road". In response, Mutshaeni declared that: "I am not afraid and will go my way, in spite of this." Beuster also made it clear that he would interpret any attack on Mutshaeni as an attack upon himself. It would seem that, either out of fear of what Tshivhase would do if she caused a rupture with Beuster or out of fear of interfering with his policy regarding the missionaries, she called off her assassins.[121]

Against this tense background, after he had completed a small house at Ha-Tshivhase, Mutshaeni brought his wife and his two-year-old son across from Tshakhuma. Shortly after the move, his wife gave birth to a second son. Although his wife had not yet converted to Christianity, she raised no objections to their being baptised by Beuster.

Due to Beuster's first wife having died, he married Emma Koboldt (born Oberländer) on 22 August 1875. She was the widow of Missionary Heinrich Koboldt, from Modimolle/Kranskop, who had died of a nervous disorder in February 1874, two months before Beuster's wife. Accompanying her to Ha-Tshivhase were her daughter Maria, a foster-daughter and a "kitchen maid".[123] The father of the foster-daughter was Paulus Luvhengo, a MoSotho from Waterberg and a former traditional healer [*heidnischer Doktor*] who had converted to Christianity. He and his wife accompanied the party to Ha-Tshivhase to see his daughter get settled in and to help Beuster in the meantime. Mutshaeni and Luvhengo soon formed a close friendship based on their mutual "love for the Lord". They took it "upon themselves to visit the neighbouring villages in order to gather people for the Word of God".[124]

Luvhengo "had a compelling eloquence" when speaking in public. This arose directly from his previous training as a traditional healer. He therefore did most of the talking. Mutshaeni served as his interpreter. People reportedly

> came from everywhere and listened, filled with amazement and wonder at what he had to say ... "Take note of that man's words," they said, "he comes from far away. What he has to say must be important."
>
> And Johannes – who so faithfully had worked for many years without ever having reaped anything else but scorn and hatred up to now – was humble enough to be happy, without any envy, about the success of his friend.[125]

While Luvhengo was at the station, and largely persuaded by himself and Mutshaeni, David Denga moved to Ha-Tshivhase. Unlike Mutshaeni, he had not made contact with the missionaries of his own accord. Beuster had sent Mutshaeni out to find him. Although he was still practising a form of

Christianity, winning him back to orthodox mission-style Christianity was seen as one of Beuster, Mutshaeni and Luvhengo's great successes: "In this way a new stimulus had been given, and one was able to hope that the work would vigorously proceed", even after Paulus and his wife had left towards the end of the first semester of 1876. Having seen their daughter properly settled in, there was no reason for them to remain any longer.[126]

Prior to his move to Ha-Tshivhase, Denga's relationship with his family had clearly illustrated the kinds of difficulties faced by converts in those early days. His moves away from orthodox Christianity seem to have been attempts to make some concessions towards local practices in the interests of peace with his family. Beuster's judgement that "on his return home, he had fallen back into the heathen ways, as most of the others like him do" seems excessively harsh to me.[127] Even given that the whole basis of the missionary presence at this stage rested on the idea that the only acceptable interpretation of Christianity was that sanctioned by them, he was well aware of the struggle that Denga was having to wage. For example, the missionary would later record:

> Once he told me about the struggle he had had with his people [relatives]: *Mynheer*, I fought until it became bare – this means, compared to a physical struggle, he fought so long, till the grass under his feet was trodden bare.[128]

The family were convinced that Denga's commitment to Christianity was a sign of madness. Intending to protect him from the consequences of what they saw as his own deranged behaviour and folly, once he decided to move to the mission station, the family elders refused his wife and young son permission to accompany him. They hoped that this would bring him to his senses and back to the family.[129] However, they failed in these attempts and, in October 1875, he moved to Ha-Tshivhase.[130] In the absence of his wife and son, he was "lonely like a widower". He nevertheless built himself a comfortable house and was even prepared to extend it, always hoping that his wife and relatives would join him. Meanwhile, there was one change that becoming a new person in Christ did not demand – he did not start to cook for himself. The *Missions-Berichte* noted that: "Johannes's wife was very happy to prepare David's food every day."[131]

With his move to the station, Denga seemed to acquire new energy. On an eight-day evangelisation tour to various rulers beginning on 26 November 1875, he introduced Johannes Mutshaeni and Paulus Luvhengo to Mphaphuli's country. He then acted as their guide to *Khosi* Makwarela Mphaphuli, *Khosi* Gondo, Queen Netshaulu of Tshaulu and *Khosi* Lambane. "They had friendly receptions at these kings." Following this, he became Beuster's guide in the same areas when he went on a follow-up visit from 13 to 15 December of the same year.[132]

Once Denga had settled at the station, after many moves, his mother joined him. Although living at the mission station, she had only moved there so that her son and other Christians could look after her. She never converted to Christianity and was extremely worried about the new cultural practices that her son had adopted. One of the things that worried her was that he was constantly striving to do everything to the best of his ability and outshine others. I suspect that, beyond his own personal industriousness, he was trying to prove to others the difference that God had made in his life. His mother feared that he ran the risk of doing better than his neighbours and standing out from the norm. This opened him up to the jealousy, and evil machinations, of *muloi* and other evil persons. For example, standard agricultural procedure was to hoe, rather than plough, fields. When hoeing, many local people tilled the top part of the soil only, chopping out the shoots of the weeds without removing the deeper roots. This meant that, as soon as the rains came, the underground roots start growing again, requiring more hoeing. In Beuster's summation of the situation:

> David was a hard worker. He did not work like the other people of his tribe, who left the stones in their gardens [fields] and in their yards and did not pull out the weeds, roots and all. With him everything had to be cleared away and clean. This is also why his old mother scolded him, because she maintained that this was the reason why the *Zauberer* would notice him and he would therefore not be successful in his life.[133]

Denga was equally thorough, and enthusiastic in his preaching. It is clear that he had found a new niche for himself as Beuster and the Native Assistants' guide. Fulfilled in his new role, he was able to resist the pressure of his relatives, who continued to attempt to entice him to come home. Just before he left for the synod at the end of August 1876, Beuster summed up to Denga what he meant to him: "David, you make my heart very happy and you behave just as a Christian and a man should. Persevere in this way, God will bless you for it. He will not abandon you." Little did the missionary realise that, after this conversation, he would be able to "count the words [which he] ... exchanged with David in this life". On one level, this praise became his epitaph.[134]

Beuster and his wife were gone for six weeks. Demonstrating the dual role of Native Assistants as both evangelists and workers on the mission stations, during this time, both Mutshaeni and Denga thatched the new missionary residence. They also continued with the evangelisation work which would result in their deaths.[135]

On his return from the synod, on 14 October 1876, Beuster found Denga seriously ill with smallpox. Mutshaeni was nursing him.[136] Denga had apparently caught the disease from contact with the body of a dead girl who he had personally buried on an evangelisation trip to Mphaphuli's area. It seems that other people were too scared of contracting smallpox to bury her. There was also the possibility that he had contracted it when he and Mutshaeni were preaching and visiting houses in a neighbouring village. At that stage, nobody had known that there was an outbreak of smallpox there. The normal practice was to keep outbreaks of the disease secret from strangers for as long as possible. In Beuster's words: "Nobody in the village will give away the secret that this disease is raging there. Lies are told until it becomes impossible to hide the fact any longer."[137] Similarly, Schwellnus pointed out that: "Should anyone get this disease, it is kept secret ... Every death amongst the people is carefully concealed." In his view, this made it extremely difficult to "discover where there is an outbreak of this disease and how serious it is and how many people died of it"[138]. This was because once it became known that a family or a village had smallpox present, they would be shunned and would be unable to get food or assistance from anywhere. So, it is hardly surprising that they kept it a secret for as long as possible.

Denga's health failed rapidly. As it became clear that he was close to death, his "old mother summoned all her resources to call a traditional healer [*Doktor*] who lived far away". However, since it was certain that Beuster "would chase him away", he refused to come.[139] In a further clear example of the clash between the old and the new ways, it is also likely that Denga would have refused his treatment. Throughout his sickness, even in his last days, he refused to allow the "heathens" to treat him in the only way that then knew for this illness, namely by "washing him" by rubbing "the enormous pox off his body by means of a mixture of bark and herbs". Since he was "convinced of the uselessness of this torture", Beuster supported him in refusing the treatment. As a result, after his death, "the heathen blamed it all on the missionary and said: 'Had he allowed them to wash him, he would have been cured.'"[140]

In the early hours of the morning of 20 October 1876, Denga passed away. In order to avoid contagion, the funeral could not be put off and took place that very morning.[141] Already on the day of the burial, Mutshaeni had felt ill. The following day he was in bed with what would turn out to be smallpox.[142]

Beuster visited Mutshaeni two days before he died. He "found all the relatives and many other heathens gathered around the suffering patient". They were urging Mutshaeni to give them permission to "wash" him, reminding him of what had happened to David. "His wife also implored him to try this last cure. The patient shuddered at the thought of this shocking treatment" and Beuster also spoke strongly against it.[143] However, hardly had Beuster left when Mutshaeni "declared himself ready to be subjected to the cruel torture". In Beuster's opinion, this was either because "the pleading of his wife" had "forced him to capitulate" or because it was "the last act of faithful love, which he wanted to present to his teacher". It was only in this way that he would have been able to protect "the teacher from renewed hostilities and suspicions".[144]

Because of the danger of infection, Mutshaeni had been housed in a hut in the bush during the time of his illness. As Beuster approached it on the next day,

> he already from afar heard a soft, heart-rending whimper. Frightened, he hurried to the hut and saw how the poor tortured one was squirming like a worm in the hands of his friends. "They have killed me," he breathed [whispered], sinking back onto his bed. Beuster did all he could to ease his pain, but his hope for a recovery was broken.[145]

During the course of that night, Mutshaeni passed away. Again because of fear of infection, he was buried on the following day, 4 November.[s] One can get some sense of Beuster's desolation in his statements that "My congregation lay buried in the graveyard, next to my dead wife!"[146] and:

> The cemetery was properly demarcated with trees and roses. There are already three graves next to one another. They could most probably be referred to as proof of a congregation. But they have no congregation behind them – they themselves are the congregation![t]

Similarly, remarkably poetically for them, the *Missions Berichte* noted that:

> All flowers had been broken off. It looked as if the station had died out. God's arm had laid severe tests of patience on them. The two faithful believers lay under a grass covered mound. Those who had intended to move onto the station had got such a fright, that they stayed away. The people of that nation, who had already got in the habit of attending church services, now called out: "The people of the Book also die. Faith does not help at all," and they stayed away.[147]

---

s. Denga and Mutshaeni had succumbed to the great outbreak of smallpox that hit the northern areas of South Africa, including the whole of Vendaland, during the latter part of 1876 and for much of the following year. This caused many deaths (*BMB*, 1877, pp. 485, 489, 490; 1879, pp. 312–313). Luckily, unlike the case for malaria, preventative treatments for smallpox were already well developed. The Swiss-French Misionary Paul Berthoud, from Valdezia, worked closely with the Berliners in setting up a vaccination program at the mission stations (*BMB*, 1878, p. 251). However, controlling the disease there did not prevent it from running rife in other parts of Vendaland (*BMB*, 1878, pp. 482–483; 488–489).

t. A congregation consists of baptised people. Beuster had only had two baptised people with him at that stage, David and Johannes, now both dead. The other people at the station were still attending baptism classes. The wife was Beuster's first wife of the three who would die at Ha-Tshivhase.

More Native Assistants would arise to take the place of those who had fallen. However, because of their dedication, their untimely deaths and because they were the first local Native Assistants, Johannes Mutshaeni and David Denga came to be regarded as heroes of the missionary endeavour in Vendaland. The story of their lives leads us to those whom the Berlin Mission saw as its other heroes in the area – the missionaries themselves.

1. *BMB*, 1875, p. 401.
2. B. Sundkler and C. Steed, *A History of the Church in Africa*, Cambridge, Cambridge University Press, 2000, p. 394.
3. *Ibid.* p. 383.
4. P. Delius, *The Land Belongs To Us: The Pedi Polity, the Boers and the British in the Nineteenth Century Transvaal*, Johannesburg, Ravan Press, 1983, pp. 108–110. Cf. P. Delius, "Migrant labour and the Pedi, 1840–80", in S. Marks and A. Atmore (eds.), *Economy and Society in Pre-Industrial South Africa*, pp. 293–312; P. Harries, *Work, Culture and Identity: Migrant Labourers in Mozambique and South Africa, c.1860–1910*, Social History of Africa Series, Portsmouth, Heinemann, Johannesburg, Witwatersrand University Press and London, James Currey, 1994, Chapter 2.
5. P. Delius, *The Land Belongs To Us*, p. 63.
6. C. Beuster, *Johannes Motscheni. Ein Lebensbild aus der Missionsarbeit in Nord-Transvaal*, Neue Missionsschriften Nr. 26, Berlin, Buchhandlung der Berliner evangelischen Missiongesellschaft, 1890, pp. 1–2.
7. *Ibid.* p. 3.
8. *Ibid.* pp. 3–4.
9. *Ibid.* p. 4.
10. *Ibid.*
11. *Ibid.* pp. 4–5.
12. *Ibid.* p. 5.
13. *Ibid.* pp. 5–6.
14. *Ibid.* p. 6.
15. *Ibid.*
16. See, for example, P. Delius, "Migrant Labour and the Pedi", pp. 296, 297, 300–302, 303–304, 307–308; P. Harries, "Work, Culture and Identity", pp. 32, 84, 85, 99–101, 104–105; J. Kimble, "Labour migration in Basutoland, c.1870–1885", in S. Marks and R. Rathbone (eds.), *Industrialisation and Social Change in South Africa: African class formation, culture and consciousness 1870–1930*, London and New York, Longmans, 1982, pp. 121, 124–125; S. Marks and A. Atmore, "Introduction", in S. Marks and A. Atmore (eds.), *Economy and Society in Pre-Industrial South Africa*, pp. 31–32; B. Sundkler and C. Steed, *A History of the Church in Africa*, p. 392; and R. Turrell, "Kimberley: labour and compounds, 1871–1888, in S. Marks and R. Rathbone (eds.), *Industrialisation and Social Change*, p. 50.
17. C. Beuster, *Johannes Motscheni*, p. 7. For discussion of Allison's life, see especially W.J. de Kock (ed. in chief), *Dictionary of South African Biography*, Volume I, Cape Town, Published for the National Council for Social Research, Department of Higher Education by Nasionale Boekhandel Beperk, 1968, pp. 11–12; J.S.M. Matsebula, *A History of Swaziland*, Third Edition, Cape Town, Longman, 1988, pp. 38, 39–43, 103–104, 248–249; and S.M. Meintjes, "Edendale 1850–1906: A Case Study of Rural Transformation and Class Formation in an African Mission in Natal", Ph.D. thesis, School of Oriental and African Studies, University of London, 1988, pp. 33–34, 46–47, 62–64, 65–81, 98, 102, 104–117, 146–148. See also S. Meintjes, "Law and Authority on a Nineteenth Century Mission Station in Natal", University of the Witwatersrand, History Workshop Conference, Class Community and Conflict: Local Perspectives, February 1994, pp. 7–9.
18. C. Beuster, *Johannes Motscheni*, p. 7.

19. *Ibid.* p. 8. For a comparative discussion of the goods taken home by returning workers, the dangers and hardships of the journey and the seizure of guns by white farmers and government officials, see P. Harries, *Work, Culture and Identity*, especially pp. 30–31, 32, 101, 115–118, 176; J. Kimble, "Labour migration in Basutoland", p. 127.
20. C. Beuster, *Johannes Motscheni*, p. 8.
21. *Ibid.* p. 9.
22. *Ibid.* pp. 9–10. I have not been able to learn anything of their subsequent fate.
23. *BMB*, 1875, p. 401.
24. *Ibid.* p. 415.
25. C. Beuster, *Johannes Motscheni*, p. 9.
26. *BMB*, 1875, p. 415.
27. *BMB*, 1873, p. 136; 1874, pp. 134, 174.
28. C. Beuster, *Johannes Motscheni*, pp. 2, 6, 7, 9; *BMB*, 1874, pp. 174, 175; 1875, pp. 402, 408; 1878, p. 439.
29. *BMB*, 1878, p. 439.
30. C. Beuster, *Johannes Motscheni*, pp. 9–10.
31. *BMB*, 1874, p. 175.
32. Among numerous references, see for example: *Der Bawenda-Freund*, 14(54), 1896, pp. 294, 295; 1912, p. 20; *BMB*, 1874, p. 138; 1875, pp. 175, 368, 400, 401–402, 406, 407, 410, 411, 412, 415–416; 1877, p. 484; 1878, pp. 488, 492; 1879, p. 413; 1880, p. 211; 1881, pp. 185, 358; 1883, p. 368; 1886, p. 218; 1888, p. 533.
33. *BMB*, 1874, p. 175.
34. Personal communication Dr W.F. Malunga, Department of History, UNIVEN; H.A. Stayt, *The Bavenda*, p. 242.
35. See pp. 160–161.
36. *BMB*, 1874, p. 175.
37. N.J. van Warmelo in collaboration with W.M.D. Phophi (a) *Venda Law: Part 2, Married life*, Ethnological Publications No. 23, Pretoria, Government Printer, 1948, p. 403 (1035–1039) & (b) *Venda Law: Part 4, Inheritance*, Ethnological Publications No. 23, Pretoria, Government Printer, 1949, pp. 919 (2311) – 923 (2323); 925 (2327) (quotation).
38. *BMB*, 1874, p. 175. See also C. Beuster, *Johannes Motscheni*, p. 10.
39. C. Beuster, *Johannes Motscheni*, pp. 9–10.
40. *Ibid.* p. 14.
41. *Ibid.* p. 9.
42. *Ibid.* p. 10.
43. See pp. 239–240.
44. *BMB*, 1879, p. 308.
45. *Ibid.*
46. *BMB*, 1879, p. 310.
47. *Ibid.* pp. 308–309.
48. *Ibid.* p. 309.
49. For male initiation, the so-called "bush schools" without circumcision and the adoption of circumcision after Makhado was circumcised at a Lemba circumcision school at Mashau, see pp. 203–240.
50. *BMB*, 1879, p. 309.
51. *Ibid.*
52. *Ibid.*
53. *Ibid.* pp. 309–310.
54. *Ibid.* p. 310.
55. *Ibid.*

LOCAL BEGINNINGS 77

56. P. Delius, *The Land Belongs To Us*, p. 111.
57. See p. 26.
58. *BMB*, 1874, pp. 126–127 (quotation p. 126). See also *BMB*, 1873, p. 133.
59. *BMB*, 1874, pp. 128–129.
60. *Ibid.* p. 134. See also *BMB*, 1873, p. 136.
61. *BMB*, 1874, p. 135.
62. *Ibid.*
63. C. Beuster, *Johannes Motscheni*, p.11.
64. *Ibid.*
65. See pp. 151, 154–156.
66. C. Beuster, *Johannes Motscheni*, p. 11.
67. *Ibid.* p. 12.
68. *Ibid.* Cf. pp. 249–250.
69. *Ibid.*
70. *Ibid.* (quotation); and *BMB*, 1874, pp. 143, 144, 148.
71. C. Beuster, *Johannes Motscheni*, p. 13. See also *BMB*, 1874, p. 184 for Beuster's illness on the journey.
72. C. Beuster, *Johannes Motscheni*, p. 13.
73. *BMB*, 1874, p. 181.
74. *Ibid.* pp. 181–182.
75. See especially *Ibid.* pp. 139–140, 142–143, 148–150, 152.
76. Consultation with Dr Wim de Villiers, Makhado/Louis Trichardt, 28 January 2000. Note that untreated malaria is usually not prolonged and usually lasts for eight to ten days if it does not result in death.
77. *BMB*, 1874, p. 153.
78. *Ibid.* p. 164.
79. *Ibid.*
80. *Ibid.* pp. 181–182.
81. *Ibid.* p. 182.
82. See, for example, *BMB*, 1875, pp. 359, 360, 403–404, 405, 406, 448–449; 1877, p. 485; 1878, pp. 311, 312, 486; 1879, pp. 202, 407; 1886, pp. 414–430.
83. *BMB*, 1874, p. 176.
84. *Ibid.* p. 241; 1875, p. 359.
85. *BMB*, 1875, p. 410.
86. *Ibid.*
87. *Ibid.*
88. See, for example, *Ibid.* pp. 400, 414.
89. *BMB*, 1874, p. 174.
90. *BMB*, 1875, p. 412.
91. *Ibid.*
92. *BMB*, 1874, pp. 174–175.
93. *Ibid.* pp. 175–176.
94. *BMB*, 1875, pp. 399–402.
95. *Ibid.* p. 399.
96. *Ibid.* p. 400.
97. *Ibid.* p. 408.
98. *Ibid.* p. 402.
99. *Ibid.*
100. *Ibid.* p. 409.

101. *Ibid.* p. 412.
102. *Ibid.* pp. 414–415.
103. *Ibid.* p. 415.
104. *Ibid.*
105. *Ibid.* pp. 420–421.
106. *Ibid.* p. 439.
107. *Ibid.* p. 440.
108. *Ibid.*
109. *Ibid.* p. 442.
110. *BMB*, 1876, p. 395.
111. *BMB*, 1879, p. 408.
112. C. Beuster, *Johannes Motscheni*, p. 14.
113. *Ibid.*
114. *BMB*, 1875, p. 402.
115. C. Beuster, *Johannes Motscheni*, p. 15.
116. *BMB*, 1875, p. 423.
117. C. Beuster, *Johannes Motscheni*, p. 16.
118. *Ibid.* p. 17.
119. *BMB*, 1875, pp. 448–449.
120. C. Beuster, *Johannes Motscheni*, p. 17.
121. *Ibid.* p. 15.
122. *Ibid.* pp. 17–18.
123. Acta der Berliner Missionsgesellschaft betreffend Personalia: Beuster, Carl, Abt. II, Fach 3, Nr. 14, 1865–1902; [Anon.] *75th Anniversary of the Berlin Mission Station Tshivhase*, pp. 3, 4; *BMB*, 1876, p. 184; and C. Beuster, *Johannes Motscheni*, p. 18.
124. *BMB*, 1876, p. 395; C. Beuster, *Johannes Motscheni*, p. 18.
125. C. Beuster, *Johannes Motscheni*, p. 18.
126. *Ibid.* See also *BMB*, 1877, p. 487.
127. *BMB*, 1876, p. 395.
128. *BMB*, 1879, p. 311.
129. *Ibid.* pp. 310–311.
130. *BMB*, 1876, pp. 395–396. See also *BMB*, 1879, p. 31.
131. *BMB*, 1879, pp. 311–312.
132. *BMB*, 1876, pp. 397–401; 1879, p. 312 (quotation).
133. *BMB*, 1879, p. 312.
134. *Ibid.*
135. *Ibid.*
136. *BMB*, 1877, pp. 217, 488–489; C. Beuster, *Johannes Motscheni*, p. 19.
137. *BMB*, 1879, p. 313.
138. *BMB*, 1877, p. 485.
139. *BMB*, 1879, p. 313.
140. C. Beuster, *Johannes Motscheni*, p. 19.
141. *BMB*, 1877, p. 489 (quotation); 1879, p. 313; C. Beuster, *Johannes Motscheni*, p. 19.
142. *BMB*, 1877, p. 489; 1879, p. 313; C. Beuster, *Johannes Motscheni*, pp. 19–20.
143. C. Beuster, *Johannes Motscheni*, p. 20.
144. *Ibid.* p. 21.
145. *Ibid.*
146. *BMB*, 1877, p. 489.
147. *BMB*, 1878, p. 481.

CHAPTER 3
The mission and its missionaries

THE MISSION

The arrival of the Berlin Missionaries transformed the situation in which Christians, and even followers of African religion, operated. It also raises questions about the nature of the Mission Society, the kind of people that the missionaries were and the kind of training that they received. The Berlin Mission Society (as it was known from 1908) had been founded by a group of Prussian notables on 29 February 1824 as the Society to Promote Evangelical (or Protestant) Missions among the Heathen (*Gesellschaft zur Beförderung der Evangelischen Missionen unter den Heiden*). Included among the founders, and subsequent committees of the organisation, were military officers, lawyers, government officials and theologians – generally members of the conservative Prussian elite. When the society was founded, none of its founders held an official position in the hierarchy of the church. As with many other mission societies at the time of its foundation, it was thus an interdenominational, voluntary organisation tied to no established church.[1]

The control of the Society was in the hands of a selected committee which initially consisted of nine members, but, in the course of time, their number was increased to between twenty and twenty-five. Because of the high percentage of committee members who were civil servants and army officers, the society's constitution was submitted to the Prussian King for approval. Indeed, Kaiser Wilhelm II was a member of the committee.[2] It is clear that, in addition to any religious motivations held by the founders, they also had a Prussian nationalist one. They wanted their state to be among those establishing churches in other parts of the world.[3]

Seeing that most of the committee members faced possible transfer, it was decided to appoint at least one permanent committee member. He was to ensure continuity in the functioning of the society and make day-to-day management and policy decisions. The post of Mission Inspector was first held by J.C. Wallmann, who served from 1857 to 1863. His successor, H.T. Wangemann (who would serve from 1865 to 1894) only accepted the position on condition that he was given extraordinary powers. The position of Mission Inspector was thus changed to that of Mission Director.[4] Accompanying these developments, the society had moved away from its original "non-aligned" status and anchored its mission work in the Evangelical

Lutheran Church of Brandenburg. The status of the Berlin missionaries was equivalent to that of pastors in Prussia.[5]

In its origin, establishment and expansion, the society had its roots in early nineteenth-century Pietism. The founding father of this reform movement was Philip Jacob Spener (1635–1705), whose religious significance is generally regarded by some German-speaking theologians as being second only to Luther.[6] In essence, Pietism was a spiritual reaction against "the cold rationalism of the eighteenth-century Aufklärung [Enlightenment]".[170] Convinced that "Protestant Scholasticism exercised a petrifying influence and thus threatened the living truths of the Reformation", as it developed, Pietistic theology emphasised "faith as 'living faith' which must bring forth 'fruits of faith'".[8] One of the ways that it was manifested was in a rejection of the orthodox Lutheran and Calvinist doctrine that rejected mission work as human interference in the will of God.[9]

During the nineteenth century, Pietism came to play a crucial role in the mission movement. In fact, the whole concept of Christian conversion as we know it today has its roots in the Pietistic tradition. Kritzinger, Meiring and Saayman have argued that:

> Conversion for the Pietists hinged on the conscious personal decision of the individual after a fierce (one can even say cataclysmic) penitential struggle. This was considered to be a once-forever decision of such overwhelming importance that the date and time of this decision should be indelibly engraved on the heart and mind. It concerned mainly (very nearly only) the affairs of the soul, the religious sphere of life, and therefore accepted a dualistic understanding of human reality with clear compartments: (holy) church/(sinful) world, (holy) soul/(sinful) body, (holy) religion/(sinful) politics, etc. ... Repentance and conversion would therefore imply a move out of the realm of sin, into the realm of holiness, and it is difficult not to interpret this move as essentially a withdrawal from the (sinful) world.[10]

They continue by arguing that, with some modification, this was the understanding of mission that "was predominant in the mission societies and churches which were the main agents of mission in the nineteenth century".[11]

This conception of conversion was closely bound to the classic Lutheran doctrine of the two kingdoms. As Gunther Pakendorf has argued, "though non-conformist by origin," German Protestant missions "were mostly committed to the Lutheran creed and there is no doubt that they consciously applied" this doctrine when dealing with secular authority.[12] Based on Luther's interpretation of Romans 13, this asserted that both the civil and ecclesiastical authorities had been instituted by God. The divinely-ordained task of the civil government was to provide the people under its rule with external righteousness and peace. The ecclesiastical government was similarly tasked with arranging for the preaching of the Gospel and the administration of the sacraments (Holy Baptism and Holy Communion). As a general rule, the two governments were not to interfere in each other's realms.[13]

As Kritzinger *et al.* have pointed out, this understanding of the nature of conversion and authority "left little scope for social involvement ... Yet it was exactly this very strong concern for the salvation of souls that propelled Pietists and evangelicals into social involvement". Deeply committed to

> winning souls, they came very close to the people, especially the outcasts, the poor, the slaves and the oppressed ... This involvement should not be understood to mean that the importance of conversion was revitalised in any way. On the contrary, social ills were contested exactly because they hindered the conversion of the heathen.[14]

According to this way of thinking, conversion "could only be brought about in one of two ways: by way of a verbal challenge or invitation, or through the example of a godly life (i.e. a life according to the Pietist understanding of the Gospel)". The verbal challenge or invitation could take the form of personal testimony, a sermon or a tract. Even in cases where emulation of a godly life served as the power of attraction of the Gospel, it was expected that this would be explained by a Pietist missionary in a pastoral discussion or testimony. Thus, according to the Pietist understanding, "The word is ... the central and overwhelming dimension of a call to conversion ... Deeds were in a decidedly second position, and then only deeds expressing the sincere faith of the missionary himself or herself."[15]

Thus, German Pietist thinking played a major role, if not the major role, in the development of the concept of conversion and the theory underlying the practice of mission activity during the nineteenth century. This situation also prevailed for much of the twentieth century. In drawing attention to the significance of specifically German societies in this mission activity, Pakendorf has argued that "In global terms, German Protestant missions were never very significant numerically". Quoting Genischen, he stated that, in 1881, "they had a total of just about half a thousand workers in the fields – merely one third of the non-Roman British missionary forces and no more than about 17% of all Protestant mission workers from North Atlantic counties".[16] During the nineteenth century, there were only four major German societies "in the field" – Moravian, Rhenish, Berlin and Hermannsburg. However, viewing this differently, of the total of 475 mission stations established in South Africa between 1737 and 1904, 169 – more than a quarter – belonged to German societies. In addition, "In some areas, notably in the Transvaal Republic (ZAR), where the British were viewed with great scepticism, German missions were for a long time practically the only mission societies present."[17]

Against this background, the initial aim was for the Berlin Mission Society to support the already established and successful missionary societies based mainly in Basel, London and Paris. However, they soon decided that this was not enough. Within ten years of the foundation of their society, the Berliners had sent five missionaries to South Africa.[18] This decision could be implemented because of the great success that they had achieved in collecting funds from the Prussian church congregations.[19]

The first Berlin Mission Station to be established in South Africa was that of Bethanien in the Orange Free State, established on 24 September 1834. A station was opened at Cape Town in 1837 to work among the Khoikhoi and slaves. The same year saw the expansion of the society's mission activity into British Kaffraria, with the Bethel Mission Station being established to work among the Xhosa. Work among the Zulu began in 1847 with the establishment of the Emmaus Mission Station in Natal. Work among the Pedi in the Transvaal began in 1860 with the establishment of Gerlachshoop Mission Station. From these original bases, the Mission Society spread out its operations to work in other areas and among other ethnic groups so that, in spite of closures and movings of some mission stations, there were thirty-one Berlin mission stations in South Africa in 1870. Of these, three were in the Orange Free State, five in the Cape Colony, five in British Kaffraria, six in Natal and twelve in the South African Republic.[20]

The society and the scope of its operations continued to grow. In addition to significant expansion in South Africa, mission work expanded into Mashonaland in 1892, using the stations established in Vendaland in the 1870s as a springboard. However, this move overtaxed the Southern African resources of the mission and this part of the mission work was handed over to the South African Mission Society in 1906. This essentially marked the end of the rapid expansion of the society's mission work in South Africa.[21] Outside South Africa, the Berlin Mission expanded the scope of its operations into China in 1882 and East Africa in 1884.[22]

The great influence of the Prussian elite on the committee of the society, its close links to the crown, its theological *raison d'être* and the expansion of its activities raise crucial questions about the kinds of people who became its missionaries, the training they received and how this impacted on the ways that they interpreted their experiences in the mission field.

At first, the Berlin Mission Society did not train its own missionaries. Instead, they sent their candidates to the seminary of Pastor Johannes Jänicke. When efforts to unite this seminary with the Society failed, they were forced to establish their own seminary in 1829. Some other German mission societies, such as the Leipzig Missionary Society, insisted that only the best university-trained theological students were properly equipped to present Lutheranism to the non-German peoples.[23] In marked contrast, the minimum educational qualification for admission to the seminary of the Berlin Mission

THE MISSION AND ITS MISSIONARIES 83

Society was "a primary education from a well-established Elementary School (*Volkschule*)". The main requirement for admission was that

> anyone who wishes to be admitted into the Berlin Missionary Seminary must, of necessity, have a heart fully converted to the Lord Jesus Christ and must also have sufficient Christian maturity and steadfastness. He must lead a life of prayer and know sufficiently about sin and grace, contrition, faith and sanctification out of his own experience.[24]

Because of the lack of advanced educational requirements, the Mission Society drew its candidates for mission work largely from the lower-middle class. Most candidates had only an elementary primary training (*Volkschule*). The decision to follow a missionary career often followed some kind of conversion experience – a central theme in Pietism.[25] The missionaries who served in Vendaland were no exception. Moreover, their background and the moulding process of the seminary training played a strong role in influencing the ways that they experienced, wrote about and illustrated what they had encountered in Vendaland.

THE MISSIONARIES

Only two of the ten missionaries who served in Vendaland during the nineteenth century differed from the norm as far as their background was concerned. One differed dramatically, the other only in superficial details. Klaas Koen, a black man of South African origin, differed so dramatically that his life history was captured in a tractate by the mission to demonstrate how one could rise above all obstacles and become reborn as a new person in Christ. These events will be considered shortly.

Erdmann Schwellnus differed in that he was Lithuanian, rather than German, and his father was a relatively prosperous farmer. Thus, he was both "foreign" and from a slightly higher social class than his colleagues. Entering the seminary just before he turned 25, he was also a little older than the other candidate missionaries at the time of entering the mission seminary. Of the four whose fathers' occupations were listed in their personnel files, one father was a townsman who farmed a smallholding (as opposed to a farm), one was a shunter on the railways, one was a trader and one was a railway worker. One candidate was 20 years old at the time that he joined the seminary, two were about to turn 21, two were already 21 years old and three were 22. In their life-stories (*Lebenslauf*) written when joining the mission, three wrote specifically of life-altering conversion experiences.

The remaining eight missionaries employed in Vendaland during the period under review were all German-speaking, all had an elementary school education at the time of their entry into the mission and were all of lower-middle class background. Two were bakers at the time of their entry into the mission, one worked for a trader in glass and porcelain goods, two were locksmiths, one was a shoemaker, one was a builder and one was an office worker. Two of these missionaries, Stech and Wessmann, would be expelled from the mission for sexual peccancy. Since the circumstances of Wessmann's expulsion, and his behaviour thereafter, were deemed to be sufficiently serious as to pose a real threat to the mission, his case will be considered after the others, prior to Koen's life history. This will contrast what the mission saw as its greatest failure in the training of a Vendaland missionary with the person whom they deemed their greatest success in the area.

Considering the remaining missionaries, in the order of their arrival in Vendaland, **Carl Beuster** was born on 7 July 1844 in Liebenwalde.[26] The son of the townsman with the smallholding, his occupation prior to entering the mission was that of a baker. In true Pietist mould, during a period of illness in the Charité Hospital, he had his first encounter with the Mission and with a missionary: "Christ called me, to pull for him in his field." He joined the mission in 1865 and was sent out to South Africa on 24 June 1870. He at first assisted the overworked and stressed Heinrich Koboldt at Modimolle near Kranskop. In January 1871, he was sent to Malokông to help Bruno Köhler. Following this, in September of the same year, he was sent to Thutloane for a few months to nurse the sick Robert Kühl back to health. This was followed by a short spell at Botshabelo.[27] Beuster and Stech's attempts to start a mission station in the lands of *Kgoši* Mutle in 1872, Sekhukhune's refusal to allow this to happen and the foundation of Ha-Tshivhase have already received attention. So too has his first marriage, to Ida Haak, in 1873.[28]

Beuster proved an inspired choice as head of the station at Ha-Tshivhase, where he remained until his death on 5 November 1901. From the time that he was first stationed there, he began translating the Mission Liturgy into Tshivenda. Together with Schwellnus and Koen, he also played a major role in producing a first reader for school use, Luther's *Small Catechism* and the rudiments of the Venda Hymnbook. In 1892, Beuster also produced a Tshivenda translation of Old and New Testament Bible stories.[29] Beuster also put together a collection of insects "so that through this science can also profit". From 14 February 1893 until his death, he was Berlin Mission Society Vice-Superintendent of the Northern Districts of the Northern Transvaal.[30]

During this time, Beuster's first wife died on 23 April 1874. She developed a fever a week after having given birth to a baby daughter, and died a few days later. The baby was taken over by the Kühls of Ga-Matlala. In spite of the best care, the baby also died, two months later.[31]

On 7 April 1897, Emma Koboldt, whom Beuster had married on 22 August 1875, passed away. He was left to care for her daughter, Maria Koboldt.[32] On 17 February 1900, he married Elisabeth Brache, who died on 24 March of the same year.[33]

THE MISSION AND ITS MISSIONARIES

In summarising Beuster's contribution to the development of the mission in Vendaland, the pamphlet produced for its 75th anniversary proclaimed that:

> Mr Beuster was the pioneer of the Venda mission, and the era from 1872 to 1901 bears the imprint of his character. Throughout the whole of Vendaland, which he so often traversed on his extensive gospel tours, his name is well known in the heathen villages. At Tshivhase it was he who laid the foundations on which his successors could go on building. In his last exhortation to his congregation he said: Whoever of you shall refuse to listen to the missionaries who will come to you after me and takes no heed of the teachings of the gospel, will be guilty before God.[34]

Carl Stech was born on 29 June 1844 in Quedlinburg. He seems to have been an illegitimate child and his mother died when he was young.[35] Before joining the mission, he worked for a trader in glass and porcelain goods. Stech seems to have had a reputation for wildness and the Mission Society had its doubts about him before they sent him out. He was sent to a Christian Institute for a further year, after he had completed his studies.[36]

Sent out to South Africa on 5 March 1872, Stech was first stationed at Botshabelo and Ga-Matlala.[37] His posting to Ha-Tshivhase, his relationship with Solomon and his transfer to Blauberg in November 1873 have already been discussed.[38] In 1875, Stech married Emile Meineke, born in 1848 in Derben bei Parey, on the Elbe. His bride had been chosen for him by the Director of the Missionshaus in Berlin from among women who had declared themselves willing to do mission work. Together they would have six children.[39]

The mission's early fears about Stech would ultimately prove to have been well-grounded. In 1891, while his wife was recovering from general ill-health at Port Elizabeth, and in response to meetings with Superintendent Krause, Stech produced a memorandum requesting that he be recalled to Germany, transferred from Blauberg to a more climatically-favourable place or be put on pension by the Mission Society.[40] This was because his wife's health was "very weak" and he had no doubt that this would prevent them from returning to Blauberg.[41]

Stech was placed on pension. However, in response to complaints received, Superintendent Krause had an interview with Christine Fisher, who had formerly worked as a childminder for the Stech family, on 27 July 1892. During the course of this interview, it emerged that she had had an affair with Stech. When she became pregnant, he had bound a horse girth tightly around her, either to hide the fact that she was pregnant or in an unsuccessful attempt to induce an abortion. When the baby was born, Fisher drowned it. Stech had been away at Synod at the time of the birth. Upon his return, he and his wife sent Fisher away. The missionary also told her to lie about the paternity of the child.[42] As a result of this investigation, Stech was expelled from the mission on 11 November 1892.[43] As he was already back in Germany at this time, since Fisher was white or so-called "coloured" and not a person local to Vendaland or Blauberg, and since Stech's actions do not seem to have been widely commented on locally, this case did not pose much of a threat to the mission and was not seen as requiring any attention subsequent to the missionary's expulsion.

Erdmann Schwellnus was born on 2 December 1841 at Lutkomanscheit (near present-day Tilsit) in Lithuania. His father was a farmer, with Schwellnus and his brother helping on the family farm. Believing that he "had a calling", and because he "hated drunkenness and card gambling", he joined the mission in 1866. His brother remained behind on the farm.[44]

Schwellnus only learned to speak and write German while he was at the Mission Seminary. Impressed by the speed with which he managed this, the *Missions-Berichte* would later comment that: "Despite the surprising way in which he mastered this language, the well disposed readers will gladly pardon some words, which appear every now and again, which have remained in the way our Brother expresses himself."[45] The editors did not show the same sensitivity towards the Lithuanian spelling of Schwellnus and "Germanised" it to Schwellnuss until the 1875 reports.[46]

Leaving Germany for South Africa at the end of 1872, Schwellnus spent his first months in South Africa at Botshabelo, learning Northern Sotho while teaching at the school there. Confirming his previously-demonstrated flair for languages, by September 1872 he was proficient enough in Northern Sotho to be left alone at Thutloane. He moved to Ha-Tshivhase in November 1873 and was with Beuster for about six months before starting the new mission station at Tshakhuma on 14 May 1874. Again, his obvious talent for languages and his ability to speak Northern Sotho had helped him to pick up quite a bit of Tshivenda in the first six months of his stay here. He did not need an interpreter when he preached for the first time at Tshakhuma.[47]

Before he came out to South Africa, Schwellnus had been engaged to a Lithuanian girl, Dorothea Manz, who was born in Stendal on 6 August 1846. In the spring of 1874, with the house at Tshakhuma complete, he left for Natal to marry her. Having married at Christianenburg, the couple returned to Tshakhuma on 24 December. They would have four sons and two daughters, all born at Tshakhuma. All the sons became missionaries.[48]

After being called home to Germany for a period of home service, largely arising from Dorothea Schwellnus' poor nervous and physical health, the family took their leave from Tshakhuma at the end of May 1894.[a] In 1904, at his own request, Erdmann Schwellnus and his wife returned to South Africa,

---

a. Dorothea suffered from a nervous condition which included attacks of dizziness and convulsions, and which got worse after the birth of each of her five children. See, for example, *BMB*, 1886, pp. 218, 360–361; 1887, pp. 222, 481; 1888, pp. 507–508.

leaving their sons Georg and Hans behind in the Mission Seminary. They were first temporarily stationed at Waterberg (Middelfontein). From here, Erdmann requested a transfer back to Vendaland. Later in the year, Otto Klatt, Beuster's successor at Ha-Tshivhase was transferred to Gertrudsburg. Schwellnus was then made missionary in charge at Ha-Tshivhase, working with his son Theodor. One of their first tasks was to rebuild the mission station further up the hill. In doing so, they renamed it Beuster.[49]

On 21 August 1904 Dorothea Schwellnus died at Beuster. She is buried there, next to the graves of Beuster and his three wives. After the death of his wife, Erdmann's health and interest steadily declined and he left more and more of the work to his son. He retired in 1907 and spent his last years alternately living with his children. In April 1910, while suffering one of his high fevered malarial attacks, he left his bed and went outside to watch Halley's Comet. This led to a serious cold and pneumonia. Even the dedicated nursing of his daughter could not save him, and he died at Georgenholtz, visiting his daughter and son-in-law on 6 May 1910. He is buried next to his wife at Beuster.[50]

Dietrich Baumhöfner was born on 7 November 1855 at Bielefeld. His father was a shunter on the railways.[51] While attending elementary school, he reportedly had a teacher who "first awakened the love of the Lord Jesus Christ in his heart". The tractate about his life would state that, despite the fact that he would later be tempted by evil, the message that this "teacher had engraved on his heart in his earliest years remained with him from then and wakened in him the desire to take the Word of the Lord Jesus Christ to others".[52] In his own description of these events, Baumhöfner would recount that he left school at the age of 7 years and performed "hard labour" for his uncle until the age of 12 years. He then was apprenticed as, and succeeded in becoming, a baker. His brother also qualified as a baker. He and his brother worked together. While working as a baker, he often worked on Sundays and "ignored God". However, he had a conversion experience and then asked for time off to attend church. He eventually felt a strong calling to work among the "poor heathens". While preparing to become a missionary, he worked with epileptics. He completed his compulsory national military service in Bielefeld.[53] He left Germany for South Africa in October 1881, arriving in Port Natal on 1 December.[54] Leaving on the following day, he finally arrived at Botshabelo after a nine-week journey. Here he studied Northern Sotho. After "five months, he gave his first sermon in the native language" on 28 May 1882. He was then transferred to Mp'hôme.[55] From here, he was transferred to Old Georgenholtz to assist the seriously-ill Koen on 1 August 1882.[56] With Koen's death on 10 February 1883, Baumhöfner was left in charge of the station. In the opinion of the mission, not only did he have "all the keenness of youth" but he was also "highly talented".[57] Against this background,

> glowing with the love of God and burning with enthusiasm, he very soon mastered the language. He had already made consid-

erable inroads amongst the heathens, when suddenly, a few months after Brother Koen, he also passed away due to fever. Much to our deep sorrow, we cannot keep silent about the fact that, speaking in human terms, his enormous over-enthusiasm became the cause of his early death. This enthusiasm made him ignore the warnings of those who know this country: that he should save his energy for the sake of his health; and the suggested precautions he should take.[58] ... He would only work until Easter ... Then he became sick. Beuster took him to Ha Tschewasse [Ha-Tshivhase], where his young life came to an end on 26 April 1883.[59] ... The ways of the Lord are unfathomable – he so often calls away the best and most indispensable people.[60]

Johann Meister's life provides a clear illustration of the Pietistic ideal of a gradual process of turning to God, followed by a conversion experience and then a growing in the Ways of God. He was born on 28 February 1864 in Königshütte, Kreis Beuthen (in present-day Poland). His father, also named Johann, had been born on 7 March 1823 in Kreutzburg. His occupation is not recorded in Meister's personnel file. Meister had two sisters and four brothers.[61]

In the summary of his life (*Lebenslauf*) that he wrote on joining the mission seminary, Meister stated that his parents were "strong Christians" and he was brought up in an extremely religious family. At an early age, he learned "to know the Lord Jesus in my [his] heart". His mother passed away when he was twelve. On 21 April 1851, his father remarried. His second wife was a widow named Karoline Jaunich, born Breit-Scheidel.

Meister attended elementary school between 1871 and 1878. His final grading was that of "Satisfactory" (Mark 3).[b] After school, he was apprenticed as a locksmith (*Schlosser*). He also explained that the other apprentices set a bad example to him of how to behave and he became less religious. Because of a shortage of work, his master moved to Eastern Poland, on the Russian border. Meister went with him. He was then fifteen years old. Moving away from the control of his parents at this age was not good for his spiritual and moral development. He fell "deeper and deeper into the hands of Satan". From time to time, he attempted to turn back to God but "it is very heavy [difficult] to come out of the influence of Satan and back to God".

After his apprenticeship, he went back home and worked for one-and-a-half years in a machine factory. He testified: "My father recognised my character and ways and demanded that I return to God ... My father was crying

---

b. The grading system went from Mark 1 (Very good); Mark 2 (Good); Mark 3 (Satisfactory); through to Mark 6. Thanking Dr Jürgen Becher of the Afrika Seminar at Humboldt Universität zu Berlin for this information.

about me and this made a deep impression on me, my heart became soft and I took my first steps back to God ... In my fight against sin, sin was sometimes the winner." This made him "depressed".

In the spring of 1883, he left home again because of *Wanderlust*. He went to Breslau and then to Liegnitz. He worked for a time at Liegnitz and then went on to Görlitz, working at a machine factory. Here he began to feel that he could turn his spiritual life around and that forgiveness was possible. A missionary from the "Berlin Town Mission" held evangelisation meetings there. He went along one evening and was deeply moved by what he heard. He explained: "My heart changed." After the end of the meeting, he went to speak to the missionary. It was not possible to speak to him for long, and the missionary suggested that he come back the following day. This he did. After the missionary had asked him a lot of things, he said that his heart was broken and he felt like the worst kind of person. However, the missionary comforted him and told him that only Jesus could help him. He wanted to follow the advice to turn to Jesus and left for Berlin eight days later.

"Sometimes I fell into bad ways again," he explained, saying that this was because of friends from home who he met and who led him into temptation. But he knew that he could not continue like this and "broke with them and went back to God". He joined the YMCA, which he described as "the tool with which I came nearer and nearer to God and Jesus' Kingdom".[c]

After some time, he started to work in this Association. On Sundays and Wednesdays, he went into the streets and asked young men to join the Association. Through these works, he became more and more interested in mission work and he testified that he felt within himself a strong demand to join the Mission. He went to the Mission House and became a member of the candidate's circle for a year. Then he joined the Mission Seminary. He ended by expressing the wish that: "God will give me his grace and assistance to let me become a tool for him."[62]

On 18 April 1890, Meister joined Schwellnus at Tshakhuma as a non-ordained probationary missionary. He served there until 6 July 1891, when he was sent to assist Beuster at Ha-Tshivhase.[63] Before this, he had already accompanied Beuster on a mission journey from 14 to 29 July 1890 and had also been sent to help Wessmann at Georgenholtz when needed.[64] Serving as Beuster's assistant, beyond the normal tasks on the station and accompanying Beuster on his journeys, he assisted the missionary in his attempts to negotiate peace in the wars involving Makwarela Mphaphuli and *Khosi* Tshivhase, in treating the injured in these battles and in attempting to secure better treatment for prisoners.[65] He was also sent out with Native Assistants on preaching journeys and assisted Wessmann at Georgenholtz from time to time.[66]

---

c. The YMCA had been founded in the 1850s by the founders of the Swiss Mission.

At the beginning of the fourth quarter of 1891, Meister left for Botshabelo to wait there for his bride, Luise Stärke. He arrived on 24 October 1891 and was married on 11 November. While he was on honeymoon, Johannes Wedepohl took his place.[67]

Meister and Johannes Wedepohl were delegated to start the new mission station at Gutu in Mashonaland. Wedepohl had been sent out to South Africa at the end of 1889. He spent some time at Adamshoop and Waterberg before moving to Ha-Tshivhase in 1891. After passing his probationer's exam in 1892, he was a fully-fledged missionary.[68] Accompanied by Beuster, Meister and Wedepohl and their two assistants, Johannes Madima and Matthaus (Matthew) Maluma, set off for Zimbabwe on 23 May 1892. The two sons of the deceased Missionary Poss_elt, who had started mission work in Natal, accompanied them as guides. Beyond the task of establishing the station, the Brothers took the trip as an opportunity for spreading the Gospel in the northern parts of South Africa and over wide stretches of Mashonaland. The station of Gutu, near Fort Victoria, was finally founded on 10 August 1892. Beuster and the Brothers Posselt remained with them until 15 August, when they began their journey home. Beuster arrived back at Ha-Tshivhase on 19 September.[69] By the end of the year, both Luise and Johannes Meister were dead from "fever", having passed away on 28 October and 8 December respectively.[70] This left Wedepohl, Madima and Maluma at the station. Wedepohl himself was ill with fever and was admitted to the Victoria Hospital in January 1893, leaving the assistants in charge at Gutu. He only returned in mid-May. Due to personnel shortages in Germany, Johannes Neitz only arrived to help them in August. Wedepohl married Therese Franke in November.[71] After the handover of the mission's operations in Zimbabwe to the Dutch Reformed Church, Wedepohl moved to the Eastern Cape in 1907. He subsequently served at Kreuzburg and Pietersburg. He died in Johannesburg on 13 June 1956.[72]

Carl Gernecke was born on 4 June 1856 in Schwarzenholz. His father died when he was two years old and he "did not know" him or his occupation. His mother was Elizabeth, born Lindeke in Walsleben, who died in 1896. Having obtained Mark 4 (below average) results at school, his occupation prior to joining the mission was that of shoemaker. He did not do military service and joined the mission in September 1878. Gernecke's wife was Paula Bertha Heese, born at Riversdale in the Cape Colony on 9 June 1868. Her father was the missionary Daniel Heese, who died in 1906 and her brother was Paul Heese, a missionary in East Africa. They had twelve children between 1887 and 1907.

Gernecke was stationed at various places in the Cape between 1883 and 1894. He moved to Georgenholtz in September 1894 and remained there until July 1898. Gernecke had lost his Prussian citizenship in October 1894 by having been in a foreign country for more than ten years. After spending a period back in Germany (July 1898 to September 1899), he was stationed at

THE MISSION AND ITS MISSIONARIES 91

Cape Town (1899 to June 1902) and then at Ladysmith from June 1902 until he retired from the mission on 1 October 1927. He died on 22 March 1932.[73]

Ernst Friedrich Gottschling was born on 10 June 1856 in Adelsdorf. He had an older sister. His father was a trader and he was a builder prior to joining the mission in 1877. Postings recorded in his personnel file are: Amalienstein (1882 to 1883, 1884 – two periods, and 1886 to 1888), Herbertsdale (1883), Riversdale (1884 – two periods), Laingsburg (1884 to 1886 and 1888 to 1894), Mossel Bay (1894 to 1897), a period back in Germany (1897), [Old] Georgenholtz (1897 to 1899), Gertrudsburg (1899 to 1904), Johannesburg (1904 to 1905 and 1907) and Botshabelo (1905 to 1907). After his transfer from Botshabelo to Johannesburg in 1907, no further details are recorded on the relevant form in his personnel file. Gottschling married Wilhelmine Elfert in Pietersburg on 12 January 1886. She had been born at Amalienstein in the Cape Colony on 29 October 1866. Her father, Ferdinand A. Elfert, was a trader. She had two sisters and three brothers. They had five children. Friedrich Wilhelm Ferdinand was born at Amalienstein on 26 November 1886.[74]

Carl August Otto Klatt was born on 3 May 1874 in Berlin. He was the oldest of four children. His father was a railway worker and he was an office worker before joining the mission in 1894. Postings recorded in his personnel file are: Pietersburg (November to December 1899), Gertrudsburg (December 1899 to 31 August 1900 and 1 August 1904 to 14 April 1914), Tshakhuma (1 September 1900 to 4 November 1901), Ha-Tshivhase (5 November 1901 to 30 July 1904). He married Auguste Louise Helene Auerbach at Christianenburg, Natal, on 10 September 1902. Helene had been born on 27 July 1873 in Berlin. Her father was a craftsman. Otto and Helene Klatt had three children. Otto died on 17 October 1943.[75]

Spiritual drive and the desire to win souls for Jesus obviously played a major role (if not the major role) in the choice of a missionary career. This is demonstrated in the summary of Beuster and Baumhöfner's lives and even more dramatically in the case of Meister. On a more secular level, one may also presume that, despite the high death rate of missionaries in the field from malaria and other tropical infections, the desire for adventure also influenced candidates to make this choice. However, in my reading, it is clear that here was also a far more material force at work and that this exerted an extremely powerful influence. These brief life histories of missionaries who served in Vendaland clearly reveal that missionary service provided a form of upward social mobility for the missionaries. This point has also been made for mission service in South Africa as a whole by Daniel van der Merwe, who argued in a thesis completed in 1980 that:

> In the mission-field, the social status of the missionary was remarkably different to the status that he had in Germany. As a missionary on his mission-station, he was responsible for the

spiritual and material welfare of a great number of inhabitants. In some cases, he even fulfilled the functions of a traditional chief. All in all, the status of the missionary in the mission-field was comparable to that enjoyed by the majority of Prussian *Junkers* – a status that no member of the lower-middle class could aspire to in Germany.[76]

I would argue that, whatever their spiritual motivations, the opportunity for social advancement offered to candidate missionaries must have been a powerful force not only in motivating their choice of a mission career but also in pressurising them to assimilate the training and ideologies of the Mission Society to the greatest possible degree. Seminarians "found unfit" as pupils could "be dismissed from among the complement of pupils at any time without compensation", thus throwing away their opportunity for social advancement.[77] By throwing himself wholeheartedly into the regimen of the Seminary, and accepting and internalising its teachings, both theological and social, a student was able to demonstrate his suitability for the calling of missionary work. Offered a chance at a new and seemingly better life at the relatively impressionable age of between twenty and twenty-five years of age, with some years of hard work in relatively menial jobs behind them, students tended to grasp the opportunity offered to them with both hands. Moreover, the whole structure of the curriculum in the Seminary and the intensive nature of the teaching, coupled with the autocratic and conservative nature of society outside its walls, would have moulded seminarians to internalise both the stated and hidden ideologies and guiding principles of the committee and their instructors.

Indeed, to ensure this kind of success, the mission ensured that its study plan at the seminary kept students extremely busy and assisted in driving these ideologies deep into their conscious and unconscious minds. The ideas that they so inculcated reinforced the early socialisation that the students had received as members of German society, ensuing that they became rigidly Germanic – more particularly, rigidly Prussian – in outlook. This was accompanied by the development of extreme loyalty to the mission – the kind of loyalty that *Junkers* would have shown to the *Kaiser* – and the wholesale adoption of bourgeois nineteenth-century mindsets.

THE TRAINING

The curriculum that candidate missionaries were exposed to in the Seminary focused on the fundamentals of Lutheran Christianity – knowledge of the Bible and Lutheran dogmatics. This was accompanied by training in practical theology – putting the theoretical training into practice in the mission-field. Seminarians were also equipped with a knowledge of modern and ancient languages – German, English, Dutch, Hebrew, Latin and Greek being compulsory – and were also given a limited knowledge of "heathen languages".[78] General knowledge courses included instruction in history, geography, accounting and bookkeeping.[79] Even prior to acceptance into the Seminary, candidates were encouraged to become teachers or receive training in practical professions. Once at the Mission House, they received instruction in, and were also strongly encouraged to equip themselves with, practical skills such as building, carpentry, agriculture, handicrafts and general ability in all forms of manual work. This was because missionaries often had to build mission stations from scratch. They also had to be able to feed themselves and their congregations from the produce of their fields. Each student also had to follow a short but intensive course in medical and surgical science. This course was taught by well-known professors in Berlin. It was only during the first decade of the twentieth century that a course in the most important tropical diseases was also offered.[80] Lastly, the candidate missionaries also received instruction in music and singing.[81]

The training, which lasted for six years,[d] was thorough. While in training, with the exception of breaks for meals, students were kept busy with formal instruction from eight o'clock in the morning until ten o'clock at night.[82] The degree to which the lives of the pupils was regulated is clearly illustrated by the following extract from the Seminary Instruction Plan:

> The gardening component begins at 5 minutes past 12 o'clock in the store where the gardening equipment is kept and, after receiving instructions and being issued with the necessary equipment, they [the pupils] move to the garden with spades, shovels, hoes, pickaxes, [and] garden hoses, and five minutes later they are at their work, which lasts until 3 minutes before 1 o'clock so that they are left with time to wash their hands, remove their overalls and take their place before the well-filled soup plates to enjoy a hearty lunch, their appetites having been doubled by the preceding labour.[83]

Van der Merwe has argued that the Mission Society "would have rejected the criticism of the liberal theologian Ernst Langhans that 'The Seminary was cloistered and despotic and bound to turn out pharisaic missionaries.'" However, in the Seminary, in its daily management and in the management of the missionaries in the field: "The Society fully supported the autocratic and conservative character of Prussian and, after 1870, German social and political life."[84] Similarly, Marcia Wright has argued that: "In describing the Berlin Mission, the word paternalism must come to the fore" and that:

> The regime of the Seminary, with its stress on obedience and humility easily became the regime of the mission-field, with the

---

d. The introductory year when candidates had to base themselves in Berlin and be in frequent contact with the authorities of the Mission house, followed by five years of study.

missionaries assuming the role of the paternalists over converts. Even the Superintendents, however, were never allowed to forget the superiority of the authorities at home whom they addressed as "Hochverehrte Herrn und Väter" (Most Reverend Masters and Fathers). The contrast between the formal brotherhood of the Moravians and the hierarchical paternalism of the Berliners symbolised a world of difference in social values and concepts of authority.[85]

Similarly, in commenting on their "typically conservative" world view, Pakendorf has argued that:

> German missionaries ... shared with their counterparts from other countries, by and large, the petty bourgeois worldview that shaped their thinking and which they sought to impart to their converts in Africa. It was the manifestation of an individualism that had developed in Europe in the post-medieval period; theologically, it revolved around concepts of sin, redemption and salvation, economically it expressed itself in terms of the work ethic, that is, high productivity based on an internalised self-discipline, and ideologically it consisted of values such as orderliness, diligence, cleanliness, frugality.[86]

In common with their fellow seminarians, this was the kind of training that the missionaries who would serve in Vendaland received, and these were the kinds of ideologies and authority structures that they experienced and internalised. Admittedly, as was the case with Carl Stech, the Berlin Mission sometimes failed to produce the kinds of missionaries they set out to mould. This was even more dramatically demonstrated in the case of Reinhold Wessmann, whose career and trial will be considered next. However, despite these failures, they succeeded in the majority of cases. The degree to which close contact with missionaries in general, and a seminary training in particular, could transform what the missionaries saw as a descendant of the "contemptible Hottentots" into the product that the Berlin Mission desired is clearly illustrated by the life of Klaas Koen.

REINHOLD WESSMANN AND THE HEART OF DARKNESS

Reinhold Wessmann [see Illustration 1][87] was born in Guben on 23 December 1859. Before joining the Berlin Mission in 1880, he was a locksmith.[88] After the completion of his training at the seminary, he was delegated to the Northern Transvaal Synod to "be initiated into the mission service there". He arrived at Mp'hôme just before Christmas 1885.[89] On 28 May 1886, he joined Beuster at Ha-Tshivhase to begin his period of orientation into the "Bawenda Mission".[90] Having married Maria van der Goltz, he was stationed at Old

Georgenholtz from 21 July 1887 to October 1894 and at Tshakhuma from then until his expulsion from the mission on 22 July 1905.[91] This expulsion was for various cases of sexual harassment of local African women, at least one of which turned into a prolonged extra-marital affair.[92]

Significantly, the charges against Wessmann had been brought by local Christians from Tshakhuma. Two letters complaining about the missionary had been received by the Mission. One was anonymous and the other had been signed by eight people.[93] In response, a hearing to consider the evidence against Wessmann was convened on 3 and 4 February 1905. It was alleged that five women – namely Ruth; Maria Moafé; Johanna; Grita and Magdalena – had refused to work for the missionary because of his behaviour towards them.[94] His actions included showing Maria a book with pictures of women giving birth,[95] fondling Grita's breasts when she went to him for Holy Communion,[96] and showing Ruth pictures of sexual acts and discussing "a lot of sexual things" with her. He had also reportedly told Ruth that "he was sleeping with a woman from Makoarele's [Makwarela's] Land without any consequences".[97] This could either have meant that she had not become pregnant or that nobody was taking any action against him because of this.

A second group of complaints presented to the same hearing regarded the fact that Wessmann's son, Günter, had "written a letter to obtain girls for white policemen".[98] Instead of punishing him according to church law, as would have been the fate of other (black) Christians, his parents had punished him. As Jeremiah Dombu, one of the complainants, pointed out, Wessmann had "strongly spoken against the drinking of beer" by Christians. This he had done in spite of the fact that "whites were sinning in his house. Günter Wessmann had procured girls for the police".[99]

The previous chapter clearly demonstrates that the relationship between the missionaries and the local converts was an extremely paternalistic one. This paternalism became even more intense when dealing with the authority structures of the mission standing above the missionary in the field. The mission consciously strove to imbue these structures with a sense of awe and power. Even the missionaries were supposed to feel this and obey. One can imagine how much more intense this was once it reached the level of the ordinary converts. Beyond these ideological dimensions, the missionaries also wielded the very real power to excommunicate Christians and expel them from the mission station.

Against this background, it is easy to understand why the authors of the first letter were too afraid to append their names to it. Those who signed the second letter showed considerable courage. They clearly hoped that these complaints would be acted upon. However, it is clear that the action that they were given was not what they expected. It would seem that they expected a hearing where they could meet with a representative, or representatives, of the mission as a group and have their complaints against Wessmann heard and discussed in his presence. Instead, they were put in front of an inquisition. The panel was chaired by Superintendent Oswald Krause. Additional members were Friedrich Reuter, Rasmus Jensen, Otto Klatt and Theodor Schwellnus, all missionaries from the Northern Transvaal and peers of Wessmann's.[100] One at a time, instead of as a group, the complainants were called in front of a panel consisting only of white missionaries and cross-examined. It will become clear that this was not only unexpected but also seriously disorientated the witnesses. In addition, Wessmann's race, occupation and ability to cross-examine witnesses clearly identified him as a part of this group. Where was the complainants' champion? Even those who did not crumble before this were treated with what they would have interpreted as hostility. It was almost as if they, rather than Wessmann, were on trial.

Clearly intimidated by the presence of the missionaries and the nature of the proceedings, Martha stated that "I know nothing about all of this ... and do not know why my name has been mentioned." Similarly Margaretha stated that she did not know why her name appeared: "I have no guilt." Magdalena simply refused to answer questions: "I do not want to say anything."[101]

Wessmann's defensive strategy focused on simply denying the charges, attacking the character of the witnesses and using their lack of knowledge of western judicial procedure as a means of confusing them, setting them against each other and discrediting their testimony. The panel also gave him considerable leeway in attempting to do this. It is difficult to interpret the panel's actions in this regard as reflecting anything other than their bias in favour of their brother missionary and against the local informants.

Local judicial proceedings were held in public in the *khoro*. All present had the opportunity to hear evidence and to take part in the proceedings. The plaintiff presented his case first. The defendant then addressed the court. Thereafter, the witnesses were called to give evidence. Any man was then free to ask questions. It was, nevertheless, usually the older men who had the most prestige and the most experience who availed themselves of this opportunity. Beyond interjections by a single designated important councillor to keep order, should these prove necessary, nobody had the right to interrupt speakers. The plaintiff and defendant had the right to argue privately over any matter. Official proceedings were suspended while this took place. When the whole case had been thrashed out to the satisfaction of those present, the *khosi* or judge summed up, declared the customary law and delivered judgement and sentence. The possibility also existed for the case to be postponed for further evidence.[103] Colleagues and friends who had taken part in trials at the *khoro* emphasised that, in most cases, the emphasis was on restoring harmony and consensus rather than merely punishing the offender.

Wessmann's manipulation of the western system and the panel's sanctioning of this was totally foreign to this concept of justice. This was most eloquently expressed by the complainant Nicholas, who "complained" to the panel: "Why do you call us one at a time, instead of all together, we are becoming confused in our heads."[104]

During the second group of complaints, Superintendent Krause himself, the person in charge of the region and the chair of the inquiry, jumped to the defence of his Brother. He argued that he had a feeling that, with time, the blame that should have been placed on the boy was being transferred to the father. Similarly, Reuter pointed out that Günter had been punished by his parents and not by church law because he was still "a young boy".[105]

Given the fact that Günter's role in organising women for the policeman seems to have been uncontested, it would seem that only bias on the part of the panel can explain their lack of probing reaction to Wessmann's attempts to place the blame on local women and also to completely distance himself from these events. The missionary stated that a police-corporal had come and asked permission to spend the night at the mission. Since he "knew nothing bad about him", he had given him a guest room. "The next morning, we found the clean bed dirty with red earth." Upon inquiry, he was told "The two girls Abigail and Ella had been there with the policemen" and that "they had a long friendship with the policemen on the hill".[106]

Wessmann continued these tactics on the second day of the hearing. In an act clearly designed both to demonstrate innocence and to enlist the support of his brethren, before any witnesses had been called, he made a plea that his wife be allowed to attend that day. She would be able to help him in places where his memory was unclear. He was suffering "great stress". He then swung straight into defensive mode, attempting to discredit the testimony and witnesses of the previous day. He asserted that he had only discussed "sexual matters" with men and not with women. Women had perhaps overheard or been told of such discussions. The missionary concluded by stating that one of the Christians at Tshakhuma, Timotheus, had told him: "*Mynheer*, if you make promises to the Bawenda they will give false witness for you." Wessmann felt that this was happening.[107]

The panel were clearly predisposed to accept the word of their brother missionary against the black Christians. Superintendent Krause stated that there was no need for Sister Wessmann to be present. The authors of the first letter were unknown. There was no real evidence in the second letter. Witnesses had given incoherent and conflicting testimony and were "lying".[108] Supporting this interpretation, Reuter stated that: "We heard so many lies yesterday that we do not need to hear those who were to have been called today repeat these lies again." He continued by arguing that it was possible that Wessmann may have shown pictures of a woman giving birth from a book in talking about childbirth for instructional purposes and touched a woman's breast to illustrate a point he was making about childbirth or breast-feeding. While this was "thoughtless ... the evidence is that he is clean".[109] The final finding of the Committee was that there was "no evidence" to support the complaints. The complainants had gone about matters "in the wrong way and could not do this again". They were also told that "their complaints would be sent to the high-ups [*Grossen*] in Berlin for their answer".[110]

Presented with the findings of the panel, the Committee in Berlin were faced with what they saw as a "difficult situation". In their opinion, if they asked Wessmann to take a break from his station, his "enemies" would think that the accusations against him were true. They did not want this situation to develop as they wanted to give him a job at another "Bawendaland" station. Worried that rumours about Wessmann's sinfulness were continuing to circulate and that the matter had not been finally and decisively laid to rest, they requested Krause to prepare a new commission and make a new examination to finalise the matter.[111]

This time, the panel took the form of a proper commission. Frederich Reuter and Rasmus Jensen were again members, this time as Commissioners. They were joined by Christoph Sonntag. This time, the Commissioners were much more exhaustive in their inquiries, which began in April with the collection of evidence. In the face of testimony by Dorka Rammba (Dorkus Rambau? – illegible) that she was involved in a sexual relationship with Wessmann, he finally broke down and confessed.[112] Admitting that he had been "overcome" by the "evil enemy", he begged forgiveness. He knew that he would be expelled as a missionary. However, noting that he had spent many years working for the mission and for God and that this was his life, he stated that he longed to continue in their service, even "at a low level".[113] This was to no avail and he was expelled from the mission.

Wessmann's expulsion was not discussed in the *Missions-Berichte* or *Der Bawenda-Freund*, which simply stop referring to him except when discussing earlier events. Indeed, after his expulsion, all reference to him in public documents of the Mission Society, in anything but the past tense, disappeared. That this was deliberate policy is illustrated by Mission Inspector Karl Axenfeld's reply to a communication from Pastor Dietrich, from Wessmann's home area in Germany, requesting information on what had happened to him. In this communication, he requests the Pastor to handle his report on the reasons for Wessmann's expulsion "with the greatest possible discretion", both in mission circles and in the wider community, because "It is a Satanic humiliation for the labourers in such Holy Service when one of them falls into such great sin." Not only the local congregants and "heathens" but also their fellow missionaries could be affected by this.[114] Indeed, so strong was their feeling against Wessmann that they did everything in their power to drive him out of the area. With his expulsion from the mission, Wessmann moved to the farm Laastgevonden. Having failed to persuade the owner to evict him, the mission bought the farm with the express purpose of doing so themselves. This was specifically so that his bad example would be removed from the sight and consciousness of his colleagues, the local converts and the local "heathens".[115] Wessmann subsequently settled in the territory of *Khosi* Masia south of the Levuvhu River, near Davhana at Mpheni. His affairs with local women continued. He died on 20 March 1928.[116] Just how successful the missionaries were in suppressing memories of their fallen brother's actions is demonstrated by the fact that the seals on the records of his disciplinary inquiry (the so-called *Protokoll*) remained inviolate for nearly a hundred years until they were opened in 1996 while the current research was being conducted in the archives of the Berlin Mission.

The fear of contagion by Wessmann and the extreme measures taken to prevent this, strongly suggest that his fall was viewed as being more than a lapse into sin.[117] While the mission did not directly state this, it is clear that they saw him as having a *Tropenkoller*, as suffering from tropical madness or having "gone native". Drawing on the descriptions of Marlow's journey up the river towards the horror in portrayal of the figure of Conrad's *Heart of Darkness*, Harries has argued that, for the Swiss Missionary and ethnographer Henri-Alexandre Junod, and for middle- and upper-class Europeans in the nineteenth century, "Africa was a place of rediscovery, a place where 'our own ancient history surges up before our eyes'."[118] This imagined encounter between Europeans and their origins, or genesis, in Edenic Africa has also been commented on by Brantlinger and White.[119] However, Brantlinger has traced, and White has commented on, the Victorian creation and development of an opposing myth of Africa, that of the "dark continent".[120] In this worldview, which became the dominant one as imperialism and the colonisation of Africa gained momentum, "going native" was the "ultimate atrocity" that the traveller, settler or missionary could commit. It represented the betrayal of the ideals of civilisation that he was supposedly bringing from Europe and the triumph of the darkness of Africa over the light of Europe.[121]

This point is well illustrated by the figure of Kurtz in *Heart of Darkness*. Echoing Brantlinger, Hampson has argued that in this work: "The narrative carries the implication that Kurtz's 'evil' is signalled by his 'going native', and that 'evil, in short, is African'."[122] Similarly, there is a strong theme in the work that Kurtz had been a man of great potential, destined to go far. He is variously described as "a first class agent", "a very remarkable person", "an exceptional man, of the greatest importance to the Company", "a prodigy ... an emissary of pity, and science, and progress and devil knows what else ... a special being" and "a 'universal genius'".[123] Explaining the triumph of "darkness", Conrad argued that "there was something wanting" in Kurtz. While this deficiency would only become apparent to him much later on, the African wilderness "found him out early" and wreaked "a terrible vengeance" on him.[124] Thus, while Kurtz had originally had "immense plans", Africa had corrupted him.[125]

In my reading, from the perspective of the missionaries, this is exactly what had happened to Wessmann. In his fall and his degradation, he had betrayed the image of the missionary as hero and servant of God. This suggested, and his continuing sinfulness confirmed, the image of the missionary as servant of Satan. In the view of the mission, they had no alternative but to protect others from corruption. Purchase of a farm with the express purpose of evicting Wessmann and attempting to expunge him from public consciousness were small prices to pay when souls were at stake.

KLAAS KOEN – THE IDEAL MISSIONARY

The career of Klaas Koen stands in marked contrast to that of Wessmann. Far from being forgotten about, the mission celebrated his life and "blessed" death, portraying him as exemplifying the degree to which one could be reborn, becoming a new man, in Christ. In conformity with the idea of the written word as a challenge that leads to conversion, Koen's refashioning of his body and soul to become as "German" as any native of Germany, the painful suffering which wracked his body and his ultimate supreme sacrifice were celebrated in *Der Bawenda-Freund*, the *Missions-Berichte* and a tractate about his life.

Klaas Koen was born at Haarlem in the Cape Colony on 22 May 1852, the son of Piet Koen, first an elder and later the verger of the small Christian community there.[126] His father had been instrumental in getting Missionary Friedrich Prietsch to go to Haarlem in 1860 and establishing the mission station of Anhalt-Schmidt. In time he became "a friend of the house". Always prepared to offer advice and help, he became a favourite of Prietsch's wife. "Klaas was the 6th child of his numerous swarm of children."[127]

Hans Heese has argued that Klaas Koen was a direct descendant of Johannes Casparus Koen van Roeksem, the Koen progenitor from Germany, who arrived at the Cape in 1741. His mother was Christina Catharina Leeu or Leen (also named De Laine). On the Koen side, his grandmother was Betje Oosthuizen, from the Cape. His great-grandmother on this side was Maria Geertruy Beyers.[128]

The Berlin Mission seems to have been unaware of Koen's distant German roots. Although they noted that he himself spelt his name as Klaas Koen, they did not find this German enough. Instead, in mission writings, his name was usually "Germanised" to Klaus Kuhn or Klaas Kuhn.[129] Moreover, it suited them to emphasise the fact that he was a South African of mixed descent. On a practical level, when they assigned him "to the high, hot northern area where he would work", they "hoped that, as a born Hottentot and an African, he more than anybody else would have the constitution which could resist the hot climate there".[130] On a more abstract, ideological, level, in their terms, as a "Hottentot", Klaas was descended from people who had gone around "half-naked ... [living] in appalling filth and still more wicked foolishness and in all sorts of heathen sins and disgraces". In time, these "weak and very lazy" people had adopted the Dutch language and

> replaced their skin clothing with European cast-offs. Because nobody was teaching them, they remained wretched heathens, going to neglect in their bottomless foolishness, especially through the vice of drunkenness. Some became even more wicked when the English, into whose possession the Cape had come, gave them unconditional freedom.[131]

However, the Berlin Missionaries believed that their "patient" work among these "degenerate heathens" demonstrated that even they could be "awakened to a new life" in Christ. Piet Koen had been one of their earliest successes.[132] In their opinion, their success with his son would be even greater. Although descended from the "contemptible Hottentots", he would go on to "work more than others whose forebears were so-called Christians" and provide a shining light for others to follow.[133] While not directly stated, the strong implication was that the Vhavenda, among whom he would spend his mission career and offer his life as a sacrifice, could also break away from their dark present and experience such a rebirth. This situation had come about by a combination of piety and good fortune.

Koen's path to ordination began with one of his father's offers of help to the Prietsch family. One of the first things that Missionary Prietsch did after his founding of the station was to establish a garden in which peach trees flourished. A great deal of the produce of these trees was dried, so that it would not go to waste. The fruit was laid out to sun-dry in front of the house. Piet Koen noticed that the chickens often ate the drying fruit. He told the missionary:

> You cannot carry on like this, you must have somebody to chase the chickens away, otherwise they will destroy everything. I will give you my Klaas, if this is acceptable to you. I want to give my son Klaas to you, he will keep the chickens away.[134]

So, the nine-year old Klaas came to live in the Prietsch's house. When the last of the peaches had been dried, Mrs. Prietsch asked the old man:

> "Piet, what now? The fruit is ready, what shall now become of Klaas?" Piet scratched his head in a somewhat embarrassed manner and eventually said ... "I do not know what to do with Klaas at home. He is not like my other children. When I say to them: Do this or that! ... they understand me and do it but Klaas, when I have said a lot to them, then he looks in the clouds and has not understood anything. The boy is extremely stupid! Do you not want to keep him here?"[135]

The answer from the Prietsch family was:

> Good, Klaas can stay with us and we want to keep him. But then we must do this in writing and you and your wife have to sign the contract.[136]

This was done, and Klaas became their stepson. In time, they also took other children into their home, giving them a "good upbringing" and sending them to school. It soon became apparent to them that, far from being stupid, Klaas in fact far outshone his peers and had the capability to become a teacher or minister one day. The problem was finding funds to finance his training.[137]

This money was eventually provided by "a distinguished benefactress in Germany", Frau von Kröcher, who had "lost her only son and heir in an accident. Because she no longer had her son to care for, she decided to do some good for a heathen boy." Hearing from her sister that, at that time, the Prietschs had a "couple of girls and three boys" living in their house, she contacted Mrs. Prietsch through her sister. Having received written reports about, and letters from, these children, she selected Klaas and offered him financial support for private lessons in English, German and the violin.[138]

When Frau von Kröcher died, her will made provision for Klaas to study in Germany to become either a teacher or a missionary.[139] The seventeen-year-old boy took the opportunity offered to him. For two years, he studied in a preparatory institution in Ducherow in Pomerania. He then moved over to the Mission House in Berlin to study in the seminary there. For his first year, this was still the old Mission House in Sebastianstrasse. However, after this it moved to the site that it still occupies in Georgenkirchstrasse. There, he studied hard with the other candidate missionaries. Through his strenuous efforts, "this Hottentot Christian of heathen ancestry made such progress as to be an example to others". He even made better progress "in Greek and Hebrew than many other candidates".[140]

As he progressed in his training, Koen began to attend and preach at Mission revival meetings. He proved to be extremely popular and made many friends among the clergy and the laity, rich and poor alike. "Above all, ... he won the friendship of the God-fearing Verger and teacher Bröse, and the heart of his daughter Maria, who was prepared to brave all dangers to join him in his homeland to preach the gospel to the heathens." However, they decided that they would only marry after he had spent a year back in Africa as a missionary.[141]

References to Koen's popularity and his success in winning the heart of a girl from "God-fearing" solid German stock demonstrate that the Berlin Missionaries, and their wider church circle, accepted this "Hottentot" as a being who had been transformed by Christ and by his exposure to the "civilising" influence of German culture and a German Seminary education. The extent to which he had become "white", or "German", through this process is also clearly demonstrated in the account of his farewell sermon given in the tractate about his life and in the photograph of him used as an illustration in the tractate *Neu-Georgenholtz im Wenda-Lande* [see Illustration 2].[142]

After six years of study in the Mission House, on 29 August 1875, Koen preached his farewell sermon in the Bartholomäuskirche, the church that served as the home church for the Mission Society. The man who entered the pulpit "was scarcely darker than any of our own when he has been really burned by the sun. That his hair, crinkled in small bushes, stands a little curly on the head, one does not see from a distance." In addition, his face was drawn into a "sensible and serious expression. He preached about the parable of the talents (Matt. 25, 14–21)".[143] Ending his sermon with thanks, "the stranger took his leave from the Christian congregation with which he had been tied in the worship of God for seven years".[144]

In the photograph, Koen wears the standard high-necked and dog-collared uniform of the Berlin Missionary. His hair has been combed in such a way that it indeed appears curly but not "crinkled". The photograph has also been exposed or retouched so that his skin does not appear to be dark. He has indeed become "white" or "German" in looks as well as in ideology.

Having completed his examinations, Koen set sail for Africa on 1 January 1876.[145] As with his fellow missionaries, in taking his leave, Koen was not only leaving his German brothers and sisters in Christ and the highly-structured learning environment of the Mission House. He was also taking his leave from the highly-structured physical environment of the church and the Seminary. Friedrichshain, the district in which the seminary was situated, was a highly ordered, densely built-up area. Buildings from three- to six-stories high were common. The only open space of significant size was the Friedrichshain Park, opened on 18 July 1847. Here, beneath carefully planted trees, and amidst fountains, nature was vigorously pruned and clipped into aesthetically-pleasing straight lines. Outside the park, nature was represented by straight rows of evenly-spaced trees.[146] Even Koen, who had spent his childhood in the Cape Colony, was unfamiliar with the kind of country that he was going to. This was the region on the Tropic of Capricorn where nature, and the inhabitants, had not as yet been brought under what he and his colleagues would have seen as "civilised" control.

Koen eventually arrived "in the lands of the Bawenda" in April 1876.[147] His first posting was at Tshakhuma. As was customary for new missionaries, he was to be stationed here for a year to "be initiated into his calling and to study the language and customs of the Bawenda". He did this under the direction of Missionary Erdmann Schwellnus and his wife.[148]

On 10 May 1876, Koen wrote to mission Director Wangemann:

> I am writing to you for the first time from the Northern Transvaal. I am really entering the proper mission work now ... learning the language. I have taken the preparatory classes over from Br. Schwellnus and am teaching the people reading, writing and singing. Polygamy is part of the consciousness of the people. Those who are not married are regarded as children here and very little attention is paid to them. They love me but it is offensive to them that I am not a married man. Therefore I wish to ask, if it is possible, that my bride (Miss Maria Bröse) can come together with Sister Grützner next year. I am certain that as long as one remains unmarried, one cannot be a missionary here.[149]

His progress was reasonably rapid. On November of the same year, he wrote to Director Wangemann: "Now that I have been here for five months, I am able to preach in the local language here."[150]

On 13 July 1877, Koen, then twenty-five years old, visited the Vhavenda *Khosi* Makwarela at his capital village of Tshikwarakwara to make final arrangements with him for the establishment of a mission station in his territory.[e] Having negotiated these details, Koen returned to Tshakhuma. On 26 July, he returned to Makwarela's area, this time to stay. Demonstrating the energy expected of a German Missionary, Koen wasted no time in starting work on the establishment of Georgenholtz. His first task was to build a small house on the side of the mountain. The costs for this and later buildings were borne by a faithful friend of the Mission, Georg Holtz, Lord of the Manor of Manow in Pomerania, hence the naming of the new station after him.[151]

Koen immediately began to preach to the people. Because he had no bell, he called them together by beating on a pot or a piece of iron. "They came also – sometimes only 10, although often up to 500."[152]

Although he received a great deal of support from Makwarela, it took some time before the preaching of the Gospel made any real impact on the local people.[153] Also, in spite of the fact that Koen enjoyed and deeply appreciated the companionship and support of Makwarela, the latter was still a "heathen". This meant that he could not fulfil all of the missionary's needs for companionship and support. These needs could also only partially be met by the African converts. Koen's first Christmas at Georgenholtz demonstrated just how "white" – just how acculturated by German culture – he had become:

> Kuhn would have felt very lonely among these people had he not had at least one Christian with him. He was one of the converts from Tsakoma (Johannes, later [joined by] one other called Samuel), who supported him faithfully. In spite of this, he was extremely lonely on his first Christmas [there]. On Christmas Eve, he sat next to a gum tree decorated with quite a few candles (the spruce tree is not found there). His heart was so heavy that this carried over to his eyes [and he cried]. Then Brother Schwellnus came riding over bringing comfort. He also brought hearty greetings and a Christmas cake from Brother Beuster, decorating the small [Christmas] tree with this. On the next day, he could again stand before the heathens full of joyfulness and give testimony about the greatest Christmas present given by the Heavenly Father.[154]

Having been revitalised by his German brothers, Koen would work hard to save souls.[155] However, his mission career would continue to be plagued by

---

e. Tshikwarakwara was recorded as "Schibngarragarra" in mission sources at this time. The first meeting between the missionary and the *khosi* is discussed in more detail on p. 249.

illness. Already in March 1877, Koen had written to Mission Director Wangemann that: "I have been ill with climate-fever [*Klimafieber*] and still feel sick more often than healthy."[156] Again, in February 1878, Koen was confined to his bed with a severe fever. He was at first nursed by Makwarela himself.[157] When it became clear that the missionary was not improving, Makwarela sent messengers to Missionary Beuster. He came and fetched Koen and took him back to his mission station. After several weeks, he was well enough to return to Georgenholtz. His recovery from what had appeared to the local people to be an almost-certainly fatal illness reportedly led to an increase in those attending church services and seeking conversion.[158] The mission took pride in the fact that Koen was, and continued to be

> driven by his enthusiasm for God's Word. Untiringly he strained all his bodily and spiritual strength – yes, he even went beyond his strength – to serve his Saviour. He did not spare himself, even it if meant visiting the villages in the hottest heat of the sun. Then, in this overheated condition, he was surprised by drenching bouts of rain, or had to ride or swim through swollen rivers. These surely were contributing factors which caused the nagging illness within him to lead him to an early end.[159]

In addition to continuing his mission work, Koen also built the "first solid dwelling-house at Georgenholtz" to replace the "small hut" that he had lived in until then. This was completed in September 1878. Revealing the idea of the missionaries as imposing order on nature, the mission recorded that this had "a delightful small garden, laid out as prettily as possible, in front".[160]

Once this was done, on 1 October, Koen left for Natal to marry his fiancée. Since he expected to be away for some months, he appointed one of his pupils, the as yet unbaptised Nathanael (Nathaniel) Lalumbe, to run services as best he could in his absence.[161]

Not only Koen but also Missionary Mars from Botshabelo, who had travelled together with him, were waiting for their brides to arrive at Königsberg Mission Station from Germany. They had to wait five weeks before they arrived. Koen and Maria Bröse were eventually married on 30 December 1878. "The black Christians also celebrated together with them. A goat had been slaughtered for them and a large urn of coffee prepared."[162]

After their lengthy return journey, the couple arrived back at Georgenholtz on 21 February 1879:

> When the wagon was sighted from Makoarele's village, and it was noticed that it contained two "school people", people came out to meet them with great jubilation. A huge crowd of joyful people, accompanied by many drawn out of curiosity, came shouting and dancing and made noise.[163]

The situation that they found gave them great hope for the future. Not only had regular Sunday services been held in Koen's absence but the congregation had also made progress in their learning. Nine new pupils, including an uncle of Makwarela, had joined those receiving instruction.[164] To top all of this off,

> The mission work was going well. There were still large numbers of attentive people coming to attend the church services and Makoarele [Makwarela] was still ... [among the most regular attendees]. Many of the pupils were also asking to be baptised and were being prepared for this.[165]

However, on earth, in the face of joy, we still have our "cross" to bear. Koen's "young wife had to fight against severe attacks of fever". Georgenholtz lay

> right in the fever lands. Also Kuhn himself periodically became very ill, so that Beuster had to come over from Ha-Tshivhase to nurse them both. With God's help, they withstood these tests.[166]

On 27 July 1879, the new bell at Georgenholtz, donated by children at the Sunday school in Fürstenwalde, was rung for the first time. "Its first ringing called Makoarele's people to a real celebration. The first four [adult] converts would be accepted into the Christian Church through baptism."[167] It will be seen in chapter 8 that in the interpretation of the missionaries, the fact that Makwarela was not among those baptised led to tensions between him and them. They also believed that, because of this, there was a great increase in hostility towards them shown by all of Makwarela's people.[168] In addition to the situation at the capital, the spreading of the Gospel in surrounding areas also "came to a halt".[169] However, Nathanael Lalumbe, who had been appointed as the Native Assistant [*Nationalhelfer*] of Georgenholtz on 1 January 1880, "went quickly to the surrounding kraals" to attempt to defuse the situation. He reportedly had to "endure ridicule and scorn" because of this.[170]

In spite of these setbacks the Christian congregation grew gradually. Although "a few were baptised" every year, "many pupils also turned away again".[171] Klaas and Maria Koen would have two children, a son named Gerhard August Peter, born on 4 January 1881, and a daughter named Hedwig, born on 18 July 1882.[172] The year 1882 also saw the completion of a new house at Georgenholtz. The old dwelling became a church.[173] At this stage, "there were but 28 Christians at the station who held faithfully to God's Word".[174] Also, in time, the relationship between Koen and Makwarela was partly restored.[175]

In the interpretation of the mission: "Heavier for the progress of Christianity at Georgenholtz than the hostility of the heathens was the illness of the missionary. It became increasingly clear that he was beginning to fade away."[176] I have already mentioned Koen's illness while still at Tshakhuma, his serious illness during his first year at Georgenholtz and his and his wife's periodic bouts of fever. In December 1881, Koen wrote to Mission Director Wangemann that:

> It has become difficult for me to carry out my duties, and I am very worried that in the future I will become a spectacle ... I suffer from [a] sore throat and pain in the chest, the sore throat comes and goes but the chest pain remains, and the coughing of blood becomes ever more serious ... Speaking has become difficult for me.[177]

By the beginning of 1882, "he was really deteriorating" and spent long periods confined to his sickbed.[178]

His wife also suffered from fever again, so she could not offer a hand, and also their one-year-old son was without the necessary care and supervision, which made the hearts of the parents even more heavy.[179]

In spite of the serious condition that he found himself in, Koen set an impressive example of devotion to duty and paternal care for his congregation:

> However, also this time of trial passed. After fourteen days, *Frau* Kuhn could get up again and her husband also recovered so that he could take up his work again. On the fourth Sunday after Easter, the little church could be officially opened. Kuhn faithfully preached although speaking had become very difficult for him. He taught the school pupils daily; but, so that he did not have to talk too much, he had to let one of the black Christians help him. He regularly assembled those who had made progress and gave them instruction, so that they could spread the gospel in the surrounding kraals. Out of spiritual care for the congregation, he appointed a congregation-guardian ... [to take over the work that he was no longer strong enough to do himself]. But he himself admonished and comforted as far as his strength allowed. In particular, he had to severely punish the members of the congregation on account of the old lethargy. The words of their sick teacher, who they all loved, had a great effect. The Christians set themselves apart from the heathens by their diligence. For the most part, they walked well, only some women with their quarrelsomeness and gossip mongering made the missionary's heart heavy. Above all other work in the community, he also used many free hours working on the translation of the Gospel of John into the language of the Bawenda. He did not fail in moving devotion to his calling.[180]

However, after this period of slight remission, his old illness returned in its full severity. In June 1882 he wrote to the Committee of the Berlin Mission Society:

> Because, due to my illness, I feel as if I am incapable, I beg you to relieve me of my duties and send another missionary to Georgenholtz ... During the 7 years of my duty, I have done as much as has lain in my weak strength.[181]

In response to Koen's declining health, the young [as yet, not ordained] missionary Dietrich Baumhöfner was sent out from Berlin and arrived at Georgenholtz on 1 August 1882. He also received an extremely warm welcome from Makwarela.[182]

Baumhöfner found Koen "so changed that he did not recognise him". However, at times when he felt strong enough to force himself out of bed, "he did not relent from his work". In October, he was again confined to his bed, often in such great pain that he begged to be released from it. In spite of his suffering, in times of lucidity he concerned himself with the "poor Bawenda" and the "poor Makoarele [Makwarela]".[183]

Baumhöfner reported that:

> On the 16 October [1882], the dear patient suffered great pains. He called out: "Oh please give me a cloth and tie my body together, because everything seems to be falling apart." Half an hour later he shouted: "Oh my heart, my heart! It is breaking! My Saviour, free me." Even he now thought his hour had come. He gave instructions about guardianship, and sent greetings to the Brothers Beuster and Schwellnus. Then he lamented about the misery of the poor Bawenda [Vhavenda] nation: "Oh, these poor Bawenda people, the poor people! Oh, poor Makoarela [Makwarela]! I have loved him so much and would have so liked to see him again up there!"[f] When his wife then asked him: "My dear husband, do you not also have a word for me?" he replied: "Mama, I feel I am still staying with you. I'll tell you that I am going Home, before I go." From then on he improved and he could sleep a little.[184]

Towards the end of the year, Koen had a slight remission of the fever. At this time,

> a severe famine prevailed in the lands of the Bawenda. Many even cooked and ate their own skin clothing. With great diffi-

---

f. A reference to Heaven. Koen would have believed that, since Makwarela was not baptised, they would not meet in the hereafter.

culty, Kuhn managed to have maize fetched from outside [Vendaland] and shared this with the starving [people], until he himself was also suffering privation.[185]

Even as his life drew to a close:

> His mercy was also seen in the adoption of a poor boy, who had been picked up along the way by Makoarele [Makwarela], when he wanted to be free of him, because he was causing so much trouble through his stealing. Kuhn took him as his stepson, in faithful memory of the good deed that he himself had received from Missionary Prietsch. He had the satisfaction of being able to baptise the young lad himself [on 21 January 1883].[186]

Again revealing what the missionaries saw as his great devotion to duty, and his care for the Vhavenda, shortly before Christmas:

> Kuhn had once again been able to deliver a sermon. But the old pain attacked him more strongly again after this. In spite of this, he led the Christmas celebrations. Under the decorated tree, the Christian children told the Christmas story and sang Christmas carols. Baumhöfner was an accomplished blower and accompanied them on his horn. "Perhaps the Lord will give me another year so that I can spread his word wider among the Bawenda!" Kuhn said at that time; however, shortly thereafter, when the pain became worse, Kuhn said to his wife: "Do not pray any more for my life, the Lord is coming shortly."[187]

Koen carried out his last official duty – the marriage of Paulus and Mavhungo, a daughter of *Khosi* Ranwedzi Mphaphuli – on 29 January 1883. "He had to sit at this, Baumhöfner had made him a pair of crutches, with their help he could slowly take a few steps. His last hour was coming and he was fully prepared for this."[188]

Despite Koen's weak physical state, and his sense of his impending death, he was not prepared to give an inch on dogma. It would seem that Paulus had impregnated Mavhungo before marrying her. Koen would only allow the marriage to go ahead after Paulus had done penance in church. Normal practice in such cases, and that which was followed in this particular case, was that the guilty parties had to attend special penance classes for a set period of time. After this, they were made to express their regret (do penance) in front of the congregation. Only then were they again regarded as true members of the congregation, allowed to partake in Holy Communion again or allowed to be married in church. In the text, the penance is only mentioned in conjunction with Paulus. This suggests that Mphaphuli's daughter was not yet a

Christian – she might have attended classes but she had not yet been baptised. As she was not yet part of the congregation, she did not have to do penance!

Even with his crutches, Koen was so weak that he could only take a few steps at a time. From time to time he cried out: "Is my Saviour not coming soon?" To his wife he said: "Do not pray that I get better. The Lord's will be done. May the Lord soon have pity on me and change things soon!" Then again he asked her: "Is it not wrong to wish for the end so ardently?" He bore his suffering patiently and never complained. He was not at all afraid of death, because he was assured of the forgiveness of his sins. Once he said to his wife: "Death is almost a good friend to me!"[190]

Koen's last days are movingly described in a letter written by his wife two days after his death and in the tractate about his life:

> It has pleased the Almighty God to take my beloved husband, the father of my small children. After long and heavy suffering, he passed away on 10.2. at one o'clock in the afternoon ...[191]
>
> On Invocative Sunday, Missionary Beuster from Ha Tschewasse was due to hold the service at Georgenholtz. As a result of an unexplained uneasiness, he made the journey on Friday ...[192] When Br. Beuster bent over him to greet him, he embraced him with both arms and called out loudly: See, now he is here! Then tears came to his eyes ... Br. Beuster was shocked to find him so emaciated and suffering. In the last days, his voice was only a quiet whisper. The terrible pain also sometimes made him terribly listless. When Br. Beuster asked him in the evening if he still had anything on his heart, he said: Yes, I still have one matter, there is an area where I really wanted to put an evangelist, there are some people there who want to learn.[193]

What he wished for was an outstation to be established at Paulus's homestead and for Franz (another convert) to live there as an evangelist. "So, until the end, he looked after the mission work."[194] His wife wrote:

> Once I had told Br. Beuster everything about this matter, he was satisfied. On Sunday morning, he often asked: Has my saviour not yet come? Oh, I still trust [in him]. He was often so [wracked by] suffering and so sick and had always recovered ... He often said to me: Do not pray for healing, the Lord's will be done, and may the Lord soon show his mercy! Then he also wished, if it was not wrongful, for the end to come ... Only one week before his death, when his throat had become a little better, he wanted to travel to Synod ... He really wanted his sins to be forgiven and also did not fear death at all. He once expressed the wish: If only I could live and work for this year. Still, he was later completely satisfied [to accept] how the Lord wanted to end it.[195]

The end was very near:

> Early on Saturday, he wished for Holy Communion, to make ready for his last passing. Beuster had brought a medicine-bottle of wine along. So the sacrament could be celebrated. Thereafter, he lay for some hours with half-opened eyes in slumber. Many times he sighed in deep pain, but his folded hands showed that he was looking for support in the right place in his last struggle. Once more, he asked to stand up from his chair, but he sank back. It moved towards the end. As the breath became shorter, his wife thought of a promise that she had given her husband earlier and said to him: "Jesus' blood and justice."[g] Thereafter, those gathered there sang the last three verses of *O Haupt voll Blut und Wunden* ["Oh Head full of Blood and Wounds"].[h] The dying [man] attempted to say some of the words together with them. Shortly before the end of the hymn, he took his last breath.[196]

Shortly after Koen breathed his last, at about 13:00, Beuster and Baumhöfner made a coffin for him from planks which he had already put aside for this purpose. Earlier, when Baumhöfner had been making a coffin for a congregation member who had passed away, "Koen had said to him: 'Please leave two for me'". These proved to be insufficient and they had to chop up a door as well. The selection of planks for his coffin was not the only thing that Koen had done to prepare for his death: "In his last days, he had put the station books [records] and accounts into the best order. Even in this, he was diligent."[197]

Due to the summer heat, the funeral could not be delayed. It would take place on the very next day, Sunday 11 February 1882. Messengers were sent to Makwarela and to Schwellnus but there was not enough time for them to get there before the funeral. At the funeral, not only was Koen's wife distraught and Beuster deeply saddened but reportedly "many of the Christians and heathens were weeping". As the body was conveyed to its final resting place, the funeral hymn *Kha ri yeni!* ("Let me Go") was sung.[198]

Harking back to the parable of the talents about which he preached before leaving for South Africa, the tractate about Koen's life commented:

> So rests under a large wild fig tree the first missionary in his faraway land. The faithfulness, about which he first preached to the congregation of the Bartholomäuskirche, he had himself

---

g. This is the first line of a verse from a hymn, *"Christi Blut und Gerechtigkeit"*. Koen had told his wife earlier that "he would like to die while the verse: 'Christ's blood and justice' was being prayed, and if he could not speak any longer, she should pray it for him" (*BMB*, 1883, p. 363).

h. A Passion-tide hymn of ten verses. The last three verses deal with death and us leaving this earth. It is Hymn 54 in the Venda Hymnal (*Nyimbo dza VhaTendi*) – *"Naa vho U ita hani?"*

achieved. Although he was descended from the contemptible Hottentots, he worked more than many whose forebears were so-called Christians. It is certain that God's words: "You are a pure and faithful servant, you have been among the few who have been really faithful. I wish to place you above many. Go forth to the peace of your Lord," apply to him.[199]

Against the background of its history, the dominant ideologies of those who determined mission policy, the officials and the raw material that it had to work with in its candidate missionaries, Koen was both the ideal Christian and the ideal missionary that the Berlin Mission were attempting to produce. During the late nineteenth century, most of his colleagues in Vendaland certainly rose above Stech and Wessmann. The others, I would argue, either came close to matching or equalled the standards set by Koen for fortitude and zeal. Having focused on their background and training in Germany, the question remains as to how they viewed the landscape of the area that they were sent to in South Africa and how they depicted this, and its inhabitants, textually and ichnographically.

1. H. Lehmann, *150 Jahre Berliner Mission*, Stuttgart, Ev.-Luth. Mission Erlangen, 1974, p. 9; U. van der Heyden, "The Archives and Library of the Berlin Mission Society", in *History in Africa: A Journal of Method*, 23, 1996, pp. 411–412; D.W. van der Merwe, "Van Paternalisme tot Selfbeskikking: Die Berlynse Sendinggenootskap en Kerkstigting in Transvaal, 1904–1962, D.Litt. et Phil. thesis, University of South Africa, 1980, pp. 1–2; and M. Wright, *German Missions in Tanganyika 1891–1941: Lutherans and Moravians in the Southern Highlands*, Oxford, Clarendon Press, 1971, p. 3. In addition to these sources, the most useful general histories of the Berlin Mission Society are H. Lehmann, *Zur Zeit und zur Unzeit: Geschichte der Berliner Mission, 1918–1972*, Drei Bände, Berlin, Berliner Missionswerk, 1989; D.J. Richter, *Geschichte der Berliner Missionsgesellschaft, 1824–1924*, Berlin, Buchhandlung der Berliner ev. Missionsgesellschaft, 1924. For the Transvaal, the most useful works are W. Gründler, *Geschichte der Bawenda-Mission in Nord-Transvaal*; D.W. van der Merwe (a) *Die geskiedenis van die Berlynse Sendinggenootskap in Transvaal, 1860–1900*, Argiefjaarboek vir Suid-Afrikaanse Geskiedenis, Pretoria, Staatsdrukker, 1984, Deel I & (b) *Die Berlynse Sendinggenootskap en Kerkstigting in Transvaal, 1904–1962*, Argiefjaarboek vir Suid-Afrikaanse Geskiedenis, Pretoria, Staatsdrukker, 1987, Deel II.

2. D.J. Richter, *Geschichte der Berliner Missionsgesellschaft*, p. 143; D.W. van der Merwe, "Van Paternalisme tot Selfbeskikking", pp. 5–6.

3. D.W. van der Merwe, "Van Paternalisme tot Selfbeskikking", p. 2; M. Wright, *German Missions in Tanganyika*, p. 3.

4. *BMB*, 1894, p. 278; D.W. van der Merwe, "Van Paternalisme tot Selfbeskikking", p. 5.

5. D.W. van der Merwe, "Van Paternalisme tot Selfbeskikking", pp. 2–3.

6. S.B. Ferguson and D.F. Wright (eds.), *New Dictionary of Theology*, Leicester and Illinois, Inter-Varsity Press, 1988, p. 516.

7. D.W. van der Merwe, "Van Paternalisme tot Selfbeskikking", p. 2.

8. L. Berkhof, *The History of Christian Doctrines*, Edinburgh, The Banner of Truth Trust, 1969, p. 30; S.P.P. Mminele, "The Berlin Missionary Enterprise at Boshabelo, 1865–1955: An Historical-Educational Study", Master of Education thesis, University of the North, 1983, p. 11.

9. S.P.P. Mminele, "The Berlin Missionary Enterprise", p. 1. See also D.G. Warneck (a) *Abriss einer Geschichte der protestantischen Missionen von der Reformation bis auf die Gegenwart*.

Ein Beitrag zur neueren Kirchengeschichte, Auflage, Berlin, Verlag von Martin Warneck, 1901, pp. 54–76 & (b) *Outline of a History of Protestant Missions from the Reformation to the Present Time: A contribution to Modern Church History*, Authorised translation from the Seventh German Edition [see above], Edinburgh and London, Oliphant Anderson & Ferrier, 1901, pp. 53–73.

10. J.J. Kritzinger, P.G.I. Meiring and W.A. Saayman, *On being Witness*, Halfway House, Orion Publishers, 1994, p. 27. Cf. D.J. Bosch, *Transforming Mission: Paradigm Shifts in Theology of Mission*, New York, Orbis Books, 1991, pp. 253–255.

11. J.J. Kritzinger et al., *On being Witness*, p. 27.

12. Gunther Pakendorf, "For there is no power but of God": The Berlin Mission and the Challenges of Colonial South Africa" (Article originally published in *Missionalia*, the Journal of the South African Missiological Society), at http://www.geocities.com/missionalia/germiss1.htm, accessed 16 October 2000, p. 3.

13. *Ibid*.; S.P.P. Mminele, "The Berlin Missionary Enterprise", p. 11.

14. J.J. Kritzinger et al., *On being Witness*, pp. 27–28.

15. *Ibid*. p. 28.

16. H.-W. Genischen, "German Protestant Missions", in T. Christensen and W.R. Hutchinson (eds.), *Missionary Ideologies in the Imperialist Era: 1880–1920. Papers from the Durham Consultation, 1981*, Aarhus, Aros, 1982, p. 181, quoted in Gunther Pakendorf "For there is no power but of God", pp. 1–2.

17. Gunther Pakendorf, "For there is no power but of God", p. 2.

18. U. van der Heyden, "The Archives and Library of the Berlin Mission Society", p. 412.

19. D.W. van der Merwe, "Van Paternalisme tot Selfbeskikking", p. 2.

20. *BMB*, 1871, pp. 185–186.

21. *BMB*, 1870, pp. 217–218; and U. van der Heyden, "The Archives and Library of the Berlin Mission Society", pp. 412–413. For the history of the Berlin Mission in South Africa from 1834 to 1914, see D.J. Richter, *Geschichte der Berliner Missionsgesellschaft*, pp. 91–318, 357–418.

22. S.P.P. Mminele, "The Berlin Missionary Enterprise", p. 17 n 26; D.J. Richter, *Geschichte der Berliner Missionsgesellschaft*, pp. 521–631 (China, 1882–1922), 632–694 (East Africa, 1884–1914); U. van der Heyden, "The Archives and Library of the Berlin Mission Society", p. 411; and M. Wright, *German Missions in Tanganyika*.

23. D.W. van der Merwe, "Van Paternalisme tot Selfbeskikking", pp. 2–3; H.T. Wangemann, *Motive und Erläuterungen zu der Missions-Ordnung der Berliner Gesellschaft zur Beförderung der Evangelischen Missionen unter den Heiden*, Berlin, Selbstverlag des Evangel. Missionshauses, Friedenstrasse 6, 1882, p. 10.

24. *BMB*, 1873, p. 224. The full list of requirements for acceptance into the Seminary of the Berlin Mission is given on pp. 224–225.

25. D.W. van der Merwe, "Van Paternalisme tot Selfbeskikking", p. 3. For a similar focus on the lower-middle and artisan classes in the recruitment of missionaries in Britain, see, for example, J.L. Comaroff and J. Comaroff, *Of Revelation and Revolution: Christianity, Colonialism and Consciousness in South Africa*, Volume One, Chicago, University of Chicago Press, 1991, pp. 75, 80–81, 84–85; A.E. Coombes, *Reinventing Africa: Museums, Material Culture and Popular Imagination*, New Haven and London, Yale University Press, 1994, p. 163; L. de Kock, *Civilising Barbarians: Missionary Narrative and African Textual Response in Nineteenth-Century South Africa*, Johannesburg, Witwatersrand University Press, 1996, p. 42; R. Elphick, "Africans and the Christian Campaign in Southern Africa", in H. Lamar and L. Thompson (eds.), *The Frontier in History: North America and Southern Africa Compared*, New Haven, Yale University Press, 1981, pp. 279–280; and A.L. Stoler and F. Cooper, "Between Metropole and Colony: Rethinking a Research agenda", in F. Cooper and A.L. Stoler (eds.), *Tensions of Empire: colonial cultures in a bourgeois world*, Berkeley, Los Angeles and London, University of California Press, 1997, p. 27.

26. The towns and villages where missionaries were born may all be traced on any good road map of Germany. For example, I traced all with the exception of Schwellnus's birthplace in Lithuania on *Deutschland 5–19 GK 1:700 000, Strassenkarte*, Bern, Hallwag AG, n.d.

27. Acta betreffend Personalia: Beuster, Carl.
28. See pp. 26–27 and 56–57 respectively.
29. Acta betreffend Personalia: Beuster, Carl; [Anon.] *75th Anniversary of the Berlin Mission Station Tshivhase*, p. 4; *BMB*, 1881, p. 356; 1882, pp. 152, 425; 1886, pp. 218, 413–414; 1887, p. 222; 1889, p. 535.
30. Acta betreffend Personalia: Beuster, Carl. I have been unable to trace the subsequent fate of the collection of insects.
31. *Ibid.* [Anon.] *75th Anniversary of the Berlin Mission Station Tshivhase*, p. 3; *BMB*, 1874, p. 466; 1875, pp. 231, 359, 369, 370, 419–420, 424.
32. Acta betreffend Personalia: Beuster, Carl; [Anon.] *75th Anniversary of the Berlin Mission Station Tshivhase*, pp. 3, 4; *BMB*, 1876, p. 184. See also p. 70.
33. Acta betreffend Personalia: Beuster, Carl; [Anon.] *75th Anniversary of the Berlin Mission Station Tshivhase*, p. 4.
34. [Anon.] *75th Anniversary of the Berlin Mission Station Tshivhase*, p. 5. For Beuster's life history, see also D.W. Krüger (ed. in chief) & C.J. Beyers, *Dictionary of South African Biography*, Volume III, Cape Town, published for the Human Sciences Research Council by Tafelberg Uitgewers Ltd., 1977, p. 63.
35. Acta der Berliner Missionsgesellschaft betreffend Personalia: Stech, Carl, Abt. II, Fach 3, No. 1, 1866–1911 (Bd. 1); *BMB*, 1874, p. 167.
36. Acta betreffend Personalia: Stech, Carl (Bd. 1); *BMB*, 1874, p. 149.
37. *Ibid.*
38. See pp. 26–27 and 56–57.
39. Acta betreffend Personalia: Stech, Carl (Bd. 1); *BMB*, 1876, p. 183.
40. In. No. 114, written on 26 August 1891 and received in Berlin 20 September 1891, in Acta der Berliner Missionsgesellschaft betreffend Personalia: Stech, Carl, Acta betreffend die Disziplinare-Untersuchung gegen dem Missionar Carl Stech, 1892, Abt. II, Fach 3, No. 1 (Bd. 2).
41. In. No. 158, pp. 3–3A, 29/12/1891 – 3 pages, in Acta betreffend die Disziplinare-Untersuchung gegen dem Missionar Carl Stech, 1892 (Bd. 2).
42. Beilage A zu Krauses Brief, 10. August 1892, In. No. 175, pp. 56–58 (5 pages – back pages are not numbered), in Acta betreffend die Disziplinare-Untersuchung gegen dem Missionar Carl Stech, 1892 (Bd. 2).
43. Acta betreffend Personalia: Stech, Carl (Bd. 1).
44. Acta der Berliner Missionsgesellschaft betreffend Personalia: Schwellnus, Erdmann; and H. Giesekke "The History of Erdmann Schwellnus in Venda", circular letter and sheet seeking more information from family members [15 typed A4 pages], p. 1.
45. *BMB*, 1875, p. 368.
46. The first correct spelling was in *BMB*, 1875, p. 415.
47. Acta betreffend Personalia: Schwellnus, Erdmann; *BMB*, 1875, pp. 231–232; and H. Giesekke, "The History of Erdmann Schwellnus in Venda", pp. 1–2.
48. Acta betreffend Personalia: Schwellnus, Erdmann; *BMB*, 1876, p. 391; and H. Giesekke, "The History of Erdmann Schwellnus in Venda", p. 2.
49. Acta betreffend Personalia: Schwellnus, Erdmann; H. Giesekke, "The History of Erdmann Schwellnus in Venda", pp. 12, 13, 14.
50. Acta betreffend Personalia: Schwellnus, Erdmann; H. Giesekke, "The History of Erdmann Schwellnus in Venda", pp. 14, 15.
51. "*Lebenslauf*" in Acta der Berliner Missionsgesellschaft betreffend Personalia: Baumhöfener, Dietrich, Abt. II, Fach 3, Nr. 9, 1875–1883.
52. [Anon.] *Dietrich Baumhöfner, ein Missionar aus dem Ravensburger Land*, Neue Missionsschriften Nr. 18, Berlin, Buchhandlung der Berliner evangelischen Missionsgesellschaft, 1890, p. 1.

53. *"Lebenslauf"* in Acta betreffend Personalia: Baumhöfener, Dietrich.
54. [Anon.] *Dietrich Baumhöfner*, pp. 7, 9.
55. Acta betreffend Personalia: Baumhöfener, Dietrich; [Anon.] *Dietrich Baumhöfner*, p. 13 (quotation).
56. Acta betreffend Personalia: Baumhöfener; *BMB*, 1883, p. 364; and Stationschronik von Georgenholtz, pp. 1, 2.
57. *BMB*, 1884, p. 222; G. Sauberzweig-Schmidt *Klaas Kuhn*, p. 30. See also *Der Bawenda-Freund*, 14(54), 1896, p. 294.
58. *BMB*, 1884, p. 222.
59. *Der Bawenda-Freund*, 14(54), 1896, p. 295.
60. *BMB*, 1884, p. 223. See also Acta betreffend Personalia: Baumhöfener, Dietrich; *Der Bawenda-Freund*, 14(54), 1896, pp. 294–295; G. Sauberzweig-Schmidt *Klaas Kuhn*, pp. 30–31; and Stationschronik von Georgenholtz, p. 1. For an overview of Baumhöfner's time at Georgenholtz, see *BMB*, 1883, pp. 364–374.
61. Acta der Berliner Missionsgesellschaft betreffend Personalia: Meister, Johann, Abt. II, Fach 3, No. 6, 1884–1892.
62. *Ibid.*
63. *Ibid.*; *BMB*, 1891, pp. 222, 240, 245, 451–452; 1892, p. 554.
64. *BMB*, 1881, pp. 455–456, 487.
65. See, for example, *BMB*, 1892, pp. 271–272, 552–554. See also p. 269.
66. See, for example, *BMB*, 1892, pp. 522–524.
67. *Ibid.* p. 554.
68. *Ibid.* pp. 93, 297, 554; 1893, p. 448.
69. *BMB*, 1893, pp. 75, 76, 86–88, 98–111, 448–449.
70. Acta betreffend Personalia: Meister, Johann; *BMB*, 1894, p. 202.
71. *BMB*, 1894, pp. 202, 380–381.
72. M.I. Bressani (Comp.), *Im Dienst der Mission*, p. 60.
73. Acta der Berliner Missionsgesellschaft betreffend Personalia: Gernecke, Carl, Abt. II, Fach 3, No. 28, 1856–1948.
74. Acta der Berliner Missionsgesellschaft betreffend Personalia: Gottschling, Ernst, Abt. II, Fach 3, No. 27, Band 1, 1877–1956.
75. Acta der Berliner Missionsgesellschaft betreffend Personalia: Klatt, Carl Otto, Abt. II, Fach 3K, No. 42, 1891–1943.
76. D.W. van der Merwe "Van Paternalisme tot Selfbeskikking", p. 4.
77. *BMB*, 1873, p. 225.
78. S.P.P. Mminele, "The Berlin Lutheran Missionary Enterprise", p. 19; D.W. van der Merwe, "Van Paternalisme tot Selfbeskikking", pp. 2, 5; and T. Wangemann, *Unterrichtsordnung des Berliner Missionsseminars*, Berlin, Verlag des Evangelischen Missionshauses, 1882, pp. 16, 25–36.
79. T. Wangemann, *Unterrichtsordnung*, pp. 16, 36–38.
80. *BMB*, 1873, p. 225; S.P.P. Mminele, "The Berlin Lutheran Missionary Enterprise", p. 19; D.J. Richter, *Geschichte der Berliner Missionsgesellschaft*, p. 356; D.W. van der Merwe, "Van Paternalisme tot Selfbeskikking", pp. 2, 5; and T. Wangemann, *Unterrichtsordnung*, pp. 38–45.
81. T. Wangemann, *Unterrichtsordnung*, pp. 31–32.
82. *Ibid.* p. 19.
83. *Ibid.* pp. 38–39.
84. D.W. van der Merwe, "Van Paternalisme tot Selfbeskikking", p. 6.
85. M. Wright, *German Missions in Tanganyika*, pp. 13, 16.

86. Gunther Pakendorf, "For there is no power but of God", p. 2. For a discussion of this in regard to British missions, see J.L. Comaroff and J. Comaroff, *Of Revalation and Revolution*, Volume One, pp. 54–85.
87. Originally titled "The Author, R. Wessmann", in R. Wessmann, *The Bawenda of the Spelonken (Transvaal): A contribution towards the psychology and folk-lore of African peoples*, translated from the original German text by L. Weinthal, London, 'The African World' Ltd., 1908, facing p. 7.
88. Acta der Berliner Missionsgesellschaft betreffend Personalia: Wessmann, Reinhold, Abt. II, Fach 3W, No. 16, 1880–1907; *BMB*, 1881, p. 165; M.I. Bressani (Comp.), *Im Dienst der Mission*, p. 57.
89. *BMB*, 1886, p. 216.
90. Acta betreffend Personalia: Wessmann, Reinhold; *BMB*, 1887, p. 48.
91. Acta betreffend Personalia: Wessmann, Reinhold; M.I. Bressani (Comp.) *Im Dienst der Mission*, p. 57; and Stationschronik von Georgenholtz, pp. 1, 2.
92. Protokoll [3–4. Februar 1905]; Letter from Missionsdirektor Martin D. Genischen to Sup.Krause, Berlin, 25. März 1905; Report of Kommission [Reuter, Jensen, Sonntag], Tschakoma, 27. Mai 1905; Letter from Wessmann, Tsakoma, 23. Mai 1905 to Gesellschaft zur Beförderung der evangelischen Missionen unter den Heiden zu Berlin; Letter from Missionsinspektor [Karl] Axenfeld to Herrn Pastor Dietrich, 22. August 1905; Letter from Missionsdirektor Martin D. Genischen to Herrn Sup. Matthes, Hochwürden, Kolberg, Berlin 30/6/1907, all in Acta der Berliner Missionsgesellschaft betreffend Personalia: Wessmann, Reinhold.
93. Protokoll [3–4. Februar 1905], pp. 11, 12 (3. Februar).
94. *Ibid.* pp. 15–16 (3. Februar).
95. *Ibid.* p. 17 (3. Februar).
96. *Ibid.* p. 22 (3. Februar).
97. *Ibid.* p. 23 (3. Februar).
98. *Ibid.* p. 12 (3. Februar).
99. *Ibid.* pp. 12, 18–19 (3. Februar). Dombu was recorded as "Domboe".
100. *Ibid.* p. 11 (3. Februar).
101. *Ibid.* pp. 17, 22 (3. Februar) respectively.
102. *Ibid.* p. 12, 13, 14, 15, 20, 21, 22, 23 (3. Februar).
103. H.A. Stayt, *The Bavenda*, pp. 219–220.
104. Protokoll [3–4. Februar 1905], p. 23 (3. Februar).
105. *Ibid.* pp. 12, 19 (3. Februar).
106. *Ibid.* pp. 14–15 (3. Februar).
107. *Ibid.* pp. 24–25 (4. Februar).
108. *Ibid.* p. 26 (4. Februar).
109. *Ibid.* p. 27 (4. Februar).
110. *Ibid.* pp. 28–29 (4. Februar).
111. Letter from Missionsdirektor Martin D. Genischen to Sup. Krause, Berlin, 25. März 1905, in Acta betreffend Personalia: Wessmann, Reinhold.
112. Commission Reuter, Jensen, Sonntag, pp. 8–9; Letter from Wessmann, Tsakoma [Tshakhuma] 23. Mai 1905 to Gesellschaft zur Beförderung der evangelischen Missionen unter den Heiden zu Berlin, in Acta betreffend Personalia: Wessmann, Reinhold.
113. Letter, Wessmann, Tsakoma [Tshakhuma] 23. Mai 1905.
114. Letter from Missionsinspektor [Karl] Axenfeld to Herrn Pastor Dietrich, 22. August 1905.
115. Letter from Missionsdirektor Martin D. Genischen to Herrn Sup. Matthes, Hochwürden, Kolberg, Berlin 30/6/1907.

116. C.J. Conerly, "The Surrendering of the Lands", p. 34; Stationschronik von Georgenholtz, p. 37 [161 of file].

117. For missionary fears of contagion by the "darkness" of Africa in other parts of the continent, see B.V. Street, *The Savage in Literature: Representations of 'primitive' society in English fiction, 1858–1920*, London, Routledge & Kegan Paul, 1975, p. 24.

118. P. Harries, "Through the Eyes of the Beholder: H.A. Junod and the Notion of Primitive", in *Social Dynamics*, 19(1), June 1993, p. 3. See also J. Conrad, *Heart of Darkness*, Harmondsworth, Penguin Books, 1995, p. 59.

119. P. Brantlinger, "Victorians and Africans: The Genealogy of the Myth of the Dark Continent", in *Critical Inquiry*, 12(1), Autumn 1985, p. 170; A. White, *Joseph Conrad and the Adventure Tradition: Constructing and deconstructing the imperial subject*, Cambridge, Cambridge University Press, 1993, p. 23.

120. P. Brantlinger, "Victorians and Africans", pp. 166–203; A. White, *Joseph Conrad*, p. 29.

121. P. Brantlinger, "Victorians and Africans", pp. 193 (quotation), 194, 196; A. White, *Joseph Conrad*, p. 24. In comparative perspective, Street has noted that: "The Englishman who 'went native' in Kipling's tales always pays the penalty" (B.V. Street, *The Savage in Literature*, p. 34). For discussion of perceptions of the roots of the Bounty mutineer Peter Heywood's "deviance" as lying in his having "gone native" in Tahiti, see G. Denning, *Mr Bligh's Bad Language: Passion, Power and Theatre on the Bounty*, Cambridge and New York, Canto (Cambridge University Press), 1994, pp. 257–262.

122. P. Brantlinger, *Rule of Darkness: British Literature and Imperialism, 1830–1914*, Ithaca Cornell University Press, 1988, p. 262; R. Hampson, "Introduction", in J. Conrad, *Heart of Darkness*, p. xxxiv.

123. J. Conrad, *Heart of Darkness*, pp. 37, 43, 47, 51.

124. *Ibid.* p. 95. See also R. Ambrosini, *Conrad's Fiction as Critical Discourse*, Cambridge, Cambridge University Press, 1991, pp. 107–108; I. Watt (a) *Conrad in the Nineteenth Century*, London, Chatto and Windus, 1980, pp. 144–145 & (b) *Essays on Conrad*, Cambridge, Cambridge University Press, 2000, pp. 90–91; and A. White, *Joseph Conrad*, pp. 171, 174.

125. J. Conrad, *Heart of Darkness*, p. 106.

126. Letter: Missionar F. Prietsch an Missionsinspektor X in Berlin, 24. April 1883, also reproduced in "Aus dem Leben des Missionars Niklas Koen", both in Acta der Berliner Missionsgesellschaft betreffend Personalia, Koen, Klaas, Abt. II, Fach 3K, No. 7, 1876–1883; G. Sauberzweig-Schmidt, *Klaas Kuhn*, p. 8. For a short biography of Koen, see also D.W. van der Merwe, "Niklaas Theunissen Koen, 1852–1883, Lewensskets van 'n pioniersendeling onder die Bawenda", in *Kleio*, IX (1&2), Junie 1977, pp. 22–30.

127. Letter: Missionar F. Prietsch an Missionsinspektor X in Berlin, 24. April 1883; "Aus dem Leben des Missionars Niklas Koen".

128. H. Heese, "Diakonie en Digitalisering: Sendingrekords en geskiedenis in die 21ste eeu", in *Historia: Journal of the South African Historical Association*, 43(2), November 1988, p. 32 n 11.

129. See, for example, Letter: Missionar F. Prietsch an Missionsinspektor X in Berlin, 24. April 1883, "Aus dem Leben des Missionars Niklas Koen"; G. Sauberzweig-Schmidt, *Klaas Kuhn*, p. 5.

130. *BMB*, 1882, p. 358.

131. G. Sauberzweig-Schmidt, *Klaas Kuhn*, pp. 7–8.

132. *Ibid.*

133. *Ibid.* p. 30.

134. Letter: Missionar F. Prietsch an Missionsinspektor X in Berlin, 24. April 1883; "Aus dem leben des Missionars Niklas Koen" (quotation); G. Sauberzweig-Schmidt, *Klaas Kuhn*, p. 8.

135. *Ibid.*

136. *Ibid.*

137. G. Sauberzweig-Schmidt, *Klaas Kuhn*, p. 9. Piet Koen would later die of consumption, at approximately fifty years of age. A sketch by Mission Director Wangemann of five people at Haarlem in 1866 includes Koen and one of his sisters. An extremely grainy reproduction of this appears in H. Heese, "Diakonie en digitalisering", p. 32.

138. *Ibid.* (quotations mixed among sources).

139. "Aus dem leben des Missionars Niklas Koen"; Letter: Missionar F. Prietsch an Missionsinspektor X in Berlin, 24.4.1883; G. Sauberzweig-Schmidt, *Klaas Kuhn*, p. 9.

140. G. Sauberzweig-Schmidt, *Klaas Kuhn*, pp. 9–10 (quotations, p. 10).

141. *Ibid.* p. 10.

142. P. Heimbach, *Neu-Georgenholtz*, p. 18.

143. G. Sauberzweig-Schmidt, *Klaas Kuhn*, p. 6.

144. *Ibid.* p. 7.

145. Ergänzungen aus den Stationsakten in Acta betreffend Personalia: Koen, Klaas.

146. J. Feustel, *Spaziergänge in Friederichshain*, Berlinsche Reminiszenzen No. 64, Berlin, Haude + Spener, 1994. See also especially Märkishes Museum, Berlin (a) Map Collection: "Plan von Berlin", Blatt IA, 1894–1903, N63/3437R & (b) Photographic Collection: "Georgenkirche" [Max Missmann], 1904, no number; "Georgenkircheplatz 8–9", no date, N65/556V; "Landsberger Tor & Strasse" [Max Missmann], 1906, N67/138V & (c) Post-Card Collection: No title, N61/3885V.

147. G. Sauberzweig-Schmidt, *Klaas Kuhn*, p. 11.

148. *Der Bawenda-Freund*, 14(54), 1896, p. 292; *BMB*, 1877, p. 216; and G. Sauberzweig-Schmidt, *Klaas Kuhn*, p. 12.

149. Letter: Missionar Koen an Direktor Wangemann aus Tshakoma [Tshakhuma], 10. Mai 1876, also reproduced in "Aus dem Leben des Missionars Niklas Koen", both in Acta betreffend Personalia: Koen, Klaas.

150. Letter: Missionar Koen an Direktor Wangemann aus Tshakoma [Tshakhuma], 1. November 1876, also reproduced in "Aus dem Leben des Missionars Niklas Koen" in Acta betreffend Personalia: Koen, Klaas.

151. *Der Bawenda-Freund*, 14(54), 1896, pp. 292–293; *BMB*, 1878, pp. 256, 490–492; Ergänzungen aus den Stationsakten: Koen, Klaas; Stationschronik von Georgenholtz, p. 1; *Mitteilungen des Vereins "Heidenfreund"*, V(19), 1887, n.p. (p. 2–3); G. Sauberzweig-Schmidt, *Klaas Kuhn*, p. 14; and Tagebuch der Station bei Ha Makoarela (Nicolaus Koen), 13. Juli 1877, 26. Juli 1877, in Berlin Mission Archives, Berlin, Acta der Berliner Missionsgesellschaft betreffend Missionsstationen: Tagebücher der Missionare auf Makoarela (Georgenholtz), Abt. III, Fach 5, No. 16, (I).

152. G. Sauberzweig-Schmidt, *Klaas Kuhn*, p. 15.

153. *Der Bawenda-Freund*, 14(54), 1896, p. 293; G. Sauberzweig-Schmidt, *Klaas Kuhn*, pp. 15–16.

154. G. Sauberzweig-Schmidt, *Klaas Kuhn*, p. 16.

155. *Der Bawenda-Freund*, 14(54), 1896, pp. 293–294.

156. Letter: Missionar Koen an Direktor Wangemann aus Tshakoma [Tshakhuma], 28.3.1877, also reproduced in "Aus dem Leben des Missionars Niklas Koen", both in Acta betreffend Personalia, Koen, Klaas.

157. *Der Bawenda-Freund*, 14(54), 1896, p. 294; *BMB*, 1878, pp. 496–497; G. Sauberzweig-Schmidt, *Klaas Kuhn*, pp. 17–18; Tagebuch der Station bei Ha Makoarela (Nicolaus Koen), 11. März 1878, pp. 9–10, 17. März 1888, pp. 10–11.

158. *BMB*, 1879, pp. 410–411; G. Sauberzweig-Schmidt, *Klaas Kuhn*, p. 18.

159. *BMB*, 1883, pp. 358–359.

160. G. Sauberzweig-Schmidt, *Klaas Kuhn*, p. 18 (quotation); Stationschronik von Georgenholtz, p. 1.

161. *BMB*, 1879, p. 413; Ergänzungen aus den Stationsakten: Koen, Klaas; G. Sauberzweig-Schmidt, *Klaas Kuhn*, pp. 18–19.

162. Ergänzungen aus den Stationsakten: Koen, Klaas; G. Sauberzweig-Schmidt, *Klaas Kuhn*, p. 19 (quotation).
163. G. Sauberzweig-Schmidt, *Klaas Kuhn*, p. 19.
164. *Ibid*. p. 20. See also *BMB*, 1880, pp. 413–414.
165. G. Sauberzweig-Schmidt, *Klaas Kuhn*, p. 21.
166. *Ibid*. See also *BMB*, 1880, p. 414.
167. G. Sauberzweig-Schmidt, *Klaas Kuhn*, p. 21. See also: Stationschronik von Georgenholtz, p. 1; *Mitteilungen des Vereins "Heidenfreund"*, V(19), 1887, n.p. (p. 3); *Der Bawenda-Freund*, 14(54), 1896, p. 294; and *BMB*, 1880, p. 211.
168. See pp. 255–257.
169. *Der Bawenda-Freund*, 14(54), 1896, p. 294; G. Sauberzweig-Schmidt, *Klaas Kuhn*, p. 23.
170. G. Sauberzweig-Schmidt, *Klaas Kuhn*, p. 24 (quotation); Stationschronik von Georgenholtz, p. 1. See also *BMB*, 1880, p. 417; 1881, p. 360.
171. G. Sauberzweig-Schmidt, *Klaas Kuhn*, p. 24.
172. Letter: aus Georgenholtz von Missionar Koen an Missions-Direktor Wangemann in Berlin, 26. Mai 1881, also reproduced in "Aus dem Leben des Missionars Niklas Koen" and Ergänzungen aus den Stationsakten, all in Acta betreffend Personalia, Koen, Klaas.
173. Stationschronik von Georgenholtz, p. 1.
174. G. Sauberzweig-Schmidt, *Klaas Kuhn*, p. 24.
175. *Der Bawenda-Freund*, 14(54), 1896, p. 294.
176. *Ibid*.
177. Letter: aus Georgenholtz von Missionar Koen an Missions-Direktor Wangemann in Berlin, 30. Dezember 1881, also reproduced in "Aus dem Leben des Missionars Niklas Koen", both in Acta betreffend Personalia, Koen, Klaas.
178. G. Sauberzweig-Schmidt, *Klaas Kuhn*, p. 25.
179. *Ibid*. p. 26.
180. *Ibid*. pp. 26–27.
181. Letter: aus Georgenholtz von Missionar Koen an Komitee in Berlin, 23. Juni 1882, also reproduced in Ergänzungen aus den Stationsakten, both in Acta betreffend Personalia, Koen, Klaas.
182. *Der Bawenda-Freund*, VI(20), 1888, p. 54; *BMB*, 1883, p. 364; *Mitteilungen des Vereins "Heidenfreund"*, V(19), 1887, n.p. (p. 4); Stationschronik von Georgenholtz, p. 1.
183. G. Sauberzweig-Schmidt, *Klaas Kuhn*, p. 27.
184. *BMB*, 1883, pp. 359–360.
185. G. Sauberzweig-Schmidt, *Klaas Kuhn*, p. 27. See also *BMB*, 1883, p. 360.
186. G. Sauberzweig-Schmidt, *Klaas Kuhn*, pp. 27–28. See also *BMB*, 1883, p. 360.
187. G. Sauberzweig-Schmidt, p. 28. See also Letter: Brief vom 12. Februar 1883 aus Georgenholtz von Frau Koen, also reproduced in "Aus dem Leben des Missionars Niklas Koen", both in Acta betreffend Personalia, Koen, Klaas; *BMB*, 1883, pp. 360, 362.
188. *BMB*, 1883, p. 362; G. Sauberzweig-Schmidt, *Klaas Kuhn*, p. 28 (quotation).
189. *BMB*, 1883, p. 362.
190. *Ibid*.
191. Letter: Brief vom 12. Februar 1883 aus Georgenholtz von Frau Koen. For Beuster's account of the events which follow and Koen's official obituary, see *BMB*, 1883, pp. 139–140. Koen's life and death are also discussed on pp. 358–364 of the same source.
192. G. Sauberzweig-Schmidt, *Klaas Kuhn*, pp. 28–29.
193. Letter: Brief vom 12. Februar 1883 aus Georgenholtz von Frau Koen. See also *BMB*, 1883, p. 362; G. Sauberzweig-Schmidt, *Klaas Kuhn*, p. 29.
194. G. Sauberzweig-Schmidt, *Klaas Kuhn*, p. 29.
195. Letter: Brief vom 12. Februar 1883 aus Georgenholtz von Frau Koen.

196. G. Sauberzweig-Schmidt, *Klaas Kuhn*, p. 29. See also also *BMB*, 1883, pp. 362–363.
197. *BMB*, 1883, p. 364; G. Sauberzweig-Schmidt, *Klaas Kuhn*, pp. 29–30.
198. Ergänzungen aus den Stationsakten: Koen, Klaas; *BMB*, 1883, p. 364; G. Sauberzweig-Schmidt, *Klaas Kuhn*, p. 30. With her husband's death, Koen's widow first moved to Ha-Tshivhase with her two children. Here she taught the mission children. Later, on 9 December 1884, she would marry Missionary Jensen, who was training the evangelists at the Mp'hôme seminary (*BMB*, 1883, p. 364; 1885, p. 75; G. Sauberzweig-Schmidt, *Klaas Kuhn*, p. 30).
199. G. Sauberzweig-Schmidt, *Klaas Kuhn*, p. 30.

CHAPTER 4
The landscape[1]

A number of authors have pointed out that landscapes are exceptionally complex and powerful creations. On the one hand, they are an aesthetic product that is culturally created and defined. On the other, they are created, and re-created, by people through their experience of, and interaction with, the world around them.

Against this background, it is clear that landscape has to be contextualised. The way that people see and engage with their world depends upon the specific time, place and historical conditions in which they are operating. Similarly, their age, gender, class, caste, social and economic situation will also play a significant role. These forces may operate at a conscious, a partly-conscious or an unconscious level. Depending on changing situations, they may also be reformulated over time and place. Thus, far from being inert, landscapes are reworked, appropriated and contested.[2]

THE LANDSCAPE OF VENDALAND

The relationship between the Berlin missionaries, the landscape of Vendaland and the Vhavenda was an extremely complex one. Even with individuals, it varied both over time and with influences such as mood, the particular circumstance prevailing at any given time, and similar intangibles that are extremely difficult, sometimes impossible, to recapture over a hundred years later. However, it is possible to identify and deconstruct certain tendencies.

In extremely broad outline, what remained constant in missionary thinking and writing in Vendaland during the late nineteenth century was a sense of the land and its people as being inextricably bound. Whether the particular interpretation placed on this relationship was predominantly positive, negative, or – as was frequently the case – contained mixed elements of both of these absolutes, the "heathen Bawenda [Vhavenda]", as the missionaries called them, were portrayed as blending into, or being created by, the landscape that nurtured, succoured and concealed them.

At one end of the scale, the missionaries celebrated the natural beauty of Vendaland and praised its fecundity and its ability to support and feed its inhabitants. In attempting to create meaning, and a sense of belonging, by relating the strange to the familiar, both for their authors and for their intended audiences, these accounts tended to draw favourable comparisons with scenic spots and resorts in Germany and other parts of Europe. They also compared conditions in Vendaland with those at other pre-existing Berlin Mission stations and areas of operation in South Africa. These accounts tend to focus on light, open vistas, running water, the breaking of the forest by rolling fields and meadows and the successful mastery of the challenges posed by the environment to the missionaries. While the forests are present here, and while their darkness and hidden dangers are mentioned, the emphasis is on the biodiversity of shrubs, creepers and flowers within them; on their beauty rather than their menacing nature. In general, the earliest missionary descriptions of the area fell into this category.

At the other end of the scale, well-versed as they were in Biblical semiotics, and viewing the landscape through German eyes, the missionaries saw the physical environment of Vendaland with its mountain ranges, rivers and forests as threatening and as conspiring with the local inhabitants to hinder their work in the region. These accounts tend to focus on "darkness", concealment, impenetrability, dangers, fears, swamps or marshes and other manifestations of wild landscape, wild animals and "wild" people. "Fever" (malaria) recurs as a deadly enemy and the challenges of the environment are seen as stumbling blocks to be overcome gradually, rather than mere irritations to be swept aside.

As the missionaries began to establish themselves in Vendaland, the challenges posed by the environment (and its inhabitants) began to assume greater importance in their perceptions. As it dawned on them that their whole task would be much more difficult than they had envisaged, the environment became more of a foe to be overcome than a pleasing backdrop against which the missionaries operated. This does not mean that they became completely blind to its beauties. In missionary thinking, the "pleasant", friendly and peaceful exterior (or persona) of the inhabitants of Vendaland often masked a far "darker" hidden "heart". Similarly, for them, the external beauty of the landscape coexisted with, and tended to mask, a far more sinister core. Moreover, due to the prevalence of malaria, this dark core could, and often did, prove to be fatal. This could provide the key to understanding the shift in the way that the missionaries constructed, and related to, the landscape of Vendaland. I illustrate this first by looking at early textual accounts and how they reveal the changing relationship between the missionaries and the environment. This leads into a discussion of the core elements of their experience of the landscape.

Thus, the earliest descriptions of this landscape by Berlin Missionaries, prior to their having established themselves in the area, focussed on describing the area both for themselves and for their readers. This was done in a way that enabled them to situate themselves on the land and plan for the future. Starting from known landmarks, they went on to describe the unknown. The beauty concealed difficulties, hardships and dangers. However, due to the excitement of entering and exploring what for them was new terrain, and

THE LANDSCAPE

given their hopes for a bright future, no obstacle seemed too great to be overcome and the great beauty of the landscape lay exposed to the eye of the beholder (and the reader).

Missionary Grützner described the May 1871 visit of himself, Beyer and Beuster to Makhado's village, high in the mountains. In doing so, he began by comparing what for the missionaries, their colleagues and readers was the unknown landscape and resources of Vendaland to the known situation in the vicinity of Blouberg Mission Station. Beyer was very familiar with this area as he was stationed there. It was also well known to the other missionaries and the wider circle of friends of the mission from the frequent reports emanating from the station, which had been established in 1868:

> Like in the Blouberg, as soon as one has climbed to a certain height up the mountain, a different vegetation greets the wanderer and here and there fresh mountain streams bubble forth. Here it is much more the case. It is clearly visible that the further east one goes along the Blouberg-Soutpansberg mountainchain, the more springs and water there are ... and the richer the rain which descends from heaven. Here at Makchato [Makhado], for example, there is so much rain that the people cannot plant any sorghum [*Kafferkorn*]. They just plant maize which, although the gardens are mostly on steep mountain slopes, grows very well. A further four to five hours on horseback, east of the so-called Spelonken, at Sewasse [Tshivhase's area], there is so much water that, during the rainy season, great surfaces of water, similar to lakes, restrict communication almost totally.[3]

From here, the party continued to Makhado's capital:

> It was just after midday when we arrived at Makchato's [Makhado's]. In front of the actual kraal [village], there are quite a number of big rocks, which are connected to one another by a six to nine-feet wall, so forming a reasonable fortress for these conditions. From the other side, the already-mentioned high rock-face protects the village. These make it difficult to capture the village. In the background, behind the houses, the beautiful dense forest of mostly yellow-wood trees rests easy on the eyes.[4]

This visit established the route into Makhado's kingdom as familiar territory. It was thus not described in any great detail in Beyer's description of his and Baumbach's visit to Makhado and Tshivhase in March 1872. Instead, it was merely reported that "the mountains [there] prevented them from riding on and the journey had to be continued on foot". However, on their departure from Makhado's capital, with Samuel as their guide, the group were again entering areas unexplored by Berlin Missionaries. Arising from this, the landscape and its people were described in much greater detail. In reporting on this, Beyer clearly attempted to present his companions' experiences in a manner which, while "factual", also captured some of the beauty of the countryside. He also clearly set out to illustrate the ways in which (in his view and that of his colleagues) the landscape and its inhabitants flowed seamlessly into each other:

> All of us, except our guide, were going into an unknown land with strange people who had strange customs. But our hearts were lifted as the beauty of the mountainous nature unfolded before our eyes; the ravines densely forested at places, and the evergreen cover of lush grasses, mixed with thousands of different kinds of beautiful flowers. The low-lying sun cast a magnificent light on the round, pointed, jagged mountains and the millions of dew drops sparkled in the rays like diamonds ...
>
> Soaked in sweat, we reached the road which went past the steep road which led up to the chief's village ... [Here], we rested and marvelled at the beautiful view into the distance. In the south-west lay the flat-topped mountain of Makchabeng [Makgabêng]; in the south the pointed mountains of Moletsche [Moletshe] stuck out of the plain – this is where Missionary Hofmeyr had previously lived; behind that, slightly to the left of the granite-black mountains of Matlale [Matlala] arose and even further back were the mountains of Makapanspoort. In the south-west [sic.] were the mountains of Maune, Metle [Mutle] and Sekukuni [Sekhukhune] ... In the villages everywhere, people were busy grinding [stamping] maize and cooking; the shepherds blew their horns, which the animals in the kraals seemed to understand well, as the cattle, sheep and goats all lowed and bleated together. Yes, if it were not for the bee-hive-shaped houses and the almost naked Black people before us, one could have thought one was in a mountain village in the Sudeten Mountains or Harz Mountains.[5]

The account erroneously placed the mountains of Mutle and Sekhukhune in the south-west. Viewing from Hanglip (the *khosi*'s village), they actually lie in the south-east. The mountains are named from the centre eastwards – Mutle's area was east of Chuniespoort River but west of the Olifants River; Sekhukhune's area was south and east of the Olifants River. In addition, locally, maize was (and is still) usually stamped in a stamping block, rather than ground. The description of the houses as "bee-hive-shaped" was also fanciful, perhaps being designed to resonate with what German readers already knew about Zulu architectural patterns. Archaeological remains in the area, and illustrations and descriptions which will follow, demonstrate that houses were round with cone-shaped roofs.

Journeying into areas where no Berlin Missionary had been before, the landscape and its inhabitants blended together harmoniously in the vision of their observers. As with the comparisons with the Sudeten and Hartz Mountains in Germany, in an effort to ground himself in the landscape, and interpret it for the intended readers of his report, Beyer looked for similarities in birdsong between African and German birds. His description of meadows and cultivated lands is also extremely evocative of the German countryside:

> Our path led us into a beautiful dark forest which stretched along the steep rock cliffs; a charming setting, intoxicating to both the eye and the heart. The silence and coolness of the forest, the smell of the forest flowers; the mighty, tall, thin and stunted trees whose roots make the pathway uneven, the sun-rays piercing the forest darkness, the magnificent songs of the red, blue, green and yellow birds, of which some sang like the German quail; yes, even the shrieks of the monkeys [baboons?][a] on the cliffs – all of these move the heart to praise God.
>
> Then we reached the top of the mountain with a view over gorges stretching out to the left and the right and beautiful meadows and cultivated fields; as far as the eye could see, village upon village, field upon field stretched out along the edges of the gorges.[6]

According to the local people, every mountain or range which could be seen from the Zoutpansberg was inhabited. As the party continued in the direction of Tshivhase's country, "The path became more mountainous and uneven." The local people whom they met seem to have thought that they were traders "as only traders occasionally come into these mountains". Crossing "a beautiful big river", the border between Makhado and Tshivhase's kingdoms at present-day Ha-Vhulaudzi, that night they "camped under Marula trees where thousands of fruit lay on the ground". In Beyer's description:

> The closer we came to our destination, the more lush the vegetation became; we saw bananas with leaves measuring over 12 feet; giant palm-like ferns, over 15 feet high.[b] At places we had to force our way through grass and bush which grew as high as

---

a. Monkeys are usually found in trees. Baboons are generally on the rocks. Beyer seems to have gotten the two confused here.
b. Cf. Illustration 3.

a rider, but which was also the favourite haunt of wild pigs and tigers [leopards], as the many spoors indicated. Or else we marched through beautiful mealie fields in which the mealies grew well, because of the moisture in the ground. Besides maize, the natives also plant sweet-potatoes, pumpkins, beans and peanuts. The usual sorghum is seldom planted here – mainly just to brew beer.[7]

Having worked in the lands of the Basotho, the missionaries were used to seeing extensive cultivation of sorghum, since it was planted in the drier regions. This is why Beyer, stationed in an area where sorghum was extensively grown, expressed surprise at seeing only a little sorghum in the mountainous and wetter Vendaland.

From there, their path took them onto the plateau again – like Makhado, Tshivhase lived "high up, under a mountain cliff". In Beyer's interpretation:

Here the large plains and hills were more in character to the highveld in the vicinity of the Drakensberg – bare, but covered with a green carpet; only in the river valleys and the mountain crevices and ravines and along the bottom of the cliffs the thick impenetrable forest grows abundantly. Many mountain buffalo live in these forests. These buffalo are smaller than those living in the plains.[8]

From the plain "the actual view into the vast Batschuëtlaland" (Vendaland) lay exposed.[c] This provided Samuel with an opportunity to further educate the missionaries about the landscape, inhabitants and etiquette of Vendaland. In interpreting the landscape and its inhabitants for his superiors and a wider German audience, Beyer was serving the same function as an ecological and cultural interpreter as Samuel had done for him and his companions. Overlooking large sections of the countryside, Samuel "named eleven big independent chiefs", including Makhado and Tshivhase, and explained the borders of their territories to the missionaries. Beyer reacted by bemoaning what he saw as the sorry situation of these rulers who all had "to live without the Word of Life" and posing the question:

When will the hour of salvation of these people strike? Oh, Africa is big and richly populated, more than anyone would believe, and all these people are still caught up in the bonds of darkness. Here, ... one is more shocked than when one glances at the many longitudinal and latitudinal degrees of heathendom on a map, because here one can see the misery; oh, and the heathendom here is stronger than in all other countries, because

---

c. This is the name given to the Vhavenda by the Basotho.

> these heathen gods are not wooden, or made of stone, or any other dead creatures – they are their kings.[9]

From their vantage point, Samuel also pointed out the mountain that was their end destination. They reached this within one-and-a-half hours. However, since Tshivhase's capital village was concealed "in the middle of a thicket", they "could not see the village of this great king before" they got to it. They could nevertheless clearly hear "the sounds and shouts" emanating from it.

Samuel must again have acted as a cultural interpreter since, following correct etiquette, the missionaries remained outside the village while sending a messenger to announce their arrival. He soon returned, inviting them to appear before Tshivhase. In describing their first impressions of the village of this powerful *khosi*, Beyer drew heavily on comparisons with his homeland:

> So we climbed down into a dark forest of tall yellow-wood trees. At first the path was stony and uneven but then the road became a beautiful avenue which reminded us of the sacred Halls of Tharant in Saxony, because above us the branches grew together, forming a ceiling. After twenty minutes we reached the village of the feared chief Sebase [Tshivhase].
>
> The view of the village came as a surprise; imagine a village at the top of a mountain, below cliffs, in the middle of a forest of trees which are as tall as the majestic German Beeches and Oaks, overgrown and entwined by masses of climbers and creepers, so forming big natural arbours, more beautiful than those found in the botanical gardens in Germany. Steep cliffs form the backdrop of the village; the foreground (facing south) presents a view over vast domains. Yes, I admit, this place is the most romantic which I have yet seen in Africa. The village itself was surrounded closely with banana plants.[10]

In order to locate and ground himself and his intended readers, Beyer also drew comparisons with the architecture of his station at Blauberg:

> While everybody was staring at us, we stepped into the village. The only difference between these houses and those of the people at Blauberg is their size. The doors are also higher, so that one need only stoop when entering them, compared to Blauberg, where one has to crawl into them.[11]

Tshivhase was obviously a man of great astuteness and ability. Not only was he multilingual, speaking Tshivenda, Northern Sotho and Tswana fluently, he was also an accomplished gunsmith. While they admitted this, the mission also portrayed him very much as we would expect the savage-cum-slightly clown-like king of the jungle people of African adventure literature. Thus, on the one hand, the views of the editors of the *Missions-Berichte* (and hence the official position of the mission) were that:

> Sebase is a clever and judicious, friendly and energetic man. He also does not like to spend his time being idle, as most other chiefs do. He would rather be industrious and active, and the veranda of his house, his favourite place, is at the same time his work-room. This is where his vice, hammer and files are found and where he repairs his guns. He speaks the language of Blauberg and Makchabêng [Makgabêng] [SeSotho] as he does his own rather different language [Tshivenda]. The Brothers therefore did not need a translator which, understandably, they preferred.[12]

However, on the other hand, in missionary consciousness, the *khosi* was also a creature of his environment – a lion. Although he also acknowledged Tshivhase's skills, in a view with which the mission authorities concurred, he pointed out that:

> When we entered the courtyard, it was filled with people who were almost all lying on their knees in the direction of a house with a railed veranda. Behind the railings of the house, a miss-shaped thick figure was moving. That was Sebase [Tshivhase], who was constantly saluted: "Big Lion, Almighty Ruler, Lord of the Heavens and the earth." As a matter of fact, the enormous gentleman in his cage looked like a lion in a zoo ...
>
> This 38 year-old man might have been big and clumsy, but he had an intelligent look, not sinister but friendly, and especially talkative with his people. In his eyes one saw cleverness and liveliness, and that this enormous lion can also occasionally show his teeth is shown by the way his people cower before him in dog-like submission. Almost every word, even every movement of the king is accompanied by shouts of commendation and praise, so much so that any listener is soon irritated by the whole affair.
>
> The women and girls may not pass before him without his permission; already from afar, they throw themselves to the ground before him, and when he has granted his permission, they do not go about their work walking, but crawling. As a support and a backrest, he has the services of a grown-up girl, who kneels behind him, while he sits.[13]

The next meeting with Tshivhase was that in October 1872 associated with the founding of Ha-Tshivhase Mission Station.[14] The hope for the future which this engendered is clearly discernible in the report presented in the *Missions-Berichte* and in Grützner's eyewitness description of the landscape.

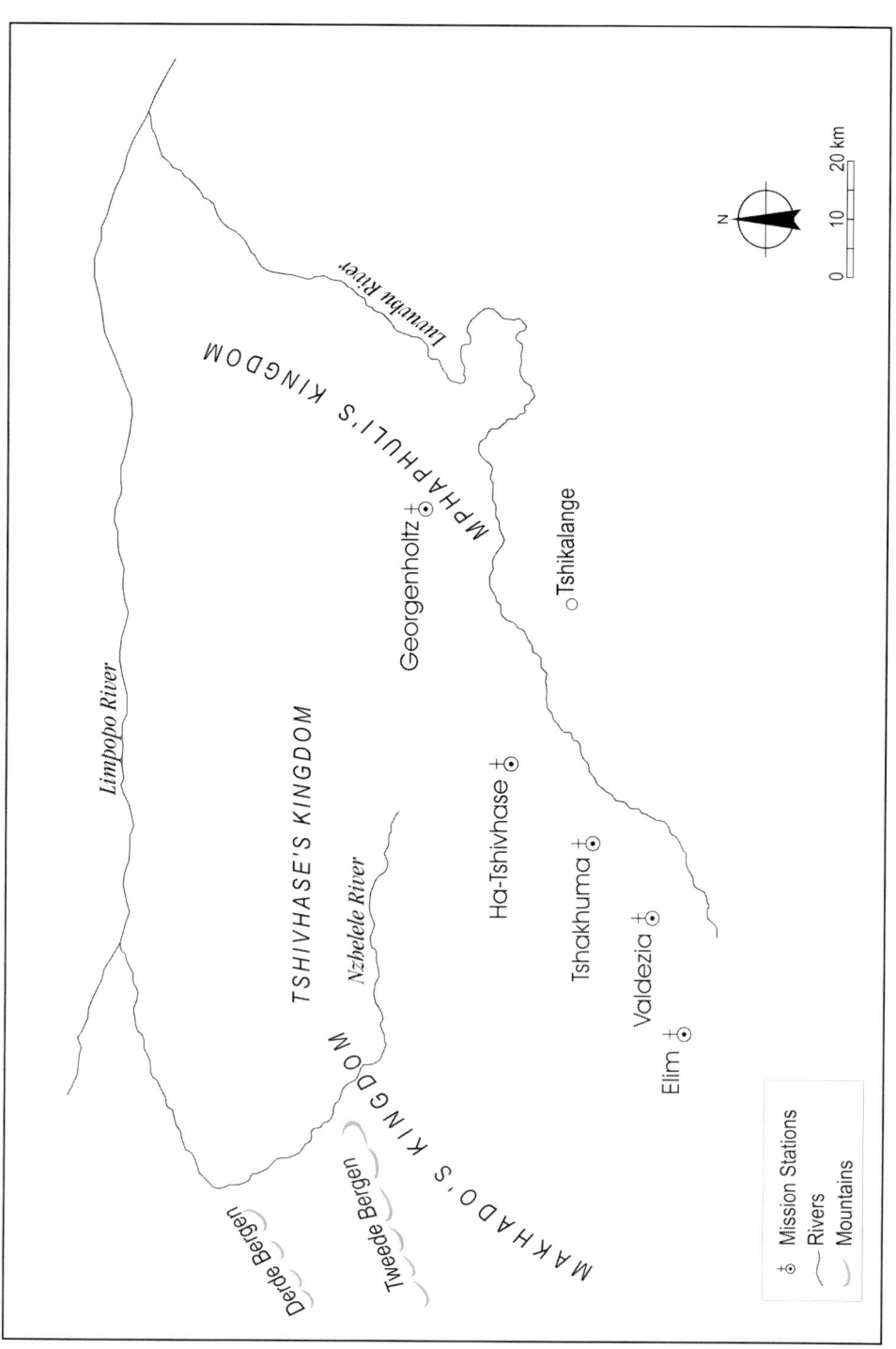

MAP 1: Rulers and Mission Stations in Nineteenth-Century Vendaland

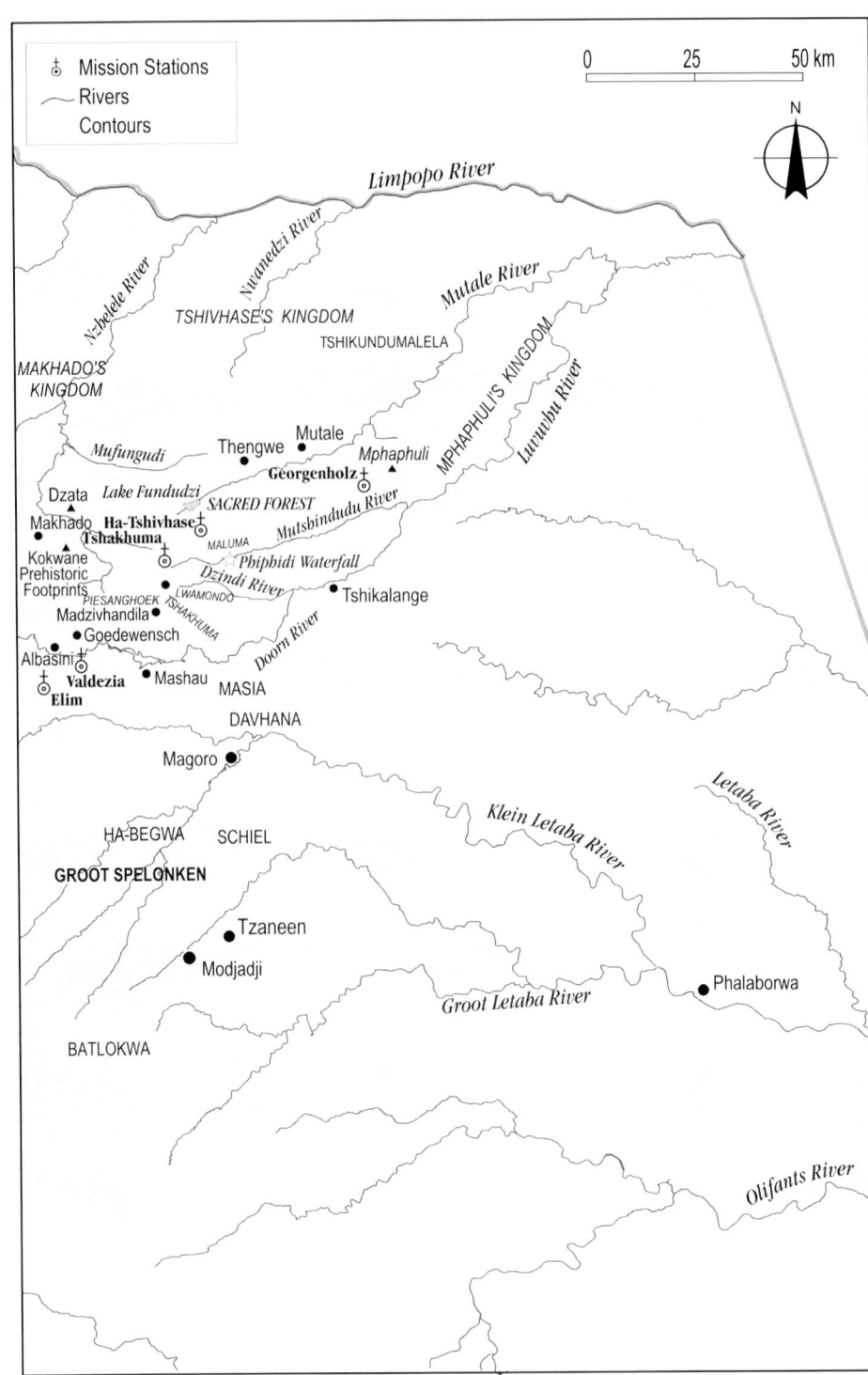

MAP 2: Nineteenth-Century Vendaland and Surrounds

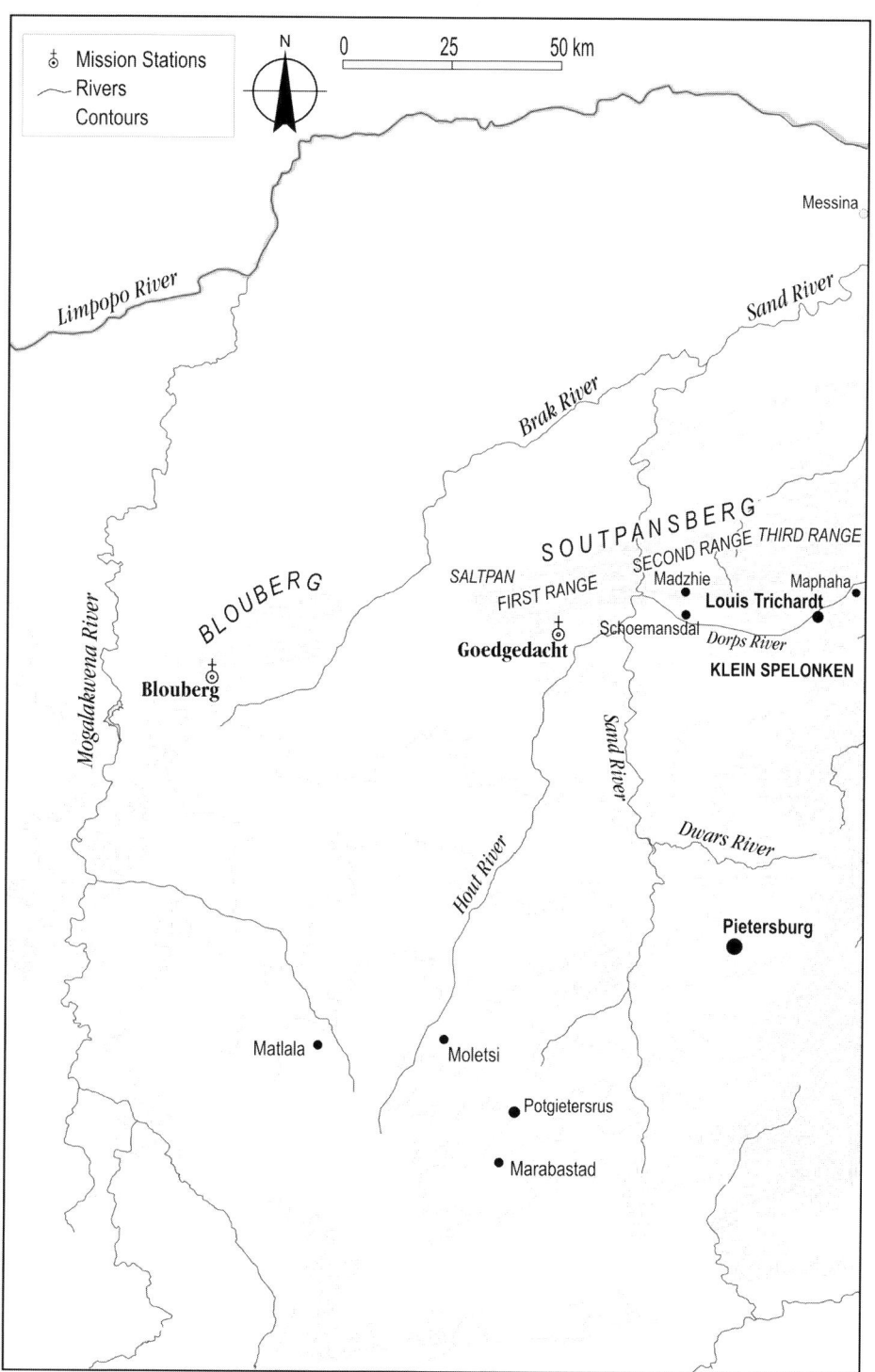

MAP 3: The Zoutpansberg District

1. Reinhold Wessmann
   Originally titled "The Author, R. Wessmann", in R. Wessmann, *The Bawenda of the Spelonken (Transvaal): A contribution towards the psychology and folk-lore of African peoples*, translated from the original German text by L. Weinthal, London, "The African World" Ltd., 1908, facing p. 7.

2. Klaas Koen
   Appears as "Klaas Kuhn" in original, P. Heimbach, *Neu-Georgenholtz im Wenda-Lande*, Neue Missionsschriften [Neue Folge] Nr. 25, Berlin, Berliner Missiongesellschaft, n.d. [1909], p. 18.

3. "Missionary Schwellnus"
   Berliner Missions-Berichte, 1893, p. 433. See also W. Gründler, *Geschichte der Bawenda-Mission in Nord-Transvaal*, frontispiece.

4. "Crossing a river in Bowenda"
   Berlin Mission Archives, Berlin: Album Nr. XXIX, Nord-Transvaal, Nr. 15197.

5. Masthead of *Bawenda-Freund*
   Bawenda-Freund, Nr. 3, 1916.

6. "The Missionary in the Palm-forest"
   Berliner Missions-Berichte, 1880, p. 409.

7. "Ha Tschewasse" [Ha-Tshivhase/Beuster/Maungani]
   Berliner Missions-Berichte, 1886, p. 401.

8. "Tchakoma" [Tshakhuma]
   Berliner Missions-Berichte, 1887, p. 201.

9. "Georgenholtz"
   Berliner Missions-Berichte, 1894, p. 365.

10. "Bawenda [Vhavenda] Children"
    W. Gründler, *Geschichte der Bawenda-Mission in Nord-Transvaal*, p. 83.

11. "A Northern Transvaal Native Belle"
    R. Wessmann, *The Bawenda of the Spelonken*, facing p. 11.

12. Warrior (untitled and undated in original)
    Berlin Mission Archives, Berlin: Album, Vendaland von Missionar G. Westphal, Nr. 8632. Westphal was stationed in Vendaland from 1912. This photograph seems to have been taken at Georgenholtz, where he was stationed from September 1919. [Acta der Berliner Missions-Gesellschaft betreffend Personalia: Westphal, Gotthardt, Abt.II, Fach II 20, Nr. 5A, Angefangen 1902, Beendigt 1929.] The only photographs dated in the Westphal album are dated to 1922, 1924, 1927 and 1928.

13. "THEN: A Native Dance in Vendaland some years ago"
    R. Wessmann, *The Bawenda of the Spelonken*, facing p. 33.

14. "Tshikona Dance in Ngovela at Ha Tschewasse [Ha-Tshivhase]"
    Berlin Mission Archives, Berlin: Album Nr. XXIX, Nord-Transvaal, Nr. 15188 and M. Wilde, *Schwarz und Weiss: Bilder von einer Reise durch das Arbeitsgebiet der Berliner Mission in Südafrika von M. Wilde, Missionsinspektor*, Berlin, Buchhandlung der Berliner evangelischen Missionsgesellschaft, 1913, p. 113.

15. "Dancing Heathens"
    T. Wangemann, *Geschichte der Berliner Missionsgesellschaft in Südafrika*. Also in the private collection of Dr Ulrich van der Heyden, Seminar für Afrikawissenschaften, Prenzlauer Promenade 149–152, 13189 Berlin.

16. "Bawenda Huts"
    W. Gründler, *Geschichte der Bawenda-Mission in Nord-Transvaal*, p. 63. Also appears in *Berliner Missions-Berichte*, Oktober 1899, p. 657.

17. "Out-Station Ha-Begwa"
   Berlin Mission Archives, Berlin: Album, Vendaland von Missionar G. Westphal, Nr. 8616.

18. Miryam, wife of Nathaniel, cooking (untitled in original)
   Berlin Mission Archives, Berlin: Album, Vendaland von Missionar G. Westphal, Nr. 8620.

19. "The Village-Tailor of Beuster"
    Berlin Mission Archives, Berlin: Album, Vendaland von Missionar G. Westphal, Nr. 8530.

20. "The Helpers [Native Evangelists] at Tschakoma [Tshakhuma]"
    M. Wilde, *Schwarz und Weiss*, p. 188. Also appears in Berlin Mission Archives, Berlin: Album XXIX, Nord-Transvaal 1, Nr. 27.

21. "AND NOW: Converts to Civilization in the Zoutpansberg"
    R. Wessmann, *The Bawenda of the Spelonken*, facing p. 33.

22. "Gertrudsburg 1926, Candidates for Confirmation, Pentecost, 1925"
    Berlin Mission Archives, Berlin: Unlabelled File [Gertrudsburg], Nr. 1134.

23. *Ndilo* [Divining bowl]
    South African Museum. Thanks to Lindsay Cooper, Collections Manager, Human Sciences, South African Museum for providing the photograph.

24. "Cannibal"
    A. Merensky, *Die Menschenfresserei in Afrika*, back cover.

25. Audience with *Khosi* Makwarela Mphaphuli
    "In the area of the ruler of the lands", in M. Wilde, *Schwarz und Weiss*, p. 73 and "Audienz mit Mpafudi (Mkwarela)"/"Audience with Mpafudi (Makwarela)", in Berlin Mission Archives, Berlin: Album XXIX, Nord-Transvaal 1, Nr. 40].

The *Missions-Berichte* noted that, riding ahead of the wagon carrying their equipment and provisions on horseback, the four Brothers travelled

> through the most magnificent land with lush vegetation; excellent country where the high mountains alternate with beautiful green patches [valleys]; and large rivers with ample water roar along; at the top of the mountains there are beautiful meadows [open countryside] where the cattle graze, and there are forests which are so cool and homely that the travellers felt as if they were journeying through the Harz Mountains or Sudeten Mountains.[15]

Beyond its potential for grazing, the land was also bountiful in what it supplied for the sustenance of its inhabitants, who were prepared to share nature's bounty with the missionaries. Grützner reported that:

> On the top of the mountain, over which we had to climb in order to get to Sewásse [Tshivhase] ... there were beautiful alpine meadows – just as beautiful as those in the German mountains. Up to now I have not seen such beautiful grassland in Africa. Although it was the end of October, that means spring-time here, many of the wild trees were covered with ripe and semi-ripe fruit. And right next to the fruit, on the same branch, there were bunches of new blooms. The people carried away baskets full of these ripe fruit which have the structure of a big plum [greengage] and looked like a rough-skinned potato. At our request, they gave us some to taste – the taste is not unpleasant. We also gathered fruit freely.[16]

However, being true men of their times, the glories of nature were not enough for the missionaries. Nature had to be perfected through agriculture. Pastoralism and subsistence agriculture were not enough – the land had to be irrigated and worked in similar ways to the emerging capitalist agricultural concerns of Natal. By implication, this transformation of the agricultural economy would transform the African inhabitants of the land. There was also the hidden implication that Africans would not be able to achieve this by themselves. Presumably Grützner felt that the missionaries would lead them part of the way. However, total transformation would have to rely on the establishment of white farms in the area, utilising African labour:

> The whole country of Sewásse [Tshivhase] – in diameter about five to seven German miles – would also be excellent for White farming, as it could be watered without the irrigation schemes which are so indispensable in Africa. It could be cultivated like the coastal stretch of Natal. Admittedly there are many more ravines in the coastal stretch of Natal.[17]

But that was all for the future. In the meanwhile, there were smaller beginnings to make. From discussing the landscape, Grützner's report flowed seamlessly into discussing its inhabitants:

> We crossed two mountain ranges and on each peak, the Brothers discussed whether these peaks were higher than those of the Harz ... Sewásse [Tshivhase] lives on the third range, close to the highest peak. I was pleased to experience that I can still walk well, and even climb well. Outwardly the people seem friendly; the language is very different from that of the Basutho or Matabele [Basotho or Ndebele]. Our mission will again be entering a new language area! and Brother Beuster, who has just learned to speak the language of the Basutho, has the work, as well as the pleasure, to start at the beginning for a second time.[18]

Now that they were entering the area to stay, rather than to reconnoitre possible areas for the expansion of mission work, it began to dawn on the travellers that the environment would pose serious difficulties to be overcome before mission work could even begin. Even getting their wagon and equipment, which they had left at Albasini's place while going ahead to complete the final negotiations for the establishment of the mission station, proved to be a major undertaking. The journey began on 6 November and

> it did not take long before picks, crowbars, spades and axes were needed to open up a passable track. People with axes ran ahead, to remove trees and bushes [from the path]. Eventually the boundary-river of Schewasse's [Tshivhase] land was reached, and it took several days of effort, during which the Brothers often stood in water up to their chests, to first remove the biggest boulders and make a passable ford, before a load could be brought through the same. It was thanks to the skilfulness of the labourers that another difficult ford was crossed on the next day, and the place where, according to Schewasse's wishes, the Brothers could make their first halt, was already reached by Friday, 8 November ... And now there was one rainy day after another.[19]

Just how difficult life could become in the incessant rain, and with the accompanying "fever" (malaria) soon became clear to the missionaries. Beuster and Stech were hard at work on the construction of the first mission station at Ha-Tshivhase in November and December 1872. Due to the fact that *Khosi* Tshivhase did not send labour in the quantities which the Brothers felt that the work demanded, and due to local perceptions that the missionaries did not pay adequately (or at all) for work done, they had to do much of the early work, such as the cutting of trees and the actual building, themselves. All of this labour was occurring at the height of the rainy season during a particularly wet year. In the opinion of the editors of the *Missions-Berichte*: "The rain alone made the work doubly difficult and finally the Brothers' strength collapsed under the enormous strain."[20] Stech was the first to succumb to a variety of tropical infections, culminating in a bout of malaria.[21] Within a month, Beuster had followed suit.

Some idea of the feelings of dread that illness could evoke in the missionaries is revealed in a letter from Stech to Mission Director Wangemann, written on 1 December 1872 and subsequently published. Describing events over the preceding week, he wrote that reference to his and Beuster's medical books had indicated that his symptoms could be those of enteritis. "Oh what a wretched time lies ahead!" To make matters worse, there was no Western doctor in the area. Botshabelo was at least fourteen days away and Matlala at least nine. In addition, there were no messengers available. Stech also felt that travelling back on his own was

> out of the question as the wagon is also our home and the fords across the rivers have all been washed out and are impassable. So, with the fear that fever [malaria] could also set in, of which the signs are there already, I handed myself over to the mercy of my Saviour, towards the evening of last Monday (25 November). That was a terrible struggle. Over and over again the heart with all its youthful courage shied away from death. Over and over again, my words of prayer became almost without exception: "Oh Lord, do not take me while half my days are done. I have not yet achieved anything which I could present to you as payment for the pain you suffered for the sins of the whole world." It took a long time until I could willingly and with my whole heart say: "Lord, but not my will, but Thy will be done." At last the quiet handing over to the will of God took place. As difficult as the punishment was before, when all my sins appeared before my soul, I could now throw it all onto the forgiveness of the blood of my Saviour. After all, he is my Saviour. By the end of the week my condition improved visibly, so that I could again do some light work … I almost felt strong again, although I was a long way off from healthy. But today, … I am quite strong.[22]

The suffering and debility caused by, and the very real danger of death through, malaria and other tropical diseases, played a crucial role in transforming missionary attitudes towards the landscape – in exposing the darkness within the light.[23] This was compounded by the difficulties they encountered in establishing themselves in, and operating in, what for them was an alien and alienating, inhospitable, as well as harsh and unforgiving environment with few support structures from fellow whites. To compound this even further, since medical science had not yet identified the mosquitoes and amoebae that carried malaria and the other tropical fevers, they did not even understand the aetiology of the diseases that were making their lives a misery and, later, killing them, their wives and their children. In Beuster's words on burying "his faithful servant Nako", who had died of malaria on 22 March 1878: "I have now already buried five people here.[d] Must I be an undertaker here amongst the heathen? And yet I should be one who raises people from the dead!"[24]

Even before they moved into the Zoutpansberg area, the missionaries were aware of the problems of fever (malaria) there. As early as 1860, Merensky noted that many Boers living in the villages of the Zoutpansberg area died of fever each year. In his opinion, "no white man" was able to "live in the northern parts of the lands of the Swazi and the lands of the Knopneusen" because of fever.[25]

Knowing that there was fever and knowing how to combat it were two entirely different matters. On 2 October 1874, Beuster noted that he had been visited by "A German man from the neighbourhood ... in the company of a German Jew". Since his fellow countryman had lived in the area for a long time, and knew "the nature of the land", Beuster saw his advice as invaluable. At that stage, the mission station lay to the west of the river. Beuster noted that the German

> was the first person to suggest that we move the station away from the fever-ridden area to a mountain which was east of the river ... which is at present east of the station. In this wet and marshy country it is important that one builds firstly high and secondly, east of any water. Almost all the winds blow from the East, from the sea, and these winds bring the fever-ridden air to the homes and the people if they have built in the west. That is how it was here. What we newcomers did not at first know and what we did not immediately notice at that time, because of the bush and the rain, that has now become visible: An extensive marsh lies to the east of the station. From there, with every wind, the fever-ridden air (*miasma*) is blown over the station; sickness and death is therefore inevitable. To re-arrange the flow of the river, i.e. to drain all the springs and puddles of the marsh into one river would, after much hard work, only partly reduce the danger. This is why a quick decision and firm resolve were taken. The life of a missionary is worth more than a few

---

d. Over the preceding four years, he had already buried his wife who had died of malaria, his first two Native Assistants who had died of smallpox, and another local Christian who had died of malaria.

> houses which will in any case not stand there for much longer.[e]
> A start must be made on the new house ... I went to Schewase [Tshivhase] on Monday to report the matter to him.[26]

Not yet realising that malaria was carried by a mosquito, they thought that it was the *miasma* – the bad air from the marshes – which caused the disease.[f] However, moving the station away from the marsh where the mosquito larvae bred would certainly have reduced exposure to the disease. The move higher up the mountain would have had a similar effect. As September is the beginning of the pre-rainy season showers, the German visitor must have advised Beuster to move as soon as possible before the next malaria season. After the first spring rains in September, October and November are usually dry. The real rainy season, when it rains for months on end, usually starts in mid-December. The malaria season usually started in mid-January or February. So Beuster had October and November to move the station up the hill. In an effort to provide some kind of protection against malaria, over the first sixteen years of the presence of the mission in Vendaland, the missionaries constructed summer houses in the mountains and each of the three mission stations would be moved from their original sites to higher ground.[27] Other control measures included clearing bush and forest from around the mission stations to let in fresh air and planting Eucalyptus trees in the cleared space. The missionaries believed that "the lush vegetation prevented the wind from blowing fresh air over the countryside". They also reported about Eucalyptus trees that "it is said that they keep the air clean and prevent the fever".[28] There was actually some truth to this as the trees require a tremendous amount of water and hence dry out the soil. At a later date, they were used in malaria eradication programs in the area since they dried up swampy and marshy areas, the breeding places of the mosquito larvae. In a desperate attempt to control the malaria which "raged violently amongst the people" in March and April 1880, Beuster also took

> all the important precautions to ensure that his people did not come into contact with the water. Because one washing of clothing at the river, one walk through the man-high, dew-drenched grass, or over-exertion while working, would surely result in an outbreak of fever.[29]

Again, while he still did not understand the causative process, there was some sense in these measures. The mosquitoes were at the river and in the wet

---

e. The houses were built of mud bricks and plastered with mud. In the rainy season even sun-dried mud bricks did not last long – the moisture made them soft and the mud walls had to be replastered every winter (during the dry season).

f. The root of the term is the Latin "bad air" (*mal-aria*). Malaria was also commonly known as "marsh fever".

grass. Also, overexertion breaks down the resistance of the body, giving the parasites in the blood a chance to multiply, resulting in a fever attack.

Despite these precautions, through the nineteenth century and beyond, not only the local converts but also the missionaries and their wives and children, were subject to recurrent bouts of malaria and other tropical diseases, which frequently proved to be fatal. Every Berlin Missionary who served in Vendaland suffered from fever at some stage in his career, as did their wives and children.[30] We have already seen that Carl Beuster lost three wives and his infant daughter to malaria between 1874 and 1900 and died himself, also of general debility caused by repeated bouts of malaria, in 1901.[31]

Koen and Baumhöfner's battles with, and subsequent death from, malaria have also received attention, as have Koen's wife's bouts of fever.[32] Only two of Carl Gernecke and his wife's twelve children were born at Georgenholtz. Both of these died as infants, one at just under twenty-three months and the other at just over eight months old. With the exception of one other child, who was born at Ladysmith and died in her sixteenth year, the others all lived to adulthood.[33] As late as the 1930s, the Giesekke family were suffering from a variety of amoebiases, and other infections resulting from the tropical climate.[34] This suffering was borne in the name of the Lord. The victims were seen as "sacrifices" and fondly remembered in tractates and the pages of the *Missions-Berichte* and *Der Bawenda-Freund* as pioneers of Christianity in "heathen Bawendaland".[35] This did not make it any easier to bear. During the time that Beuster was away in Natal to get married, Stech's accounts of life at Ha-Tshivhase dealt more with his suffering from malaria and other illnesses and fear of death than with events at the station.[36] Dietrich Baumhöfner's descriptions of Klaas Koen's final illness and death in letters sent back to the Mission Director in Berlin are extremely moving accounts.[37] Wessmann likened suffering from malaria to experiencing the effects of "a slow-acting deadly poison".[38] Beuster was prostrated with grief when fever took his family members.[39] Describing the effects of repeated bouts of malaria on his constitution by 1877, the *Missions-Berichte* noted that: "The illness had so weakened him that one of the Brothers, who visited him, hardly recognised the previously strong, cheerful Brother in the almost senile figure which came towards him."[40] Missionaries at home on their sickbeds or in the Swiss Mission Hospital at Elim were unable to work for the period of their illness, sometimes for months at a time.[41]

These very real uncertainties, dangers, fears and stumbling blocks to the missionary endeavour in turn influenced, and interacted with, missionary attitudes to other core features of the local environment.

Numerous reports in the *Missions-Berichte* and the reports for friends of the Bawenda Mission contained in *Der Bawenda-Freund* refer to the mountainous nature of the landscape of Vendaland.[42] At first, the mountains provided a scenic background to the mission stations, established on land obtained from the *mahosi* in low-lying areas. However, this scenic backdrop was not without its hidden dangers and evils. In the heights of the mountains, with their entrances well-hidden among a maze of footpaths and dead ends through the lush vegetation, lay the villages of what the missionaries called the "heathen Bawenda".[43] At the crudest level of analysis, the missionaries often could not reach the mountain villages on horseback. Evangelising the people there often meant undertaking a strenuous and time-consuming climb.[44] At a deeper level, in the perception of the missionaries, from their mountain strongholds the local people could see the approach of strangers for miles, while themselves remaining unseen.[45] There they lived under what the missionaries saw as the (often) tyrannical rule of the *mahosi*,[46] ruled by superstition and *Zauberei*.[47] A whole way of life was being lived out hidden from the eyes and the direct influence of the missionaries.

The mountain strongholds of the Vhavenda were not the only hindrance to the work of the missionaries. The land was criss-crossed by rivers and streams.[48] While these could be narrow, or even dry, in the dry season, during the rainy season they could become raging torrents. As late as the 1920s, parts of Vendaland were cut off in the rainy season because of the lack of bridges over rivers and streams.[49] Even a report on the then so-called independent state of Venda in 1979 stated that: "Owing to the seasonality of the rainfall, small streams can become raging torrents which are often impassable in summer".[50] When rivers were in flood, those attempting to cross them faced great danger of drowning and a number of missionaries and local people had narrow escapes from a watery grave.[51] At times, wagons carrying equipment for the missionaries or missionary personnel either became stuck or capsized in rivers. Freeing them and salvaging equipment often took some time. Equipment and provisions were sometimes also lost or damaged beyond repair.[52]

Given the wasted hours and losses involved in wagons capsizing, getting bogged down or getting stuck, the missionaries were forced to devote considerable time and effort to constructing bridges and crossings over rivers.[53] This was one way in which they inscribed themselves on the landscape. In doing so, they also unintentionally created sites of tension with local communities. During the early years of Ha-Tshivhase Mission Station in particular, Beuster referred disputes over the ownership, use and treatment of these bridges and crossings to *Khosi* Tshivhase for arbitration. He also made allegations that local people deliberately vandalised both them and the furrows supplying water to the mission station. Inhabitants of areas adjacent to the mission stations occasionally damaged these structures by using them as crossing and drinking places for cattle. Sometimes they also removed conveniently-sized stones from them for the building of terraces, courtyard walls and other structures. The missionaries believed that these tensions and disputes led to their having to waste a great deal of time and energy in repairing damage and attempting to obtain redress from local rulers. As such, they saw them as having a strong negative impact on their mission work in the area.[54]

Rivers also hampered mission work as they often formed the boundaries between the lands of the different *mahosi*. While he allowed missionaries to cross his boundary river and preach on occasion, Makhado consistently forbade them to do so to establish a mission station in his territory.[55] In this sense, the river formed a symbolic, impassable barrier. More concretely, because of their role as boundaries, from the point of view of the missionaries, crossing a river often meant entering into a new set of time-consuming polite meetings with yet another *khosi* in order to gain permission to preach in his area.[56] The missionaries experienced rivers and streams as but further dangerous and time-consuming obstacles to be overcome in the important work of spreading the gospel.

These dangers were compounded by the fact that rivers and streams served as further graphic reminders of the wildness of the area for the missionaries. On a practical level, rivers teemed with crocodiles and hippopotami, posing dangers to those who attempted to cross them.[57] Some of the trepidation which this engendered is amply reflected in the Georgenholtz Missionary Brother Koen's diary entry of 7 March 1882, when he recorded that:

> On my journey to Tsakoma [Tshakhuma], I was in great mortal danger. When we had outspanned, … it was already a beautifully moon-lit evening. I took out my fishing tackle in order to fish a bit, while supper was being prepared at the wagon. I stood there for a long time, but no fish would bite – it was as if here, where there are usually so many fish, there were no fish to be had. Suddenly [the Native Assistant] Solomon, whom I had taken with me, tapped me lightly on the shoulder and ran away. At that same moment, I saw the enormity of the danger. A crocodile lay in the water in front of me, ready to leap at me. I quickly jumped to one side, but my fishing line was stuck. I gave a sharp tug; the strong fishing line snapped and I followed Solomon, just as speedily, to the wagon. I got such a fright that I feel a cold shiver run through me, every time I think of the danger – I had seen that monstrosity so close to me. It had got hold of the hook, then followed the line till it almost reached me. Thanks be to God for having protected me so mercifully.[58]

More abstractly, as with mountains and forests, this wildness was reinforced for the missionaries by the fact that Africans viewed some rivers, pools, waterfalls and lakes as being sacred.[59] In missionary discourse, these "lying gods of the Bawenda" were another great obstacle to be overcome in the spreading of the gospel.[60] Moreover, on at least one occasion, the sacred beings of the rivers fought back against the missionaries. On 17 August 1873,

Beuster recorded that his assistant, Johannes (Mutshaeni), had assured him that

> Schewase [Tshivhase] is not at all such a bad person. It is the old councillors who constantly encourage him to beg; who want to incite him to despise the Word. They are the ones who see the gods in the Moschindote [Mutshindudi River] and who speak to them. The gods have seen white people going through the river.[g] So they asked: "Who are those people?"
> "Those are teachers," they answered. "Teachers? What do they do? They destroy the land! It is not good that you let them into the land!", that is what the gods called out.[61]

This accusation obviously touched a nerve in Beuster. On a number of occasions, he again referred to, and refuted, it.[62]

For the missionaries, the danger and wildness of the environment was especially reflected in the forests that surrounded, and covered the slopes of, the mountains and through which the rivers and streams flowed. Indeed, forests, in particular, came to serve as icons of the fears and tensions – many of which were unconscious or only partly conscious – that they faced.[63]

This tied in with core notions of contemporary European environmental thinking. Since classical times, forests and mountains had served to signify a liminal space of wilderness in European thought, whether Christian or not, of a life outside humanity and an animal existence as symbolised by the wildman of the woods of medieval imagination, a naked hairy figure with both human and animal traits, and a club as his only tool.[64] Carl Ritter, the father of modern geography, and Friedrich Ratzel (his disciple), who together dominated scientific geographical thought in much of the nineteenth and early twentieth centuries, did their best to move away from old stereotypes of ancient and Biblical versions of the world. They thought that environment and society were closely related in a way that reduced the power of the creator. But they also took the degree to which a landscape had been transformed as a yardstick for cultural development. Hence people living in an area with dense forests were imagined as people without "culture" and "civilisation". The forest remained an icon of wilderness and savagery even for the *maître penseurs* in modern science.[65]

For the Berlin Missionaries, the forests of Vendaland teemed with game, which could be hunted and eaten. On the other hand, lions and "tigers" (leop-

---

g. When Tshivhase left the Nzhelele valley with the breakup of the Dzata empire, he first settled at Phiphidi. There were people living here who venerated their ancestors and other spirits in the Mutshindudi River. Although these were not Singo spirits, Tshivhase's people also adopted this practice. If one goes from Maungani (Ha-Tshivhase) to Tshivhase's village, one has to cross the Mutshindudi river near Phiphidi. This is where the spirits, who live in the indigenous forest around the Phiphidi waterfall and in the pool at its base [see Map 2], saw them cross the river (see p. 171 for a discussion of these spirits, the *zwidudwane*).

ards) abounded.⁶⁶ A number of cases where missionaries had narrow escapes from lions are reported in their journals.⁶⁷ In addition, they provided a constant threat to man's divinely-ordained dominance of nature by taking cattle and other livestock. Attempting to control them could result in serious injury for humans. For example, in commenting on events at Georgenholtz on Sunday, 5 February 1882, Koen wrote that:

> This morning battle cries were heard coming from Schecundo [Tshikundu]. It later turned out that the noise was because of a mighty lion which had broken into a goat pen during the night. The pen was situated between the huts of the people. They had come out when they had been woken up by the noise. The animal was very wild. They could not kill it, but they managed to get a shot at it and wounded it. After the lion had, before their eyes, torn nine goats to pieces and eaten one, it escaped so quickly, that nobody thought of doing anything to it – they just stared after it as it vanished in the bushes. While the people were still standing there, observing their dead goats, the lion returned. He grabbed an old man from their midst, crushed his leg and inflicted several more serious wounds on him, almost as if he was taking revenge for the shot that had wounded him – which most probably was also causing him serious pain. While he was still venting his anger like this on the old man, another person killed him with an assegai.⁶⁸

Even more insidious were the serpents which were met with in the field or invaded the houses of the missionaries, even being found under the beds of their sleeping children. Missionary accounts of encounters with snakes display an almost hysterical fear of these reptiles (the Christian icon of Satan), and treat the ultimate victory of the missionary – armed with a poker or some other heavy object – as being divinely assisted.⁶⁹ For example (in one of the more subdued accounts), in reporting on events at Tshakhuma during the first half of the year 1877, the *Missions-Berichte* reported that:

> Besides the continual illnesses, Brother Schwellnus also had to go through several life-threatening dangers ... Many a time he ... had to ward off poisonous snakes. One crept under his feet into his house, when he opened the door. He killed it with an iron wash-basin. Another which was just on its way to the house, was killed with a spade. A third one which was making its way straight for his wife, was hunted by the people, but it managed to escape. A fourth one was beaten to death right next to the front door, where the children were playing. So Brother Schwellnus has often enough had the opportunity to thank his Lord for merciful protection.⁷⁰

Even when humans were not in danger, they sometimes suffered losses because of the activities of wild animals. For example, reporting on events at Georgenholtz during the year 1889, Wessmann reported that:

> We are often plagued by wild animals here at our new station. As soon as the sun has gone down and darkness sets in, the hyenas start their work. In one night they fetched no less than five pigs at once ... They also attack dogs and even old hides [skins] are not despised by them. Unfortunately we have no gun and it would be difficult to obtain one here. A tiger [leopard] killed a calf on our station the day before yesterday. Even one of the lions worried us – they are nowadays active here in the area, yet without really getting up to anything serious.[71]

Against this background, what the missionaries saw as the dark and dangerous forests were perceived as surrounding and threatening the mission stations[72] – which they saw as "God's gardens in the heathen wilderness".[73] They argued that the mission stations in Vendaland had been "created out of the wild" and there was an ever-present danger of them reverting to this state.[74] Moreover, for the missionaries, the hidden menace and darkness of the forests were also reflected in the character of their inhabitants, who were obscured and sustained by them. As late as 1912, an article in *Der Bawenda-Freund* referred to "the dark forests of Bawendaland and the dark hearts of the heathen Bawenda".[75]

To counteract this, they clearly believed that their task was in the service of the only true God and that it was his will that they convert the people of Vendaland. The "darkness" of the environment was a trial to be overcome to bring the "light" of Christianity. They also had a very clear perception that, in opposition to the darkness and wildness of Africa, the "light" that they were bringing was the light of "civilisation" – more particularly, "German culture".[76] The Berlin missionaries saw themselves as the "pioneers of culture" in Vendaland.[77] In texts such as the *Missions-Berichte*, *Der Bawenda-Freund* and various tractates, "heathenism" was frequently referred to in terms of darkness and the progression to Christianity was seen as a progression to light.[78]

Thus, the Berlin missionaries had moved a long way from their original naïve optimism and wonder. Their early, almost rhapsodic, attempts to ground themselves (and the mission authorities and friends of the mission at home in Germany) by comparing the landscape of Vendaland with the tamed German landscape, pruned, trimmed and replanted into pleasing straight lines, floundered on the harsh reality of the local situation. The very real hidden danger of the anopheles mosquito, the difficulties to be overcome in establishing themselves in what they experienced as an extremely foreign and "untamed" environment, and what they perceived to be the hidden hazards and resistance of the dark and dangerous forest – its natural features, animal life, inhabitants and even the supernatural beings which it was said to shelter and succour – brought a discordant note to the symphony of birdsong. They introduced a sense of foreboding, even, at times, despair. In missionary experience and discourse, the light was still there. However, so too was the darkness at its heart.

These were the major trends that emerged in the missionary interpretation of the landscape of Vendaland over time. This raises the issue of the problems faced by the missionaries in illustrating what they saw as the hardships, dangers and "darkness" of the environment, and the "light" of Christianity, for their readers. Due to the missionary identification of the local people with their environment, their treatment of the human inhabitants of the area forms a core element of this analysis.

1. This chapter draws heavily on A. Kirkaldy, "The Darkness within the Light: Berlin missionaries and the Landscape of Vendaland, c. 1870–1900", in *Historia*, 48(1), May 2003, pp. 169–202.

2. See, for example, B. Bender, "Introduction: Landscape-Meaning and Action", in B. Bender (ed.) *Landscape: Politics and Perspectives*, Oxford, Berg, 1993, pp. 1–3, 9, 11; D. Cosgrove, "Landscapes and Myths, Gods and Humans", in B. Bender (ed.), *Landscape*, pp. 281–305; G. Finley, *Landscapes of Memory: Turner as Illustrator to Scott*, Berkley, University of California Press, 1980; S. Kügler, "Landscape as Memory: The Mapping of process and its Representation in a Melanesian Society", in B. Bender (ed.), *Landscape*, pp. 85–106; T. Mitchell, "The world as exhibition" in *Comparative Studies in Society and History*, 31, 1989, pp. 217–236; H. Morphy (a) "From dull to brilliant: the aesthetics of spiritual power among the Yolngu", in *Man* (N.S.), 24(1), 1989, pp. 21–41 & (b) *Ancestral Connections: Art and an Aboriginal System of Knowledge*, Chicago, Chicago University Press, 1991 & (c) "Colonialism, History and the Construction of Place: The Politics of Landscape in Northern Australia", in B. Bender (ed.), *Landscape*, pp. 205–243; P. Sutton, *Dreamings: the Art of Aboriginal Australia*, Asia Society Galleries, New York, George Braziller, 1988; and J. Thomas, "The Politics of Vision and the Archaeologies of Landscape", in B. Bender (ed.), *Landscape*, pp. 19–48.

3. *BMB*, 1872, p. 159. This visit is also discussed on p. 26. For earlier reports from Blauberg, see, for example, *BMB*, 1869, pp. 100–107; 1870, pp. 23, 136–138, 147–155, 163–167, 214–215; 1871, pp. 183–184.

4. *BMB*, 1872, p. 160.

5. *BMB*, 1874, pp. 127–128. The visits to Makhado and Tshivhase, and Makhado's supplying them with the Christian guide, Samuel, are also discussed on pp. 27, 52–54.

6. *BMB*, 1874, p. 128. For Wangemann's version, see *BMB*, 1873, pp. 133–134. For discussion of incorporating alien landscapes by finding (or creating) links between them and the familiar European landscape, see B.V. Street, *The savage in literature*, p. 26.

7. *BMB*, 1874, p. 129.

8. *Ibid.*

9. *Ibid.* p. 130.

10. *Ibid.* Cf. *BMB*, 1873, pp. 134–135.

11. *BMB*, 1874, p. 131.

12. *BMB*, 1873, p. 135. For discussion of the adventure literature trope of "despotic" and "buffoon-like" rulers of "primitive" societies, see B.V. Street, *The savage in literature*, p. 133.

13. *BMB*, 1874, p. 131. Cf. D. Livingstone, "Marenga im Kreise seiner Frauen. (Nach Young)", in *Livingstone, der Missionar, II*, Leipzig, Spamer, 1869, also appearing as L594 in R.F. Kennedy

(comp.), *Catalogue of Prints in the Africana Museum and in books in the Strange Collection of Africana in the Johannesburg Public Library up to 1870, Volume Two: L–Z and Index*, Johannesburg, Africana Museum, 1976. Beyond Beyer's eyewitness account, Livingstone's various works were available (both in English and in German) in the Berlin Mission Library during the nineteenth century. It is likely that many of Beyer's colleagues would have thought of this etching when reading his account.

14. See pp. 27.
15. *BMB*, 1874, p. 136.
16. *Ibid.* pp. 67–68.
17. *Ibid.* p. 68.
18. *Ibid.*
19. *Ibid.* pp. 137–138.
20. *Ibid.* pp. 138–139 (quotation p. 139).
21. See pp. 58–59.
22. *Ibid.* p. 141.
23. For the role played by malaria in the "darkening" of Africa, see also P. Brantlinger, "Victorians and Africans", p. 174.
24. *BMB*, 1879, p. 435.
25. *BMB*, 1860, p. 63.
26. Tagebuch der Station bei Schewase (Carl Beuster), 2. Oktober 1874, in Berlin Mission Archives, Berlin, Acta der Berliner Missionsgesellschaft betreffend Missionsstationen: Acta: Tagebücher der Missionare auf der Station Ga Sebase, 1872–1891, (I), Abt.III, Fach 5, No. 14. See also *BMB*, 1875, pp. 446–447.
27. *BMB*, 1878, p. 256; 1886, pp. 360–361; 1887, pp. 210–211, 222, 223, 481, 485, 486; 1888, pp. 507, 508, 533–534; 1889, pp. 249, 530.
28. *BMB*, 1878, p. 483; 1879, pp. 434–435 (quotations); 1885, p. 182.
29. *BMB*, 1880, p. 405.
30. See, for example, *Der Bawenda-Freund*, VII(26), 1889, p. 82; 8(30), 1890, p. 98; 11(42), 1893, p. 158; 11(43), 1893, p. 166; 12(44), 1894, pp. 174–175; 13(51), 1895, p. 246; 15(59), 1897, p. 363; and *BMB*, 1866, p. 199; 1874, pp. 125–126, 143, 152, 241; 1875, pp. 419, 446–447; 1876, pp. 390–391; 1877, pp. 485, 488–489, 490; 1878, pp. 251, 480, 481, 482–483, 488–489, 494; 1879, pp. 203, 411, 434–435; 1880, p. 405; 1883, pp. 372, 374, 434–435; 1885, pp. 71, 74, 182; 1887, pp. 481, 485, 486; 1888, pp. 222, 223, 507; 1889, pp. 249, 238; 1890, pp. 463, 465, 488; 1891, pp. 221, 449; 1893, p. 460; 1894, pp. 200, 201, 367, 373–375; 1897, p. 107; 1898, pp. 8, 314, 318, 519, 593; 1899, p. 93; 1900, pp. 305, 306, 691, 692, 694. In addition, the letters of missionaries contained in their personal files frequently discuss fever among themselves, their immediate family members, members of their congregation and/or the "heathens". See Acta betreffend Personalia: Baumhöfner, Dietrich; Beuster, Carl; Endemann, Christian, Abt.II, Fach IIIG, Nr. 8, Angefangen 1891, Beendigt 1976; Giesekke, Ludwig, Abt.II, Fach IG, Nr. 2a, Angefangen 1898, Beendigt 1955; Gottschling, Ernst, (a) Abt. II, Fach 3 & (b) Abt. II, Fach 3G, No. 27, Band 2, Angefangen 1913, Beendigt 1952; Klatt, Carl Otto; Koen, Klaas; Meister, Johannes; Schwellnus, Erdmann; Sonntag, Christoph, Abt. II, Fach 3, No. 13, 1878–1952; Stork, Hellmuth, Abt. II, Fach St 3, Nr. 8, Angefangen 1926, Beendigt 19–; Wessmann, Reinhold and Westphal, Gotthardt, Abt. II, Fach II20, Nr. 5A, Angefangen 1902, Beendigt 1929.
31. See pp. 84–85.
32. See pp. 87–88, 105, 106–111.
33. Acta betreffend Personalia: Gernecke, Carl. See also pp. 90–91.
34. See numerous medical reports contained in Acta betreffend Personalia: Giesekke, Ludwig.
35. See, for example, [Anon.] *Dietrich Baumhöfner*; *BMB*, 1875, p. 232; 1883, pp. 139–140, 358; G. Sauberzweig-Schmidt, *Klaas Kuhn*.

36. See especially *BMB*, 1874, pp. 143, 150–153.
37. Letters, D. Baumhöfner to Mission Director, Berlin Mission Society, 3. August 1882; 7. Januar 1883; 13. Februar 1883, in Acta betreffend Personalia: Baumhöfner, Dietrich.
38. *Der Bawenda-Freund*, 12(44), 1894, p. 175.
39. For the most moving account, see Berichte der Station bei Schewase (Carl Beuster), 7. Juli 1874, pp. 15–16 (also in *BMB*, 1875, pp. 423–424).
40. *BMB*, 1878, p. 482.
41. See, for example, *Der Bawenda-Freund*, 11(42), 1893, p. 158; 11(43), 1893, pp. 166–167; 12(44), 1894, pp. 174–175 which discuss Reinhold Wessmann's "months of illness".
42. See, for example, *Der Bawenda-Freund*, VI(21), 1888, p. 63; VI(23), 1888, p. 67; VII(25), 1889, p. 80; 10(36), 1892, pp. 121, 122; 11(40), 1892 (*sic* – corrected by hand on volume to 1893), p. 146; 13(52), 1895, p. 267; 14(56), 1896, p. 329; and 15(57), 1897, p. 343; *BMB*, 1874, pp. 68, 125, 128, 133, 135, 136; 1875, pp. 369, 446; 1876, p. 390; 1878, pp. 481, 490–491; 1879, pp. 435, 438, 441, 442; 1882, pp. 428, 431, 432; 1885, pp. 72, 74, 77; 1888, p. 515; 1889, p. 530; 1890, pp. 466, 470, 471, 476, 500; 1894, p. 376; 1895, p. 191; 1897, p. 107; 1898, p. 18; 1899, pp. 93, 94, 564, 643; 1900, pp. 692, 694. As with the other environmental features discussed here, the sheer number of references indicates the degree to which these influenced the lives and work of the missionaries.
43. See, for example, *BMB*, 1872, pp. 432, 433; 1873, pp. 134, 135; 1874, pp. 67, 130, 131; 1875, p. 365; 1878, pp. 497, 498; R. Wessmann, *Philippus Thai*, pp. 3, 5.
44. *BMB*, 1873, p. 133; 1874, p. 126.
45. *BMB*, 1874, pp. 126, 129.
46. *Der Bawenda-Freund*, VII(24), 1889, pp. 73–75; VII(26), 1889, p. 83; 8(30), 1890, p. 98; 10(36), 1892, pp. 121–123; 10(39), 1892, pp. 139–140; 13(50), 1895, pp. 223–224; 14(55), 1896, pp. 308–310; *BMB*, 1872, pp. 158–160; 1873, pp. 132–137; 1874, pp. 68, 126–127, 130–135; 1875, p. 369; 1878, pp. 291–292, 490; 1885, pp. 75–76; and *Mitteilungen des Vereins "Heidenfreund"*, V(16), 1887, n.p. (pp. 3–4); V(18), 1887, n.p. (pp. 2–3).
47. *Der Bawenda-Freund*, 8(30), 1890, p. 99; 10(36), 1892, p. 123; 10(39), 1892, pp. 136–191; 11(40), 1892 (sic – corrected by hand on volume to 1893), p. 144; 13(52), 1895, pp. 258–259, 262–263, 267; 14(53), 1896, pp. 278–279; 15(59), 1897, pp. 360–361; 30(3), 1913, p. 36; 31(1), 1914, p. 8; *BMB*, 1870, p. 332; 1872, pp. 154–155; 1874, pp. 179–180; 1875, p. 401; 1876, pp. 392–393; 1877, p. 485; 1878, pp. 455, 484–486, 492–494, 495; 1879, pp. 312, 435; 1880, pp. 3–4, 344, 403, 408, 414; 1883, pp. 443–444; 1886, pp. 416–417, 420; 1887, pp. 485, 488; 1888, p. 515; 1889, pp. 547–548; 1890, pp. 239, 484, 500–501; 1893, pp. 469–470; 1894, pp. 369–370; 1897, pp. 87–89, 728, 735; 1899, pp. 603–604, 699; 1900, pp. 448, 683–685, 688–689, 692; and *Mitteilungen des Vereins "Heidenfreund"*, V(18), 1887, n.p. (p. 4). For the trope of the lives of Africans or "primitives" being completely dominated by "superstition", see also L. de Kock, *Civilising Barbarians*, p. 101; B.V. Street, *The savage in literature*, pp. 137, 163.
48. These are referred to almost as often in reports as mountains. See, for example, *Der Bawenda-Freund*, 6(23), 1888, p. 67; 10(36), 1892, pp. 121, 122, 123; 11(40), 1892 (sic – corrected by hand on volume to 1893), pp. 145–148; 14(54), 1896, p. 297; 15(57), 1897, p. 344; *BMB*, 1874, pp. 129, 136, 144, 145; 1875, pp. 369, 373, 409–410, 416–418, 446; 1876, p. 390; 1878, pp. 491, 496, 498; 1885, pp. 74, 78; 1890, p. 463; 1894, p. 375; 1897, p. 726; and 1899, p. 643.
49. D. McDonald "Vendaland", February 1933, p. 12.
50. Benso, *The Independent Venda*, p. 16.
51. D. McDonald "Vendaland", February 1933, p. 12; *BMB*, 1892, p. 524.
52. See, for example, *BMB*, 1874, pp. 145–149, 184; 1875, p. 373.
53. See, for example, *BMB*, 1875, pp. 360, 418–419, 448.
54. See, for example, *Ibid.* pp. 425, 438–439, 443, 448; 1876, p. 394; 1878, p. 483.
55. See, for example, *BMB*, 1874, pp. 126–127; 1877, pp. 482–483, 484; 1882, p. 423; 1885, p. 410; 1886, p. 217; 1887, p. 481; 1888, p. 507; 1889, pp. 249, 529; 1891, p. 221; 1891, pp. 450, 451, 455, 456; 1892, p. 270, 520; 1894, pp. 200, 366; 1895, p. 350.

THE LANDSCAPE 143

56. *BMB*, 1874, pp. 129–130, 137; 1875, pp. 365–366, 369; 1878, p. 498; 1882, pp. 433–434; 1890, p. 478; and Tagebuch der Station Ha Tsevase (Carl Beuster), 12. Mai 1889, pp. 50–51.

57. *Der Bawenda-Freund*, VII(25), 1889, p. 80; 10(36), 1892, p. 122; and 11(40), 1892 (*sic* – corrected by hand on volume to 1893), pp. 145–146.

58. *BMB*, 1882, p. 451.

59. For sacred rivers, river spirits/sprites and sacred river stones, see *Der Bawenda-Freund*, VII(27), 1899, p. 86; *BMB*, 1874, p. 375; 1875, pp. 361, 371; 1879, p. 444; 1889, p. 546; 1894, p. 375. For sacred mountains and mountain Gods, see *Der Bawenda-Freund*, VII(25), 1899, pp. 79–80; *BMB*, 1879, pp. 441–442. For sacred forests and forest spirits, see *Der Bawenda-Freund*, VII(27), 1899, p. 88; *BMB*, 1875, pp. 371–372, 373, 374, 417; 1878, p. 498; 1879, p. 443; 1897, p. 84. These categories of sacred beings, ancestral beings, objects and features of the landscape are also discussed on pp. 168–174, 181.

60. *BMB*, 1878, p. 496.

61. *BMB*, 1875, p. 361. These themes are discussed in more detail in chapter 6.

62. *Ibid.* pp. 364, 371–372; 1875, pp. 419, 443.

63. See, for example, *Der Bawenda-Freund*, 13(52), 1895, p. 267; 14(54,) 1896, p. 288; 15(57), 1897, p. 343; *BMB*, 1873, pp. 133–134; 1874, pp. 128, 130–131; 1875, pp. 371, 373, 374; 1879, pp. 435, 443; 1882, pp. 429, 430; 1885, pp. 72, 77; 1897, p. 84; 1899, p. 643.

64. S. Moser, *Ancestral Images. The Iconography of Human origins*, Stroud, Sutton Publishing, 1998. Thanking Prof. Albert Wirz for drawing my attention to this source.

65. A. Kirkaldy and A. Wirz, "Picturing the soul: missionary encounters in late 19th and early 20th century South Africa", in *Working Papers on African Societies*, 44, Berlin, Das Arabische Buch, 2000, p. 4.

66. See, for example, *Der Bawenda-Freund*, VII(25), 1889, p. 80 (duck shooting and hyenas); VII(27), 1889, p. 87 (lions); 10(36), 1892, pp. 121–122 (unspecified wild animals and lions), 11(40), 1892 (*sic* – corrected by hand on volume to 1893), p. 145 (lions); *BMB*, 1872, pp. 159, 160 (lions), 252 (lions); 1873, pp. 133–134 ("quaggas" (zebra?), wild pigs and "tigers"); 1874, pp. 124 (lions and "quagga"), 125 (wild pigs and hyenas), 129 (wild pigs and "tigers"), 130 (buffalo); 1875, pp. 417 (lions), 423 ("tigers"); 1878, p. 492 (buffalo, elephants, lions and "wolves" (wild dogs or hyenas?); 1879, p. 442 (lions); 1880, p. 412 (lions and "tigers"); 1885, p. 75 (buffaloes, giraffe, hippopotami and rhinoceri); 1894, pp. 373 (lions), 410–411 (lions).

67. See, for example, *Der Bawenda-Freund*, 9(33), 1891, p. 109; 12(46), 1894, pp. 192–194.

68. *BMB*, 1882, pp. 450–451.

69. See, for example, *Der Bawenda-Freund*, VII(24), 1889, 75–76; 14(53), 1896, pp. 281–282. For discussion of the snake as "Satan (alias the African as other)", see M.L. Pratt, *Imperial Eyes: Travel Writing and Transculturation*, London, Routledge, 1992, pp. 209–211.

70. *BMB*, 1888, p. 508.

71. *BMB*, 1889, p. 545.

72. See in particular *BMB*, 1873, pp. 133–134; 1874, p. 128; 1879, p. 435.

73. *Mitteilungen des Vereins "Heidenfreund"*, V(16), 1887, n.p. (p. 3). For mission stations as "God's gardens", horticultural imagery and the idea of "cultivating the heathens" in other parts of South Africa, see J.L. Comaroff and J. Comaroff, *Of Revelation and Revolution*, Volume One, pp. 80, 88, 120, 121, 170, 175, 243; L. de Kock, *Civilising Barbarians*, p. 149. For missionary imagery of "the re-creation of the spoiled English garden in Africa's 'vast moral wastes'", see J.L. Comaroff, "Images of Empire, Contents of Conscience: Models of Colonial Domination in South Africa", in F. Cooper and A.L. Stoler (eds.), *Tensions of empire*, p. 175.

74. *Der Bawenda-Freund*, 32(1), 1915, p. 13.

75. *Der Bawenda-Freund*, 29(1), 1912, p. 1. For the idea of wild landscapes as harbouring "wild" people, see also J.L. Comaroff and J. Comaroff, *Of Revelation and Revolution*, Volume I, pp. 173, 174; L. de Kock, *Civilising Barbarians*, p. 147.

76. *Der Bawenda-Freund*, 32(3), 1915, p. 17; *BMB*, 1878, p. 483; 1880, pp. 346–348; 1886, pp. 361–362.

77. *BMB*, 1878, p. 483.

78. See, for example, *BMB*, 1875, pp. 232, 369, 401; 1877, p. 484; 1882, pp. 434, 435; 1883, p. 40; 1884, p. 216; R. Wessmann (a) *Der Häuptling August Makhahane, ein Lebensbild aus der Bawenda-Mission*, Berlin, Buchhandlung der Berliner evangelischen Missionsgesellschaft, 1892, pp. 1, 10, 16 & (b) *Philippus Thai*, pp. 2, 8–9. Cf. P. Brantlinger, "Victorians and Africans", especially pp. 176, 178, 183; L. de Kock, *Civilising Barbarians*, pp. 46–47, 84; and B.V. Street, *The Savage in Literature*, pp. 23–24.

CHAPTER 5
Missionary images[1]

In recent years, great strides have been made in the use of photographs as a source for the writing of history. Due especially to the efforts of Christraud Geary, Paul Jenkins and others, new ways have been discovered of using pictures to document the colonial discourse and the processes of "othering" that are inherent in the colonial situation. We have also learnt to read missionary photographs as mirrors of missionary ideology, to use them as guides to missionary ideas of what is right and what is wrong, proofs of their ambivalence towards African cultures and – more recently – as a privileged source for the study of material culture in African societies.[2]

As a result, even historians without formal training in art history have familiarised themselves with different conventions of representation, especially with the pictorial traditions that inform and direct the photographer's eye. In short: we have learnt to read pictures as attentively and as critically as we read texts.

CONSTRUCTING VENDALAND AND THE VHAVENDA

Against this background, for me, the photographic image that captures the way that the Berlin Missionaries felt about Vendaland and the "Bawenda" (Vhavenda) most effectively was that of "Missionary Schwellnus" which appeared in the *Berliner Missions-Berichte* in 1893 [see Illustration 3].[3] It would appear that the Mission Society felt the same way, as they also used this image for the cover and frontispiece of their published history of the mission in Vendaland (1897). In the last-mentioned position, it is more suitably titled "Forest-stream in Bawendaland. Missionary Schwellnus and natives".[4]

The carefully-composed image uses trees, ferns, creepers and other riverine bush to give the impression of a suitably dense jungle, lush, uncontrolled and untamed. There is no clearing – the missionary stands impressively in the undergrowth of the river bank and the three young black boys who accompany him are perched on the rocks that surround a tiny waterfall. While the caption makes no reference to this being the source of the river (and, indeed, this was not so in "reality" either), the idea of a source is strongly evoked. This suggests the idea of the missionary as a source of knowledge – both about the world and about God and the road to salvation.

The subjects are positioned around a banana tree – a sign of cultivation. On one level, this draws the viewer's eye away from the background forest and towards those grouped around it. Viewed differently, the grouping serves to separate the missionary from the African other. Separation and othering is also linked to dominance and subordination – Schwellnus is standing on the left-hand side, slightly elevated above the young boys, two of whom are seated and one squatting slightly lower down on the right. The missionary's head and shoulders protrude into the upper left-hand quadrant of the photograph (the strongest part), while the boys are clustered in the lower right-hand quadrant (the weakest part). This serves both to balance the picture and to accentuate his dominance over them. Moreover, his dominance extends to nature. While the jungle stretching out behind the missionary is clearly extremely dense, his positioning in the foreground, and the fact that he has his back to it, lead us to suppose that he knows the paths through the darkness to the light and is able to safely avoid the dangers of the forest. While the jungle is much more massive than himself, it is clear that he is not swallowed by it. The idea of a lush, dense, hostile and (to the uninitiated) impenetrable jungle is enhanced by careful cropping of the image and shading and enhancing of the original photograph so that it acquires many of the characteristics of an etching.

Missionary Schwellnus's hat is his only concession to the climate – he wears a high collar, frock coat, waistcoat and long trousers. While we cannot see his feet, we may safely presume that they are encased in suitably well-made German leather shoes or short boots. The three young boys with him are obviously converts as they wear jackets, one of them a rather impressively tailored and well-fitting one, and long pants. Two of them wear hats. However, they are all barefoot.

This photograph stands apart from all the others from Vendaland in its ability to capture the feelings that the missionaries were attempting to convey to their readers. It would appear that, given the technological constraints of photographic equipment at the time and the limited abilities of most of the Vendaland missionaries as photographers, one of the main difficulties that they faced was the ability to visually illustrate the metaphors of darkness and light used in their texts. This is partly illustrated by the enhancements made to the image just discussed. It is also clearly illustrated by a photograph entitled "Crossing a river in Bowenda" [see Illustration 4], which appears in the photographic albums of the Berlin Mission but never appears to have been published, apparently because it was not adjudged to be of sufficiently high quality.[6] In addition, the presence of a disembodied African arm (belonging to a person standing behind the missionary out of the view of the camera) subverts the ruggedly macho scene the picture seeks to create.

This image is undated. However, photographs from the same album appear in M. Wilde's *Schwarz und Weiss: Bilder von einer Reise durch das Arbeitsgebiet der Berliner Mission in Südafrika*, Berlin, Buchhandlung der Berliner Missionsgesellschaft in Berlin, 1913. It may be presumed that this image dates from around this time.

The image gives a clear sense of the kind of gung-ho sense of adventure that the missionaries needed in order to survive in Vendaland. Positioned slightly to the left of the photograph with his head, shoulders and chest protruding into the dominant upper left quadrant, the missionary immediately draws the eye of the viewer and clearly dominates the photograph. This dominance is reinforced by the sense of movement, the patch of light on the water in the vicinity of the punting missionary, his reflection in the water and the fact that his white underclothing and the darkness of the craft upon which he is standing contrast fairly strongly with the rest of the photograph. While he has stripped to his long underclothing to cross the river, he still wears his pith helmet, boots and gun belt with revolver. Using a long branch to punt the rather Heath Robinson-looking craft across the wide river (apparently the Luvuvhu), the missionary displays obvious bravery and resourcefulness. While we cannot see them, we know there are (at least potentially) crocodiles lurking in the vicinity.

The image manages to generate a sense of excitement and adventure. However, it does not clearly convey a sense of hidden menace in the lush riverine bush in the background. While wild animals and wild people may possibly lurk there, it is lit far too brightly by the sun to evoke any kind of eerily-chilling feeling in the spine. Shading and enhancements would also not work to instil a feeling of menace or a contrast between light and darkness here.

To capture these deeper emotions equating forests, darkness and heathenism, the Mission Society used etchings. For example, from July 1916, the masthead of *Der Bawenda-Freund* [see Illustration 5] depicted a missionary clad in jacket, tie, waistcoat and hat standing with a group of two scantily-clad men and a child.[7] The direct gaze of the missionary suggests his earnestness, trustworthiness and strength. His manner of dress strengthens this impression. As the men wear only loincloths and the child only a singlet, they are obviously "heathens". This is further reinforced by the fact that they stand in front of the edge of the luxuriant tropical forest. Their facial features are rather coarse, suggesting a race not as well evolved as that from which the missionary comes – perhaps even suggesting a closer link with creatures of the forest than with their European missionary. Support for this interpretation is provided by the broad, muscular and naked backs and arms of the two African men. Due to the contrast provided by their facial features, their exposure to the viewer is not homoerotic, instead it emphasises the physical strength and virility of these "creatures of the forest", a strength which, in the interpretation of the mission, is far more "earthy" than, and hence not nearly as powerful as, that given to the missionary by his faith and his culture.

The Africans look across a mountain valley, which contains a settlement, to a full sun rising over the mountains on the other side which contains a cross. The settlement is obviously a Christian one as it lies exposed and unconcealed at the foot of the mountains. Were it a "heathen" one, it would be concealed in mountain forest.[8] This village is protected by the Lord and needs no such crude defensive measures. With an expansive gesture, the missionary points the way to salvation. Despite the fact that it is he, rather than the Africans, who should be the "outsider", in the eyes of the mission and its friends, his position as the agent of Christ puts him in the dominant role of guide to the Africans in their own country. This position of dominance, and what the Europeans saw as his superiority, is reinforced by his hand resting paternally on the naked shoulder of the African man nearest to the viewer. One can imagine what his reaction would be if the African man dared do the same to him! Once again, we are left with an extremely clear idea of missionary beliefs about their superiority, and eventual victory, over the African other.

The equation of heathenism and the dark and dangerous forest is also seen in illustrations in the *Missions-Berichte*. A picture entitled "Der Missionar im Palmenwalde" (The Missionary in the Palmforest) [see Illustration 6] appeared amongst the reports from Vendaland in the *Berliner Missions-Berichte* for 1880.[9] This depicts a missionary and what appears to be a local evangelist walking on a path through a dense forest. They are clearly separated from the "other" – the remaining people in the illustration. Trees, some straight and some crooked, are randomly arranged under a dense tropical canopy. With the exception of the narrow path through the forest, the undergrowth is lush. This is no forest planted or tamed by the hand of "man" – it is primordial forest, dark and "pregnant" with fecundity and, presumably, hidden danger. It is also peopled with hidden indigenes. Their dress makes it clear that they are "heathens". Those in front of the missionary and his assistant, who both wear European clothing and carry Bibles, hide themselves from view. They either peer round trees or hang from vines and branches like apes, or, in the case of the figure on the left, cherubs or angels in Renaissance paintings, seeing but attempting to remain unseen. Seen as apes, they represent the creatures of the forest. If they may indeed be seen as angels, they represent what (in missionary discourse) the creatures of the forest are capable of becoming if they accept the Gospel and the teachings of the missionary and his assistant.

The people behind the missionary and his companion are not as well concealed, apparently since there is less danger of their being seen. A few move away to the right quickly, possibly to find better hiding places or possibly out of fear of these men and the message that they bring. The child running onto the path is being pulled back, presumably as it runs the risk of being too exposed. In spite of their slightly greater visibility, one gains the impression that, should either the missionary or his companion turn around, those behind them would be able to disappear from view quickly enough to remain undetected or to be merely glimpsed. They are unarmed and thus do not appear to present any immediate danger to either of the bearers of the Gospel. However, their concealing themselves could possibly be interpreted as threatening in itself. If not threatening, from the point of view of missionary discourse, it certainly demonstrates the cunning nature and resistance to the adoption of the teachings of Christianity exhibited by these creatures of the forest. On a more symbolic level, what is needed is for them to follow the missionary and his companion on the narrow path out of the dark and gloomy forest to light and salvation. However, in missionary thinking, at present, their misplaced fear or their clinging to the shallow and misleading security offered by the forest – the "darkness" and "superstition" of "heathenism" – is preventing them from doing so.

Interestingly, this illustration of "Der Missionar im Palmenwalde" was not specified as relating to Vendaland. It may nevertheless be argued that its placement amongst reports emanating from that area would have created this link in the minds of readers. Moreover, the kind of dense tropical forest depicted is evocative of that described in many reports emanating from Vendaland and in the photograph of Missionary Schwellnus in this area first published in 1893.

The failure to source this picture, and others, to a specific area is significant. On one level, in many cases, the artists who drew them had never been to the areas that they drew. For illustrations of specific mission stations, which are often recognisable from structures or other features still existing today, they presumably relied on drawings, descriptions or photographs made by missionaries from these areas. For less specific background features, and illustrations of general themes, such as missionaries in the palm forest, they would presumably have relied on their imagination to a greater extent. This imagination saw "heathen lands" as areas of dense tropical forest with all of the hidden dangers and the darkness described above. It made no real difference where these forests were, or which "tribe" of "heathens" lived in them. Forests, "darkness", "superstition" and "dark practices" were common features of "heathen" life in all parts of Africa and, indeed, in other "heathen lands" as well.

Arising from the multi-purpose nature of these less-specific illustrations, they could also be reused in, and utilised to meet the needs of, a variety of different situations. Perhaps the most versatile example is a vignette by the artist C. Roux. This began its published life in 1859 as "Guerrier mossouto" in the French edition of E. Casalis' *Les Bassoutos* and appeared as "A Mosuto Warrior" in the English edition two years later.[10] In 1895, the heroic warrior's picture was titled "Menschenfresser" [Cannibal] in Merensky's *Die Menschenfresserei in Afrika*, the guise in which it is discussed in chapter 8 of this work [see p. 249].[11]

Less dramatically, the wood engraving entitled "Tanzende Heiden" [Dancing Heathens] discussed later in this chapter (which appeared in Theodor Wangemann's *Geschichte der Berliner Missionsgesellschaft in Südafrika*, published in 1877),[12] originally appeared in Dutch and German versions of Livingstone's *Narrative of an Expedition to the Zambezi*, published in various forms in 1865 and 1866. Here, the dancers were described as "Landeens, or Zulus, who lift tribute of the Portuguese at Senna exhibiting war exercises".[13]

GOD'S GARDENS IN THE HEATHEN WILDERNESS

Moreover, just as sketches or engravings – or their titles – could be utilised to capture "primitiveness", they could also be called into service to fulfil the opposite function. Just as the forest of Vendaland was not wild enough, so the mission stations were not controlled enough. Here too, drawings were used to convey ideas that photographing "reality" could not.

In the illustration of "Ha Tschewasse" [Ha-Tshivhase/Beuster/Maungani], two neat lines of trees (which still exist) border the road to the mission station [see Illustration 7].[14] In a manner reminiscent of German meadows, the ground is covered in low-growing grasses and ground cover. Missionary Beuster, in hat and frock-coat, walks down the road towards the viewer. Behind him walk two Africans, a man (in front) and a woman. Judging by their dress, they are "heathens" (perhaps following Beuster to conversion). The mission buildings stand neatly behind them. Behind all of this lies the rather neat-looking forest and impressively high and rocky Soutpansberg. The whole idea that is conveyed to the reader is one of neatness, control and tranquillity. Similar emotions are evoked by illustrations of "Tchakoma" [Tshakhuma] and "Georgenholtz" [see Illustrations 8 and 9].[15]

Thus, for the missionaries, Africans had to choose between the "darkness of the forest" and the light of "God's gardens in the heathen wilderness". As illustrated by textual comments about "the dark forests of Bawendaland and the dark hearts of the heathen Bawenda" and my comments on the illustration "Der Missionar im Palmenwalde", Africans were very much seen as an integral part of the forest which concealed and succoured them. This point is also clearly made in descriptions of Missionary Koen's first sight of Vendaland on his arrival in April 1876. In missionary description, upon entering this area, he found himself in

> a completely different area. A wonderful view from heavily-forested mountain ranges lay before them. In between were to be seen light-green mounds surrounded by meadows as fine as those in the Alps, and many crystal-clear streams and magnificent rivers rushing through the valleys. Here and there could be seen reddish-green spots – these were gardens, and not far from them could be seen the pale, pointed grass roofs of the villages set between the great plantations of bananas. Here and there, a herd of cattle grazed in the long grass.[16]

Because of Koen's "Germanised" world-view, and because the tractate from which this description is taken was intended for a German audience, this description of his first impressions of the environment draws on Alpine imagery familiar to Germans. Viewed from high in the mountains, and at first sight, the panoramic view that lay exposed before him was very beautiful, clear and filled with varying hues of colour – the "darkness" of the forest of missionary stereotypes is not visible from above, to experience it, one has to descend from the light and live in it. Also, even danger can have its beauty.

In the continuation of the missionary description of what Koen saw on his first contact with the Vhavenda, the people themselves in turn merge into the environment. In the eyes of the missionaries, as "primitive" people of the land, they are only revealed once their environment has been revealed. The first sighting of the Vhavenda occurs when they are engaged in *dzunde*, communal labour for the *khosi*. They are at work in the gardens. Although the comparison is not drawn directly, there is a strong implicit suggestion that these people are very different to German peasants. German peasants would have been seen as imposing order on the environment and working hard to make a living from it. The Vhavenda are portrayed as being much more dominated by the environment than their European counterparts. Rather than imposing order on it, they are its products. Because of the demands that the environment makes on them, they are strong. They wear only the minimum clothing, made from skin, thus displaying another core item of "primitive" life according to European thought. Skin garments, in European eyes, indicated an absence of cultural skills such as sewing and weaving:

> In one of these gardens, they saw for the first time the people of the tribe among whom ... [he] was to preach the gospel. There, black-brown men, handsome, strong figures, only clothed with a small piece of skin around the hips were hard at work with their broad hoes, while others were making music with their drums, pipes [flutes] and other instruments. Some were dancing, jumping together in time. A large group was also standing with the beer, valiantly drinking. After a while, some of the workers left the musicians and took hold of the hoes. Conspicuous were their shaved heads, on them only a patch of woolly hair was left standing. In such gardens, maize and so-called kaffir-corn, a variety of tall-growing millet, are grown, also pumpkins and beans. Usually it is the women who do most of the work.[17]

In less complimentary vein, Beuster also drew parallels between local people and their environment, and described their bodies. On 24 August 1881, Beuster, two Native Evangelists and two catechists set out on a reconnaissance journey to the northern parts of the country. This would take them up to the banks of the Limpopo River and would last until 1 September 1881.[18] Commenting on their journey northwards from the capital village of Thengwe on 27 August 1881, Beuster noted that:

> As soon as we left the capital village, we were continually presented with ever changing interesting sights. Here we found the first fruit-bearing Baobab and many Mahogany trees. A shower

of rain drove us into a village along the road. This village distinguished itself by its excessive dirt and disorder. The cattle kraal was in the middle of the people's huts. Because of the rain, the wet manure flowed from the kraal everywhere – through everything, into everything; one could hardly walk through there. The people living there were also not unlike their surroundings – they were rough, unobliging, dirty youths.[19]

The missionaries clearly had a special interest in people's bodies – whether "handsome" or "dirty" – because, for Christians, the body is God's temple. David Livingstone had set the tone when he hailed Commerce, Christianity and Civilisation as the true trinity of progress.[20] The Berliners may have been less enthusiastic supporters of commerce than Livingstone but they too were convinced that industrious labour and, to a lesser extent, trade in the products of this labour, lay at the heart of rebirth in Christ. Building on this foundation, they also shared the Scottish Missionary's conviction that Christianity was a way of life and that the Gospel asked for deep-reaching changes – changes demanding that the body and mind of each individual be reformulated according to contemporary European notions of propriety and moderation. Hence they entered into a war against nakedness or what they considered improper dress. Transformation had to be total – the ecology, the economy, social relationships and the people themselves.

Thus, when Beuster wrote an overview in the *Missions-Berichte* ("The Mission and Culture") in 1879, he focused on the opportunities for trade and industrious labour which the missionaries had opened up by constructing a wagon road to Ha-Tshivhase:

> What a source of income has opened up for the people of this area in that they can now sell the surplus of their crops – a short while ago these surpluses were as good as worthless. Now they can trade the surplus for valuable articles like salt, clothing, beads. By obtaining a market for the produce, the people are stimulated to greater industry and more diligence. It will be no exaggeration, if we estimate the amount of maize exported along this road in the year 1879 as 6000 bushels.[a] If we calculate further, the seller receives an amount of goods to the value of 4 Marks for each bushel, we get to a sum of 24 000 Marks worth of goods which were imported here and which were of benefit to the local population.[21]

According to this argument, it was also not only the local African population who benefited, directly or indirectly, from the road. Most of the surplus maize was bought or bartered by traders who made 100% profit on each trip.[22]

---

a. One bushel is about 36,5 dry litres – one big bucket.

Lastly, in Beuster's opinion, white inhabitants of the northern areas and even the British administration of the Transvaal had benefited from these developments. Prior to the opening of the trade with Vendaland, "the White population within a radius of five to six days travel ... had often found it necessary to go hungry." They were now able to "obtain a good proportion of their food requirements from this country". Even the administration had "to thank the German missionaries", since most of the grain being stockpiled for the approaching campaign against Sekhukhune had been bought in Vendaland:

> It might not be an exceptional work of culture, which I occasionally allow myself to represent. But in the face of the facts that this all has been brought about in a short space of time, through the work of a few missionaries, it could be regarded as proof that the missionaries are not just loafers – but that, by the sweat of their brows, they can lay claim to have the honour of being the champions of culture here.[23]

A further element of this "culture" which the missionaries saw themselves as introducing and fostering lay in a shift in focus away from pastoralism to agriculture or, were this to prove impossible, onto some other form of labour. Thus, writing on 24 October 1885, Beuster stated that he would very much like to be able to provide a significant number of jobs for local people. Having taken care of their needs for clothing and food, he would then be able to devote himself to tackling what he saw as their spiritual needs. However, he could not persuade people to grow produce, or collect wood or obtain hides from the *veld*, for local sale as there was no market – people were used to growing their own food or collecting what they needed from the *veld*. The solution, as he saw it, lay in the development of a local industry. He had seen the development of a coffee industry as a possible solution to these difficulties. This was nevertheless "rendered as good as impossible by a worm which eats up the roots till the trees die". Over time, since the establishment of the mission, he had employed close to a hundred labourers for varying periods of time. At the time of writing, he had three schoolboys and an adult Christian working for him. This meant that he had no other work available. However, until another industry was found, this type of employment would have to suffice. Commenting on this, the *Missions-Berichte* reported that "So, civilisation marches forward hand in hand with the mission, also in this far away region."[24]

The Berlin missionaries attached great importance to the transformation of the environment and economic life as a prerequisite for other changes they saw as being equally important, if not more important, stepping stones towards the ultimate aim of total transformation of the believer in Christ. In the missionary ideal, building on this foundation, changes in architecture in turn reflected changes in the covering of the body and the body itself. In turn, all of this reflected spiritual turning and spiritual change.

FASHIONING THE COLONIAL SUBJECT

Thus, building rectangular houses was not enough if they were still "built of poles like a hut".[25] Instead, when family finances allowed, they had to be built of stone and bricks, which could be collected or produced, and nails and other iron equipment, which had to be purchased (previously, all building materials could be collected or manufactured locally). Some of the difficulties involved in this are illustrated by Schwellnus' reports on building operations at Tshakhuma Mission Station during July 1885. At this stage, one house had just been rebuilt and five others were in the process of reconstruction. They had reportedly collapsed because of damage to their pole frames by termites. Schwellnus commented that:

> Because so many MaGwamba [Tsonga-Shangaan] have moved to here almost all the wood in this area, which can be used to build, has been chopped down. That is why these people formed bricks (they have learnt this craft here, from me) and tried to burn them with too little wood – this however did not work very well. They gathered stones from the veld for the foundations and started to build – I had to measure off the building sites for them. But the building of rectangular shaped houses with bricks was by no means a success. That is when I had to jump in to help them through this cultural battle – using my own hands. As I was helping the one, it was not good to desert the second; and the same went for the third, right up to the fifth. When the walls had been done, I had to instruct them on how to make rafters, one after the other. There was a shortage of nails needed for the rafters and more iron materials for the doors and more things like this – unfortunately this boiled down to money, which was needed to buy these things. That is when they had to be helped again, so that each would still experience the joy of putting a roof over the building. One brought eggs, the other coffee beans to trade with. Others did not even have these and asked for credit in this difficult cultural battle.[26]

Despite these difficulties and expenses, the converts were obviously extremely proud of their new dwellings. At least some of them had been assisted in purchasing the necessary equipment by trading coffee beans. Thus, by this stage, the missionaries must have showed the local people how to plant coffee trees and reap the beans, since coffee is not a "traditional" local brew.

A further crucial element of being reborn in Christ was the adoption of western dress. We have seen Mutshaeni's shame at being dressed in skins when he accompanied Beuster to Natal, and the trouble that his fellow Christians went to in clothing him in what they saw as the appropriate manner.²⁷ At the other end of the scale, one of the recurring themes of Makwarela Mphaphuli's story, discussed in chapter 8, is his sophisticated wearing of western dress, his possessing a square house and his use of other items of western material culture. These are interpreted as setting him apart from the mass of his subjects, and even his royal contemporaries. Before his "fall", he is seen as being "half-civilised" [semi-civilised]. Even more commendable from the point of view of the missionaries, he masters "the art of tailoring", presents "well-made European clothing" to catechists, and teaches others how to sew "decent clothes for themselves".²⁸ Some of the importance which the missionaries attached to the covering of the body with cloth clothing is also revealed by Frau Schwellnus' report to the wife of Mission Director Wangemann on her sewing club at Tshakhuma during the course of the year 1880:

> Our congregation is developing more and more. Nobody is walking about without clothing any longer. They work and so earn their clothing. I have my sewing classes every afternoon – for women, girls and also boys. Sometimes men also come to sew their trousers and coats. I have to help them with these. Our small congregation gives me great joy. Of the fifty members of the congregation, only one old grey-haired man, Nosa, goes about without clothes – he covers himself with a blanket only. All of them have to sew. I found that the traditional garments which they have sewn for themselves with great effort, are much more appreciated by them ... This year, several of our people have made big wheat [maize?] fields, so that they will be able to sell the wheat [maize?] later on to obtain money for clothing.ᵇ On the whole, the people are industrious. The heathens are amazed at their big gardens [fields] – they can hardly understand it, that one can work so much.ᶜ They say, the Christians have suddenly become rich people. But they will not admit [see] it, that the Christians are not sitting about and loafing like they are – they reckon, *Mynheer* has made the people rich.²⁹

The Comaroffs call this whole process of transformation the fashioning of the colonial subject.³⁰ This is well put. But it is important to stress that converts

---

b. She used the word *Weizen* [wheat]. However, wheat does not do well in Vendaland. I am sure she meant maize fields but used an image more familiar to Germans as a staple foodstuff.
c. In subsistence living, one just works enough to live – excess produce beyond that in private and royal grain-storage bins will just rot or be stolen. As everybody had enough to live on, nobody thought of selling off the excesses – who would buy if he already had? Buying was only done in times of drought, and then everybody in the area was in the same position. It was then a fairly recent development that the traders regularly came to buy produce and take it to other areas.

actually wanted to live in square houses and to wear western dress since this set them apart from the "heathens". This not only gave them a new sense of identity, and a sense of community related to this identity, but also enabled them to recognize each other. If a Christian entered a strange area, he or she would be able to use signifiers such as this to find fellow believers who would offer help, shelter and food. This adds another dimension to, rather than contradicts, our understanding of what the missionaries were setting out to do. In many cases, there was a coincidence, rather than a conflict, of desires. Problems would only present themselves if the convert or, perhaps, the pastor, wished to break the conventional mould.

It is also important to see that the missionary project did not only involve the clothing of the "heathen", but also the refashioning of their very bodies. Missionaries did not only fight nakedness, they also wanted people to do away with their habit of greasing and tattooing the skin, they wanted them to adopt new hair styles, they made them walk and sit in a different way, they taught them to differentiate between leisure and work, the public and the private, and they imposed new time schedules.[31]

In the present work, in missionary terms, the refashioning of bodies is seen as occurring on two main levels. On the first, there is maintaining the sanctity of the body by reserving it for only one partner through abandoning polygyny, refraining from taking part in war and the rituals surrounding warfare, protecting the bodies of twins who would otherwise have been killed (for Africans but not for the missionaries), refraining from polluting it through the drinking of alcohol and refraining from "heathen practices" in general. At a deeper level, not mutilating male genitals through circumcision, avoiding mutilating or excessively punishing the female body through initiation rituals are revealed as core elements of this process.[32] In addition, I would argue that the touchstone of all these techniques of the body, to use a term coined by Marcel Mauss, was the face, more particularly the eyes and their gaze.[33]

The reason for this stress put on the eyes lies in the fact that the missionaries thought as Europeans had thought for centuries: that the eyes are a mirror of the soul, expressing "man's" inner self. This idea has a long tradition harking back to the Romans and Greeks at least, but it gained prominence only in the early Modern period.[34] It also suited the Berliners' Pietist convictions. It is thus not surprising that they held on to this idea even though, in the eighteenth and nineteenth centuries, scientific thought moved away from it.[35]

Thus, a crucial part of remaking the convert was the remaking of his or her gaze. Eyes are prominent in most pictures in which people appear, more especially so in portraits, be they of individuals, families or other groups. The gaze of most people in early photographs is stern and staring, rare are the pictures with people smiling and laughing. This is first and foremost a product of technology – in the early days of photography, people had to hold still for quite a while in front of the camera and look fixedly with eyes wide open before they could relax again. No wonder then that they got this stern or even anxious expression on their face. Studio photographers knew about the problem. One response that they adopted was that of pointing their cameras at other parts of the body than the eyes – the bust if the person to be photographed was a woman or, if it was a man, the hands, often holding some paraphernalia or tool as symbol of his profession and social status. Alternatively, they tried to soften the expression of those photographed by means of carefully retouching the prints.

However, that there is more to the stern gaze than a simple technical problem. This is clearly demonstrated by the fact that it is carried over in sketches and other forms of illustration during the period. A good example from Vendaland is the "Sketch of Bawenda [Vhavenda] Children" appearing in Gründler's *Geschichte der Bawenda-Mission in Nord-Transvaal* [see Illustration 10].[36] The four children are suitably demure in dress and demeanour. All are smartly, but conservatively, dressed. The eldest boy seated in front wears a sedate jacket and tie. His compatriots wear demure jackets or tops influenced by Prussian clerical and children's dress. Despite their humble and devout expressions, it is their eyes that dominate the picture and draw the attention of the viewer. In marked contrast, viewing the photograph of a (non-Christian) "Transvaal Native Belle" appearing in Wessmann's *The Bawenda of the Spelonken*, it is her naked breasts, rather than her eyes, that attract the viewer. In fact, her eyes are almost closed and look away to the side of the viewer [see Illustration 11].[37]

So, rather than focusing on the technical difficulties involved in taking the photographs, I would argue that these eyes in photographs and other illustrations of Christians partly document certain contemporary ideas about what a decent person had to look like. Also, although they may misrepresent the feelings and identities of those pictured, they nonetheless had an influence on their self-image, and that of their peers as well. Establishing a new convention of self-representation, these portraits helped to mould people. Thus, photography and other forms of portraiture developed into an agent of change, in Africa no less than in Europe. They were helping to personalise men and women, giving each of them what only royals and other members of the elite had formerly had a right to, namely the right to a unique body and a face of their own. In democratising the face, portraiture was helping to create individuals.[38] In marked contrast, images of "heathens" continued to objectify them, depriving them of individual personality and portraying them as representing specific "types" – one may say, almost as specimens.

"HEATHENS"

Against this ideological background, returning to the description of Koen's first impressions of Vendaland and the Vhavenda on pp. 150–151, while the missionaries were able to appreciate the beauty of the people they encountered in the fields, they could not help but be surprised that the hoeing went hand in hand with music, dancing and drinking, turning a pastoral idyll into a festival. Since daily life looked so peaceful, tempting and Arcadian, the missionaries had to look elsewhere to better construct the African "heathens" as dangerous and depraved people. As is vividly demonstrated in chapter 8, and other descriptions of warfare in this work, what they looked for they found in Vhavenda warfare and the festivities and rituals with which the end of a raid was celebrated. Describing in graphic detail what they saw of these occasions, the missionaries focused all their attention on what people did with their own bodies and with those of their enemies, including hearsay and moral judgements in their texts.

Thus, in describing Vhavenda warfare, Missionary Reinhold Wessmann noted that:

> A war is never finished until the enemy's capital has been destroyed and the chief been killed, or has taken flight from the country; for the conclusion of peace is unknown to the Bawenda. The raids mostly take place in moonlight nights after midnight, when the enemy have grown tired and are in deep sleep. Has a raid succeeded? The victors celebrate their victory on returning; on these occasions the big war-drum is audible throughout the country. Occasionally a killed enemy is taken home by the victors and used as medicine, as they think that tasting his flesh will make them strong and give them advantages. Usually the flesh is mixed with beef. Cowardly as they are, they are also cruel, and often helpless women and children are their only targets; and when their wild nature has been awakened they allow their evil passions to run loose. A spectacularly brave warrior who succeeds in doing some deed of valour, such as murder, receives as a reward a small dignity, such as ruler over some villages, or the chief presents him with a woman.[39]

However, as with the landscape, it was difficult to capture these scenes – and the emotions that they engendered – photographically. The photograph of a warrior that appears in the albums of Missionary Westphal [see Illustration 12] is obviously posed and is far from terrifying.[40] An apparently amused crowd of onlookers dressed in items of western clothing peep into the photograph from the bushes on the right. It is probable that the subject was a Christian convert who dressed up specially for the shoot. Perhaps because this photograph was very obviously staged, it does not appear to have been published at any stage.

Moving to dancing, apparently because of the difficulties in capturing movement on photographic plates during the late nineteenth and early twentieth centuries and the amateur status of the missionary photographers, the photograph of a *domba* dance appearing in Wessmann's (1908) work *The Bawenda of the Spelonken* looks remarkably static and fails to capture the sinuous and sensual python-like movements of the dance [see Illustration 13].[41]

This dance, first illustrated by the missionaries, has become an icon for the Vhavenda appearing in tourist brochures, posters and academic works.[42] More recently, it has been illustrated in Peter Magubane's *Vanishing Cultures*.[43] It was also performed at the first Soweto Awards ceremony in February 2001, at which achievers who had their roots in Soweto were honoured. A photograph captioned the "Snake Dance" illustrated the newspaper report.[44] Similarly, the *tshikona* dance performed on solemn and special occasions – in particular for royalty – involves the combined music of reed flutes, and *ngoma*, *thungwa* and *mirumba* drums and is extremely energetic and loud.[45] However, the photograph appearing as "Tshikona Dance in Ngovela at Ha Tschewasse" in the Berlin Mission Northern Transvaal albums and "Tshikona dance" in M. Wilde's *Schwarz und Weiss* is extremely static and fails to capture the circling, advancing and retreating movements of the dancer-musicians [see Illustration 14].[46] Indeed, while clearly photographed and pleasing to the eye, due to the limited photographic technology, the dancers are arranged as stiffly as Prussian soldiers on parade.

Faced with this "tameness" of the "heathens" in photographs such as these, in order to show what they saw as the "wildness" and "satanic" nature of their dancing, the editors of the *Missions-Berichte* appropriated an image that they titled "*Tanzende Heiden*" [Dancing Heathens]. We have already seen how this had its origins in Livingstone's *Narrative of an Expedition to the Zambezi* and also appeared in Wangemann's *Geschichte der Berliner Missionsgesellschaft in Südafrika* [see Illustration 15].[47]

Village scenes were much easier to stage for photographs. An image entitled "Bawenda Huts" appeared in the Berlin Mission Society's history of its activities in Vendaland published in 1897 [see Illustration 16].[48] Two years later, the same picture was published as "Natives (Heathens) in [the] Transvaal" in the *Missions-Berichte*.[49] In this publication, it was annotated. Unfortunately, the surviving copy of the reports was not in good condition and could not be reproduced. Thus, the copy from Gründler has been included in the present publication. In the *Missions-Berichte*, the woman kneeling on the left is labelled as "woman". Moving across to the right, labels are "house", "grinding-stone", "women", "baskets", "water-pot", "women and children", "men" and "house".

The image, and its annotations, could have appeared in any of the standard ethnographic works of the time (or, indeed, for most of the following century). Draped in blankets and beads, the women are dressed suitably "traditionally". While some are barebreasted, they are less noticeably so than in many non-missionary sources. The children wear little more than beads and coverings for their genitalia. The "huts" and household implements seen in the photograph are also suitably "traditional". However, much as this "tradition" could be staged, modernity still crept in – as with the concealed onlookers in the photograph of the warrior, the men who are so far in the background as to be almost unnoticeable are wearing items of Western clothing.

Images discussed thus far were viewed by the missionaries as being "public" – capable of being disseminated to the friends and supporters of the mission and the wider public, if they were of sufficiently high artistic merit. However, the missionaries' deep interest in aspects of "heathen" life and tradition led to a situation where some images were deemed as "private" – not suitable for consumption outside of the controlled environment of the missionary's home or the mission seminary. These presumably fulfilled the exoticist longings of individual missionaries or were used for instructional purposes – as a kind of "know your enemy" exercise. Thus, an illustration about the use of a hoe to symbolise a bride from the outstation Ha-Begwa that appeared in the album of Missionary Westphal was given the explanatory label: "Offering the bride (hoe-handle) by the Makhadzi (head woman of the extended family) for a deceased young man, because he had not yet looked for a bride." However, to the best of my knowledge, this was not published anywhere in missionary sources [see Illustration 17].[50]

The missionaries nevertheless appear to have decided that it was acceptable for "private" images to be published in "scientific" anthropological sources and made these available to Stayt for use in his work *The Bavenda* (1931). According to the anthropologist, any young man over the age of puberty who died before being given a wife was "a poor foolish fellow, having left the world ignorant of the all-important subject of sex and parenthood, and dying before he has fulfilled the purpose for which he was born". Unless pacified, it was possible that he would "become a source of endless trouble to his lineage". So he was provided with an old hoe handle. A cotton string was tied near the hole. This represented the waistband of a wife, while the hole represented her vagina. The handle was then fixed by means of four pegs in a well-cleared open space at a fork in a path approaching the village where the young man's spirit could clearly see it. The handle faced towards the spirit as it approached the village, while the pegs were made of the *tshiralala* (from the verb *u ralala*, "to wander about") or the *tshilivhalo* (from the verb *u livhala*, "to forget") trees. These were then tied to the head by means of a string made of wild cotton "treated with a mixture made from the roots of the *vhulivhadza* (from u *livhadza*, to make forget) and the *mpeta* (to dissolve or tie up), with powder from the hedgehog quill, *thoni* (bashfulness)." According to Stayt, these preparations were "all used to confuse the young man's spirit so that it" would "forget its anger, become bashful and ashamed, and run away before it reached the village". The hoe was fixed by a girl who was not a sibling. After this, a woman from the lineage of the deceased, generally the *makhadzi*, poured beer into the hole in the hoe, saying: "To-day we have found you a wife; the wife is here. Do not worry us any more. If you are annoyed with us, come here." This reportedly satisfied the young man's spirit for ever.

While similar in many ways, the explanation that I was given by a member of the extended Mphephu royal family, *Vho* Lettie Mphephu-Nengudza, was far more sexually explicit. She explained that the photograph depicted the *makhadzi* pouring the viscous white residue obtained from grinding grass (*mufhoho*). The hoe handle represents the woman, the slot where the hoe would normally go through the vagina and the peg the penis of the deceased man. The white residue represents the semen.[52]

Both of these explanations are sufficient to explain why the missionaries do not appear to have published the photographs in mission publications but saw them as acceptable for publication in Stayt's work.

CHRISTIANS

In opposition to what the missionaries saw as these secret customs, Christians could be shown involved in their daily task and trades, preparing to set out to spread the Gospel, or at high-points in their lives and the lives of their communities.

Miryam, the wife of the Evangelist Nathanael, one of the first and best-loved assistants to the missionaries in Vendaland, is hard at work in the photograph of her that appears in Westphal's album [see Illustration 18].[53] As a Christian, she does not wear the bracelets and anklets (*vhukunda tshotshane* and *vhukunda ha mulenzhe*), given to a bride and wife by her husband's family to mark significant events, that a married "heathen" woman would usually wear with pride. Her children are all dressed in, at least cast-off, Western clothing. Perhaps she and the children are not dressed in their best because this is no special occasion – she is involved in cooking maize porridge. Unlike the case with non-royal "heathens", all people appearing in the photograph are individually named, attributing to each of them a history and a personal identity. The inscription in the album reads: "Miryam with the young Nathanael on her back cooks for the builder of the chapel of Old-Georgenholtz. Mashudu, next to her, holds the flour-basket [basket of maize]. Petrus, with his hand below his knee. In the background, Asaf, the oldest son."[54]

The photograph of "The Village-Tailor of Beuster", appearing in Westphal's album, clearly reveals what the missionaries would have perceived to be the diligence and self-reliance of the converts. In the inscription accompanying the image, we are told that he "uses his artistically put-together trousers as a recommendation for his art that he learned in Johannesburg" [see Illustration 19].[55]

Also ready for anything are the so-called "Native Evangelists" of Tshakhuma, pictured in the Northern Transvaal albums of the Berlin Mission and M. Wilde's *Schwarz und Weiss* grouped in front of a paw-paw tree [see Illustration 20].[56] As we have already seen, people grew food and fruit crops close to their houses prior to the extension of white settlement into Vendaland. However, friends and colleagues of mine who grew up on mission stations, or who were born into second- or third-generation Christian families, state that they always plant fruit trees wherever they stay and that this is a habit learned from their parents or grandparents who, in turn, learned it from missionaries. The idea behind this was to assist in making people self-sufficient. Paw-paws are also tropical fruits and, by their shape and the exuberance of their seeds, could be said to call to mind tropical fecundity.

Because of the grouping of people around it, the tree is very much a part of this photograph, almost like a ninth person. It emphasises the tropical setting while the usefulness of its fruits echoes the usefulness of the Evangelists. They are neatly dressed in western suits of varying degrees of shabbiness. At least one of the men is barefoot.

In Wessman's *The Bawenda of the Spelonken* and a file of photographs from Gertrudsburg in the archives of the Berlin Mission, two photographs are labelled "AND NOW: Converts to Civilization in the Zoutpansberg" and "Gertrudsburg, 1926, Candidates for Confirmation, Pentecost, 1925" respectively [see Illustrations 21 and 22].[57] These clearly illustrate the kind of men and women that the missionaries were setting out to create. The first of these, appears below the picture of the "THEN: Native Dance in Bawendaland some years ago" [see Illustration 13]. The picture is dominated by two rows of women, one seated on the ground and the other seated on chairs behind them. All of them wear headcoverings and eight out of the eleven wear white dresses symbolic of purity and humility. The three who do not wear white are nevertheless soberly dressed. Slightly in front of, but next to, the front row of women sit four young children and an older boy. A child's head also peeps out from behind the row of women sitting on the ground. Girls wear white and boys wear small suits or other items of western clothing. The women are clearly identified as the chaste mothers and nurturers of the children. This was how they were supposed to be in missionary thinking, which was strictly gendered in agreement with contemporary European bourgeois values. Two rows of largely sombre men, obviously clad in their Sunday and high holiday best stand protectively behind the women. The man in their middle is the most distinguished looking of the men, drawing the gaze of the viewer to him. He in particular, and the men in general, draw the viewer to their eyes.

Similar feelings are evoked even more powerfully by the photograph of the "Candidates for confirmation". Seen through missionary eyes, the women are suitably demure in dress and posture, the well-dressed young men exude confidence in the clear focused gaze of the convert and in their clothing and accessories, their sitting positions and the way that they hold their hats, some with their arms crossed, others with joined hands. Both of these photographs leave the viewer in no doubt that these people have been completely remade as Christians. To put it differently: the camera eye furthered the development of the Christian eye/I.

Remaking converts – and the environment that they lived in – lay at the heart of the missionary endeavour. To appropriate one of Rod Giblett's phrases, the "dark and dank ... 'nether regions'"[58] of the Vhavenda and Vendaland had to be brought under control – by being hidden beneath neatly-cut western clothing or cut and pruned into submission by the shears of diligent missionaries and eager converts. Just as skin clothing – symbols of nature and "heathenism/barbarism" – would give way to neat dresses and suits, so the "dark forests" would have to be transformed into "God's gardens". In order to make all of this possible, the upper echelons of the Mission Society, and the wider circle of friends of the mission in Germany, had to be convinced that the labour was desperately needed. Wealthy patrons had to be persuaded to give bountifully. Parishioners in the smallest parishes had to be persuaded to put their spare change into the mission collection boxes (suitably embellished with mechanised models of small black boys who nodded their heads submissively in thanks when coins were given to them). While this could be achieved easily in written texts, it frequently needed to be either embellished or pruned if suitable illustrations were to be called into service. Moreover, by attempting to remake Africa and Africans in their own image, and with their own gaze, the missionaries were enabling themselves to exert control over the unknown, to carve a niche for themselves in what they saw as the dangers and uncertainties of late nineteenth-century Vendaland.

In doing this, the missionaries were not operating in a vacuum. Their power to bring about the changes that they desired was severely constrained by the fact that they were operating in an area which had not yet been brought under colonial domination. Although under pressure from the expanding authority of the South African Republic, power in the area was vested in the local deity, other supernatural beings, the local rulers and local medico-religious practitioners. In their terms, if missionaries were to succeed, they had to wean people away from the authority and influence of these. In order to do so, they had to understand the nature of the society they were seeking to transform.

1. This chapter draws on A. Kirkaldy, "'Dark Forests and Dark Hearts': Berlin Missionary Constructions of Vendaland, c. 1870–1900", in *Psychology Bulletin*, 9 (2), December 1999, pp. 75–105; and A. Kirkaldy and A. Wirz (a) "Picturing the soul" & (b) "Writing the soul in light: missionary encounters in late-nineteenth century Vendaland, Blouberg and Beyond", *SHS Monograph Series*, 1 (1), Thohoyandou, School of Human Sciences, University of Venda for Science and Technology, October 2000.

2. C.M. Geary (a) "Photographs as Materials for African History: Some Methodological Considerations, in *History in Africa*, 13 (1986), pp. 89–116 & (b) *Images from Bamum. German Colonial Photography at the Court of King Njoya, Cameroon, West Africa*,

1902–1915, Washington DC, Smithsonial Institution Press, 1988 & (c) "Impressions of the African Past: Interpreting Ethnographic Photographs from Cameroon", in *Visual Anthropology*, 3/2–2 (1990), pp. 289–315 & (d) "Missionary Photography. Private and Public Readings", in *African Arts*, 24/4 (1991), pp. 48–59, 98–100; and P. Jenkins, "In the Eye of the Beholder: An Exercise in the Interpretation of Two Photographs Taken in Cameroon Early in This Century", in D. Henige and T.C. Mc Caskie (eds.), *West African Economic and Social History. Studies in memoriam of Marion Johnson*, Madison, University of Wisconsin Press, 1990, pp. 93–103.

3. *BMB*, 1893, p. 433.
4. W. Gründler, *Geschichte der Bawenda-Mission in Nord-Transvaal*.
5. I would like to thank the Johannesburg-based photographer Mike Goldblatt for clarifying issues of composition here for me.
6. Berlin Mission Archives, Berlin: Album Nr. XXIX, Nord-Transvaal, Nr. 15197.
7. *Der Bawenda-Freund*, Nr. 3, 1916.
8. See A. Kirkaldy, "Makoarele's return to 'the darkness of heathenism': *Khosi* Makwarela and the Berlin Missionaries in Vendaland, c. 1876–1897", unpublished paper presented to the Second CSSALL Interdisciplinary Conference, University of Durban-Westville, 26 September 1997, p. 132.
9. *BMB*, 1880, p. 409.
10. E. Casalis, *Les Bassoutos*, Paris, Ch, Meyrueis, 1859, p. 66; J. Nisbet, *The Basutos*, London, 1861, p. 63. See R.F. Kennedy (comp.), *Catalogue of Prints in the Africana Museum and in books in the Strange Collection of Africana in the Johannesburg Public Library up to 1870, Volume One*: A–K, Johannesburg, Africana Museum, 1975, C48.
11. A. Merensky, *Die Menschenfresserei in Afrika*, Missionsschriften für Kinder Nr. 25, Berlin, Buchhandlung der Berliner evangelischen Missionsgesellschaft, n.d. (1895), back cover. In discussing the same picture in 1983, Delius argued that it probably was initially intended to depict a southern Sotho warrior. However, in the same way that the missionaries used a drawing of Tswana society to depict Pedi people working the land, they frequently used the "Warrior ... to depict Pedi society". (See etchings entitled "Working the land" and "Warrior" between pp. 180 and 181 of P. Delius, *The Land Belongs To Us*.) More recently, in the *Reader's Digest Illustrated History of South Africa*, it is captioned: "An Engraving of a Sotho armed with club, spear and shield. In fact, warriors preferred more than one spear" (C. Saunders [ed.]) *Reader's Digest Illustrated History of South Africa: The Real Story*, Cape Town, Reader's Digest Association, 1988, p. 90).
12. T. Wangemann, *Geschichte der Berliner Missionsgesellschaft in Südafrika*, Berlin, Evangelisches Missionshaus, 1877.
13. David and Charles Livingstone (a) *Narrative of an Expedition to the Zambezi*, London, Murray 1865, p. 36 & (b) (same title), New York, Harper & Brothers, 1866, p. 153 & (c) *Neue Missionsreisen in Süd-Afrika*, Two volumes in one, Jena und Leipzig, Hermann Gostenoble 1866, Volume 2, p. 38. See R.F. Kennedy (comp.), *Catalogue of Prints in the Africana Museum, Volume Two*, L 603.
14. *BMB*, 1886, p. 401.
15. *BMB*, 1887, p. 201; 1894, p. 365.
16. G. Sauberzweig-Schmidt, *Klaas Kuhn*, p. 11.
17. *Ibid*. pp. 11–12.
18. *BMB*, 1882, pp. 427–436.
19. *Ibid*. p. 429.
20. R. Mackenzie, *David Livingstone: The Truth behind the Legend*, Fourth Edition, Chinhoyi, Fig Tree Publications Zimbabwe, 1997, pp. 17, 29, 47, 143, 188, 190, 196, 291, 293.
21. *BMB*, 1880, p. 347.
22. *Ibid*. pp. 347–348.
23. *Ibid*. p. 348.
24. *BMB*, 1886, pp. 421–422; 1888, p. 517 (quotation).
25. *BMB*, 1886, p. 361.

26. *Ibid.* pp. 361–362.
27. See p. 57.
28. See especially pp. 249–250, 251.
29. *BMB*, 1881, pp. 121–122.
30. J.L. Comaroff & J. Comaroff, *Of Revelation and Revolution: The Dialectics of Modernity on a South African Frontier*, Volume Two, Chicago, University of Chicago Press, 1997, Chapter 5.
31. A. Kirkaldy and A. Wirz (a) "Picturing the soul", p. 25 & (b) "Writing the soul in light", p. 30.
32. See chapter 7.
33. M. Mauss, "Les techniques du corps", in *Journal de psychologie normale et pathologique*, 32, 1935, pp. 271–293. Thanks to Prof. Albert Wirz for this reference and that which follows.
34. Cf. Jean-Jaques Courtine and C. Haroche, *Histoire du visage, XVIe – début XIXe siècle*, Paris, Rivage/Histoire, 1988, for a succinct overview.
35. See A. Kirkaldy and A. Wirz (a) "Picturing the soul", pp. 25–26 & (b) "Writing the soul in light", p. 31.
36. W. Gründler, *Geschichte der Bawenda-Mission in Nord-Transvaal*, p. 83.
37. R. Wessmann, *The Bawenda of the Spelonken*, facing p. 11.
38. Cf. D. Le Breton, *Des Visages. Essai d'anthropologie*, Paris, Éditions A.M. Métaillié, 1992, pp. 45–52.
39. R. Wessmann, *The Bawenda of the Spelonken*, p. 112.
40. (Untitled and undated in original) Berlin Mission Archives, Berlin: Album, Vendaland von Missionar G. Westphal, Nr. 8632. Westphal was stationed in Vendaland from 1912. This photograph seems to have been taken at Georgenholtz, where he was stationed from September 1919. [Acta der Berliner Missions-Gesellschaft betreffend Personalia: Westphal, Gotthardt, Abt.II, Fach II 20, Nr. 5A, Angefangen 1902, Beendigt 1929.] The only photographs dated in the Westphal album are dated to 1922, 1924, 1927 and 1928.
41. R. Wessmann, *The Bawenda of the Spelonken*, facing p. 33.
42. For tourist brochures, see, for example, B. Johnson Barker, G. Maclay and A. Steyn, *Off the Beaten Track: Selected Day Drives in Southern Africa*, Cape Town, AA The Motorist Publications, 1996, p. 16; Republic of Venda, *Venda Land Of Legend*, Sibasa, Venda Tourism, n.d. p. 3; and Republic of Venda, *Venḓa Travelogue*, Sibasa, Department of Information and Broadcasting, n.d. p. 3. For academic works, see, for example, John Blacking (a) *The Initiation Cycle: vhusha, tshikanda and domba*, at http://era.anthropology.ac.uk/Era_R...agirls/Introduction/I_GIS_Text.html, accessed 29 September 2000 (follow through links) & (b) Domba, at http://era.anthropology.ac.uk/Era_R...girls/Domba.School/D_00_Opening.html, accessed 21 September 2000 (follow through links); W.D. Hammond-Tooke (ed.), *The Bantu-Speaking Peoples of Southern Africa*, London, Routledge & Kegan Paul, Second Edition, 1974, facing p. 235; and H.A. Stayt, *The Bavenda*, facing p. 114.
43. P. Magubane, *Vanishing Cultures*, Cape Town, Struik, 1998. See especially pp. 83, 85.
44. *The Star* 26 February 2001, p. 3 (includes photograph captioned "Snake Dance" by Alf Kumalo).
45. Personal experience and N.J. van Warmelo, *Venda Dictionary: Tshivenda English*, Pretoria, J.L. van Schaik, 1989, p. 406.
46. Berlin Mission Archives, Berlin: Album Nr. XXIX, Nord-Transvaal, Nr. 15188; M. Wilde, *Schwarz und Weiss: Bilder von einer Reise durch das Arbeitsgebiet der Berliner Mission in Südafrika von M. Wilde, Missionsinspektor*, Berlin, Buchhandlung der Berliner evangelischen Missionsgesellschaft, 1913, p. 113.
47. T. Wangemann, *Geschichte der Berliner Missionsgesellschaft in Südafrika*. Also in the private collection of Dr Ulrich van der Heyden, Seminar für Afrikawissenschaften, Prenzlauer Promenade 149–152, 13189 Berlin.
48. W. Gründler, *Geschichte der Bawenda-Mission in Nord-Transvaal*, p. 63.
49. *BMB*, 1899, p. 657.
50. Berlin Mission Archives, Berlin: Album, Vendaland von Missionar G. Westphal, Nr. 8616.

51. H.A. Stayt, *The Bavenda*, pp. 241–242; facing p. 242 (illustration).
52. Personal communication, *Vho* Lettie Mphephu-Nengudza (sister of the late *Khosi* P.R. Mphephu), 23 June 1999.
53. Berlin Mission Archives, Berlin: Album, Vendaland von Missionar G. Westphal, Nr. 8620.
54. *Ibid.*
55. *Ibid.* Nr. 8530.
56. M. Wilde, *Schwarz und Weiss*, p. 188. Also appears in Berlin Mission Archives, Berlin: Album XXIX, Nord Transvaal 1, Nr. 27.
57. R. Wessmann, *The Bawenda of the Spelonken*, facing p. 33; Berlin Mission Archives, Berlin: Unlabelled File [Gertrudsburg], Nr. 1134 respectively.
58. R. Giblett, "Cities and Swamp Settling: decolonizing wetlands", in Michèle Drouart (ed.), "Postcolonial Fictions", *SPAN: Journal of the South Pacific Association for Commonwealth Literature and Language Studies*, Number 36 (1993), electronic edition at http://humpc61.murdoc.edu.au/cntinuum/ltserv/SPAN/36/giblett.html, p.1, accessed 10 February 1999, p. 5.

CHAPTER 6
Ethnographies of power

The missionaries recorded a surprising amount about local belief structures and the nature of local society in Vendaland. On the one hand, this was used to show their principals in Germany, and the wider community of friends of the mission, just how desperately important it was (in their terms) to save the "heathens", both for Christ and from themselves. However, it is also clear that they treated this collection of information as a form of intelligence gathering in their fight to win people away from "tradition" (many elements of which they saw as synonymous with "darkness" and "superstition") and remodel them as Christians. In modern military terms, what they were attempting to do was build up a corpus of "know-your-enemy" literature to assist them in their struggle against local ideologies, local social and political structures and what they interpreted as the power of Satan.

The present-day reader is situated in a different ideological background (and a different era) to the missionaries, and may not realise that missionaries viewed Satan as a very real, and an extremely active, enemy. This is clearly indicated in Missionary Karl Endemann's account in the *Missionsberichte* ("The Religion of the Bassuto [Basotho – Pedi]"), written from the newly-founded mission station of Phatametsane in 1863. He argued that:

> Their religion is a religion of the Devil ... Of God they know nothing ... It is human nature to need faith. They must have something supernatural upon which they can hang their hearts; and if it is not Jehovah, then it is Satan and all the forces of darkness.[1]

It will become clear that the attitudes of these pioneers of the Berlin Mission in the northern areas were carried over into Vendaland by those who followed them. At various times, the *malombo*, the *thondo* and various forms of female and male initiation and circumcision were all described as being satanically-inspired. In contrast to this, there were also elements of local belief structures which the missionaries felt that they could use as laying a foundation for conversion. For example, they saw local conceptions of a supreme being and the local belief that a founding ancestor would return to bring peace to the world as an ideal starting point for attempts to wean the local people away from their existing beliefs to the Christian God. However, even in engaging with beliefs such as these, the missionaries still believed that they would first have to attack the religious foundations of society. In their analysis, only then would it be possible to activate and build on their potential.

THE SUPREME BEING AND OTHER SUPERNATURAL ENTITIES

In a report compiled in 1878 and published in the following year, Beuster recorded that the supreme deity in Vendaland was Raluvhimba, the Father of Holiness or the Holy Father. He was "the active, all-creating and maintaining god through whom the trees, shrubs and everything were created and are maintained even now". His dwelling lay at Mubvumela Mountain in the lands of the Karanga people in Zimbabwe. He was also known as *Muhali-muhulu* or *Mudzimu muhulu* (in other words, the Great God).[2]

The missionary seems to have been unaware that there was no "real" or "pure" Vhavenda religion which was identical for all the groups living in Vendaland. Rather, as Dederen has emphasised, just like any religion, it was "a combination, an amalgam of contributions from a variety of groups".[3] Thus, Beuster did not mention that Raluvhimba was called Mwali by some groups. Raluvhimba was the name given to this God by the people of the eastern parts (the VhaMbedzi), who had come down in small groups before the VhaSenzi and settled in Vhumbedzi. This was the area where Beuster was working. The VhaSenzi groups (the Ramabulanas, Tshivhases and Mphaphulis) knew him as Mwali. In addition, Beuster was not yet able to comment on the fact that Mubvumela, "the place of the white seringa [*Kirkia acuminata*]", is in the Belingwe Province of Zimbabwe – apparently Mount Belingwe. Groups of VhaLemba still have a yearly pilgrimage to this place to worship there.[4] His linguistic abilities also seem not yet to have extended to understanding that *Muhali* is the name of respect given to a *khosi*; *muhulu* means "great one". So *Muhali-muhulu* means "Great chief". In addition, in informal discussions, the Reverend Martin Moremi (Department of Religious Studies, UNIVEN) emphasised that the existence of Raluvhimba demonstrates the existence of a local belief in a unitary supreme being. The fact that both the VhaMbedzi and the VhaSenzi worshipped a single deity also caused great confusion when the missionaries spoke of the One God, the Creator of the Universe. While the missionaries preached about God (the God of the Bible), the Vhavenda were thinking of God (Raluvhimba/Mwali) and for years they talked at cross-purposes without even realising it. This was even more complicated by the fact that the story of the VhaSenzi migration was so similar to that of the Exodus of the Israelites (see the story of the *Ngoma lungundu* on p. 18).

Beuster also noted that many local people falsely identified Raluvhimba as Satan.[5] While he did not comment on this, this situation seems to have arisen from the local idea of God as something to be feared (in a similar sense to the Old Testament concept of fearing God). The missionaries brought with them a new concept – a God who could be loved by his subjects. As a counter to this, they brought the idea of Satan, the evil one; the one who sought to harm and destroy people; the one whom people feared. For local people, respect was synonymous with fear – Raluvhimba had to be respected, in other words, he was feared. He provided everything good to those who feared him, but he destroyed those who did not please him. So when the missionaries spoke about Satan, the one who was able to destroy everyone, the local people immediately related him to Raluvhimba.

In the interests of getting to know this competing power more deeply, Beuster also recorded some of the "stories of wonders" surrounding the God. He described how he had been told that pilgrims to the mountain where Raluvhimba lived heard "much whistling and roaring, many shouts and screams and noises which sound like pieces of metal being beaten together or like the rattling of chains". This was often interspersed with (mostly unintelligible) words and phrases. According to the missionary's informants, Raluvhimba sometimes also moved around, settling in a cave at Luvhiumbi behind the capital village of the Tshivhases. Then one heard the same noises as were heard at the Mubvumela Mountain. It was reportedly said that: "one hears him talk inside the house and yet one does not see him" or "he speaks from a tree or from a post and yet he is never seen". When the pilgrims to his mountain asked him for sustenance for their return journey, he reportedly told them exactly where they would find the game which would serve them as food. "Up to now, they have always found the game at the designated place – it does not run away and they club it to death with a stick."[6]

Given his Western rationalist background, and the fact that he was describing a competitor for power, Beuster could not afford to even give the impression that he was attaching any truth to these accounts. Rather, he described how, in "reality", people were being deceived and exploited. Noting that these were "the stories the people generally tell", his report continued by stating that the people who had actually been sent by Tshivhase to take the annual offerings to the sacred mountain usually denied that they had ever seen anything miraculous. Offerings, both in Zimbabwe and in Vendaland, were accepted by an official called "the son of Raluvhimba". In Beuster's interpretation, the holder of this office knew: "how to use the ignorance of the heathens for his benefit ... [performing] this or that trick every now and again, to maintain his credibility and to keep up appearances".[7]

Understandably, allegations of chicanery were not enough to wean people away from their God. Even before the establishment of a missionary presence in Vendaland, *Khosi* Makhado had made it clear that he and his people viewed the white God with great suspicion. In reporting on his meeting with Makhado in October 1870, Beyer had noted that:

> What I like especially about this nation is that it is not indifferent to the Word of God like the people of Blauberg and elsewhere, instead it contradicts or agrees. Several times during the sermon, there on the mountain, the king himself, or others, voiced contradictions. Once the king said: "Yes, if we could see that one of our people, a black person like us, came down from

heaven and brought us the message, then we would all agree and believe; why should we accept the Word of God from a white man?"[8]

A crucial question indeed.

Similarly, in reporting on events during the year 1889, Wessmann recorded that he had visited *Khosi* Mutele, one of the lesser *mahosi*, at his mountain capital. Here he had found Daniel, one of the congregation members from Georgenholtz, who was preaching in the area. In reporting on his preaching journey, Daniel had informed the missionary that:

> A chief, called Maschiki [Matsheke] stood up excitedly during his [Daniel's] sermon and said: "Our God is Ralowimba [Raluvhimba] (the God of the Bakhalanga [VhaKaranga]). Should you despise our God, I will kill you here, on this spot." Filled with anger, he had already raised his spear, and now threatened to stab Daniel. "I am not afraid of your threats", Daniel said. "You will be able to kill my body, but you will not be able to kill my soul – that goes to God." But the Chief could not be pacified, he continued with his threats and finally robbed our Daniel of a he-goat [as a fine].[9]

In addition to the supreme being, local people either remembered or showed respect to a variety of other supernatural beings. Beuster also engaged a number of these in his report. While he referred to them all as "gods", only one of them seems to have held a form of divine status. This was Khuswane, whom Beuster described as "the father of Ralowimba", the creator of "everything that is pleasant and beautiful" and the original source of knowledge about "all the vital crafts". Once he had completed his task, "he withdrew himself – he has no abode amongst the people and has become an unknown god".[10] It is difficult to comment more fully on Khuswane as he retired after fulfilling his vaguely-defined role in creation. He then committed the ruling of the world, and further acts of creation, into the hands of Raluvhimba. In the scant information available, no mention is made of any form of worship being offered to him. Since he did not interfere in the lives of mortals, he was neither feared nor respected. The only trace that remains of him are the fossilised footprints which he left at Kokwane (Nzhelele) and elsewhere [see Map 2].[11]

Thovhela, a founding ancestor incorrectly identified by Beuster as a God, caught the interest of the missionaries more than many other divine, supernatural or ancestral beings. Greatly venerated, he was reportedly very sympathetic to humankind. He was also said to have made a covenant with the people that he would return and bring peace to the world. This promise seems to have been captured in the phrase "*Thovhela u a da; u a da lini?; nwana o bebwa; o vuwa o tshimbila!*" ("Thovhela is coming; when is he coming?; The child is born and learns to walk [but Thovhela has not yet come]!") By this, a longing was expressed for someone who was expected. Thovhela was also (and has remained) a synonym for the word *khosi*, and the phrase "*Thovhela; Thovhela wa vhatu*" ("King; King of the people") has continued to be used as a salutation for royalty. Similarly, *Thovhela* was (and still is) used as a respectful greeting to people in higher office and was used as a praise-name by emissaries to Mwali at Mubvumela Mountain. The phrase "*mutu wa Thovhela*" is a respectful reference to a pregnant woman. This is related to his function of protecting marital happiness and the unborn child (in addition to visitors and travellers).[12] Thovhela's rivalry with another *khosi*, by the name of Tshilonge, over sexual jealousy, kingship and power also forms the subject of a drama performed as part of the *tshikanda* initiation for girls in some areas of Vendaland and the *domba* initiation in others.[13] The missionary interest in this figure arose from the "longing for someone who should be coming". As Beuster pointed out, this could easily be incorporated "in a sermon, to bear testimony to them of the longing for a Saviour through repentance".[14]

More controversial from the perspective of the missionaries were the *zwidudwane*, the water-spirits or sprites which Beuster again incorrectly identified as gods, and various other spiritual beings associated with Holy Forests. The *zwidudwane* were of pre-Singo origin and were described as being of human shape but as being divided vertically. Thus, they had only one visible leg, one arm and one eye. (Possibly the other half of the body was invisible or spiritual.) Residing in Lake Fundudzi, nearby waterfalls and pools, such as Maneledzi and Gunhuvkuvhu (the pool below Phiphidi waterfall), and the forests surrounding these, they expected tribute in the form of beer, a potsherd, a stone, a bangle, a tuft of hair or a branch from anyone passing by their residence [see Map 2]. Residents of the nearest settlement – usually of Mbedzi, Thavhatsinde and Ngona origin – were exempted from these pacification offerings and served as guardians of their sacred places. It was believed that the *zwidudzwane* of neighbouring areas (such as Phiphidi and Fundudzi) visited each other. They travelled along invisible paths, setting alight or stoning nearby homesteads. Gottschling included discussion of these beliefs under "superstitious customs", implying that the people were shackled or exploited by them.[15]

The so-called "holy forests" were sites of far more direct confrontation between missionaries and local rulers. These sacred forests (*tshifho, tshiozwi* or *tshiendeulu*) served (and continue to serve) as the burial grounds of members of the royal families. In the case of the more powerful *mahosi* and *magota*, they covered a significant area. Lesser *mahosi* or *magota* had smaller groves which served the same purpose. Entering these forests and groves was (and remains) strictly prohibited for non-royals and was enforced both supernaturally and by guardians of the royal graves. For example, the Thathe

Vondo holy forest, sacred to the Netshitongani *magota* of Tshivhase, was believed to be inhabited and protected by a huge supernatural lion, the reincarnation either of the ancestral ruler *Khosi* Nethathe or of the successive *magota* [see Map 2, area marked as "Sacred Forest"]. At the same time, any collection of the wood of these groves was (and still is) prohibited.[16]

During the first month of the existence of the Tshakhuma Mission Station, the proposed utilization of wood from the forest for building purposes at the new mission station became an issue between Missionary Schwellnus and *Khosi* Madzivhandila. At a meeting between Schwellnus, Beuster and the *khosi* on 4 June 1874, Johannes Madima (Johannes Mutshaeni's brother) let slip that the two missionaries intended to chop down trees in the holy forest at Tshakhuma and use the wood for building purposes. It is unclear whether he let this slip out by mistake or was letting his *khosi* know out of a sense of concern or duty (and hiding this from the missionaries).

Schwellnus wrote that Madzivhandila was extremely displeased by this:

> He refused to give us permission to do so; we would make him very sad if we did that. At the same time he showed me a tree (*Mofula*) whose fruit I should please not eat before he had sacrificed some of the fruit to the gods [ancestral spirits].[a] Brother Beuster told him: We did not come to serve their gods; also not to learn their customs, but we serve the true God and we are here to teach them.[17]

In the face of this insensitivity and arrogance, and in a statement which clearly reveals the intimate relationship between the *khosi* and the land, "He replied if we did these things, we would spoil his land and he would become ill e.g. his feet would swell up etc".[18]

Again the accusation that the missionaries were destroyers of the land, which had stung them so much when thrown by Tshivhase's councillor on behalf of the spirits of the Mutshindudi River (see p. 137), had been levelled against them. The only defence that they could offer against this was that:

> If the teachers will spoil the land, why had he called them. We have not come to spoil the land but to bring it blessings, and he would also like to admit it later. We both stuck to our convictions; he would show us somewhere else where we could chop wood. He went home, thinking deeply because he is faithful towards his god.[19]

---

a. The Maroela tree, *Mufula* in Tshivenda. The fruit of the Maroela tree usually starts ripening around January. So this was still a long way away (for taboos surrounding this fruit, see N.J. van Warmelo (ed.), *Contributions Towards Venda History*, p. 184).

From the missionary side, there was no modification in their attitude towards African religion. They do not seem to have defied Madzivhandila by cutting trees in his holy forest before he later gave them permission. However, early in July 1874, a wagon bringing goods from Matlala to Schwellnus broke its axle. Schwellnus and Beuster did not hesitate to fashion an emergency axle from a tree, in Schwellnus' own words: "out of the holy forest which was dedicated to the gods, at the Bawenda Chief Tsetongulo [Tshitungulu]".[20]

The issue was again raised in a meeting between Madzivhandila and Schwellnus on 13 July. Visiting Schwellnus and finding him busy building a rectangular house, the *khosi* asked him if he would consider building a similar structure for him. Instead of agreeing outright, Schwellnus stated that, if Madzivhandila would send him his best craftsmen when he was building a wagon shed at his station, he would "teach them how to build". After that, he would come and advise them when they were building the house for the *khosi*. He had "not come to do this work here, but ... to teach them". Schwellnus also took the opportunity to remind Madzivhandila

> how he had refused to allow me to take wood from that forest ... where the gods are supposed to live. I said to him, God does not stay in the forest or in a river, but His home is in heaven; but He can be everywhere and longs to live in the hearts of people who believe in Him and love Him, when they love Him above all things and receive Him. I would also like to believe that he, the King, will later see this and be convinced of it that his opinion about the gods is false, because their gods are just lies of people, which the devil has fed them.[21]

Schwellnus was not prepared to drop this matter. He raised it again on the following Sunday, 20 July 1874. Reporting on this, he wrote that he had

> preached about the Creation; that Jehovah, the living God, *Mosika-vhato* (the creator of the people), gave the people everything to rule over; he also gave them all the fruits, which were healthy for them, as food; this is why we can use the wood in the forests, as well as eat all the fruit from the trees. What kind of customs do they have that they do not permit this? I serve only the True God and cannot follow their customs. In the conversation afterwards, he gave me permission to do both; I should now do as I please.[22]

It is not clear why Madzivhandila granted this permission. Present-day accounts from locals cannot elucidate either. It seems implausible that the *khosi* could have been convinced by Schwellnus' arguments. Perhaps he wished to avoid an open rupture with the missionaries and decided to use more subtle means of persuasion. If Madzivhandila stopped making an issue out of the collection of wood, the missionary would be convinced that he had made his point and would no longer be so keen to do so. Instead, he would concentrate his efforts on areas other than the holy forest which were actually more convenient to exploit. Moreover, even if Schwellnus continued to collect wood there, it is extremely likely that (instructed to do so by the *khosi*), the guardians of the graves would have made certain that he only did so in areas adjoining the holy forest proper, or on its periphery. He would not have been allowed near the graves themselves. This in fact seems to have been what occurred and the issue does not feature in missionary sources after this.

The missionaries found the beliefs sketched thus far interesting, able to be portrayed as a pale reflection of the "truth" contained in the Christian message and a starting point for conversion, merely "superstitious", or worthy of opposition. What they really found blasphemous and horrible was the etiquette surrounding the greeting of *mahosi*, a variety of religious practices under the ultimate control of the rulers, and various ways in which their power was displayed using the bodies of their subjects.

THE *MAHOSI*

I have already discussed the first meeting between Berlin Missionaries and *Khosi* Tshivhase in March 1872. In describing this, the missionaries commented on the praises with which people lauded Tshivhase, the subservient positions which they assumed in his presence, their affirmation of his every action and his using a "grown-up girl" as a backrest.[23] These missionary attitudes did not change significantly over time during the nineteenth century. Thus, even after his expulsion from the mission for a very *khosi*-like attitude to sexual liaisons with women, in describing what he depicted as a typical meeting with Tshivhase, Wessmann wrote that *mahosi* usually kept "their visitors waiting for a lengthy time" before appearing in person. Just before their anticipated arrival,

> A large beer-pot is carried along by a woman and deposited in the centre of the assembly. Suddenly the animated chatter is interrupted by the chief's rather thick voice in close proximity. All eyes are turned upon him, and his large, smiling, full-moon-shaped face fits the chequered company exactly. Very slowly, leaning on every prop of the veranda of the houses, he approaches, finally stopping at the entrance to the hall, partly in order to shake hands with us, partly to regain his breath; for every movement, even the shortest, has proved a great strain for him, in consequence of his enormous obesity. He is clad in trousers and a shirt, the uppermost button of which stands, on account of his fat neck, immediately below his chin. Slowly he settles down on a mat spread for him on the veranda before the entrance of the hall. He is thus able to watch the proceedings

both inside and outside the hall. The moment he squats ... the assembly shows a dog-like submission. Everybody bows low, heads nearly touching the floor, and with hands clasped in front they shout in unison and for several minutes such salutes of "God of heaven and earth", "handsome man with four eyes", "Lion", "beast", "goat stable", "cattle-kraal", "ox", "light of the world", "beast of prey", and other similar flattering expressions commenting on the chief's great wealth or splendid qualities, real or imaginary. Well pleased and glowing with satisfaction he lets his eyes muster on the assembly, and makes some jocular remarks, which, regardless of their merit, have, needless to mention, the desired effect. Soon, however, the conversation moves on the news of the day ... In the meantime the chief cup-bearer has filled the large cups and handed them to this or that native without any special selection. The chief has meanwhile made himself very comfortable on his mat. In order, however, that he may not overbalance himself, a nearly nude maiden supports him on her back, whilst another girl serves as his footstool. Still another lady sits in front of him, almost like a wax-statue, holding up a tin tray with his own always filled cup, so that he may take a drink in comfort whenever he pleases. On his left another girl holds his silver snuff-box, from which he now and then allows somebody else to take a pinch. Now and then he takes a long draught from his cup, always closing his bulging eyes as he does so, and every draught being accompanied by enthusiastic shouts from the assembly... [Similarly,] ... any coughing or clearing of his throat is accompanied by ... praises and flatteries from his loyal admirers.[24]

The praise-names mentioned in the text indicate that the Vhavenda, contrary to Europeans, looked to the animal kingdom for metaphors to describe their ruler's valour and virtues, thereby incorporating nature to a certain extent in the realm of society. But they also made use of the figurative power of the eyes and the gaze, attributing four eyes to their *khosi* as an indication of his ability to see further than common men and his ability to communicate with the ancestral spirits and the world beyond.

As in the earlier descriptions of the 1872 meeting by Beyer and the editors of the *Missions-Berichte*, Wessmann had a different agenda: denigration, not praise. And in order to achieve this, as with his predecessors, he also focused on the *khosi*'s body, his eyes and his gaze, his drinking and snuffing habits, his stride and, more generally, the shape of his body, using corpulence as a signifier of a life of passion, "savagery" and "despotism". The result was a portrait of a "savage" ruler as a powerful yet gluttonous, and therefore grossly overweight, man, self-absorbed, comical in his exercise of power, and unpredictable in his behaviour, switching from laughter to fury in no time. In brief, he transgressed again and again the limits of so-called civilised behaviour. This was the kind of ruler who, in missionary discourse, had to be outmanoeuvred to clear the way for the spreading of the Gospel. This was not only because he was a competing secular power but, equally importantly, because of the religious dimensions of his power. As with his fellow-royals, here too the missionaries saw him as transgressing in many ways, firstly because of what they saw as his vain and blasphemous adoption of divine titles and secondly because of other sacred dimensions of his office and what the missionaries saw as his use of "superstition" as a source of power. That they viewed this as an affront to the Christian God and to the norms of "civilised" society, not only from Tshivhase but also from other *mahosi*, is clearly indicated by an entry in Wessmann's diary at Georgenholtz for 13 March 1889, subsequently published in the *Missions-Berichte* under the title "Heathen Superstitions". This stated that:

> What darkness reigns amongst the Bawenda [Vhavenda] nation: ... [They] do not only venerate their Chiefs like gods – from afar already they fall down before them and call out: "The God of heaven and of earth!" – but they also venerate and pray to their ancestors like gods. The weapons of the deceased are passed down from generation to generation ... Stones are also taken from the holy river and then carried to the village, to venerate them there. Even goats and oxen are specially selected, to be regarded as holy and to be called 'God'. The people from Téngoe [Thengwe] venerate a big snake. Those from Tsaulu [Tshaulu], venerate a big river. They cheer and sing while they march to the river to pour beer into the river. When the Chief of Lambane dies, he is burnt [cremated] and his ashes are strewn into the holy river – his cattle also, as well as all his possessions, are burnt and strewn into the holy river. All these things happen here in the Georgenholtz area.[25]

As the supreme secular and religious authority, the representative of his people and the channel of communication between the natural and the supernatural, the *khosi* was indeed shown great respect. Building on the sources already cited, a strong body of missionary and anthropological writings have argued that this expressed itself in the existence of the institution of divine kingship among the Vhavenda (a conclusion with which I disagree). For example, writing in 1905, the Reverend E. Gottschling noted that so sacred was the personage of the *khosi* and, through him, the entire royal family that dangerous princes were strangled. "This is the manner of doing away with dangerous princes among the Bawenda, for the blood of the 'royal' house may not be shed."[26] Van Warmelo's royal informant Tshamaano, used in writing his

Contributions Towards Venda History (1932), and contributors to his *Copper Miners of Musina* (1940) made reference to cases where this reportedly happened or was threatened to both princes and *mahosi*, particularly in the case of succession disputes. The bodies of members of the royal family killed in this manner were believed to make extremely powerful *muti*.[27]

Similarly, Wessmann commented in 1908 that the *mahosi* were "so to say regarded as gods".[28] From an anthropological perspective, in an article published in 1930, Lestrade noted that:

> Among the Venḓa tribes, however, the chief may be said to be an absolute lord and master over his people. This may be partly due to the fact that here greater stress is laid on the sacred as opposed to the secular character of the chief's person, which, while it exists among other tribes, does not come to the fore so markedly as here. He is for many purposes high-priest as well as secular head of his people. When the villages have to be inured against the attacks of enemies or evil spirits, when warriors have to be made invincible, when taboos have to be imposed or withdrawn, it is he who administers the treatment required.[29] His very person is sacred: he must be approached on hands and knees, and addresses everyone with the condescending second person singular (*iwe*), whereas every one must address him with the polite third person plural (*vhone*). The chief's language is different from that of the others, and the names of objects and actions associated with the chief's functions are different from the names of these same objects and actions of the common people …[30] The chief's person is so sacred that it is no rare thing to see people rub on their own bodies sweat and mucus of which the chief has got rid of by way of a strengthening drug. All the chief's actions are highly lauded: when he drinks beer, or takes snuff, or coughs, or expectorates, there is always an adulatory chorus: *Ndau yau nduna* (male lion); *Ngwenyama* (meat-eater, i.e. beast of prey); *Mbolomo* (great bull); *Tshivhanda tshihulu* (great wild beast); *Nemashango* (prince of the lands), and so forth, all uttered in the reverential position of *u losha*, i.e. prostrate salutation.[31] But not only is the chief thus regarded as semi-divine during the greater part of his life; towards the end of it, or sometimes long before, he actually confers godhead upon himself, when after abjuring all contact with women, and putting away his wives, he performs a solemn solitary dance (*u pembela*) which makes him in very truth a god (*Mudzimu*).[32]

Again, in an article published in the following year, Van Warmelo, the Government Ethnologist, noted that, while the *mahosi* often "quarrelled" among themselves they nevertheless maintained "a feeling of solidarity against their subjects". He continued by arguing that the *khosi*

> is feared and honoured by the Venda like nowhere else in the South of the Continent. This unusually strong position is shared by the nobility. By contrast, in their eyes, the ordinary people are but livestock [*is maar vee in hulle oë*], and until today are indebted to perform all sorts of services at the capital village (from where they are ruled), that can only be explained through an earlier servitude.[33]

As late as 1994, in an otherwise extremely useful article, Hanisch also traced the development of what he called "divine kingship" amongst various proto-Venda groups and how this was eventually adopted by the Singo and carried by them to Dzata.[34]

In my reading, scholars arguing that Vhavenda rulers were divine or semi-divine are falling into the same trap as the early missionaries in equating profound respect with veneration or worship. This could rest upon a racist or paternalist approach to African societies which sees them as being incapable of social complexity. This view is influenced by numerous informal conversations locally and by Kantorowicz's seminal work *The King's Two Bodies* (1957), in which he explored the medieval separation of the king's two bodies, namely his "body natural" and his "body politic". People were fully aware of the frailty and mortality of the ordinary mortals who became kings. However, the medieval idea of the crown came to be inscribed with immortality and an entire political theology.[35]

Against this background, at the simplest level, the evidence surrounding the position of Raluvhimba as the supreme being (and, effectively, the only God) is extremely strong. Similarly, in common with many other African groups, the ancestors were not worshipped but rather asked – through sacrifice and other rituals – for protection, assistance and guidance. Arising from this, during the early years of his reign, the *khosi* should be seen as the link between his people and the ancestors, between the ephemeral present and the idealized past, and not as a God. The strength of this link, and the closeness of the ruler to the ancestors, gradually grew until, towards the end of his life, when he had danced the *u pembela* dance, he acquired the status of a living ancestor. His next stage was to join the ancestors themselves. The degree to which these links were viewed literally or symbolically by the various segments of society, or whether these views changed in different contexts or over time, is not recoverable from the historical record.

In addition to these objections and alternative interpretations, the conventional interpretation of the power and status of *mahosi* in Vendaland does not adequately take into account the strong checks and balances on their powers that were built into the social fabric. Lestrade mentions these but does not seem to realize the degree to which they undermine his earlier argument:

> It may be imagined that in all the political sphere the word of such a sacred person is law to an extent not met with among other South African tribes except in extreme cases such as that of Shaka among the Zulu-speaking peoples. At the same time he is not so much of an absolute tyrant as a mere consideration of the ceremony with which he is surrounded might lead one to suppose. He is in the first place bound by law and custom to act in certain well-defined ways and along certain well-defined lines, and cannot except with extreme difficulty make any alterations in these age-old laws and customs and methods of procedure, even in the purely political sphere; while in the religious sphere of ceremonial taboo, ritual, and what not, he is absolutely powerless to make any alteration whatever except in the most judicious manner and by following rather than trying to lead tribal opinion on to the point. In the political sphere too, not only is he hemmed in with restrictions, but the powerful effect of personal and other influences on him plays a very great part indeed in regulating his actions. In order to get anything done, he must first assure himself of the co-operation of his *magota* [headmen] and *dzinduna* [sub-headmen], of his *khoro*, and in fact of every one of real importance in the tribe. He cannot drive his will through without such co-operation, and if he attempts to do so, he will fail, and in olden days would run severe risk of dying by poisoning.[36]

However, this kind of interpretation did not yet feature in missionary thinking. Instead, in dealing with those from whom they would have to win the hearts and minds of the people, they generally emphasised that the *mahosi* were all-powerful and (often) tyrannical.[37]

THE ANCESTORS

Returning to the other practices surrounding the showing of respect to, and propitiation of, the ancestors mentioned in Beuster's 1878 report and Wessmann's March 1889 diary entry, Stayt has argued that the shades could be represented collectively by cattle, goats or river pebbles and individually by spears or small iron or copper rings. Between them, the missionaries covered all of these possibilities, Beuster far more "ethnographically" than Wessmann's already-quoted discourse on "darkness". In addition, although he was sometimes extremely accurate in his observations, beyond using the term "God" far too freely, Beuster sometimes misinterpreted what his informants were telling him. Thus, he recorded (apparently accurately) that a person who could afford it would "consecrate a bull to his dead father". However, he continued by writing that, since a bull was far too valuable an animal for most individuals to be able to do this, "this honour usually just befalls a chief". In arguing this, he neglected the fact that lineages were sometimes able to do what individuals could not and dedicate a bull for this purpose. He also seems to have begun to become inaccurate when he argued that:

> The bull is given the name of the dead person and is regarded as a god – he is the dead person himself who has now become a god. A cow is consecrated for a dead mother. If there is no bull available, but there is a cow, a cow can probably be consecrated as the god of the father.[38]

Stayt's much later version was apparently more accurate. He argued that the various royal families, as well as many important lineages, kept a sacred black bull which was seen as embodying all the ancestral spirits of the father's lineage. Arising from the belief that no male was complete without a mate, a cow was associated with the sacred bull. This did not represent the spirits of the mother's lineage, as this role would have been filled by a goat. The most important role played by the bull came during the harvest festival, when the ancestors were thanked collectively. For more individual requests, such as pleas for protection at the commencement of a dangerous journey, the ancestors of the mother's lineage were approached. The thinking seems to have been that the tie between the mother and her children was seen as being more intimate than that between them and their father. The woman, who had only a limited number of children, was less likely to forget them than the father, who may have had several wives and many children.[39]

Despite his intolerance over holy forests, Beuster seems to have been exceptional in showing the kind of tolerance that he did over this issue. Even Koen seems to have found his encounter with the practice more amusing than informative. Describing events at Georgenholtz during the year 1878 and during the first six months of 1879, the *Missions-Berichte* reported that:

> On another occasion he came to a small boy who was herding his cattle. But the cattle gave him so much trouble, that the little boy was beside himself and he tearfully complained to the missionary, that the gods would not listen to him. "But who are your gods?"
>
> He answered: "That bull and this cow." Koen had to laugh at this. But in most of the villages of this nation, there is the notion that an ox or a cow in the herd is a god. This village headman [*Kraalhäuptling*], a wealthy cattle owner, had turned two of his beasts into gods – a male and a female god. These animals may not be sold nor slaughtered; should one die, it is replaced by another.[40]

Not every lineage possessed a sacred bull. According to Stayt, in some cases, the functions of this animal were performed by sacred stones instead. These highly-polished, cylindrical stones had to be taken from a river bed. They were replaced by other stones of the same size. The bull was represented by a smaller stone than the cow. They were embedded side by side near the lineage head's dwelling. Offerings were made to them in a similar manner to those made to the sacred bull. There were a number of variations on this basic theme. For example, some groups possessed three sacred stones. In some cases, it would appear that the poorer lineages substituted stones for cattle for economic reasons. However, it seems that others had always shown respect to their ancestors in this form.[41] Here Stayt's version did not contradict Beuster's earlier analysis. In addition, Beuster argued that the stones were also used to represent members of the family who had been killed in wars where they could not be buried at home by their own relatives.[42]

Ancestral spears were kept by members of the royal family as a link with the ancestors and, through this, as symbols of the transmission of authority. During the *u pembela* dance, the *khosi* danced with a miniature spear that he had made for himself and with those made by his ancestors. In both the royal family and the wider community, beyond being collectively absorbed into the sacred bull after death, male members of the lineage could also be represented individually by a spear. It was the duty of the dead man's son by his great wife to provide this spear. He usually did not do this immediately after his father's death. Instead, he waited until illness or disaster overtook the family and a diviner discovered that this was because the dead man's spirit was troubled because his spear had not been put up. After the new spear had been made by a smith, the family were called. The head of the lineage brought out all of the family spears. The new spear was placed next to them and was introduced to each of them. They, in turn, were requested to accept their "grandchild". The new spear was then told to join its relatives and enjoined not to trouble the living any more. Beer was poured over each of the spears in turn. The newly-consecrated spear was then put away with those who had preceded it. Commoners also carried their sacred spears to the first-fruits ceremony. Each married male member of the lineage had the right to be represented by a spear.[43] Young men who had died unmarried were represented by the rite of the hoe handle, discussed earlier.[44]

As a male ancestor was represented by a spear, after her death, a woman had a small iron ring dedicated to her. This was made from an old Vhavenda-made hoe, preferably one which had been used by the deceased woman herself. Again, these were generally only made after a diviner had indicated that an illness or misfortune had been caused by a female ancestor spirit who desired her *dzembe* (hoe – plural *malembe*) to be put up. These were worn around the neck on a piece of string made from wild cotton.[45] Wessmann did not mention these. Beuster was non-judgemental in stating that: "Another custom [is that] ... whereby they carry round their necks their dead relatives, represented by small longish bits of iron which have been forged from old used-up axes and hoes. Each bit of iron represents the name of one of the family members who has died."[46]

One of the clear indications that Tshivenda-speakers did not form a homogenous group was the variation in mortuary practices for rulers among the various sections. It is here that the reference to the cremation of *Khosi* Lambane in Wessmann's March 1889 diary entry (see p. 176) fits in. In extremely broad outline, the Thavhatsinde, Famadi and Ngona of Tshivhale exhumed the bones of their dead rulers after a number of years, cremated them and then disposed of the ash in their sacred river pools. Sometimes the bones were broken or ground before burning. In other cases, any bones which survived the burning process were broken and ground. The Mbedzi disposed of the bones in their sacred river pool without having burnt them. On the other hand, the various Singo groups either exhumed the bones of their *mahosi* after a number of years of burial or allowed the body of the deceased ruler to decompose above ground in a sealed chamber. In either case, after a number of years, the bones were then reburied in the group's holy forest.[47] The one common theme among all Tsivhenda-speaking groups was that the death of the *khosi* was kept secret from his people for a considerable period – often a year or more. During this period, the *makhadzi* and the *khotsi-munene* continued the government, giving some of the tensions surrounding succession and possible attempts at usurpation of power time to work themselves out before the heir was installed.[48] Also, work was forbidden during the time of mourning. If not properly managed, cessation from work by the people could lead to famine. So, the timing of the announcement of the death of the *khosi* was crucial. This would only be announced after the harvest.[49]

THE *MALOMBO*

A further practice related to pacifying troubled spirits which was viewed in an extremely negative light by the missionaries was the *malombo*. As with his encounters with holy forests, Beuster lost his ethnographic detachment when writing about this practice. On 18 September 1874, he recorded that:

> For several days now, by day and by night, I heard the racket of drums, flutes and bells and the yodelling of people coming from a village. I heard that an idol-worshipping feast was being celebrated there. Today I made my way to the village. I found many people gathered there. They formed a circle around several dancing women. Four of these women were specially decorated with ostrich plumes and coloured cloths. They were the instigators of the feast. Their forefathers, who were now gods, had come to them, had spoken to them and had taught them all sorts of wonderful things, like: to heal sicknesses, to cast spells

> [*Zaubern*] etc. I was told they find the cause of the illness through smell and in the same way they find the correct remedy for the illness. There was a frightful din in the yard. From a distance, the drums had sounded deceptively like the rattling of a mill; nearby one also heard the sounds made by the other instruments. One did not only beat on the skin of the drum, but also on the wood of which the drum is made. The drummers raced across their drums with frightful fury, at the same time pulling their faces into the most abhorrent grimaces; their sweat poured down and mingled with the swirling dust. In this way these people experienced a truly devilish spectacle ... The actual idols [the four dancing women] tried to maintain a certain amount of dignity; but the dancing of the others, especially that of an old woman, was too terrible to observe. I could only speak with the people by shouting. After I had spoken with individuals for a while, I noticed that they did not treat me with hostility, as I had expected at the beginning. I used a moment of silence to walk into the circle and to speak to the crowd – I said something like: "I have come to experience your customs. But what do I see? I see people who are lost, who have left the correct path." I pointed at the idolised-people and said to them that they were impostors and that the people were deceived by them, etc. The idolised-people had withdrawn a bit; a woman was lying down; she had danced herself sick. I spoke especially to them, but they did not feel like listening.[50]

Beuster continued describing what he saw as the fraudulent practices involved here by recording that he had "heard that these dancing people pretend that they don't eat anything on the day of the dance – they are cared for by the gods. They only accept water". However, on asking a "clever boy" what the dancers had eaten besides their staple food, and how many goats they had slaughtered, he had been rewarded with the answer: "They haven't slaughtered any goats yet. But they have other food which they eat with their mealie-pap. This they only eat at night." Lastly, in the missionary's opinion, the practice of *malombo* had been imposed on the local people by outsiders from the north. The intended implication seems to have been that it was not deeply rooted in local culture and should be dispensed with as quickly as possible.[51]

On 25 March 1878, Koen also described a *malombo* dance at Georgenholtz (still called "the new station at Makoarele [Makwarela]"). He wrote that:

> Since yesterday, they have been dancing non-stop at a big village here in the neighbourhood. Even at night, there was no pause. This dance is in honour of the gods [ancestors]. They

have a lead-dancer (man or woman) who is in a state of ecstasy.[b] While dancing, the lead-dancer sings in the higher language of the gods, which no-one else can understand. Suddenly he falls down as if dead, not stirring or moving (he is now with the gods in spirit). He is carried in a house where he is watched over by men and women, while the youth continue to dance. There are two such heathen somnambulists here close to me, a man and a woman.[52]

Beyond the information that they convey, these accounts are particularly interesting in that they strongly suggest that the *malombo* was already well-established in Vendaland by the 1870s. Further evidence is supplied by Koen's reference to another *malombo* dance at Georgenholtz on 5 October 1879 (see pp. 256–257). These descriptions challenge Stayt's assertion that the practice "was rare among the BaVenda until about 1914".[53] Other interesting themes raised by these accounts are the fact that the dancing took place over several days and nights and was accompanied by its own special music. The participants were possessed and in a state of ecstasy. Beyond communion with spiritual beings, the activity was associated with healing and other supernatural activities. The participants were clothed in garments and accessories which differed from the norm. They suffered great bodily discomfort and exhaustion, resulting in collapse, as a result of their participation. While all dancers in the performance discussed by Beuster were female, both men and women took part in that witnessed by Koen. The rite was carried out openly in the village and attracted an audience who felt free to comment on aspects of what was occurring, sometimes even critically. Even outsiders Beuster and Koen were not prevented from witnessing the spectacle. Beuster was even allowed to publicly denigrate both the participants and the onlookers. The practice was described as being of foreign origin. The participants spoke in an unintelligible language. These are classic features of the twentieth-century *malombo* as described by Stayt and Dederen, and as I have witnessed myself on one occasion.

Stayt and Dederen argued that the cult was of Karanga origin. The spirit, *tshilombo* (plural *zwilombo*), which entered the host was either that of an offended ancestor, sometimes extremely remote, or a troublesome homeless spirit with no genealogical connection with the person whom it entered. In the latter case, it was often extremely ill-intentioned and had been cut off from further contact with its own kin with the help of a *nanga*. Such banished spirits wandered around searching for a host within whom they could seek refuge. In some cases, they could even be the *tshilombo* of foreigners. Although it was generally women who were possessed, on rare occasions men could also suffer this fate.[54]

---

b. A religious state in which the soul leaves the body to be united with God/the gods.

Possession by a *tshilombo* was often indicated by the afflicted person suffering a prolonged or serious illness. Once this had been diagnosed by a *nanga*, a *malombo* ritual specialist, called a *maine a tshele*, was called in. Treatment was divided into two phases. During the first, the *maine a tshele* visited the afflicted person in her homestead. A drummer who knew the *malombo* beat was summoned and word was sent out to the extended family, especially the woman's relations, and the wider community, stating that she needed their help. When the drumming began, any people in the district who had previously been possessed would arrive to take an active part in the proceedings. Their new comrade was brought into a trance by the *maine a tshele* and made to dance, accompanied by the *maine a tshele* and the other previously possessed people in the district in relays, until she collapsed. Attempts were made to get the *tshilombo* to identify itself and to state its needs. If it refused to do this, after a short pause, during which she was rubbed with various magical substances, the woman was made to dance to the point of collapse again. This process was repeated, sometimes over a number of days, until the *tshilombo* finally co-operated. It then spoke in Tshikaranga, Tshivenda, a mixture of the two or a language intelligible only to the initiated. If it proved to be a malicious homeless sprit, it was then exorcised, trapped in a stick and thrown into a tree in the forest. It would remain there unless some unfortunate individual touched the stick, releasing it and becoming possessed in the process. However, in the case of an ancestral spirit, the aim was not to exorcise the *tshilombo* but to persuade it to periodically occupy the body of the afflicted person and dance in a manner which was not injurious to her health – expressed differently, to transform her status from that of victim to that of medium.[55]

Items identified by Stayt as being among those demanded by *tshilombo* included clothes, ornaments, ancestral spears or axes (male ritual objects), or various types of cloth. Sometimes these items could not be supplied immediately but a promise was made and they were supplied later. Dederen echoed this, referring to imitation assegais or axes and male garments (a waistcoat, a tie and/or a hat). In the dance I witnessed, a woman who had previously been possessed was dressed in a white shirt, black trousers, a gold waistcoat and a grey felt hat. The spirit could also demand sacrifices of fowls or a goat. While a woman was possessed by the *tshilombo*, her husband and relations had to treat her with great consideration and respect, saluting her as if she were a *khosi*. Once possessed, a woman was never the same again. From then on, the spirit would possess her from time to time when it had requests which it wished to be fulfilled or required propitiatory gifts. Hearing the *malombo* beat played on the drums was also enough to call the spirit to re-enter her and take part in the dancing. In this, the second phase, the medium joined a society of *malombo* dancers. This consisted of previously-treated patients. In addition to assisting the newly possessed, they danced at intervals (annually at least) at the homestead of the eldest *maine a tshele* in the district or in the royal *khoro*. In the latter case, the *khosi* loaned the society some of his royal objects.[56]

In his pioneering study of spirit possession and shamanism, Lewis argued that, in many societies, this

> form of possession, which is regarded initially as an illness, is ... virtually restricted to women. Such women's possession "afflictions" are regularly treated not by permanently expelling the possessing agency, but by reaching a viable accommodation with it. The spirit is tamed and domesticated, rather than exorcized. This treatment is usually accomplished by the induction of the affected women into a female cult group which regularly promotes possession experiences among its members. Within the secluded cult group, possession has thus lost its malign significance.[57]

Thus, according to Lewis, "what men consider a demoniacal sickness, women convert into a clandestine ecstasy". Against this background, he interprets cults of this nature as "thinly disguised protest movements directed against the dominant sex" and as offering "an effective vehicle for manipulating husbands and male relatives" in societies where women are not otherwise effectively protected from the exactions of men. Responsibility and, through this, blame for the women's affliction, and the annoyance and cost which its treatment involves, does not lie with them but rather with (male) spirits. Their husbands and male relatives thus have no choice but to submit graciously to the demands for respect and gifts which these spirits demand. Moreover, as Lewis continues by arguing, possession of this nature is not "a secure female monopoly" – it also commonly embraces "downtrodden categories of men who are subject to strong discrimination in rigidly stratified societies". Thus, cults of this type "work to help the interests of the weak and downtrodden who have otherwise few effective means to press their claims for attention and respect".[58]

Being men of the nineteenth century, and representatives of the competing Christian God, the Berlin missionaries did not develop explanations of this nature. However, given the dominant position of men, and of rulers, in nineteenth-century Vhavenda society, Lewis' explanation of the *malombo* is particularly appealing. As with the other manifestations of the supernatural, and its interaction with the natural order, already discussed, the *malombo* also raises questions about the mediating role of rulers and ritual specialists in these processes of interaction.

"WITCHERY AND WITCHDOCTORS" – *ZAUBEREI, MAHOSI* AND *DZINANGA*

In general, the Berlin Missionaries in Vendaland believed that the *mahosi* and the *dzinanga* worked together extremely closely. On the one hand, this was to regulate society and relations between the natural and the supernatural. On the other, missionary discourse portrayed the rulers and what they called the *Zauberer* as colluding with each other to mislead and exploit the people. While they believed that this was sometimes conscious, the missionaries were nevertheless prepared to concede that (as they saw it) the rulers and (apparently to a lesser extent) the *dzinanga* believed in many of the "lies" and "superstitions" of African religion just as much as their people. They were thus unaware, or only partly conscious, of their role in "deceiving" their people. The missionaries also found it impossible to conceal their delight on occasions when what they saw as the scheming of the *dzinanga* backfired on them with unexpected results.

Describing events in the vicinity of Georgenholtz on 9 and 10 January 1878, Koen was clearly dealing with actions which even the missionaries conceded were performed in good faith by the participants. He wrote that on these two days, the lands of the Mphaphulis in the vicinity of Georgenholtz had been "doctored" [*Landesdoktorei*]. Other parts of the realm had been "doctored" on the preceding days. This was an annual ceremony designed to protect the area against enemy attack from outside. It was also performed once it became known that an enemy force was on its way. Once the boundaries had been protected in this manner, the legs of any enemy crossing the sticks and entering the country would swell up. They would also lose all their power and fighting spirit. In order to achieve this end, a "witch-doctor [*Zauberdoktor*]" had prepared a mixture of various herbs. This had then been taken to the capital. *Khosi* Ranwedzi Mphaphuli had then smeared this "medicine" on small sticks, each about two inches long, taken from a special tree. These sticks were then carried to all the borders of the realm by young men who buried them under the soil at crossroads. While performing these tasks, they had to be completely naked – nobody who was dressed in any way was allowed to touch the sticks. Those carrying the sticks had to be "greeted most respectfully" by all who met them on the way. They also had the right to requisition food, drink or anything else that they needed on their journey. Over the two days that this ceremony took place, nobody was allowed to work, for fear of heavy punishment. A few days previously, people from three villages near to Mphaphuli's capital had ignored this prohibition and had hoed their fields. The *khosi* had punished them by seizing all of their goats. Koen reported that he had unsuccessfully attempted to convince Makwarela Mphaphuli and others about what he saw as "the foolishness of these beliefs". They strongly believed that failure to perform these rituals would result in defeat and disaster at the hands of their enemies.[59]

During the same year, Beuster reported on a case that he clearly delighted in portraying as a *nanga* being caught out by his own attempts to be too clever for his own good, and please both the Christian and the "Heathen" communities. The editors of the *Missions-Berichte* clearly shared his views, and it was published under the title "Caught in your own trap". According to Beuster's report of 12 June 1878, for quite a while, a "heathen", named Mangale, had had a reasonably close relationship with the mission station at Ha-Tshivhase. "He had lived amongst the Boers [*Bauern*] for a long time, and experienced much there – he has a crippled arm, thanks to the malice of a burgher [*Bauer*]." Apparently utilizing skills he had learned from the Boers, upon his return to Vendaland, he had planted apple and peach trees. The missionaries had got to know him when he had arrived at Ha-Tshivahse attempting to trade peaches and apples from his trees for other goods. "For a while, he almost regularly attended church services and he understood God's Word well."[60]

Some time previously, Mangale had been extremely ill with malaria. After he had recovered, his two children died within a short time of each other. In response, the bereaved man summoned a *mungome* or *nanga* to ascertain who was responsible for the deaths.[c] Mangale was a *nanga* himself. Beuster was convinced that this meant that he knew that the whole process of throwing the bones was a fraudulent one. The missionary therefore explained the action of calling for a diviner in cynical terms:

> He himself is a doctor [*Doctor* – sic] and he therefore does not act out of ignorance, but he knows very well what is involved in casting the bones [*Würfeln*].[d] Rather than stand the risk of being regarded as a loveless father who does not care for his children, or as one who has adopted the ways of the Boers [*Bauern*] and has thrown away the ways of the ancestors, he thought it would be better to perform a clearly visible deed to counter any suspicions – a deed which would prove that he had not yet been contaminated with the ways of the teacher; but that he was still faithful to the ways of the ancestors.[61]

This cynical explanation surely misinterprets and misrepresents Mangale's motivations and actions. Admittedly, as a *nanga*, he would have been aware of some of the techniques used to impress clients. However, to extrapolate from this that he and his colleagues saw themselves as frauds preying on a gullible public is extremely Eurocentric. In numerous informal conversations

---

c. The text describes him as a "doctor" without specifying any more than this. The missionaries either had not yet realised, or were not yet interested in noting, that there were different categories of specialist supernatural practitioners. I have already discussed the *maine wa tsehle*, who dealt with spirit possession. Other categories of specialists are discussed in the glossary under the heading "Traditional Healers and Specialists". I strongly suspect that the specialist called by Mangale was a *mungome* since the allegation was one of *vhuloi*. In my reading, it is also likely that Mangale was a general practitioner, rather than a specialist. It is unlikely that he would have developed such a close relationship with the mission station were he a *mungome*.

d. *Würfeln* should actually be translated as "dice". However, the term "throwing the bones" is much more familiar locally. I therefore translate "casting" and "throwing the [divining] dice" as "throwing the bones" throughout.

locally, I have been told that even powerful *dzinanaga* and *mingome* have to resort to "trickery" on occasion either to make their clients' minds receptive or to distract their attention so that the genuine power of the ancestors and the herbs is able to operate. Not only does this argument seem extremely logical but, nineteenth-century *dzinanaga* would have thought in the same way – yes, there was illusion but this illusion allowed the real power to operate. In addition, turning to Mangale himself, he had only been attending church services and developing a cordial relationship with Beuster and the Christians at Ha-Tshivhase. He had not yet been converted to Christianity and baptised. As such, he had no reason to turn his back on local religious beliefs and practices. Moreover, even if he had converted, there was a strong chance that he would have turned to the beliefs that he had grown up with at this traumatic time. Still today, many local people who are strong Christians in the non-indigenous churches turn to *dzinanga* and other African medico-religious practitioners in times of misfortune, illness or death which are not adequately explained by western versions of Christianity or (in the case of illness) which do not seem to be responding to western medicine. In some cases, the same applies to the showing of respect for the ancestors. African Initiated Churches, such as the Zion Christian Church [ZCC], have prophets and other religious healers within their hierarchy who are able to fulfil this need. Members are also specifically taught to show respect to the ancestors.[62] Against this background, I am certain that Mangale was convinced that he was acting in the only responsible manner in attempting to ascertain who had been responsible for the death of his children.

The *nanga* identified a man from the village as the *muloi*. When he heard this, the man who had been pointed out fled to one of Tshivhase's wives for protection. People in the area reportedly were convinced that this action demonstrated his guilt: "You see, that is the murderer! ... Why else has he run away? He is afraid!" However, the accused *muloi* had another explanation. Anyone accused of *vhuloi* had the right to defend themselves before the council and the right to demand a second opinion from another *mungome*. He seems to have thought that he had a better chance if he took the second option rather than the first. To do this, he needed the protection of the queen. The accused thus reportedly argued that: "I am no murderer. I had nothing to do with the death of the children. But I did flee because I wanted to defend myself – that would be impossible amongst you. I will also call a doctor and then it will be seen whether I am guilty."[63]

Another "doctor" (again, presumably a *mungome*) was called from far away. This was (and remains) normal practice as he or she was believed to be unbiased because of being a stranger. In addition, apparently on the principle of a prophet never being acknowledged at home, the most powerful *mingome* and *dzinanga* were always believed to live far away. Again revealing his cynicism, Beuster reported that this specialist was "given a very friendly reception. While he eats and recovers his strength for this important task, he drops hints that he expects to be paid a substantial fee for settling the matter favourably".⁶⁴

Following normal practice, the queen sent along a representative to report back to her on the judgement. He and the accused (presumably accompanied by the accuser and his witnesses) went to the place where the bones would be thrown:

> The doctor throws the bones; and then he throws them again. And verily, the bones clearly contradict those of the first doctor. The man is truly no murderer! Then finally it is decided – there is no doubt about it – the parents themselves, the own mothers, have killed the children!ᵉ Many friends and relatives had stood around the accused, showing their support, and they had exercised their influence on the doctor. When now, the last decisive judgement is pronounced, shouts of joy and cheers are heard. The men grab their guns and shoot into the sky – so that we at home thought the shots were fired to welcome workers from foreign places who had returned home. Now, on top of this, the accused explains that he can not just forget about such a serious insult – he is entitled to a fee for his suffering; the one who had started it all, Mangale, should at least pay him a beast.ᶠ It seems he will also receive the beast. ... This is how things go with this man who, because of his great care for earthly advantages, turned his back on Jesus and chose instead, the services of Satan.⁶⁵

For the missionaries, these cases surrounding attempts to trace the *vhaloi* responsible for deaths within families typified the work of *dzinanga* and *mingome*. Except possibly in the case of extremely old people, local belief structures reportedly did not allow for cases of natural death – a *muloi* had to be responsible.⁶⁶ The missionaries occasionally commented (disparagingly) on attempts by supernatural practitioners to heal the sick or bring rain. However, their focus was definitely on what they saw as the injustices brought about by the so-called witch-hunts. Thus, in an overview of news from Tshakhuma for the first semester of 1880, the *Missions-Berichte* noted that one of *Khosi* Madzivhandila's daughters had died. The family had then gone to a *mungome* [*Zauberer*], who had identified the culprit who had brought about her death. Unidentified relatives, presumably acting under the orders or at least with the consent of the *khosi*, had then killed the alleged *muloi*. Schwellnus and the

---

e. It seems that the children had different mothers. Jealousy and tensions between co-wives is one of the classic causes of witchcraft accusations in a number of African societies. Beuster seems to have misunderstood the accusation here – it is most likely that the women were accused of bewitching each other's children.

f. A bull, an ox or a cow.

Missions-Berichte bemoaned the fact that, despite his having been reappointed as the Commissioner for Native Affairs in the Zoutpansberg area by the British administration of the Transvaal, Albasini had done nothing to bring these vengeance-seekers to book.[67]

In April 1885, during the time when Beuster was overseeing the running of the Georgenholtz Mission Station, he wrote of a case which he saw both as divine punishment for a person who denied the Christian God and an issue manipulated by the *khosi* (apparently Makwarela Mphaphuli). Beuster wrote that August Tshimange and Paulus Raknopa, two Christians from Georgenholtz, had informed him that they had been discussing "the existence of God with some heathens, in the presence of Makoaräla [Makwarela Mphaphuli]" at the latter's capital-village. Among those taking part in the discussion, there "was an old grey-haired man who, with utter impudence, denied the existence of God. 'If there is a God, He can prove His existence by killing me, an old man. You young ones can remain alive. He can use me to show His might.'" *Khosi* Makwarela reportedly warned the old man not to talk like this. Three days later, the old man was dead.[68]

However, while the Christians viewed this as being the result of divine retribution, the local people had other ideas. Although it was believed that *vhaloi* sometimes used an innate evil power to kill their victims, they could allegedly also use poisons (either in the context of sympathetic magic or directly), familiars or other means.[69] In this case, a whole family were suspected of having used poison to kill the old man. Beuster was horrified by what he saw as the outright manipulation of the case in order to secure income for the *khosi*:

> Already on the day after his blasphemy, the old man had become ill and by the third day he had died. Although the matter had become public knowledge, all those concerned with it kept quiet. But so that the ruler of the country should not have his income sources cut, the old man had to have been killed by a poison mixture. This is why the family of six was immediately arrested and taken to the capital village. How quickly all the excitement was calmed when it was said: "Several guilty people could buy their freedom, if two to three head of cattle were paid for each guilty person." So the auction started and after a few days we heard that it was over. The girls had been sold as wives; the boys had been bought by relatives, but some of them fled. So this death brought the chief an income of about 12–15 head of cattle.[70]

The theme of what the missionaries interpreted to be the manipulation of evidence in accusations of *vhuloi* continued to surface in reports from the mission stations. Thus, on 12 May 1885, Beuster reported that he had visited

Khosi Tshivhase. He provided a vivid description of what he saw as the antics of a famous diviner (apparently a *mungome*) who had been summoned by Tshivhase to clear his country of *vhaloi*:

> Presently a famous witch-doctor [*Zauberdoktor*] is living in the open space in the beautiful forest in front of the capital village. This man has been ordered to come here by Tshewasse [Tshivhase], to establish the high court in his country. For this reason the witch-doctor has been equipped with all the protection and might from Tshewasse. He is dressed in all sorts of trinkets like ostrich feathers, tiger [leopard] and snake-skins – a fantastically adorned man. He is now working daily on all sorts of murder [*vhuloi*] and theft cases, and the gaping masses regard the hocus-pocus which is so well presented to them in this way with clear amusement for days on end. In order that he may not be accused of receiving good remuneration for nothing, he really works by the sweat of his brow. He stamps his feet like a buffalo; he jumps and flings his hands about, like an ostrich does with its wings; he rolls his eyes like a chameleon, and froths at the mouth and sprays spittle far around him with his mouth; with his long knife, he mysteriously points in this or that direction as if he smells the culprit he is looking for there.[71]

Here again Beuster levelled accusations that judgements against *vhaloi* were used to enrich the *khosi* and that those found guilty by other practitioners were able to buy a reversal of this judgement if they were wealthy enough to be able to afford the required discrete bribes:

> Tshewasse is now reaping a good harvest. His servants sit in the background. As soon as the name of the guilty one has been pronounced, they rush to his place to get hold of him, or his wife and children, or his animals. Speed is essential as friends or relatives of the condemned person could be amongst the crowd; they could inform him of the impending danger. If the wife or children have been arrested, they can be bought back by means of cattle. Nowadays the punishment is almost always paid more in belongings and goods than also with a life. So in this case, the cruelty has been reduced. But not only condemnations are passed here; those who have been declared as guilty by other witch-doctors are also pardoned here. Even though in such cases, the capital village does not reap any benefit from this, the witch-doctor always profits from such an act, as such a pardon cannot be obtained without a good greasing of the palm. One evening we heard clear yodelling [ululation] and jubilation coming from a neighbouring village, as is usually heard on

especially happy occasions. The reason for this was that the sister of the chief of that village had been acquitted by the witch-doctor of the murder she had been accused of. With her honour now restored, she could again return to her home. Her brother had done his share in order to attain the favourable result. I spoke some words to the gathered crowd, while sitting on my horse. I found it very interesting to notice how so many of that crowd listened intently when I told them of their confusion and exposed the impotence of the witch-doctor in these matters. Yes, even the witch-doctor gave a friendly, smiling nod when I departed, as if he wanted to say: "In spite of this, let there not be hostility."[72]

During the course of the following year, 1886, there was a far more serious case of *vhuloi* at Ha-Tshivhase. Malaria was particularly bad in the area that year and many local people died as a result of this. Among their number was *Khosi* Tshivhase's second-most-important wife, Kowâla. The *Missions-Berichte* recorded that: "Amongst the heathens, every death is referred back to witch-doctors and poison-mixers [*Zauberer und Giftmischer*]." An old, grey-haired woman and her daughter were immediately pointed out as having been responsible for the queen's death and were executed. One version of the story doing the rounds at the time was that this was the end of the matter. However, there was a strong rumour that the situation was actually far more complicated. According to this version, the story that they were the *vhaloi* responsible for the death was merely a cover-up. Instead,

> an important woman like the Queen, must have a mat on which to rest (that is the old woman) and a blanket to cover her (that is the younger woman); the real murderers would still be discovered by the throwing of the bones [*Würfel*] – they will soon enough follow these two people to their graves.[73]

Beuster was not the only Berlin Missionary to encounter cases such as these. Thus, on 5 April 1889, Wessmann reported from Gerorgernholtz that:

> Towards mid-day I heard of a large crowd of people who had gathered at the foot of our mountain.[g] They were looking for the so-called murderers of three children who had died close by a few days ago. Should one of the Bawenda [Vhavenda] nation die, then, according to the superstitions of this nation, another person has killed him. This murderer may from then onwards no longer live amongst them [so that they will not be able to kill again]. The search for the culprit soon gets under way. When he

---

g. The Mavhola Mountain on which Wessmann had built the new Georgenholtz Mission Station.

is found, he is secretly attacked and killed – if he does not succeed in fleeing away in time. The women and children of such an alleged murderer are sold, or are bought back by the relatives for cattle. All other property – like the cattle of the murderer – is taken to the king in the capital village. As this is a profitable business for the king, even the murderers of relatives who work in the diamond fields – or those of any other people living in distant lands – are hunted down here as soon as the message of their death reaches here. Because of this, as a rule, only rich people are selected as murderers – people from whom one stands to gain very much. It has also already happened that people have returned from distant places, after they have been pronounced dead and their murderers have long since been killed. These poor people are indescribably blind, not to recognise such palpable deceit, and also do not want to admit its existence.[74]

On the day in question, three *vhaloi* were being sought. As soon as he heard of the gathering, Wessmann had his horse saddled and rode over to where it was taking place. As the missionary described it,

Men, women and many old grey-haired people sat closely huddled together, shivering [shaking], waiting to see what would happen. In the middle of the gathering, sat the witch-doctor [*Zauberdoktor*] with a container filled with water in which he performed his sinister intentions. In the water there were all sorts of little stones which he moved backwards and forwards in the water, with his right hand. While doing this, he uttered inarticulate sounds which reminded one of the ravings [senseless talk] of a drunkard. He held a small piece of rag [cloth] which had belonged to the deceased person in his hand. This was thrown into the water with the stones and, depending on how the cloth settles, it will point out the alleged murderer – he is found in the stones which represent the names of various people.[75]

This seems to be a variation of the "ideal" method of use of the *ndilo* described by Van Warmelo, Stayt and Loubser. According to these authors, first the *thangu* (made of ivory, bone or wood) and associated bones and objects were thrown. The main dice – the old man, old woman, young man and young woman – gave information about the *mutupo* (clan name, totem group and tabus) of the *muloi* or *vhaloi* involved. The astalagus bones and objects gave supplementary information. This gave a preliminary reading and identified the likely parties involved. The *thangu* could be thrown a number of times until there was clarity on the issue. The *ndilo*, which had been filled with water, was then consulted in the presence of all involved parties and (ideally) representatives of the *khosi* or *gota*. Before any of the parties could look at the bowl, they had to rub their eyes with kingfisher droppings as a protective measure against blindness caused by the power of the bowl. Scraps collected from the corpse were mixed with four seeds from the *muruthu* tree (*Croton megalobotrys* – these seeds are extremely light).

These seeds were then set afloat on the water. They drifted around, occasionally remaining stationary for a while and then beginning to move again. Carvings on the inside of the bowl assisted in reconstructing events. There was a small protuberance in the centre of the bowl which had a cowry shell embedded in it. The mound represented either the umbilicus or the *khosi*'s capital, the cowry the female genitals. Eventually, the seeds came to rest alongside the symbols carved on the rim of the bowl [see Illustration 23].[76] During all this time, the *mungome* was carefully watching their movements and interpreting them as they occurred. The first seed to touch the side indicated the *mutupo* of the *muloi*, the second and third the *mitupo* of the mother and grandmother of the *muloi* and the fourth provided extra information. The seeds were then removed with a small spoon or some similar object and placed on the symbols on the rim where they came to rest. The *thangu* were then thrown into the *ndilo*. They were also fished out with a spoon and the information which they revealed was read in conjunction with that provided by the seeds. This whole process could be repeated a number of times until the *mungome* and the majority of the participants (although presumably not the convicted *muloi* or *vhaloi*) were satisfied that finality had been reached.[77]

In the case which Wessmann came across, *Khosi* Makwarela's mother was sitting near to the *mungome*. She and other important councillors from the capital village had originally been discussing other matters. However, they appeared to have taken control over the witch-hunting gathering. In Wessmann's interpretation, his sudden arrival was quite unexpected. The councillors were uncertain of how they should handle this intrusion. Some gave the missionary "a friendly nod of the head", others seemed not to "know whether they should interrupt this activity immediately by speaking up". In an apparent bid to politely get rid of him, Makwarela's mother asked Wessmann to go to the capital village to see her son, who would undoubtedly be very glad to see him. The missionary was nevertheless not to be deflected in his purpose:

> "I am coming here to you," this is how I introduced my conversation. "The whole nation is gathered here today. What are you looking for?" The old lady answered in a shaking [quivering], soft voice: "We are looking for our things." Everybody listened most attentively and at this moment, my appearance was truly no unwelcome sight for the shivering figures. I continued: "Are you not looking for a murderer?" The gathering agreed to this, and it gave me the opportunity to speak of the Living God, who

will in turn demand payment for the innocent blood which is crying out to heaven. The gathering listened to this in absolute silence, without any interruption. The horse was the pulpit.[h] The murderers were not found during this gathering. Makoarele's [Makwarela's] mother tried to make light of the impression which my words left. As I was later told, she had said soon after my departure: "*Mynheer* is only cross because we are performing our rituals near his place."[78]

On another occasion, Wessmann intervened far more directly to save the lives of convicted *vhaloi*. Reporting on events at Georgenholtz in 1892, the *Missions-Berichte* stated that "Brother Wessmann strides bravely into the middle of the environment of heathen abominations, and saves many an innocent person." During the course of the year, he had heard that a man and his sister in a neighbouring village had been identified by a *mungome* as the *vhaloi* responsible for the death of a distant relative. They were reportedly about to be executed by poisoning or strangulation. Rushing there on horseback, he had found the two accused cowering in the corner of a rondavel. Having untied them, he had asked the people in the vicinity and the *gota*:

> "What do you intend doing?"
> "Yes, it is true. We want to kill this old man and his sister, and we are not afraid to even do it in front of your eyes!"
> "I have no doubt that you intend doing this, because you are totally foolish in what you do. You as a new chief [*gota*], now want to show your power. But you do not consider that you are loading a burden [of guilt] on yourself."
> "How can that be? Are they not murderers? The witch-doctor [*Zauberer*] has said so!"
> "Why does the witch-doctor not say that you are the murderer?"
> "So, don't you white people also lock up the sinners [guilty ones] in prison?"
> "Yes we do. And murderers are even hanged. But mark my words, should the white government official come into this country and hear that you have murdered an innocent person, you will also be hanged." These words seemed to make him somewhat doubtful, and he finally promised not to do anything to the two accused.[79]

Wessmann then left the village, taking the rope which had been used to bind the two along with him as a precaution against their being tied up again

---

h. In other words, he sat on his horse while he spoke.

immediately after his back was turned. The *gota* nevertheless ran after him and demanded that he give it back. He was forced to do this in order to avoid an accusation of theft. Wessmann nevertheless extracted a further promise from the *gota* that nothing would be done to the prisoners. He also learned that the whole affair had allegedly been engineered by *Khosi* Makwarela Mphaphuli. The two prisoners took the opportunity to flee out of the lands of the Mphaphulis. As a result, their extended family were stripped of many cattle. The *Misisons-Berichte* cynically noted that: "Since then the heathens prefer holding their council meetings on a Sunday, when it comes to investigating a so-called murder, because they are then safe that the missionary will not appear."[80]

Cases where *dzinanga* attempted to cure the sick received far less attention in missionary diaries and reports and in the columns of the *Missions-Berichte*. Even here, at this stage, the missionaries could not accept that local pharmaceutical knowledge could have any beneficial properties. In their opinion, it could only be based on deception. Thus, Wessmann had recorded on 18 September 1889 that:

> Today I was able to experience in which way the heathen doctors [*heidnische Doktoren*] try to deceive the people and how they make their profits. Our neighbouring Chief had a doctor [*Doktor*] called from a distant place, who should cure the illness of one of his wives. After he had made several small cuts at various places on her body, he took out a piece of a dismembered ox-horn. This served as a tube – by putting the ox-horn on the ear and at other places, he tried to draw the sickness out of her body. On this occasion, the Chief also asked the reason for the illness which his son had recently had. The boy was called and questioned by the doctor as follows: "While you were herding the cattle, you saw a snake with two heads!" The boy replied: "No!" The witch-doctor continued: "Did you not once see a leopard [*Tiger*]?" The boy again replied: "No!" The witch-doctor continued: "Did you not have nightmares one night?" The boy again said: "No!" After the boy was asked even more questions and the questions were always answered with "No!", he was sent away by the doctor, who accused him of ignorance. For this work the father paid a he-goat.[81]

Thus, the missionaries saw local religious beliefs, conceptions about *vhuloi* and beliefs in the power of *dzinanga*, *mingome* and other specialists as being manifestations of the power of Satan or as arising from superstition and duplicity. In their interpretation, a great deal of the blame for the persistence of these beliefs and practices had to be shouldered by the *mahosi*. In missionary analysis, it was only by weakening the power of these living "idols" of the people that any significant progress could be made in weaning people away from enslavement to "darkness" to rebirth in the "light" of Christianity. This kind of thinking had clearly underlain the *Missions-Berichte* report on the visit of Mission-Director Wangemann to Vendaland. Describing his and his missionaries' travels on 8 December 1884, the editors wrote that:

> The land is richly populated by Knopnösen [Knopneusen] and Bawända [Vhavenda]. The Knopnösen no longer have any chiefs – they regard Albasini as their big chief. This is why they are more open to the Gospel. But the Bawända still have their chiefs and their well developed witchcraft customs [*Zauberei-sitten*]. For this reason they are more closed and less accessible to the Gospels. Now, after 10 years of work and suffering, the ice has finally been broken. The people now care for and trust the missionaries and the mission is slowly but surely going forward.[82]

Despite the distorting effect of their ethnographic lens, the missionaries nevertheless recorded a great deal about these beliefs and practices during the nineteenth century. Much of what they recorded is in conformity with the picture painted by Stayt and Van Warmelo. On the one hand, this reflects the degree to which Stayt relied on published sources by Beuster, Gottschling, Gründler and Wessmann (a debt reflected in his bibliography as well as in the text).[i] On the other, the missionary records provide us with a contemporary source against which to compare later descriptions. In one case in particular, that of the *malombo*, they also provide strong evidence to refute later explanations of the purported origins of spirit possession cults.

Thus, it is clear that local rulers and their people did not simply passively accept missionary attempts to draw them away from their deeply-held beliefs about the nature of the world and local ways of interacting with it. Makhado clearly stated that he was deeply suspicious of the idea of a white God. Matsheke threatened Daniel, the Christian from Georgenholtz, with violence and fined him because of his preachings. Holy forests were sites of tension and culture clashes. One of Tshivhase councillors argued that the spirits of the Mutshindudi River had accused the missionaries of being destroyers of the land. In addition, "heathen" resistance to conversion to Christianity and hostility against those who took this step, is a recurring theme of this work. The struggle by Makwarela Mphaphuli to come to terms with, exert some kind of control over and retain power in the face of the new God and his representatives forms one of the main sub-themes of chapter 8. Not all of these struggles were as overtly dramatic. Beuster recorded, on 20 September 1885, that the parents of a young MuLemba man, Poroa, had been trying to win their

---

i. Van Warmelo drew extremely heavily on oral sources.

son back from Ha-Tshivhase Mission Station. In attempting to describe the situation that they found themselves in, he wrote that they

> are now greatly worried and very uneasy. They and all their relatives are exerting themselves, to get as much sympathy as possible. All the divining dice [*Zauberwürfel*] have been employed, and everybody rushes to wherever these point. In spite of all their disappointments they are still hopeful [that they will persuade him to come back] and they comfort themselves with the oracle-like pronouncements of the witch-doctors [*Zauberdoktoren*].[83]

Before moving to the case study of the Mphaphuli royal family which raises many of these themes it is necessary to discuss one more group of related beliefs and practices. These are those surrounding the inscription of power on the African body and the use of the body as a source of power.

1. *BMB*, 1864, pp. 108, 110–111.
2. *BMB*, 1879, pp. 441–442 (quotation, p. 441). Cf. *BMB*, 1888, p. 511; J.M. Dederen, "Venda for the inquisitive tourist", Tourist Workshop, Department of Anthropology, University of Venda, 1986, pp. 2–4; J. Flygare, *De Zoutpansbergen en de Bawenda Natie*, p. 7; E. Gottschling, "The Bawenda", p. 211; H.A. Junod, "Some Features of the Religion of the Ba-Venda", in *South African Journal of Science*, 17, 1920, pp. 208–211; D. McDonald, "Vendaland", in *The Blythswood Review: A South African Journal Review: A South African Journal of Religious, Social and Economic Work*, X (112), April 1933, p. 28; H.A. Stayt *The Bavenda*, pp. 43, 201, 225, 226, 230–236, 240, 310, 313, 360; and R. Wessmann, *The Bawenda of the Spelonken*, p. 80.
3. J.M. Dederen, "Venda for the inquisitive tourist", p. 2.
4. Among numerous sources on the Lemba, see L. Frobenius, "Die Waremba, Träger einer fossilen Kultur", in *Zeitschrift für Ethnologie*, 70, 1938, pp. 159–175; B. Hendrickx, "The Ancient Origin of the Lemba (Mwenye): A critical overview of existing theories", in *Journal of Oriental and African Studies* (Athens), 3, 1991, pp. 172–193; H.A. Junod, "The Balemba of the Zoutpansberg (Transvaal)", in *Folk-Lore: A Quarterly Review of Myth, Tradition, Institution and Custom*, 19(3), London, 1908, pp. 276–287; M. le Roux, "African 'Jews' for Jesus: A preliminary investigation into the Semitic origins and missionary initiatives of some Lemba communities in southern Africa", in *Missionalia*, 24(4), December 1997, pp. 493–510; M.M. Motenda, "History of the Western Venḓa", pp. 51–70; E. Mudau, "Ngoma lungundu and the early invaders of Venḓa", pp. 10–32; T. Parfitt, *Journey to the Vanished City: the search for a lost tribe of Israel*, London, Phoenix (Orion Books), 1997; [H.D.] Schlömann, "Die Malepa in Transvaal", in *Zeitschrift für Ethnologie*, 26, 1894, pp. 64–70; T. Schwellnus, "Die Valemba", in *Mission und Pfarramt: Herausgegeben im Auftrage der Berliner Missionsgesellschaft vom Missionsinspektor M. Wilde*, 5. Jahrgang 1912, pp. 116–120; H.A. Stayt, "Notes on the Balemba: An Arabic-Bantu tribe living among the Ba Venda and other Bantu tribes in the Northern Transvaal and Southern Rhodesia", in *Journal of the Royal Anthropological Institute*, 61, 1931, pp. 231–238; and L.C. Thompson, "The Ba-Lemba of Southern Rhodesia", in *NADA: Southern Rhodesia Native Affairs Department Annual*, 19, 1942, pp. 72–86.
5. *BMB*, 1879, pp. 441.
6. *Ibid*. p. 442. See also H.A. Junod, "Some Features of the Religion of the Ba-Venda", pp. 209–210; H.A. Stayt, *The Bavenda*, pp. 231–232.
7. *BMB*, 1879, p. 442.
8. *BMB*, 1874, pp. 135–136.
9. *BMB*, 1889, pp. 564–565.
10. *BMB*, 1879, p. 442.

11. *BMB*, 1890, pp. 499–500; J.M. Dederen, "Venda for the inquisitive tourist", p. 2; E. Gottschling, "The Bawenda", p. 211; D. McDonald, "Vendaland", Vol. X, No. 112, p. 28; H.A. Stayt, *The Bavenda*, p. 236; and R. Wessmann, *The Bawenda of the Spelonken*, p. 80.

12. Personal Communication, *Vho* Lettie Mphephu-Nengudza; *BMB*, 1879, p. 443; J.M. Dederen, "Venda for the inquisitive tourist", p. 4; E. Gottschling, "The Bawenda", p. 211; N.M.N. Ralushai, "Conflicting Accounts of Venda History", pp. 159–160; H.A. Stayt, *The Bavenda*, pp. 85, 112–113, 236; and R. Wessmann, *The Bawenda of the Spelonken*, pp. 80–81.

13. John Blacking, "The Drama of Thovhela and Tshishonge", at http://era.anthropology.ac.uk/Era_R...a/VendaGirls/Tshikanda/T_Text2.html (and following links), accessed 29 September 2000; N.M.N. Ralushai, "Conflicting Accounts of Venda History", pp. 160–161; and H.A. Stayt, *The Bavenda*, pp. 112–113.

14. *BMB*, 1879, p. 443.

15. *Ibid.* p. 443; J.M. Dederen, "Venda for the inquisitive tourist", p. 6; E. Gottschling, "The Bawenda", p. 214; N.M.N. Ralushai, "Conflicting Accounts of Venda History", pp. 84, 94; and H.A. Stayt, *The Bavenda*, pp. 237–239. Beuster refers to the *zwidudwane* as "*Isidodoane*", while Stayt calls them "*Zwidhadyani*".

16. *BMB*, 1875, pp. 371, 417; 1879, p. 443; 1897, p. 728; N.M.N. Ralushai, "Conflicting Accounts of Venda History", pp. 61–63, 89–90, 92, 93–94, 98, 99, 144–145; Republic of Venda, *Venḓa Travelogue*, pp. 16, 18; H.A. Stayt, *The Bavenda*, pp. 212–213; and N.J. van Warmelo (ed.), *Contributions Towards Venda History*, pp. 151, 153, 160, 161, 167, 173–174.

17. *BMB*, 1875, p. 371.

18. *Ibid.*

19. *Ibid.* p. 372.

20. *Ibid.* p. 373.

21. *Ibid.* p. 374.

22. *Ibid.*

23. See pp. 127–128.

24. R. Wessmann, *The Bawenda of the Spelonken*, pp. 15–17.

25. *BMB*, 1889, p. 546.

26. E. Gottschling, "The Bawenda", p. 197.

27. S.M. Dzivhani, "The Chiefs of Venḓa", p. 46; M.M. Motenda, "History of the Western Venḓa", p. 56; E. Mudau (a) "Ngoma lungundu", p. 25 & (b) "The Dau of Tshakhuma", pp. 75, 77; and N.J. van Warmelo (ed.), *Contributions Towards Venda History*, pp. 6, 14, 20–22. See discussion of ritual homicide in chapter 7 and rituals surrounding warfare in chapter 8 for discussion of the ritual utilisation of human body parts.

28. R. Wessmann, *The Bawenda of the Spelonken*, p. 80.

29. See also E. Gottschling, "The Bawenda", pp. 209, 213–214; H.A. Junod, "Some Features of the Religion of the Ba-Venda", pp. 216–218; and R. Wessmann, *The Bawenda of the Spelonken*, pp. 13, 53–54.

30. For discussion of the *Musanda* language of royalty, see A.E. Khuba (a) "The significance of the Musanda language in Venda: a diglossia", Ph.D. dissertation, Pretoria, University of South Africa, 1993 & (b) "The significance of the Musanda Language in Venda", in *Luvhone*, Department of Education and Culture, Venda, 3(4), April 1994, pp. 29–31; and N.J. van Warmelo (a) "Courts and Court Speech in Venda", in *African Studies*, 30(3–4), 1971, pp. 355–370 & (b) *Venda Dictionary*, p. 7.

31. See also D. McDonald, "Vendaland", X (110), p. 13.

32. G.P. Lestrade, "Some notes on the political Organisation of the Venda-Speaking Tribes", pp. 311–312.

33. N.J. van Warmelo, "Volksgebruike van die Venda", in *South African Railways and Harbours Magazine*, 25(7), July 1931, pp. 998–999.

34. E.O.M. Hanisch, "Legends, Oral Traditions and Archaeology", see especially pp. 71, 75.

35. E.H. Kantorowicz, *The King's Two Bodies: A Study in Medieval Political Theology*, Princeton, Princeton University Press, 1957.

36. G.P. Lestrade, "Some notes on the political Organisation of the Venda-Speaking Tribes", pp. 312–313. See also E. Gottschling, "The Bawenda", p. 208.
37. See p. 142 n47.
38. *BMB*, 1897, p. 444.
39. H.A. Stayt, *The Bavenda*, pp. 242–243, 245–246. See also N.J. van Warmelo (ed.), *Contributions Towards Venda History*, pp. 169, 177–178, 180.
40. *BMB*, 1879, p. 411.
41. H.A. Stayt, *The Bavenda*, pp. 243–245. See also H.A. Junod, "Some Features of the Religion of the Ba-Venda", pp. 214–215.
42. *BMB*, 1879, p. 444.
43. H.A. Junod, "Some Features of the Religion of the Ba-Venda", p. 213; H.A. Stayt, *The Bavenda*, pp. 211, 246–247, 256; N.J. van Warmelo (ed.), *Contributions Towards Venda History*, pp. 169, 174, 179, 185, 186–187; and R. Wessmann, *The Bawenda of the Spelonken*, p. 81.
44. See pp. 160–161.
45. H.A. Stayt, *The Bavenda*, pp. 247–248; N.J. van Warmelo (ed.), *Contributions Towards Venda History*, pp. 186, 187–190.
46. *BMB*, 1879, p. 443.
47. *BMB*, 1890, p. 484; S.M. Dzivhani, "The Chiefs of Venḑa", pp. 35–36; A. Jaques, "Les coutumes funéraires", pp. 256–258; N.M.N. Ralushai, "Conflicting Accounts of Venda History", especially pp. 47, 65, 73–74, 87–88, 89–90, 92, 95, 110, 118; and H.A. Stayt, *The Bavenda*, pp. 206–208, 210–213.
48. *Der Bawenda-Freund*, 14(54), 1896, p. 289; H.A. Stayt, *The Bavenda*, p. 207.
49. A. Jaques, "Les coutumes funéraires", p. 256.
50. Tagebuch der Station bei Schewase (Carl Beuster), 18. September 1874. See also *BMB*, 1875, pp. 445–446.
51. Tagebuch der Station bei Schewase (Carl Beuster), 18. September 1874. See also *BMB*, 1875, p. 446.
52. Tagebuch der Station bei Ha Makoarela (Nicolaus Koen), 25. März 1878, p. 12. See also *BMB*, 1878, p. 494.
53. H.A. Stayt, *The Bavenda*, p. 302.
54. J.M. Dederen, "Venda for the inquisitive tourist", p. 7; H.A. Stayt, *The Bavenda*, pp. 202–203.
55. J.M. Dederen, "Venda for the inquisitive tourist", p. 7; H.A. Stayt, *The Bavenda*, pp. 202, 203–206. See also N.J. van Warmelo (ed.), *Contributions Towards Venda History*, pp. 141–150.
56. J.M. Dederen, "Venda for the inquisitive tourist", p. 7; H.A. Stayt, *The Bavenda*, pp. 204–205, 206.
57. I.M. Lewis, *Ecstatic Religion: An Anthropological Study of Spirit Possession and Shamanism*, Harmondsworth, Penguin Books, 1971, p. 30. See also chapter 3.
58. *Ibid*. pp. 31, 32. See also chapter 4.
59. Tagebuch der Station bei Ha Makoarela (Nicolaus Koen), 10. Januar 1878, pp. 1–3. See also *BMB*, 1878, pp. 493–494.
60. Tagebuch der Station bei Tschewase (Carl Beuster), 12. Juni 1878, p. 25. See also *BMB*, 1880, p. 3.
61. Tagebuch der Station bei Tschewase (Carl Beuster), 12. Juni 1878, pp. 25–26. See also *BMB*, 1880, p. 3.
62. See especially A. Anderson and G. Pillay, "The Segregated Spirit: The Pentecostals", in R. Elphick and R. Davenport (eds.), *Christianity in South Africa: A Political, Social & Cultural History*, Oxford, James Currey and Cape Town, David Philip, 1997, pp. 227–241; Stephen Hayes (a) "The African Independent Churches: Judgement through terminology?", in *Missionalia*, 20 (2), August 1992, pp. 139–146 & (b) *Christian Reponses to Witchcraft and Sorcery* (Article originally published in *Missionalia*, the Journal of the South African Missiological Society, in November 1995), at http://www.geocities.com/missionalia/witch1.htm, accessed 16 October 2000; B.A. Pauw, "The Influence of Christianity", in W.D. Hammond-Tooke (ed.), *The Bantu-Speaking Peoples of Southern Africa*, pp. 415–440; H. Pretorius and L.

Jafta, "'A Branch Springs Out': African Initiated Churches", in R. Elphick and R. Davenport (eds.), *Christianity in South Africa*", pp. 211–226; B.G.M. Sundkler, *Bantu Prophets in South Africa*, Second Edition, London, Oxford University Press, 1961 (first published, 1948); and A.L. Vilakazi, "Magic and Seperatist or Independent Churches", in G.C. Oosthuizen and I. Hexham (eds.), *Afro-Christian Religion at the grassroots in Southern Africa*, African Studies, 19, Lewiston, Edwin Mellen Press, 1991, pp. 164–170. See also J.L. Comaroff and J. Comaroff (a) *Of Revelation and Revolution*, Volume One, especially chapter 6 & (b) *Of Revelation and Revolution*, Volume Two, especially chapter 2. These references include discussion on changing terminology in dealing with what have been called (among other terms) Ethiopian, Zionist, Native Separatist, Bantu Independent, African Independent, heretical, proselytic, millennial, quasi-Christian, cultic, syncrestic, magico-religious and neo-pagan churches. In using the term "African Initiated Churches", I follow the argument of Hennie Pretorius and Lizo Jafta that this focuses "on the churches' distinctive African origins (p. 211)".

63. Tagebuch der Station bei Tschewase (Carl Beuster), 12. Juni 1878, p. 26. See also *BMB*, 1880, p. 3.
64. *Ibid.*
65. Tagebuch der Station bei Tschewase (Carl Beuster), 12. Juni 1878, pp. 26–27. See also *BMB*, 1880, p. 4. For witchcraft accusations between co-wives among Tshivenda speakers, see N.J. van Warmelo in collaboration with W.M.D. Phophi, *Venda Law*: Part 2, p. 307 (754). Among other groups, see, for example, M. Gluckman, *Custom and Conflict in Africa*, Oxford, Basil Blackwell, 1973, pp. 98–100; W.D. Hammond-Tooke, "World-view II: A System of Action", in W.D. Hammond-Tooke (ed.), *The Bantu-Speaking Peoples of Southern Africa*, p. 358; L. Mair, *An Introduction to Social Anthropology*, Second Edition, Oxford, Clarendon Press, 1972, pp. 249–250; P. Mayer, "Witches", Inaugural Lecture, Rhodes University, 1954, in M. Marwick (ed.), *Witchcraft & Sorcery*, Harmondsworth, Penguin Books, 1970, p. 55; A.R. Radcliffe-Brown and D. Forde, *African Systems of Kinship and Marriage*, London, International African Institute, Oxford University Press, 1950, pp. 94, 113, 258, 275.
66. E. Gottschling, "The Bawenda", p. 207; H.A. Stayt, *The Bavenda*, pp. 280, 291; and R. Wessmann, *The Bawenda of the Spelonken*, pp. 84–85.
67. *BMB*, 1880, p. 403.
68. *BMB*, 1885, pp. 407–408.
69. H.A. Stayt, *The Bavenda*, pp. 273–279. See also S. Balic, "Change brings muti murders", in *New African*, 272, May 1990, p. 33.
70. *BMB*, 1885, p. 408.
71. Tagebuch der Station Ha Tsevase (Carl Beuster), 12. Mai 1885, pp. 19–20. See also *BMB*, 1886, p. 416 .
72. Tagebuch der Station Ha Tsevase (Carl Beuster), 12. Mai 1885, pp. 20–21. See also *BMB*, 1886, pp. 416–417.
73. *BMB*, 1887, p. 485. Allegations about the provision of a human "mat" and "blanket" for deceased royals are discussed in the next chapter (see pp. 219–220).
74. *BMB*, 1889, p. 547.
75. *Ibid.*
76. South African Museum; thanking Lindsay Cooper, Collections Manager, Human Sciences, South African Museum for photographing this for me.
77. J. Loubser, "The Venda Divining Bowl in the Museum", in *National Museum News*, 36, April 1989, pp. 18–19; H.A. Stayt, *The Bavenda*, pp. 279–300; and N.J. van Warmelo (ed.), *Contributions Towards Venda History*, pp. 197–200.
78. *BMB*, 1889, pp. 547–548.
79. *BMB*, 1873, p. 469.
80. *Ibid.* p. 470.
81. *BMB*, 1889, p. 570.
82. *BMB*, 1885, p. 74.
83. *BMB*, 1886, pp. 422–423.

CHAPTER 7
The African body

The missionaries reserved their greatest disapproval for ritual practices which reflected the power of society, and its hierarchies, through its power to command and appropriate the bodies of its subjects. In *vhutuka*, *murundu* and *vhusha*, the organisers of the schools inflicted pain on the bodies of the participants as a means of enforcing discipline and obedience not only to them but to society as a whole, as a test of fortitude and courage and as a learning-aid to heighten perceptions and assist in the retention of knowledge. In addition to secret knowledge and formulae acquired during these rites of passage, in the *murundu* and *vhusha*, the changed status of the initiate was inscribed on his or her body through circumcision (in the case of men) or lengthening of the *labia minora* (in that of women). In addition, scars acquired at all three schools would be borne proudly for life as marks of having graduated. Similarly, it would seem that the *espirit de corps* and sense of place in the community which developed through initiation into the *thondo* was as least as great as – if not greater than – the camaraderie developed between age-mates in the other three schools. The missionaries saw initiation into this military school as an even greater obstacle to conversion to Christianity and Westernisation than the other forms of initiation.

The missionaries seriously disapproved of all of these practices. Even greater was their disapproval for the killing of twins, which they saw as murder. Surprisingly, beyond brief references, they did not take up the issue of the killing of close associates and relatives to accompany members of the royal families in death. They also neglected other forms of ritual homicide. I strongly suspect that that this omission resulted from a lack of knowledge of allegations about these practices, rather than reticence to discuss them. The fact that they were prepared to uncritically accept tales of the allegedly cannibalistic nature of the Vhavenda, and participated in spreading these, provides support for this interpretation. So too do missionary accounts of the ritual consumption of parts of the bodies of slain enemies, which form one of the main sub-themes of the concluding chapter.

VHUTUKA, *MURUNDU* AND *VHUSHA*

The missionaries arrived at a particularly interesting time as far as puberty and circumcision rites for boys were concerned. Prior to the widespread adoption of circumcision, participation in the *vhutuka* puberty rite was the norm for local boys. However, at the time that the missionaries were beginning to establish themselves in Vendaland, the *mahosi* were beginning to force their subjects to attend the *murundu*, or circumcision school. In doing so, some seem to have been attempting to create a new supplementary power base among the circumcised. Others seem to have used the schools as a means of increasing revenue.

In the *vhutuka*, once a year, the boys who had attained puberty were collected together in the *thondo* military barracks. Here they would stay for several days and nights being taught *milayo* – formulae encapsulating the rules and knowledge which the rites sought to impart. At various stages, they were forced to endure pain. Pieces of wood (later, gun ramrods, which were harder than wood) were placed between the fingers. These were then pressed together, causing excruciating pain. This was a test of manhood, as the boys were supposed to endure the pain stoically. The climax of the school came when the boys were driven to a river under blows. After spending the night sitting in the water up to their necks (*u kama*), they returned as men. The newly-initiated men then danced *matangwa* – where they marched round in a circle playing on reed flutes and dancing, while girls beat an accompaniment on the drums – with women and girls being present.[1] In commenting on the beginnings of his new station at Georgenholtz in 1877, Koen recorded that:

> The men are not circumcised like the Walemba [Vhalemba] and Bassutho [Basotho], but they also have a kind of washing. They are woken from their sleep at night by young men with sticks. Under a shower of heavy blows, they are driven to the river where they have to sit in the water for about an hour. After this they return, again being beaten all the way. That completes the ceremony. But they sometimes beat them so badly that some boys have already died from the blows.[2]

Individuals seem to have attended *murundu* from about the 1840s. However, circumcision appears only to have become widespread during the last decade or decade-and-a-half of the nineteenth century. Its prevalence spread as a direct result of pressure from the *mahosi*. Force was also increasingly used as a means of ensuring participation.

Basing his argument on oral evidence collected during the 1920s, Van Warmelo argued that the first Tshivenda-speakers to be circumcised were individuals on their way southwards as migrant labourers. On their journey, they had to pass through Sotho-speaking areas. A number of these migrants were forcibly circumcised there. In order to evade this forced circumcision *en route*, Tshivenda-speakers began to voluntarily undergo circumcision. While they first went to Sotho-speaking areas, gradually, lodges began to be opened in Vendaland itself to meet the demand.[3]

At this stage, the practice seems to have had no official sanction from the *mahosi* in Vendaland. However, in about 1854, Makhado entered a circumcision lodge at Tshamatangwi in the lands of *Khosi* Mashau. It would appear that, in doing so, he was attempting to lay claim to the support of "initiates of the circumcision tradition" in any possible future succession struggle. By this act, he became the first member of the Ramabulana royal family to be circumcised. As Nemudzivhadi has pointed out, this meant that, when he ascended the throne about ten years later, he became "the first circumcised prince of the Singo royal house to ascend the throne". This action gave what would otherwise have been historically insignificant great significance.[4] This act was so radical and created such a strong bond between the *khosi* and other graduates of the *murundu* because, as Van Warmelo pointed out, for many years after this, the more culturally conservative regarded those who had been circumcised as "renegades to true Venda custom and tradition". They were "not allowed to be present at sacrifice to the spirits of their ancestors, who would only be angered by the sight of impious converts to strange and foreign ways".[5]

Details on the *murundu*, and forced participation in the school, began to appear in missionary reports from the late 1870s. Reporting on events at Tshakuma during the closing months of the year 1878, the *Berliner Missions-Berichte* noted that:

> At last the war unrest died down as another subject occupied all their minds – circumcision. It is true that circumcision is not a custom generally practised amongst the Bawenda [Vhavenda] – Chief Madzebandela [Madzivhandila] even prohibited it outright. But now, some of his people and the Batonga (Knopneusen) go to neighbouring chiefs [*Capitänen*] to participate in this atrocity. In spite of the horrors associated with the practice – which often deter the youths – this practice on the whole possesses a very great power of attraction amongst the heathen.[6]

Already, many people were also being "forced to participate through surprise attacks". The report continued by stating that, despite the fact that members of the royal families were exempted from participation, some of the relatives of *Khosi* Maphuphe of Lwamondo had been abducted and taken to the *murundu*.[a] The *khosi* mobilized troops, who "attacked the kidnappers and brought back the victims by force".[7]

---

a. This exemption was presumably introduced because participation in the *murundu* would (in theory) have precluded royals from taking part in some of the ritual activities associated with their position in society. However, as we have seen, Makhado, arguably one of the most powerful Vhavenda *mahosi* in the remembered history of Vendaland, was circumcised. I have come across no evidence that he was prevented from fulfilling his religious and ritual duties because of this. The issue is, in fact, an extremely complex one. At a later date, Stayt argued that the spread of circumcision was at first very slow. Indeed, in the eastern areas, where the influence of the conservative Tshivhase and Mphaphuli are most felt, the *murundu* was "still disliked and discouraged" in the late 1920s (H.A. Stayt, *The Bavenda*, p. 127). In addition, to this day, many members of the royal families are discouraged from attending *murundu* if they are in the likely line of succession. If they do, they do so on their individual resolve, rather than by order of the family. This has, on occasion, been used to disqualify candidates from the throne. Basically, a great deal depends on the attitudes and opinions of the *khosi* and his *makhadzi* and *khotsimunene* (personal communication Dr Nelson Musehane, Department of Tshivenda, UNIVEN).

The missionaries forbade Christians to take part in the *murundu* as they saw it as a "heathen" institution. As a result, Schwellnus did not allow his workers to go out and perform their tasks without protection. He feared that they would be attacked and kidnapped while working in the fields or away from the immediate mission surroundings – if they resisted too strongly, they would most probably be killed. The mission cattle were also withdrawn from the best grazing fields, since these fields were near the villages where the circumcision lodge was. It was likely that those participating would either steal the cattle (acceptable behaviour for participants in the *murundu* or *thondo*) or kidnap the herdsmen. The missionary also found that the thatching grass, which he wanted to use for a building, had been burnt down by participants in the school. This was apparently an act of hostility against the mission.[8]

During the course of the following year, *murundu* were held in the vicinity of both Georgenholtz and Ha-Tshivhase. Koen reported that *Khosi* Makwarela Mphaphuli had been against the holding of the school but had been overruled by his father, *Khosi* Ranwedzi Mphaphuli. In the interpretation of the missionaries, the only reason that Ranwedzi had agreed to allow the organisers to hold the school was because he would make a profit out of it – the families of participants had to pay the organisers in hoes (which were used as a form of currency) or livestock and a percentage of the profits was given to the *khosi*.[9] According to Koen, this was only the third time that the lodge had been held in Mphaphuli territory – showing what they felt about this, the *Missions-Berichte* expressed the hope that "May God let it also be the last time". In an action which earned the thankfulness of the mission, Makwarela nevertheless saw to it that no Christians were forced to attend against their will. This must have taken considerable commitment and fortitude on his part since all boys of the required age were expected to attend. Failure to do so was punishable by a heavy fine, payable to the organisers of the initiation lodge.[10]

The *murundu* in the vicinity of Ha-Tshivhase began on 7 April 1879. Beuster reported that this was the first time that it had been held in Tshivhase's lands in fifteen years:

> Messengers were sent in all directions to announce the approaching celebration. Crowds of men gathered in the plain. In their heathen way, they howled for a while and then they scattered in groups, throughout the kingdom. And then the whole devilish apparition of heathendom, which flourished in this ceremony, came to light. Certainly, not in such a way that the people realised what the intention was. On the contrary, the participants threw such a dense veil over what was happening there that any uninitiated who had had information passed on to them, together with the informer, were immediately killed.[11]

Beuster reiterated that the whole undertaking rested upon "speculation and avarice". The organisers stood to make substantial gains. They would share these with *Khosi* Tshivhase who, in turn, would share his profit with his *magota*. This ensured that nobody prevented their people from attending the school and also compensated them for the absence of their subjects from their area for about four months. The parents of each child to be circumcised had to pay two hoes or one goat. Interestingly, Beuster also noted that: "Amongst the Bawenda [Vhavenda], the leader of this ritual is not the king himself, but another person from the Bapedi [BaPedi] nation – from this it seems as if the tradition is only now in the process of infiltrating into the Bawenda culture." This assertion is in conformity with Van Warmelo's assertions about the local origins of the *murundu* in migrant labourers passing through Sotho-speaking areas discussed earlier. However, in the opinion of the missionary, nothing was too depraved for the person running the school or for the ritual itself. He reported that: "It is said that this leader and his assistants also do not scorn human flesh."[12]

The missionary continued by describing what he saw as the conditions of uncertainty which prevailed during the time that the school was in operation:

> The people tremble and shake with fear during the time of the morundo [*murundu*], because there is then total anarchy. Many of them flee to foreign areas. No-one dares to go out unarmed. The women have to do all the work in the field because the men are afraid of surprise attacks. During this time no debt may be claimed, no dance or war may be practised. Transgressors are punished [fined] by the organisers of the morundo. The chiefs, who stand to benefit from this, let such acts of violence go unpunished. Not only the lust for gain drives them to capture people, but also satanic cruelty. The people say: We had to suffer these pains, so now we want to take pleasure in the pains of the young ones.[13]

Judging by the accounts of Stayt and Van Warmelo, the missionary's account of the proceedings and methods of instruction of the *murundu* seems to have been accurate.[14] The school of 1878 at Ha-Tshivhase was established on the plain, away from the houses of the people, at the confluence of two rivers. Presumably because of the fifteen-year gap from the previous initiation, it seems to have been a particularly large one. Beuster described it as "a second village ... unlike any other village in the country". Entry to any uninitiated person was forbidden. After having been circumcised, the candidates were forced into the water, where they had to remain for a considerable length of time. Instruction at the school included learning the dances, songs and *milayo* of the *murundu*. Candidates were beaten with sticks, sometimes until their backs were bleeding, for minor infractions, to teach them to endure pain and to assist them in remembering and internalising the lessons that they were being taught. They had to eat the extremely stiff pap supplied hurriedly while crouching, choking it down non-stop without the usual accompanying vegetables or meat, until it was all finished. They were not allowed to use their hands to transfer the food to their mouths, as they usually did. Instead, they had to form the food into a pyramid and eat it directly with their mouths.[b] They also ate mice, which did not normally form part of their diet. The food was cooked by women who had set up shelters near to, but not in sight of, the initiation village. If they did not cook enough food, they were "beaten unmercifully". Revealing his Victorian sensibilities, Beuster recorded with horror that: "Throughout the whole duration of this ritual, nobody may cover himself with even the smallest piece of clothing – fathers and children mix like this, without any shame." The ritual was held in winter, to aid in the healing of the circumcision wound. Because of the dangers of infection of the circumcision cut, the hardships that the candidates had to endure, and their naked state in the winter cold, a number of the candidates became ill and some died. This was kept secret from those not taking part in the proceedings. Their parents still had to bring food for them and would only learn about their death when they did not return.[15]

Towards the end of the school, the candidates were smeared with fat, to aid in the healing of the scars from their beatings. The closing of *murundu* was marked by the burning of the village and all the equipment which had been used. This symbolic purifying ritual represented the return from the sacred to the profane. It also ensured that nothing which had been used during the school could be used for any other purpose. Those who had "stayed healthy and alive" returned home.[16]

Beuster concluded his discussion of the 1878 *murundu* by arguing that most of those who had taken part had been Vhalemba, living among the Vhavenda, rather than the Vhavenda themselves. There had nevertheless been a significant number of Vhavenda and "Knopneusen" [Tsonga-Shangaan] among the candidates. Beuster viewed this situation with considerable alarm:

> Most certainly this custom, corresponding so much to the innermost being of heathendom, will also soon become part of the Bawenda tradition, unless it is blocked by the mission and the English [British] government. The circumcision protagonists have already overcome one barrier: that people from among the Bawenda are prepared to participate at all. The second barrier: that those belonging to the king's family [royalty] are not circumcised, has been successfully defended this time – and not

---

b. There is an interesting parallel here with anthrophophagaous rituals described later, where participants allegedly had to eat a mixture of ox-meat and human flesh without using their hands, see pp. 248, 270.

without help of the missionary. Those belonging to the king's family form a state within a state – the term Bawenda has its own its own special meaning when applied to them.[17]

By this time, the wider Tshivhase royal family were divided on the issue of circumcision. Some of their number had taken part in the *murundu*, as had some of the local *magota*. Apparently under the influence of Luvhengo Tshivhase, one the *khosi*'s brothers, there had been attempts to force individual members of the royal family, as well as some of the people who lived on the mission station, to be circumcised. Secretly supported by Luvhengo, the organisers of the school had set out to kidnap several youths from the mission station, in direct contradiction to *Khosi* Tshivhase's orders. However, they met with such fierce resistance from the missionary and his converts that they were forced to withdraw.[18]

From May to July of the following year, 1880, it was again the turn of Tshakhuma. Schwellnus reported that the organisers of the *murundu* specifically targeted the mission station. The station reportedly "looked like a fortress under siege". Groups of armed men patrolled around the outside of the station waiting the chance to grab people who showed a lapse in vigilance and drag them off to the circumcision lodge. In order to defend themselves, the station inhabitants armed themselves and only moved about in groups. They also had to protect the newly-planted young trees in the station orchard – the organisers of the school reportedly wished to strip these for the young, flexible branches. These could be used as canes to lash the initiates.[19] In the end, Madzivhandila reportedly

> ordered the circumcision people not to trouble our station and instructed the residents of the station to immediately beat to death any intruders. Although, after this, the heathens then kept themselves more to the boundaries, the terrible cries which the commandos utter when they catch (often with a sling which is thrown out) an uncircumcised person, were often still heard – this noise is raised in order to drown out the cries of help from the victim. Up to now the nobility have still been excluded from the circumcision rites, but Makhato [Makhado] has already expressed the wish that all should participate.[20]

The *murundu* ended on 10 July. The initiates returned "amid much noise, singing and horn blowing". All those returning had to walk past the *khosi*. He then formally returned them to their parents, receiving a hoe for each in return. Repeating earlier assertions, the *Missions-Berichte* reported that: "This is why the chiefs are keen to introduce this custom which has, until a few decades ago, been totally strange to the Bawenda nation." For a short period immediately surrounding their return and the ceremonial handover to their families, normal patters of behaviour were overturned and the initiates wandered around amongst the people singing and blowing on their reed flutes. They were entitled to take something – a snuffbox, a knife, a spear or some similar object from everybody that they met on their way.[21]

The missionaries were not to be granted their wish that the *murundu* be abandoned in Vendaland before it ever really caught on. During the period under review, they continued to view the practice in an extremely negative light and had to continue to be vigilant that people living on the mission station were not forcibly taken for circumcision.[22] They nevertheless managed (in theory anyway) to retain some kind of agreement with Tshivhase, Makwarela Mphaphuli and Madzivhandila (the *mahosi* in whose lands the mission stations were situated) that they would at least discourage the organisers of schools from forcing those from the mission stations to attend. This situation could sometimes result in a fair amount of tension.[23]

The missionaries were equally horrified about the *vhusha* puberty rites for girls. These were the first of the three initiations marking the passage from childhood to womanhood, the other two being *tshikanda* and *domba*. The *vhusha* took place as soon as possible after a girl's first menstruation but was often delayed for a short time until at least three or four girls were ready. Marking the transition from childhood to adolescence, the rite was used to impart knowledge about local laws and customs which the girls would have to follow as women and, especially, to provide sex education. In addition, the rite was preceded by the lengthening of the *labia minora* through manipulation from the age of about ten or twelve years. This practice was continued at the *vhusha*, where a significant part of the time was spent on this. Initiates were subject to humiliation and the infliction of pain. They were also forced to immerse themselves in cold river water, sometimes for lengthy periods. This was designed to teach stoicism, humility and perseverance, and to drive the lessons of the school home to the initiates.[24] Possibly as a result of the nature of the curriculum, the missionaries did not write about the *vhusha* as often as about the *murundu*. Even women who had converted to Christianity would have been unlikely to discuss such private matters with male missionaries. Moreover, given the Victorian sensibilities of the missionaries, it is unlikely that their wives would have discussed these matters with them even if details had been revealed to them by female converts. Also, in addition to being kept secret from the uninitiated in general, these matters were particularly not discussed with men.

The first to comment on the *vhusha* was Beuster. On 19 July 1874, he noted that the sound of a drum playing next to the small river near to the mission station had attracted him to go and investigate what was happening. Accompanied by Johannes Mutshaeni, he discovered several girls immersed in the ice-cold water (there had been frost that morning). Under normal conditions, any man coming across this scene would have been driven away violently by the women. However, they appear to have made an exception for the missionary and his assistant. Beuster was even allowed to address the girls, telling the young women who were assisting that they were participating in the murder of their friends. He informed them that he knew of cases where girls had died of exposure during the rites. On one occasion, he had come across initiates who had collapsed in the river and had had to be carried out. In his opinion, in their callous disregard for the lives of their fellows, they were worse than beasts of prey. He, a white man, had more sympathy for their friends than they themselves had – he felt sorry for the initiates, while those who were assisting appeared to feel no pity. The young women reportedly replied that: "We can't do anything else, the old people will torment us if we don't do it." Feeling powerless to intervene in any meaningful way, Beuster attempted, apparently with some degree of success, to persuade Tshivhase and his *magota* to forbid any *vhusha* rites in the immediate vicinity of the station.[25]

Koen also commented on the institution. Returning from working on the wagon track to Georgenholtz on 24 August 1877, he heard "a row, singing, screaming, drums and whistles". As had been the case at Ha-Tshivhase, the noise came from the river flowing past the mission station. Apparently having been told about the rite by Beuster during his period of acclimatisation, he realised that this

> was the washing of the young maidens. Amongst these people, it is customary that, on puberty, young girls must lie in the cold water for a week, from dawn to dusk. Old and young women ... [also] jump and dance like a herd of young calves. But it is not difficult to imagine the stress which those poor naked girls have to endure by staying for so long in the cold water. Men are not allowed to go near them or they will be greeted with stones thrown by the women. The young girls do not have to do any work during these days; they merely dance. I saw that they decorate themselves with green twigs.[26]

Thus, the missionaries opposed *vhutuka*, *murundu* and *vhusha* on what they saw as a combination of humanitarian grounds and resistance against "heathen" or superstitious practices. However, their opposition to the *thondo* seems to have arisen from much more pragmatic considerations. At stake here was the role that this institution played in building up the military might of the local groups and, through this, their ability to maintain their independence and resist change. The *thondo* was also very closely tied to the power and prestige of the *mahosi* and was seen as a real impediment to weaning people away from their religious and temporal authority to the authority of the Lutheran God and his missionaries.

THE *THONDO*

As a social institution, the *thondo* was a system of military conscription for all young men capable of handling weapons. In concrete terms, this was the name given to an enclosed space in the *khosi*'s capital village with a hut in its centre. Its main function was to provide a meeting place and barracks for the warriors, *vhaḓinḓa*, who regularly spent the night in the *khosi*'s capital as a garrison, and to instruct recruits in the art of war. It was occupied every night, so that the capital was never without defenders. Secrecy as to what took place inside this *thondo* was rigidly enforced. It was surrounded by high walls and the entrance was built in a zigzag form to stop the inquisitive from glancing inside. Non-initiates were forbidden to enter the area.[27]

Initiation into the *thondo* took place when a group of boys were considered old enough to handle weapons. Sent there not only from the *khosi*'s village but from the outlying villages as well, they had to crawl through the gate on their knees, following one of the initiated who went in front. Upon entering the walled enclosure, they were lead around this a number of times, at times on their knees and at times flat on their stomachs. At every veranda pole of the central hut, they had to *losha* (greet humbly). While this was happening, they were repeatedly "being pinched, and not only for ceremony, but hard". They did not dare to shout out in pain, for this would have brought severe punishment and ridicule. At every pinch, the rules of the *thondo* were "repeated, to let them penetrate well". These included admonitions such as: "You may not betray anything", "You must honour and obey your superiors", "Do everything that you are commanded", "Do not dare to tell anything to uninitiated (people)."[28]

Instruction in the *thondo* was supervised by the oldest and wisest of the *khosi*'s councillors. In the central rondavel were stored "all the fetishes of the tribe" and a "wood-carved image of their totem and others of a man and woman about 2 feet in height". These were used for instructional purposes. According to Missionary Gottschling:

> The young people in the *tondo* are shown all these sacred things of the tribe and acquainted with their meaning and use ... The pupils of the *tondo* are also taught the full range of etiquette in the intercourse with their superiors and chiefs. They are taught to be brave in war, cunning in stealing and true to their special form of heathenism, i.e. to their ancestors. They are taught to bear pain without showing it, and are thus practised in self-restraint. Those who have undergone the discipline of the *tondo* in the same year form a special brotherhood (*morole*), and will not betray one another nor give evidence against each other.[29]

Completion of the training in the *thondo* conferred the status of adulthood on the initiate. After this, in addition to the times he was forced to spend there for defensive purposes, an initiate was free to use it as a place for socialising with his peers. Men frequently met there to barbecue meat and socialise together. "This service, *vhuḓinḓa*, is therefore a regular tribal institution, and clearly is also intended to foster the qualities of manhood and to engender a certain espirit de corps." It was also very much tied up with the power and prestige of the *khosi*. According to Van Warmelo:

> It would appear that the *thondo* is in essence or in origin a kind of sanctum of the ruling house. Some *thondos* are so small that they cannot possibly hold one-tenth of the chief's *vhaḓinḓa*. Yet it is never dispensed with. Every chief must build his own *thondo*, and the status of the different *thondos* in the country depends entirely on that of their owners, this status determining the right of all members of a certain *thondo* to be granted or refused admission to the *thondo* of another.[30]

Beuster regarded the *thondo* as "one of the most significant obstacles which stand in the way of the conversion of the heathens" and a "bulwark of Satan", while Wessmann called it "a kind of Devil's school [*Teufelsschule*]".[31] The leaders of the *thondo* did not use their troops to interfere directly in the work of the mission. However, they obviously acted to prevent their troops from deserting to the mission stations. The logic was obvious – if the troops were at the mission stations, they would not be available for their military and bodyguarding duties. Unable to concede this point, the missionaries nevertheless portrayed the military leaders in a far more sinister light:

> As soon as we make known our intentions to proclaim God's Word at a village where such a *thondo* is found – as a rule these are usually the most respected and most populated villages – all the men of the village usually disappear at the given sign of the leader of the *thondo*. They usually go behind the fence which surrounds the *thondo* and nobody may follow them there. As the leaders of these *thondos* are usually the biggest villains and enemies of the Gospel, it is very difficult to get to those under them – at least not at home, before their eyes. These *thondo* leaders, as well as the doctors [*Doktoren*] and the rulers of the country, are the main enemies and obstacles to the Gospel.[32]

In missionary interpretation, another great obstacle to the spread of the Gospel in Vendaland was the practice of killing twins. We have already seen that, for the missionaries, it was *Gota* Totane's acquiescence to the killing of his second-born twin child which marked his "real defection from the faith" which he had been converted to in Natal. Beuster reported that, despite the fact that the first of the pair of twins had been born dead, the family had insisted that, following normal practice, the second-born be killed.[33]

TWINS

It seems that the practice in fact varied from place to place in Vendaland. During the nineteenth century, three accounts state that only the second twin was killed; the other missionary reports stating that both twins were killed.[34] Stayt also noted that – unlike most other southern African groups, who only killed one twin – in Vendaland, both were put to death.[35] The birth of twins at Ha-Tshivhase mission station in 1878 took the matter from one of humanitarian intervention to save the lives of the newborns to an issue right at the heart of the position of the mission in Vendaland.

Soon after their arrival in the area, the missionaries had heard about the Christian convert Andries.[c] Although "still praying", he proved to be extremely elusive. Beuster and Johannes Mutsaheni made a number of unsuccessful attempts to meet with him and persuade him to attend services at Ha-Tshivhase.[36] Finally, during the latter part of 1875, Johannes Mutshaeni managed not only to contact Andries but also to persuade him to attend a church service.[37] Early the following year, he agreed to move to Ha-Tshivhase. However, after this he became seriously ill and did not carry out his intention. It was only on 21 November 1878, a year after the death of Johannes Mutshaeni, that he finally moved to the station. This time he had been persuaded by David Fuzane, another Muvenda Christian convert who had been baptised while working as a migrant labourer in Natal. Commenting on this, Beuster expressed the hope that this would be a turning point both for Andries and for the station.

Andries' arrival would indeed involve the mission in dramatic events – far more dramatic than they would have wished. These involved saving the lives of a pair of twins and served to establish an important point about conflicts between local law and missionary law on mission stations with Tshivhase. The missionaries were nevertheless able to see the hand and saving Grace of God in these developments.

Shortly after Andries, his wife and their child arrived at the station, his wife gave birth to twins. From the point of view of the missionaries, God had ordained that the move took place just in time:

> Both would most certainly have been strangled – according to the heathen custom – had they not been saved under the protection of the missionary. And how easily the murder of these children could have been the cause for the total regression into heathendom for these unfortunates. After the birth of these twins, the family first experienced a tremendous shock. The old grandmother was all for immediately killing the children, and she had

---

c. I use the Afrikaaans/Dutch version of his name as this is probably the name by which he was known. However, in missionary sources, his name appears as "Andreas" – the German version of Andrew/Andries.

to be closely watched that she did not commit the murders. But
she was finally pacified and Andries also agreed; the mother
said: "I have received the children from God, so I will also keep
them."[41]

By taking this step, the parents had committed a serious offence, endangering not only themselves but the whole community. Beuster well realised that "According to the laws of this country, this was a severely punishable act" and that Tshivhase "would eventually have to pronounce a sentence over their actions."[42] He thus decided to pre-empt this by visiting the *khosi*. Having lived in the area for six years, and presumably having been advised by the Christians and his assistants, by this time he realised that he would have to approach the matter extremely carefully if he was to stand any chance of success.

In keeping with local ways, he did not take any of the people directly involved in the problem with him. Showing a degree of insight unusual in the case of the missionaries, he also did not take the Native Assistant David Fuzane with him. Most probably, he realised that had a Muvenda Assistant been present, Tshivhase would have been forced to draw attention to the fact that this Assistant well knew the law and should have seen to it that it was enforced. The *khosi* himself would then have been forced to insist that the law was rigidly implemented. Instead, Beuster took along Stoffel and Franz, the two Native Assistants who had come from Waterberg-Modimulle (in March 1879) to assist him after a difficult period which lasted for more than a year after the death of David Denga and Johannes Mutshaeni. In a similar way to which I will argue that Paulus Luvhengo could be excused for not knowing local customs in the first meeting with Ranwedzi Mphaphuli, while Johannes Mutshaeni could not, I am convinced that Beuster did this deliberately so as to allow Tshivhase as much freedom of action as possible.[43]

In describing his course of action, Beuster wrote:

> I approached the topic in a round-about way. I told Tshewase [Tshivhase] that I had something that worried me and that my heart was aching very much because of an evil thing. The matter concerned an evil custom practised amongst his people. Because I am a messenger of God, I cannot cover up evil but have to speak out directly and warn people against evil. So I will speak out openly: The thing which pains my heart, is the matter that every year many children in his country are killed – those that are born as twins and those whose teeth develop first in their upper jaw.[44]

In Beuster's interpretation, Tshivhase "was visibly astonished at this speech and needed a moment to compose himself". Once he had done so, an exchange recorded by Beuster reveals that he clearly viewed allowing children of this nature to live as an abomination:

> He then answered: "*Mynheer, zi a elã,*" [*zwi a ela*] i.e. they are impure. I answered: "What is impure. Will they do any harm?" He: "It is not our custom to let such children live."
> "Are they then not also people?"
> "Yes, they are people."
> "So the person who kills them, is he not a murderer?"
> "But they are impure!"
> "They are not impure! Why do we [whites] not kill twins and other nations also don't do it and it does not harm us? Look at our kitchen maid who comes from Waterberg – you know her, don't you remember – isn't she also a twin?[d] Yet she and her sister are both alive and they live well."
> "So she is a twin and both are still alive?"
> "Yes, both are still alive."
> "That is a miracle. But we will continue to kill them."[45]

It was then that the wisdom of bringing Stoffel and Franz became apparent. Since they were outsiders, Tshivhase could see them as appendages of Beuster's. While ultimately subject to his authority, he could choose to view them as being subject to Beuster's immediate authority. Had they been Vhavenda, as a *khosi*, the overlord of the area in which they were living, he would have been forced to protect the law and local tradition. He would thus have been unable to enter into the following dialogue with them:

> Turning to the evangelists: "What do you do? Do you let them live?" They: "Oh Sire [*O Herr*], we do not kill them!" We say: "God has given them to us so we cannot kill them." Tshewase: "Oh I know very well that those who have learned do not kill. You are different people." Then Stoffel suddenly interrupted (to my mind a bit too early): "But Sire, if something like this were to happen to us, who stay with *Mynheer*, do we have to kill the children?" He: "Absolutely not! You will rear them! You will certainly bring them up!" We in unison: "So that is all right, Your Majesty [*König*]."[46]

With some justification, Beuster chose to interpret this pronouncement as setting a crucial precedent for relations between the *khosi* and the mission station. It would seem that he was not exaggerating when he stated that, had Tshivhase decided differently, they would have been forced to close the mis-

---

d. Waterberg was the mission station where Mrs Beuster had lived before her previous husband, Rev. Koboldt, had died.

sion station in his area. From their point of view, being forced to kill the twins on the mission station would have rendered their presence in the area untenable:

> I continued and said: "My heart is now calm, because it depended on these words, whether I could remain in this country and stay with you as a teacher. If you would have forced us to kill the children, we could no longer have stayed here." I then addressed the people (there were three of them): "Have you now all heard the words of the king?" They: "Yes, we heard what he said!"
>
> "Remember these words. You all have to be witnesses in this matter." And then I grasped the hand of my king and spoke with a joyful heart and sincerely (because I must admit, I love my Tshewase as much as a teacher can love his heathen ruler) saying: "Now I would like to inform you about something, King: we already have twins on our station." He, very surprised about it: "So they are there! Whose children are they?" This was explained to him and the king stuck to his original pronouncement: "Let the children live. Do not kill them but bring them up!" I again grasped the King's hand and expressed my satisfaction. Automatically the other Christians followed my example and expressed their joy over this verdict before the king.[47]

Tshivhase obviously realised the importance of this ruling just as much as the missionaries did. However, just as he was left with no option but to make the decision that he did if he wished to keep the missionaries, so he had no option but to stick to the law as far as the wider community was concerned. Certainly, he believed that failure to do so would expose his people to great dangers and cost him his throne.[e]

During the course of the following year, a second set of twins was born at Ha-Tshivhase. Since the legal precedent that twins born on the mission station did not have to be put to death had already been established, this time, the case was not even taken to Tshivhase. The twins were allowed to live.[48] In fact, both sets of twins became matters of local curiosity. For example, the mother of the *gota* whose territory neighboured Ha-Tshivhase visited Beuster in the company of some of her ladies-in-waiting on 28 April 1885. Beuster recorded that, after they had discussed a wide variety of topics:

> This heathen lady even expressed the wish to be introduced to our twin children – which is quite daring for a woman who is still so deeply steeped in heathen traditions. It is generally

---

e. The whole question of the power of *mahosi*, the limitations on their power and sanctions for the abuse of power has been considered on pp. 176–179.

feared that the sight of such children, yes even to talk about such things, or to touch the parents of such children, must bring bad luck to the person concerned ... This lady could now even speak about people who had lost several children, because they always had twins which were killed in the traditional heathen way.⁴⁹

Outside the mission station, these token rescues of twins nevertheless had little effect. Moreover, nobody was exempted from carrying out these acts. For example, on 26 June 1865, Beuster reported that *Khosi* Tshikalange had come to speak to him "about his earthly affairs – he is still fairly inaccessible towards God's Word".ᶠ A few days previously, one of his wives had given birth to twins. Convinced that he had no other alternative, he had agreed to their being put to death. In the discussion which followed, the Native Assistant Stoffel stated that he knew about four other pairs of twins in the area who had been killed. Tshikalange spoke about ten other cases.⁵⁰

Under the influence of the missionaries, Makwarela Mphaphuli seems to have acted to curb the killing of twins in 1887.⁵¹ One is not certain of how energetically he pursued this. However, on 4 October 1888, Beuster baptised what was reportedly the first pair of twins not put to death in the lands of the Mphaphulis. They were two great-grandchildren of *Khosi* Ranwedzi Mphaphuli himself. Reporting on the baptismal feast, Beuster stated that the "heathens" had also been invited:

> I heard them negotiating, whether they should take the risk of attending this feast and whether they could eat the food which would be served there.ᵍ One of them boldly said: "Come on, here with us nothing is unclean!" After this they had all started eating until they were satisfied. In this way heathendom has received another blow here. If one realises with what enormous fear the heathens are prejudiced in this regard – how they take care not to bring upon themselves the same evil, through avoiding any contact whatsoever with such twin children or their parents – then one has to marvel at these decisions and the changes in attitudes, even if at first they are of a purely external nature only. If heathen parents should experience such misfortune, the next thing to do would be to kill and get rid of the children in a

---

f. Tshikalange, son of Ranwedzi Mphaphuli and the brother of Makwarela Mphaphuli, is one of the major actors in chapter 8. As with his brother, Tshiklanage's *de jure* position was that of a *gota*. However, for similar reasons to those discussed for Makwarela, I refer to him here as *khosi*.

g. Having abandoned local taboos concerning food, it was conceivable that the Christians would have served "unclean" food. On top of this, this was the home of twins – who knew what kind of forces their continued survival would unleash. In this way of thinking, eating the food could have been dangerous.

wet [moist] spot, as soon as possible – these twin children are mostly buried in pots along the river banks. Then the doctor [*Doktor*] is called in who, through all kinds of medicine [*muti*] and good payment, has to work against the recurrence of this evil. The doctor takes with him all the clothes of the man and the woman, because they could hold the seeds of the recurrence of such an evil. One does not leave such a home through the door, but through an opening which has been broken into the wall on the back [rear] side of the house.[52]

Despite the missionary optimism here, the practice of killing twins was certainly common in Vendaland until at least the 1930s. It would seem that it only began to die out once it began to be prosecuted as murder in Western courts.[53]

BURIAL PRACTICES AND RITUAL HOMICIDE

The absence of missionary comment on the alleged ritual killing of retainers or others to accompany members of the royal family into the grave is extremely strange. In the previous chapter, reference was made to the human "mat" and "blanket" allegedly provided for *Khosi* Tshivhase's second-most-important wife, Kowâla.[54] The only other case of a similar nature traceable in nineteenth-century missionary literature from Vendaland concerned the Tsonga–Shangaan *Hosi* Njamande. An "old grey-haired woman, a young boy, a girl and a black dog were [allegedly] buried alive with him".[55]

The only explanation for this apparent reticence to expose practices which would have been perfect for accounts to gather support from Germany for the mission endeavour, was that neither their local converts nor the local people discussed the matter with the missionaries. Burial (or the first burial) of *mahosi* and members of the royal family was conducted in great secrecy. Only selected members of the royal family were present and they were sworn to secrecy.[56] It was taboo to refer directly to the death of a *khosi* – instead euphemisms such as "the pool has dried up", "the *khosi* has vanished", "the *khosi* has gone away" or "we see him no longer" were used.[57] Matters surrounding the death of *mahosi* were simply not spoken about. Commoners would not have known the details while members of the royal families would have refused to discuss them with the missionaries.

It was only much later that S.M. Dzivhani, a Christian convert, made accusations about ritual homicide in the context of the burial of *mahosi* in an essay published in N.J. van Warmelo's *The Copper Miners of Musina and the Early History of the Zoutpansberg* (1940). Dzivhani noted that, among some Vhavenda groups:

> The corpse of a chief is not buried in the ground and covered with earth. For him they slaughter a black bull and skin it, and

> sew the corpse in the hide in the evening. A small hut is built and plastered with mud inside and outside, and even inside the roof. A platform is erected inside. They then summon those who used to live in close contact with the chief, who waited on him and ate with him, and these are killed by strangling with a girdle. They are tied hand and foot with the creeper bopa-vha-fu and placed upon the platform. They are called the mat of the chief. Then the corpse, sewn up in the hide, is bent up and placed upon the corpses of the retainers, and others are placed over it. Under the platform they make a hole into which the moisture from the rotting corpses runs. A retainer who wants to save his life when he sees that the chief is about to die and there is no hope, will immediately go on a visit very far away in another country, for there is no other means of escape. A retainer who they fear might show fright, is enticed into the *thondo* and strangled there. Another they might send on a distant errand with others who are to strangle him on the road, and nobody will ever hear where he went, for the stranglers will return and say "We became separated on the road and thought he had returned home."[58]

During the period that the death was kept secret from the people, the corpses were left to decompose in the sealed hut. On an appointed day, the royal servants blew *tshikona* in a way known as *tshikumo*. This was a clear sign to the initiated that the *khosi* had passed away. However, this was still not publicly acknowledged – cases were still brought to court and settled in the name of the *khosi* and orders were still given in his name. Things continued in this manner until the day was fixed for the installation of the new ruler. According to Dzivhani, at first, the new ruler would not decide cases on his own. Instead, he would

> listen to those who are his elders, until the time is come for the little hut to be broken down and the royal bones to be sewn up in the hide of another bull. In the cavity underneath the platform there will remain the bones of the retainers who formed the mat of the dead chief, and a branch of the mubvumela tree is planted there, earth is cast over all and a wall built around it. Then the bones of the chief are taken to the sacred grove of his ancestors, where they bury the dead ... In this place they hold their annual rite of sacrifice, and the chief has no power to decide cases until the bones of his predecessor have been taken there.[59]

Because of his core position in the life of his group, the installation of the new *khosi* necessitated rebuilding the supernatural defences of his village. Related to the rituals for the supernatural protection of the borders discussed in chapter 6 (see p. 187), Wessmann drew attention to similar protective devices for villages:

> In times of distress and war the Bawenda try to protect themselves by witchcraft, and medicine which they lay across the roads in order to make the country strong, so that the enemy cannot enter their land. In the same manner they protect themselves against illnesses, and put a pail with medicine across the entrance of their village, by which they believe they will exclude even death.[60]

Again, during the nineteenth century, Wessmann and the other Berlin Missionaries did not describe the role of ritual homicide in this process. Presumably, they had not yet been able to penetrate the veil of secrecy which surrounded it. However, the anthropologist H. du Plessis, writing in 1945, recorded that:

> At the village of a chief, where every time when a new chief succeeds [to power] a new entrance is built, besides these different things, skulls of people who are killed on this occasion are also buried under both gates. In addition, at the back-side of the village, outside the surrounding fence, pegs are driven into the ground after they have been smeared with medicines.[61]

In a footnote on the same page, he explained further that:

> For three chiefs following each other, a certain family is appointed and the head of this family then, at such an occasion, has to kill an old man and two children and the skulls of these three are then buried in the entrances. These persons' skin is removed and is stretched over the sacred drum(s) of the chief. A cattle-hide was [placed] over this human skin.[62]

In a number of descriptions, the institution of chieftainship was thus closely linked to the appropriation and use of the bodies of subjects of the *mahosi* through ritual homicide. Changes in leadership were marked by rituals to safeguard the village which involved the use of human bodies, or body parts. A final year undergraduate student also argued in an assignment that, from time to time, the *khosi* (or his close relatives acting in his interest) would order a ritual homicide to strengthen his power and vitality.[63] However, beyond the ritual use of body parts in the context of warfare (which will be discussed in chapter 8), during the course of the nineteenth century, much of this seems to have escaped the scrutiny of the missionaries. At this stage, they also seem to have been unaware of the alleged role of ritual homicide in ensuring a bountiful harvest for the community.

As agro-pastoralist communities, the Vhavenda were dependent on an adequate supply of rainfall for grazing-lands and fields. Moreover, since the harvest provided both food for the months ahead and the seeds for the following season's planting, hardy seed which would store well and survive variable weather conditions after its planting was of crucial importance. Once these elements had been satisfied, it was primarily the labour of the community that ensured success in farming. As the central guardian of the community, it was the *khosi*'s task to ensure that these requirements were met. Since success or failure depended largely on human initiative, it was reportedly to the human body that he turned in order to attempt to gain control over the fickle forces of nature. All the community would bring seeds to the *khosi*'s capital. In great secrecy, these seeds would then reportedly be mixed with others which had been treated with medicines containing a mixture of herbs and human body parts. The people would then take seeds from the common stock to plant in their own fields. This ensured a good harvest.[64]

Support for the argument that the missionaries did not engage themes of this nature because they did not know about them is provided by the fact that, in other contexts, they offered a complex reading of what they saw as local people's perceptions of the power contained in human flesh. This is clearly revealed in their analysis of some of the events surrounding the burial of David Denga (whose life history was discussed in chapter 2), in their tales of cannibalism and in their discussions of anthropophagous rituals in warfare.

At the funeral of his comrade David Denga, Johannes Mutshaeni had said that he would like to guard the grave for a few nights, as he was afraid that the body would be stolen. He dismissed Beuster's counterargument that nobody was likely to disinter the body of a man who had died of smallpox. Instead, he argued "that David had been a hard-working man, so one could ascribe very special characteristics to his flesh, and therefore his flesh would be much sought after". Unlike the case in local burials, the cemetery was not near to people's homes and it would be relatively easy to rob the grave at night. However, since he was feeling so sick with what would turn out to be his own fatal bout of smallpox, Mutshaeni was unable to guard the grave. Instead, he and the missionaries

> took the precaution of putting many pieces of broken glass into the soil when we filled up the grave, in this way hoping to prevent the grave-robbers – who scrape the soil of out the grave with their hands – from invading the grave. (Human flesh is especially used by these heathens, when making hoes. The iron is improved and more effective if human flesh is first mixed with the ore, before it is smelted. This flesh is much sought after, because such a high value is laid on this flesh. For this reason, those who remain behind try to protect their dead from these hyenas in human form. They do this by burying their dead

near their homes and they usually guard the graves for a few nights.)[65]

Beyond these explanations of fears of sinister happenings, it is also likely that Mutshaeni was scared that David's "heathen" relatives would attempt to recover his body for burial according to Vhavenda rites. However, the fact that he had died of smallpox seems to militate against this interpretation. As indicated by the secrecy surrounding smallpox cases, and the fact that people had been too scared to bury the child whose dead body possibly infected Denga in the first place, people were well aware of how infectious the disease was. It is unlikely that they would have dug him up to rebury him. By a similar argument, even were freshly-buried corpses on occasion dug up so that body-parts could be used in *muti* or iron-smelting, it is likely that people would have been disinclined to exhume Johannes because of the manner of his death.

Similarly, without denying the possibility that fresh graves were situated near people's homes and guarded for a few days for the reasons stated in the text, there were also less sinister explanations. A dead person is an ancestral spirit. When disturbed, you disturb the ancestral spirits. There is always the possibility that an enemy, or somebody who is ill-disposed towards you, will disturb or desecrate the grave. On the other hand, to this day, when families celebrate important occasions, such as marriages, or need assistance in times of trouble, rituals are performed at the ancestral graves. Only senior members of the immediate family participate in these. Having the graves situated at the houses makes it easier to keep these occasions private.

One should also not forget that the missionaries constantly had their principals in Berlin, and the wider mission community in Germany, in mind when writing their reports. The wider public expected such things to happen. It was also important to impress upon them just how important mission work among these "raw" and "dark" "heathens" really was, so that more donations would be made. Thus, even if they did not blatantly falsify their reports, the missionaries had reason, on occasion, to emphasise the dramatic, the unusual and the bloodthirsty. This is clearly revealed in their descriptions of the allegedly cannibalistic habits of the Vhavenda.

TALES OF CANNIBALISM

Stories about cannibalism were arguably the most extreme form of "othering" perpetuated by Europeans against Africans. In their racist obsession with cultural evolutionism, they dichotomised what they saw as their own developed "civilisations" and African "savagery" or "barbarism"; the "light of civilisation" and the "darkness of heathenism".

It is nevertheless important to go deeper than this in attempting to make sense of the sources. In conformity with one of the conventional strategies to demonise strangers or enemies, other African groups seem to have portrayed Tshivenda-speakers as being cannibals. This impression, in turn, was uncritically accepted by explorers and the Berlin Missionaries. Both of these groups had been preconditioned by their European upbringing to accept the "reality" and prevalence of African cannibalism. The missionaries had been further influenced by what they had been told by their Pedi converts before coming to Vendaland. The Berliners soon came to be seen as the resident experts on "the Bawenda" and their ways. Their pronouncements about the supposedly cannibalistic habits of the inhabitants of Vendaland were repeated and rehashed by others.

The German explorer Carl Mauch provided the first textual description of Tshivenda-speaking groups as cannibals in July 1871. Describing his visit to *Khosi* Lwamondo, he stated that:

> Lomondo [Lwamondo] himself is of an uncouth appearance and his face is almost animal-like. While his devouring tools, behind extremely averted lips, have grown to perfection, the lids partly hide the small, cruel eyes and a once red-coloured piece of cloth makes the forehead appear still lower by the manner in which it is tied around the head. His behaviour matches fully one's expectations; crude talk in a shrill voice. I believe he would make a perfect character to portray a cannibal, and I can hardly doubt the pronouncement of one of my companions to the effect that he actually is one. In fact all the Berg Kaffirs [Vhavenda[h]] are still such.[66]

It is easy to dismiss this kind of description as resting on hearsay evidence and as being a reflection of the prejudices of nineteenth-century Europeans, rather than any kind of African "reality". Indeed, Mauch's description is a good example of the kinds of descriptions that Brian Street was thinking of when he discussed cannibalism in his work on representations of "primitive" society in English fiction between 1858 and 1950. In this discussion, Street noted that:

> If ... cultural differences can be put down to racial heritage, then even cannibalism, supposedly one of the greatest distinctions between a gentleman and a savage, can be cited as a hereditary characteristic of inferior races. The Englishman, it is assumed, doesn't practise it because his instincts, passed down to him through his race, revolt against it. Thus Tarzan, with no

---

h. According to Gottschling, writing as late as 1905: "Among Europeans very few know the real name of the Bawenda; either they mix them up with the Basotho or simply call them 'Mountain Kaffirs', because they live in the Zoutpansberg mountain range" (E. Gottschling, "The Bawenda", p. 195).

cultural training in an English environment, nevertheless has inherited the instinct which tells him that the cannibal breaks a natural law ... The natives, of course, have no such inhibitions and proceed to break natural law with relish, revelling in meals of human flesh ... That cannibalism is natural to primitive people is implied by Gilson in a description that links it with their physical appearance. They are "bestial, gorilla-like creatures, with exceptionally powerful jaws and teeth like fangs, hunting human flesh".[67]

Thus, in deconstructing Mauch's account (and others like it), one is provided with a window into the unconscious forces which shaped the way that explorers and missionaries interpreted and made sense of the world – both physical and psychological – that they found themselves inhabiting in Africa. It may be argued that Mauch's description of Lwamondo tells us more about his prior conditioning which made him see an independent African ruler, whose lands had not yet been colonised by European settlers, as a cannibal, than about Lwamondo himself. Even the description of the *khosi's* physical features and dress was shaped by European stereotypes.

Similarly, I have no difficulty in rejecting the account of the Reverend D.F. Ellenberger of the Paris Evangelical Mission Society mission to the Basotho which appeared in his book *History of the Basuto*. In writing his account of the travels of semi-legendary Batebang king Mohlomi before his accession to power, Ellenberger used oral tradition describing events during the 1780s as his main source. The description of the prince's encounter with the Vhavenda could easily have come from the pages of Rider Haggard or one of the other African adventure writers and it portrayed them as cannibals in stereotypical terms:

> Far away in the North Mohlomi arrived at the abode of some cannibal tribes, but they did him no hurt, perceiving that he was a man of peace, though Segoaela, one of his companions, who was rather quarrelsome, nearly served as a meal for these hungry people. Mohlomi arrived at one of their villages unexpectedly about noon. The sun was very hot, and everyone in the village slept. Nothing was seen but the cattle lying in the shade, and one heard no sound but the barking of the dogs and the buzzing of the flies. But little by little the inhabitants came out of their huts and the chief appeared and invited Mohlomi to sit down in the shade with his people. To their great horror, he offered the travellers some human flesh to eat; but they excused themselves, saying that this kind of food was strange to them, and they dared not partake of it, whereupon an ox was killed for them. They and the cannibals conversed together, asking and

> answering questions. These cannibals (*Ma-ya-batho*) were black and stout, resembling Bechuana in speech and appearance. Their hair was long and frizzled, and they kept it greased with human fat. Their bodies were smeared with red ochre; their huts were covered with reeds and thatching grass; their villages were large and built in a circle. They drank much thick milk, and ate the flesh of their fellows as a delicacy. They even seem to have devoured the flesh of those who died. They were at one time well known by reputation to the Basuto, who called them Bamahlabaneng ("people of the antipodes"), because they lived so far away.[68]

In Ellenberger's terms, people practised cannibalism because they lusted after the taste of human flesh, rather than because they had no other food. This was evidenced by the fact that they had cattle, drank milk and also owned dogs for hunting. He further alleged that they had originally become cannibals through eating prisoners of war and that "according to the missionary Beuster they remained such, until finally subjugated by the Government of the South African Republic at the recent date of 1898".[69]

According to Ellenberger, at the time of Mohlomi's travels, there was no cannibalism amongst the Basotho. However, he detailed numerous cases of this practice among them during the first three decades of the nineteenth century. These he ascribed largely to what he saw as the holocaust of wars set in motion by the rise and growth of the Zulu kingdom, the so-called *Mfecane* or *Difaqane*. He argued that groups were driven into cannibalism by starvation as a result of their having lost their cattle and crops to raiders or by their defeat in battle. People either ate their own dead or consumed those they managed to kill. Cannibals and robbers infested the country and one of the reasons for state formation among the Basotho was the protection offered against these conditions.[70] Cannibalism and lawlessness were eventually largely brought under control by the efforts of Moshoeshoe.[71] In attempting to explain this "aberration", he laid the original blame directly at the door of the Vhavenda, the people who saw human flesh as "a delicacy". For the Paris missionary, it was "improbable that the idea of eating their fellow-men would have occurred to the South African Bantu had the example not been set by ... the Bavenda".[72]

Even though he himself had seen no real evidence of cannibalism, Ellenberger had been preconditioned by his upbringing in Europe to accept the idea of Africans as savages and cannibals. He was thus prepared to accept uncritically the testimony of his informants and Beuster's tales about Vhavenda cannibalism. Moreover, the account that they gave him, and which Beuster's evidence could be used to support, enabled him partly to excuse "his Africans" for their aberration as they had learned it from others and only been driven into it by necessity. In turn, his informants had no scruples about portraying another group, who were conveniently far away and with whom there was a history of warfare in the nineteenth century, as cannibals. Distant people and enemies alone were seen as being capable of eating people for pleasure, local people first resorted to it only out of dire need. Related to this, Ellenberger's account also fails to engage the idea that, as David Coplan has pointed out, the image of cannibalism has long served "as an unsavoury emblem of social pathology, parasitism and disintegration in Sesotho".[73] Thus, there was no "hard" evidence of cannibalism in Ellenberger's account – merely a clear example of the interaction of European and African preconceptions of the Other, and a failure to understand the local linguistic symbolism of "cannibalism".

The second missionary account that I would like to consider comes from the Swiss Missionary Auguste Jaques of the Mission Station at Elim and was written on 18 April 1887. In discussing the then current fears of war between the Boers and the Vhavenda, Jaques chose to draw attention to the possible "scenes of savagery" which would result. Significantly, although still extremely paternalistic and heavily influenced by ideas of the superiority of western Christianity and "civilization", his analysis attempted to be sympathetic. He moved beyond the idea that people were eaten out of a "revolting taste for the flesh of warriors". Rather, he looked to the "superstition" which enslaved the local people as the root cause of the practice. This, he argued, was slowly being dispelled by the "light" brought by the missionaries:

> There is an opinion, that if war sparks out, there is the prospect of scenes of savagery which will give little reason to be cheerful. During summer, the people of Mpafouri [*Khosi* Ranwedzi (Masindi) Mphaphuli] ate their prisoners of war, and Mr. Beuster himself was witness to all preparations of the feast. Our neighbour Ndjabane, of Tsofim, also ate one of his brothers who offended him about fifteen years ago, and it can be supposed that he would do this again, if a good occasion arose. This eating of people should not be attributed to a revolting taste for the flesh of warriors. A few people actually only attend these horrors because they have been pressed by their chiefs or the relatives of those who are being sent into battle. It is just that there exists amongst our Bavenda [Vhavenda] and amongst many Africans the inveterate belief that whoever tastes human flesh is invulnerable in battle. Of all medicines, this one is the most effective to repel the blows of the enemy and to give victory. So it is more superstition and not cruelty or a depraved taste that leads these unfortunates to the exercise of such horrible practices.[74]

Thus, Jaques "made sense" of the practice. In other words, he did not label it as diabolical but as rational (within another way of thinking). However, his

German colleague seems to have been less subtle. Again, we have Beuster, the first white missionary in the heart of Vendaland, asserting that the local people were "cannibals". As the longest-serving missionary in Vendaland, he could claim to be the "expert" and speak with authority. However, reading deeper into what we are told, again there is no evidence that he actually witnessed any kind of cannibalistic act – he merely allegedly watched the (unspecified) preparations for the feast.

Moving on to the second part of the account, Jaques was not yet in South Africa at the time that Ndjabane's allegedly ate his brother. In addition, his account was based on hearsay evidence from an unidentified informant (or group of informants). We should thus be sceptical of viewing it as an "accurate" description of any "real" events.

With this account, we have nevertheless moved one step further. In drawing attention to the idea that eating a part of the body of an enemy would transfer invulnerability in battle to the person who ate it, Jaques moved beyond mere "superstition" and introduced the concept of the human body as a source of power. His position as a missionary of the Swiss Mission Society, and his view of African societies, seems to have prevented him from pursuing this line of inquiry any further.

Considering all of these cases together, it is clear that none of the authors or their informants quoted had actually witnessed an act of anthropophagy or the consumption of human flesh in any form. They either recounted the tales of others (who had not actually witnessed the act itself) or witnessed what were allegedly the preparations for the feast, but not the actual feast itself. In addition, in these accounts, cannibals usually look, and always act, the part. Lwamondo's "uncouth appearance", "almost animal-like" face, large teeth, "averted lips" and red bandanna serve to set him apart from others. His "crude talk in a shrill voice" completes the picture of the savage cannibal ruler. Ellenberger's Bamahlabaneng (had they actually ever gone around like this) would have looked extremely ferocious with their "stout" bodies "smeared with red ochre" (presumably, the colour of blood, danger and death) and their "long and frizzled" hair "greased with human fat". In addition, even when he portrayed them as following common African custom by offering their guests food, Ellenberger still had the Bamahlabaneng behaving like cannibals – the meat offered was not beef but human flesh. Moreover, eating even troublesome guests (although they allegedly only nearly did this) presumably would have offended all African groups' customs of hospitality. If this did not set them apart, their lust for human flesh and their consumption of their dead, certainly did.

In Jaques's account, Ranwedzi Mphaphuli was not described in enough detail to comment on his appearance or his actions, except to note his peoples' (and, presumably, his) consumption of their prisoners. However, descriptions of his person and actions discussed in the following chapter more than make up for this. In addition, colonial authors would have taken it for granted that African rulers would torture, maim or otherwise commit atrocities upon, their prisoners. Although Ndjabane has only one sentence devoted to him, he eats his brother in this – an act which strikes at the very core of the family and, through this, of society in general.

These descriptions fall squarely into the kinds of accounts analysed by the anthropologist William Arens – probably the scholar most vociferous in his attempt to debunk the notion that cannibalism has been a characteristic feature of any society.[75] Arens' analysis covered most societies which have been accused of cannibalism, including – amongst others – prehistoric humans, the Aztecs, North American, New Guinean and African societies. In attempting to find credible witnesses who had actually witnessed the acts that they were describing, he found that these so-called witnesses were merely recounting what they had been told. In dismissing these "second-hand" accounts of explorers, missionaries and anthropologists, he noted that they fortuitously seemed to enter areas just after the inhabitants, or – more usually – their neighbours had given up cannibalism. Only a handful of the masses of second-hand accounts purported to be by direct witnesses of cannibalism. In each of these cases, and in the case of modern anthropologists who claimed to have witnessed cannibalistic rituals, he found reasons to throw doubt on either the credibility of the witness or on the accuracy of their observation.

Similarly, in discussing what he calls "the myth of cannibalism", the sociologist Agner Fog has argued that:

> The belief that primitive peoples habitually eat one another for nutrition, leads to such a high degree of psychological excitation that this myth has been told and retold for centuries and until recently has been believed by even the most reputable scientists, despite the fact that no anthropologist or ethnographer ever has seen the alleged cannibalistic act.[76] Most tales about cannibalism can be traced back to demonising images that a people have created in order to bring disgrace upon their enemy, just like accusations of witchcraft, etc. These accusations have often been used to justify war, slavery, and colonialism ...
>
> The imaginary cannibal is not only a bogey but a perfect model for how not to behave – a prototype on barbarism and wickedness. Humans need such negative identification models, and therefore the myth is kept alive.[77]

In attempting to explain how these myths work, Richard Buckhorn has argued that:

> In the era of colonisation, "They are cannibals" could be loosely translated, "We want their land". The perception of indigenous peoples as primitive, savage and inferior helped justify both the process and its brutality.[78]

Joan Smith also raised issues such as these in an essay in *Granta*. Here she argued that, for most Europeans during the nineteenth century, cannibalism was "an index of savagery" and that the belief in "the widespread existence of cannibal tribes in the non-European, 'uncivilized' areas of the world" was shared by a range of authors. Thus:

> Cannibal narratives ... are one of the ways in which colonial cultures differentiate themselves from other races – particularly ones they regard as troublesome or unwilling to accept their subject status ... This is not to argue that cannibalism does not exist but to suggest that its unacknowledged function in supporting an otherwise dubious hierarchy of racial superiority has predisposed too many commentators to believe almost any anecdote, no matter how vague or unlikely the details.[79]

Moreover, for Smith, these "credulous and strikingly similar narratives" reveal far more about "a prurient curiosity within *developed* cultures about cannibalism than of its widespread practice outside them".[80]

Smith's comments about the suspension of normal critical facilities when it comes to accounts of cannibalism are clearly borne out in the South African context. Here, the debate has focused largely around the so-called *Mfecane/ Difaqane*. With varying degrees of bloodthirstiness, and underlying racism, accounts of skeletons littering the veld and cannibalism have been a recurring theme in discussions of the presumed holocaust of wars and destruction. Even liberal historians like Leonard Thompson and John Omer-Cooper fell into this trap.[81]

Conversely, in dismissing the whole concept of "The 'mfecane'", Julian Cobbing has argued that allegations of cannibalism played an important role in building up the alibi which was used "to legitimate South Africa's racially unequal land division". In particular, cannibalism was used in the construction of the concept of the Mantatees – "a word deliberately used to convey at once the idea of terror, and that of the black man as *Untermensch*." Through the use of this stereotype: "Genuine refugees from the slave raids were converted into marauding bands of semi-demonic women and children, as well as men, who ravaged the countryside like locusts and threatened the entire colonial civilization." As cannibals, "Mantatee hordes had to be subject to laws of behaviour and motion completely mysterious to rational people". Moreover, "Black 'irrationality' became 'truer' with each repetition".[82] Later, he argued that "Many of the cannibal stories belong to the genre of European fairy tales and represent the export into Africa of fantasies historically embedded in the collective European unconscious." After examining African tales about white slave-hunters as cannibals, he concluded by arguing that it was extremely likely that local accounts of cannibals were, for the most part, records of the raiding for "labourers" and slaves which he saw as the driving force of the destruction and devastation.[83] Also casting doubt on accounts of cannibalism at this time, John Wright has argued that many of the so-called cannibal bands "were probably bandits".[84]

This raises the question of how the Berlin Missionaries saw cannibalism. Three tractates produced by the Berlin Mission Society give reasonably detailed biographies of a number of people who claimed to have been forced into "cannibalism" at this time. The first two (originally published in 1871) were the products of interviews with sixteen self-confessed former cannibals, who had subsequently converted to Christianity and were living at Botshabelo, by Missionary Alexander Merensky. These interviews were then reworked by Hermann Theodor Wangemann, Director of the Berlin Mission Society. He also carried out follow-up interviews of his own.[85] The third tractate, this time authored by Merensky, drew both on these interviews and on missionary and travellers' accounts from other parts of Africa.[86] They are crucial texts providing windows into the missionaries' thinking. In addition, the first two were originally published the year before Ha-Tshivhase was established. Beuster, Stech, Schwellnus and Baumhöfner were all stationed at Botshabelo (at different times) prior to their posting to Vendaland. They would certainly have heard these stories (possibly from the informants themselves) and it is extremely likely that they had read the published works before their move. In addition to other influences on their thinking, these (extremely farfetched) accounts contributed to the ways that they thought, spoke and wrote about their experiences in Vendaland. They would also have influenced the way that they taught the probationary missionaries, such as Koen, Meister and Wessmann, who served under them in the area.

As with the colonialist orthodoxy, Merensky and Wangemann ascribed widespread cannibalism to the disruption and devastation caused by the *Mfecane/ Difaqane*. Scattered refugees from Shaka's and Mzilikazi's wars living in mountains and other places of refuge were forced into cannibalism in order to survive. As the dislocation spread further northwards, so did cannibalism. Raiding bands usually captured people who were alone but, when they felt strong enough, also attacked villages, taking captives who were subsequently either eaten or incorporated into their bands.[87] In making "human flesh their food ... what they first did out of need, they later did out of enjoyment".[88]

Wangemann described what he saw as the lives of the *Makchema* – the supposed cannibal bands among the Pedi – in considerable detail. In doing so, he was obviously influenced as much by European preconceptions about the nature of cannibal bands as by whatever his informants told him. Dehumanising and brutalising his subjects, the missionary wrote that paternal bonds were non-existent – children were in danger of being eaten by their own fathers. Skulls and other remains of their victims were treated as utilitarian objects, such as drinking bowls and children's toys. Human fat was used as an unguent. Human flesh was ranked on a scale of preference for its taste, both by "cut" and by the ethnic origin of the victim. Normal social relations were either absent or distorted and captives were treated like domestic animals, to be worked, fed and fattened. When the time came, they were either strangled or had a sharpened stake pushed through their body from the rectum. They were then cooked and eaten.[89] For a time, they "did not bury their dead, they ate them".[90] For years, the *Makchema* inspired terror in their neighbours. People were too scared to go out in the rainy periods to plant crops in case they were tracked and hunted down by the cannibals. However, even living together in villages did not provide much protection. Often, entire villages were attacked and plundered, and their inhabitants slaughtered or carried away as victims.[91] This only stopped once they were crushed by Sekwati, Sekhukhune and other rulers.[92]

All of the life histories in the tractates followed the same basic pattern. Informants claimed that they had been captured by "cannibal" bands. They then gave horrific tales of the lifestyle of the "cannibals", the terrible deeds that they were forced to perform and the horrors that they were forced to witness in order to avoid being eaten themselves. In time, and to varying degrees, they came to accept this way of life. The suppression of cannibalism by the rulers had prevented them from continuing to enjoy the "terrible meals" of human flesh but did not remove the deep craving. However, in true Pietist fashion, the informants reported that they were gradually exposed to the Word of God. They then had a conversion experience. It is only with their conversion to Christianity that they completely broke with their terrible past and became "new beings in Christ". The depth of this change was demonstrated by the fact that, when persecuted by Sekhukhune, who had turned against the Christians, they chose their new faith over their people and their families and fled to Botshabelo.

In the eyes of the mission, the horrific tales of life among the *Makchema* provided ample justification for the occupation of Sekhukhuneland by settlers. Coupled with this, the transformation of the "cannibals" by life in Christ was a powerful testimony for the need for continued, and extended, mission work among the Pedi and other "heathen" nations. Even although local rulers had managed to suppress "cannibalism", it was only colonial rule and the "light" of the Gospel that would eradicate the practice totally.[93]

To come to the conclusions that they did, it is obvious that the missionaries interpreted the testimony of their informants in the worst possible light and were prepared to believe whatever they told them. Leaving aside the possibility that the missionaries completely invented the material, we have to ask ourselves why their informants told them the kinds of things that they did. While, as suggested by Wangemann, they may have been reluctant at first, they certainly became extremely loquacious once they got going.

Delius has argued that accounts of cannibalism in the lands of the Pedi at this time should be approached with caution. The practice was used in traditions as "a way of showing the dire consequences of the destruction of properly constituted authority". Missionaries used talk about cannibalism as "evidence which confirmed their suspicions that these societies teetered on the edge of barbarism". In marked contrast to the picture painted by these traditions and, particularly, the missionary accounts: "A close examination of the evidence suggests that it was restricted to relatively few groups who were principally distinguished by the fact that they secured their subsistence almost exclusively through raiding, and were thus seen as living on their fellows."[94] This convincing argument seems to explain the hidden messages behind many of the tales prevalent at the time. However, it does not adequately account for what Merensky and Wangemann's informants told them. There is a big difference between saying that "people were eaten" and testifying that: "I ate people." While the first statement may be interpreted as a comment on social dislocation, and missionary prejudice, the second is far more complicated.

The most obvious answer, and one that seems plausible, is that the informants simply told the missionaries what they thought they wanted to hear. Asked to tell tales about "cannibalism" by white missionaries who stood in a paternalistic relationship to them, they presumably did just this, inventing and embellishing where necessary. Moreover, it is likely that they would have played on the horror and excitement of the missionaries and shaped their tales to get the best reactions from listeners who wanted to hear – and believe – the worst that they could tell them.

A second, less obvious, influence on the content of the tales would presumably have been the desire of converts to show just how far they had been transformed by Christ. One just has to think of pentecostalist revival meetings today. In presenting their testimonies of how they came to the Lord, few, if any, speakers will say that they were actually very nice people, living fulfilled lives, before they saw the light. In the overwhelming majority of cases, they had to defeat the demons of drink, drugs, violence, sexual perversion, Satanism or other self-destructive behaviour through the power of God. A few years ago, a student who is a staunch member of a pentecostalist church told me in great excitement about the testimony of a former *muloi* which he had heard the previous night. This woman told a packed tent how she had flown to Johannesburg on a loaf of bread to strike her victims. Partly as a result of testimonies like this, membership of the church soared and they now occupy a huge church complex instead of their former tent. They are considering starting their own television station. For me, one is as likely to confess to indulging in a *braaivleis* ball of human flesh as flying to Johannesburg on a loaf of bread. Similarly, if the audience wants to believe it, they will.

Added to this, a corpus of adventure literature prepared the missionaries to believe the accounts that they heard. These kinds of tales were also reflected in instructional material housed in the library of the Mission Seminary. H.J. Meyer's *Neues Konversations-Lexikon* was available there at the time that the missionaries who would record the case studies of "cannibalism" were studying in the seminary. It is thus extremely likely that they would have consulted it when studying. Here, nineteenth-century trevellers' accounts of cannibalism in Africa were reproduced uncritically. For example:

> among the Fan ... human flesh is their main foodstuff and, because of this, even forms an article of trade; they do not only eat those they have killed and their captured enemies but also eat their own fellows who have died, yes, they even dig up bodies from graves to eat them.[95]

The same kind of uncritical approach that the editors of the *Lexikon* showed to the material about the supposedly cannibalistic Africans was reflected in Merensky and Wangemann's treatment of the tales of their informants. One should also not underestimate the probable impact of the tractates. Wangemann's *Die Menschenfresser im Bapediländer* and *Gerettete Menschenfresser in Botshabelo* ran to three editions each – a sign of great success. Presumably his position as Director also ensured him a wider readership than that commanded by some of his subordinates. Similarly, Merensky's position as Superintendent would probably have increased his potential readership. In both cases, their position would also have lent credibility to their work. In addition, the tractates as a whole had extremely large print runs. For example, between 1890 and 1895, 110 257 copies of *Neue Missionsschriften*, 149 893 copies of *Missionsschriften für Kinder* and 28 754 copies of the *Berliner Missionstraktate* were produced.[96] In the period of self-examination prior to being accepted as candidates for training in the Society's seminary, aspirant missionaries were required to have "thoroughly" read its publications.[97] The presence of tractates in the mission library also strongly suggests that they were used in teaching. Merensky's specific target audience was Sunday-school children, the group most likely to internalise the bloodthirsty tales of African depravity and rebirth in Christ. Moreover, much as I hesitate in saying this, the tractates were written in an extremely gripping and lucid style and are difficult to put down once one starts reading them.

Against this background, one comes to the conclusion that the only way of attempting to make sense of missionary (or any other) accounts of cannibalism was to contextualise them in a detailed case study which engaged far wider issues than the alleged consumption of human flesh. Moreover, for me, the most crucial task is not that of deciding whether or not the Vhavenda "really" ate bits of their enemies. What is important is the fact that the explorers and missionaries said that they did. So too did at least some of their African informants. Rather than trying to look at which of the cases "actually" occurred and which did not, one may spend one's time far more usefully in deconstructing the missionary accounts and seeing what they tell us about the missionaries, the Vhavenda and their interaction. In a similar way to Luise White, one may set out to see the unexpected aspects of their interaction, not beneath, but through, tales about anthropophagy.[98] I have attempted to achieve this through the case study and what may be termed a strategy of close reading – a process whereby first readings are often counterposed with second readings. In addition, following the lead of Gananath Obeyesekere, I differentiate between cannibalism and anthropophagy, the former indicating "cannibal talk" in the wider context of contact and othering, the latter a complex ritual practice.[99] I turn now to this case study of the relationship between the Mphaphuli royal family and the Berlin Missionaries.

1. N.J. van Warmelo (ed.) (a) *Contributions Towards Venda History*, pp. 104–108, 192–196 & (b) *Venda Dictionary*, pp. 222, 474. See also H.A. Stayt, *The Bavenda*, pp. 105–106, 124–125.
2. Tagebuch der Station bei Ha Makoarela (Nicolaus Koen), 24. August 1877, p. 10. See also *BMB*, 1878, p. 493.
3. N.J. van Warmelo (ed.), *Contributions Towards Venda History*, p. 125.
4. S.M. Dzivhani, "The Chiefs of Venḓa", p. 39; W. Grant, "Magato and his Tribe", in *Journal of the Royal Anthropological Institute*, Vol. 35, London, 1905, pp. 267–268; M.H. Nemudzivhadi, "The attempts by Makhado to revive the Venda kingdom", pp. 17, 22–23 (quotations); N.J. van Warmelo (ed.), *Contributions Towards Venda History*, p. 25 (see also pp. 125–133 for discussion of the *murundu*); and R. Wagner, "Zoutpansberg", p. 336. For discussion of the *murundu*, see also H.A. Stayt, *The Bavenda*, pp. 125–138.
5. N.J. van Warmelo (ed.), *Contributions Towards Venda History*, p. 125.
6. *BMB*, 1879, p. 409.
7. *Ibid*.
8. *Ibid*.
9. Van Warmelo and Stayt attribute the spread and continued existence of the *murundu* to the profit motive on the part of the organisers and the rulers (H.A. Stayt, *The Bavenda*, p. 127; N.J. van Warmelo (ed.), *Contributions Towards Venda History*, p. 125).
10. *BMB*, 1879, p. 413.
11. *Ibid*. p. 444.
12. *Ibid*. pp. 444–445. I have been able to find no evidence of the consumption of human flesh at the *murundu*. Van Warmelo recorded that the severed foreskins were collected and roasted. From this, a medicine called *lutala* and *muuluso* was made for protection against shadows. He explained that, when a woman had a newborn infant, she always had to have a small pouch of this medicine with her to protect the child against the shadows of paramours and its parents. Before the umbilical cord had dropped off, the child was kept inside the rondavel. It was made to swallow a little of the medicine. Otherwise, if someone who had committed adultery with the child's father or mother were to come along, the child would die (N.J. van Warmelo (ed.), *Contributions Towards Venda History*, p. 127). Rumors of a ritual homicide to open and close some *murundu* were rife in the 1990s. However, no such cases were brought to court. While I am prepared to accept that some of these ritual homicides may have occurred, I seriously doubt that anthropophagous rituals or cannibalistic feasts have ever formed a part of the ritual. I return to cannibalism and anthropophagy at the end of this chapter. The reported consumption of the flesh of fallen (or butchered) enemies also forms one of the main sub-themes of chapter 8.
13. *BMB*, 1879, p. 445.
14. H.A. Stayt, *The Bavenda*, especially pp. 128–135; N.J. van Warmelo (ed.), *Contributions Towards Venda History*, pp. 126–133.
15. *BMB*, 1879, pp. 445–446 (quotation, p. 446).
16. *Ibid*. p. 446.
17. *Ibid*.
18. *Ibid*. pp. 446–447.
19. *BMB*, 1880, p. 403 (quotation); 1881, p. 359.
20. *BMB*, 1881, p. 359.
21. *Ibid*.
22. See, for example, *BMB*, 1895, p. 191.
23. See, for example, *BMB*, 1889, p. 534.
24. See John Blacking (a) "The Initiation Cycle: vhusha, tshikanda and Domba" & (b) "Vhusha", at http://era.anthropology.ac.uk/Era_R...ra/VendaGirls/Vhusha/V_Opening.html, accessed 29

September 2000; H.A. Stayt, *The Bavenda*, pp. 106–110; and N.J. van Warmelo (ed.), *Contributions Towards Venda History*, pp. 37–51.
25. Berichte der Station bei Schewase (Carl Beuster), 19. Juli 1874, p. 16. See also *BMB*, 1875, pp. 424–425.
26. Tagebuch der Station bei Ha Makoarela (Nicolaus Koen), 24. August 1877, pp. 9–10. See also *BMB*, 1878, pp. 492–493.
27. Berlin Mission Archives, Berlin: Album, Vendaland von Missionar G. Westphal, Nr. 8541 "Eine 'Thondo' Mauer" and accompanying text; E. Gottschling, "The Bawenda", p. 203; H.A. Stayt, *The Bavenda*, pp. 101–102; and N.J. van Warmelo (a) "Volksgebruike van die Venda", p. 999 & (b) (ed.) *Contributions Towards Venda History*, p. 109.
28. E. Gottschling, "The Bawenda", p. 204; H.A. Stayt, *The Bavenda*, pp. 102–104; and N.J. van Warmelo, "Volksgebruike van die Venda", pp. 999 (quotation).
29. E. Gottschling, "The Bawenda", pp. 203–204 (quotation, p. 204). See also H.A. Stayt, *The Bavenda*, pp. 104–105.
30. E. Gottschling, "The Bawenda", p. 204; N.J. van Warmelo, "Volksgebruike van die Venda", p. 109 (quotation). See also H.A. Stayt, *The Bavenda*, p. 105.
31. *BMB*, 1888, pp. 515, 516 (Beuster); 1889, p. 566 (Wessmann).
32. *BMB*, 1888, p. 516.
33. See pp. 45–46.
34. See especially *BMB*, 1880, pp. 4, 344; 1888, p. 533; G. Fischer, "Die Bawenda, ein neues Bild in der Mission", in *Der Missions-Freund: Ein Volksblatt, die Liebe zur Mission im deutschen Volke zu wecken und zu erhalten*, XXXII(4), 1877, p. 60 (one twin only); E. Gottschling, "The Bawenda", p. 203; and G. Sauberzweig-Schmidt, *Klaas Kuhn*, p. 13 (second twin only). In 1936, Mission-Inspector Siegfried Schoene stated that both children were killed (S. Schoene, "Zwillingskinder! Von Heidenelend und Christenglück in Südafrika", in *Der Missions-Freund*, 88. Jahrgang, 1936, p. 68).
35. H.A. Stayt, *The Bavenda*, p. 91. See also S.S. Dornan, "Some Beliefs and Ceremonies connected with the Birth and Death of Twins among the South African Natives", in *South African Journal of Science*, Vol. XXIX, October 1932, pp. 690–700 (especially pp. 693–694).
36. *BMB*, 1875, pp. 409, 439–440.
37. *BMB*, 1876, p. 395.
38. *BMB*, 1877, p. 487.
39. Recorded as "Funzane" here. Later, it also appears as "Fanzane" (see, for example, *BMB*, 1880, p. 4). David Fuzane and his family settled at Tshakhuma in June 1876. Beyond the fact that he was a Christian, his decision to move to the station was sparked by the fact that his wife, who was not yet a Christian, wanted to attend catechism classes and convert. Her brother took the opportunity to do the same (*BMB*, 1877, p. 481). Early the following year, their two children were baptised. The elder was four years old (*BMB*, 1877, p. 484). In the Annual Report for 1878, David was described as a "talented Native Assistant" who "faithfully stood at Brother Schwellnus' side". In order to keep his large extended family, he thought that he would have to go to the diamond fields. However, determined not to lose his assistance, Schwellnus managed to obtain a salary of 15 Mark a month for him. This meant that he was required to do extra evangelist duties for Beuster at Ha-Tshivhase and also to preach in Maluma and Matidza's areas. The Annual Report also recorded that "The people have high respect and great regard for him" (*BMB*, 1879, pp. 202 (quotations), 408).
40. *BMB*, 1879, p. 438.
41. *BMB*, 1880, p. 4.
42. *Ibid*.
43. See p. 247.
44. *BMB*, 1880, p. 5.
45. *Ibid*.
46. *Ibid*.
47. *Ibid*. pp. 5–6.
48. *Ibid*. p. 344.
49. Tagebuch der Station Ha Tsevase (Carl Beuster), 28. April 1885, pp. 17–18. See also *BMB*, 1886, p. 415.
50. Tagebuch der Station Ha Tsevase (Carl Beuster), 24. Juni 1885, pp. 25–26. See also *BMB*, 1886, pp. 417–418.

51. See p. 265.
52. Tagebuch der Station Ha Tsevase (Carl Beuster), 4. Oktober 1888, pp. 56–57. See also *BMB*, 1889, pp. 537–538.
53. C. Hoffmann, "Die Sünde der Welt im Heidentum", in *Mission und Unterricht: Missions-Pädagogische Handreichung der Berliner Missionsgesellschaft*, 24. Jahrgang, 1936, Heft 1, p. 26; D. McDonald, "Vendaland", in *The Blythswood Review: A South African Journal Review: A South African Journal of Religious, Social and Economic Work*, X (111), March 1933, p. 28; W.L. Spreight, "Human Sacrifice in South Africa", in *The Nongqai*, February 1935, p. 152; and H.A. Stayt, *The Bavenda*, p. 93. Note that Hoffmann and Spreight refer to the same case.
54. See p. 193.
55. Tagebuch der Station Ha Tsevase (Carl Beuster), 10. Januar 1885, pp. 2–3 (quotation, p. 3). See also *BMB*, 1885, pp. 396–397 (quotation, p. 397).
56. See especially E. Gottschling, "The Bawenda", p. 208; H.A. Stayt, *The Bavenda*, pp. 206, 207; and N.J. van Warmelo (ed.), *Contributions Towards Venda History*, pp. 134–140.
57. C.J. Conerly, "The Surrendering of the Lands", p. xviii; S.M. Dzivhani, "The Chiefs of Venḓa", p. 35; T.N. Huffman, "Snakes and birds: expressive space at Great Zimbabwe", in *African Studies*, 40(2), 1981, p. 133; H.A. Stayt, *The Bavenda*, p. 207; and N.J. van Warmelo (ed.), *Contributions Towards Venda History*, p. 14.
58. S.M. Dzivhani, "The Chiefs of Venḓa", p. 35.
59. *Ibid.* pp. 35, 36.
60. R. Wessmann, *The Bawenda of the Spelonken*, p. 83.
61. H. du Plessis, "Die Territoriale Organisasie van die Venda", in *African Studies* (Formerly *Bantu Studies*), 4(3), September 1945, p. 126.
62. *Ibid.* p. 126 (footnote).
63. M.P. Nemadodzi, "Main themes in the history of Venda over the past twenty-five years", unpublished History 300 Assignment, University of Venda, 10 June 1991, p. 7.
64. P.J. S[ampson], "'Fertilising The Corn.' Being the true story of the weird and terrible Bawenda special rite of 'Mokuku wa mabeli' whereby the seed corn is made fertile and brings forth abundant crops", in *The Nongqai*, 12, January 1921, pp. 18–19; H.A. Stayt, *The Bavenda*, pp. 314–315. See also S. Balic, "Change brings muti murders", p. 33; E. Koch and E. Ritchken, "The political economy of witchcraft", in Weekly Mail, 23–29 March 1990, p. 10.
65. *BMB*, 1879, p. 314. For the reported use of human flesh in iron-smelting, see J.B. de Vaal, "Yster vir Assegaai se Lem", in *Die Brandwag*, 14 June 1946, p. 12 (see also pp. 13, 56 for the continuation of the description of iron-smelting and smithing). See also E.D. Giesekke, "Der Eisenindustrie der Bawenda", in *Die Brücke*, 7, July 1930, pp. 5–9.
66. E.E. Burke (ed.), *The Journals of Carl Mauch: His travels in the Transvaal and Rhodesia 1869–1872*, transcribed from the original by Mrs. E. Bernhard and translated by F.O. Bernhard, Salisbury, National Archives of Rhodesia, 1969, pp. 120–121.
67. B.V. Street, *The savage in literature*, pp. 75–76. Sources cited or quoted by Street in this section include E.R. Burroughs (1917), *Tarzan of the Apes* and C. Gilson (1919), *In the Power of the Pygmies*.
68. D.F. Ellenberger, *History of the Basuto: Ancient and Modern*, London, Caxton Publishing Company, 1912 (translation from French by J.C. Macgregor), pp. 94–95. The Paris Evangelical Mission Society began working among the Basotho in 1833. For discussion of cannibalism in the African adventure tradition, see especially P. Brantlinger, "Victorians and Africans", pp. 175, 176, 184, 185, 190, 196; M.L Pratt, Imperial Eyes, pp. 83, 208, 218; and B.V. Street, *The Savage in Literature*, pp. 17, 70, 75–76, 159.
69. D.F. Ellenberger, *History of the Basuto*, p. 95.
70. *Ibid.* pp. 32, 34, 54, 89, 122, 137, 144, 146, 150, 158, 161–163, 190, 191, 192, 203, 217–226, 233.
71. *Ibid.* pp. 192, 203.
72. *Ibid.* pp. 217–218, 224.
73. D.B. Coplan, *In the Time of Cannibals: The Word Music of South Africa's Basotho Migrants*, Johannesburg, Witwatersrand University Press, 1994, pp. 1, 3.
74. A. Jaques, "Craintes de guerre", in *Bulletin Missionnaire des Églises Libres de la Suisse Romande*, 6(73), Lausanne, August 1887, pp. 281–282. Thanking Pippa Davies for translating this for me.
75. W. Arens, *The Man-eating Myth: Anthropology and Anthropophagy*, Oxford, Oxford University Press, 1979.

76. For attempts at producing a cultural materialist account of cannibalism/anthropophagy based on nutritional requirements and available food resources, see M. Harris (a) *Cannibals and Kings: The Origins of Cultures*, Glasgow, Fontana/Collins, 1978, especially pp. 110–125, 134–136 & (b) *Cultural Materialism: The Struggle for a Science of Culture*, New York, Vintage Books, 1980, especially pp. 188–190, 333–341.
77. Agner Fog, *Cultural selection* © 1996, chapter 8: Sociology of deviance, at http://announce.com/agner/cultsel/chap8.html, accessed 25 November 1997, pp. 4–5.
78. Richard Buchhorn, *A Taste for Chinese* [first appeared in *Skeptic* 14(1)], at http://www.skeptics.com.au/journal/canib-chinese.htm, accessed 15 February 1999, pp. 3–4.
79. J. Smith, "People Eaters", in *Granta*, 52, Winter 1995, Food: The Vital Stuff, pp. 73, 76.
80. *Ibid.* p. 78.
81. See, for example, F. Ellenberger, *History of the Basuto*, pp. 217–226; J.D. Omer-Cooper, *The Zulu Aftermath: A Nineteenth-Century Revolution in Bantu Africa*, London, Longman, 1966, especially pp. 96, 100, 102; and L. Thompson, "Co-operation and Conflict: The High Veld", in M. Wilson and L. Thompson (eds.), *The Oxford History of South Africa, Volume I. South Africa to 1870*, London, Oxford University Press, 1969, pp. 391–405.
82. J. Cobbing, "The Mfecane as Alibi: Thoughts on Dithakong and Mbolompo", in *Journal of African History*, 29 (1988), pp. 487, 499–500, 519.
83. J. Cobbing, "Grasping the Nettle: The Slave Trade and the Early Zulu", unpublished paper privately circulated by the author, September 1990, p. 15.
84. J. Wright, "Political Transformations in the Thukela-Mzimkhulu Region in the Late Eighteenth and Early nineteenth Centuries", in C. Hamilton (ed.), *The Mfecane Aftermath: Reconstructive Debates in Southern African History*, Johannesburg, Witwatersrand University Press and Pietermaritzburg, University of Natal Press, 1995, p. 176.
85. H.T. Wangemann, *Die Menschenfresser im Bapediländer*, Berliner Missionstraktate, Neue Folge, Nr. V, Dritte Auflage, Berlin, Selbstverlag des Missionhauses, 1883; and *Gerettete Menschenfresser in Botshabelo*, Berliner Missionstraktate, Neue Folge, Nr. VI, Dritte Auflage, Berlin, Selbstverlag des Missionhauses, 1883.
86. A. Merensky, *Die Menschenfresserei in Afrika*.
87. *Ibid.* pp. 5–6; H.T. Wangemann, *Die Menschenfresser im Bapediländer*, pp. 2–3, 12–13.
88. H.T. Wangemann, *Die Menschenfresser im Bapediländer*, p. 3.
89. *Ibid.* p. 12.
90. *Ibid.* pp. 12, 14–15.
91. *Ibid.* p. 15.
92. *Ibid.* pp. 10, 15; A. Merensky, *Die Menschenfresserei in Afrika*, pp. 9–10.
93. See especially A. Merensky, *Die Menschenfresserei in Afrika*, pp. 10–11.
94. P. Delius, *The Land Belongs To Us*, p. 24.
95. H.J. Meyer (ed.), *Neues Konversations-Lexikon*, 15 Bänden, Zweite Auflage, Hildburghausen, 1869, Band 1, p. 833 (*Anthropophagen*).
96. R. Bodenstein, *Die Schriftenreihen der Berliner Missionsgesellschaft*, Berlin, Berliner Missionswerk Bibliothek, 1996, p. 7. In comparison, Rider Haggard's works *King Solomon's Mines* (first published in 1885), *She* (first published in book form in 1887) and *Allan Quatermain* (first published in book form in 1887) were the blockbusters of their day. *King Solomon's Mines* sold 31 000 copies in its first year of publication, *She* sold 30 792 copies in June of 1887 and the author received payment for 29 403 copies of *Allan Quatermain* in the first year of its publication (G. Ching-Liang Low, *White Skins/Black Masks: Representation and Colonialism*, London, Routledge, 1996, p. 6; B.V. Street, *The Savage in Literature*, p. 13).
97. *BMB*, 1880, p. 272.
98. L. White (a) "Cars out of place: vampires, technology and labor in East and Central Africa", in F. Cooper and A.L. Stoler (eds.), *Tensions of Empire*, pp. 436–460 & (b) *Speaking with vampires: rumor and history in colonial Africa*, Berkeley, Los Angeles and London, University of California Press, 2000.
99. See G. Obeyesekere, "'British Cannibals': Contemplation of an Event in the Death and Resurrection of James Cook, Explorer", in K.A. Appiah and H.L. Gates (eds.), *Identities*, Chicago, Chicago University Press, 1995, pp. 7–32.

CHAPTER 8
The Mphaphulis

The missionaries in Vendaland faced many setbacks in their attempt to win the hearts and minds of the local people and to wean them away from their culture and their ancestors. Due to the great difficulties that they were experiencing in making, and keeping, a significant number of converts, from very early on, they saw it as essential that they convert a *khosi*. They believed that only this would make conversion acceptable to society-at-large. Due to the ruler's central position in the life of his people, if they succeeded in doing so, his followers would follow.[1]

None of the Vhavenda *mahosi* of any significance converted to Christianity during the nineteenth century. Because of this, the missionaries did not go to any trouble to reconstruct the personal histories of the rulers before the establishment of mission stations in any great detail. However, Makwarela Mphaphuli was "the person whose understanding the Gospel has come the closest to penetrating". Arising from this, the missionaries recorded a great deal more about his life than they did for other *mahosi*. They also collected oral testimony about his life from him and from his subjects.

BEFORE THE MISSION – MAKWARELA MPHAPHULI

According to missionary accounts, this "curious man" was born in Miluwani in about 1850. This large village was situated in the area where Georgenholtz would later be established. His father was Masindi (Ranwedzi), "the son and sub-chief of the mighty Chief" Ratsibi Mphaphuli and his mother was Matshekeketsheke, Masindi's "'great' (that is, respected) wife".[a] At the time of his birth, Masindi already had three sons by other wives. However, as the first son of the "'great' wife", Makwarela was the *de jure* successor. As was (and still is) common for members of the royal family, he

> spent his youth simply and it did not differ visibly from that of his age-mates. Dressed only in a goat-skin, he looked after the cattle with the other boys and took part in their many games, in

---
a. Before his accession to the throne, missionary sources refer to Ranwedzi as Masindi, his birth name. Ranwedzi and Mphaphuli was respectively his name and title after he ascended the throne. From here on, mission sources refer to him as Mpafudi, Pafuli or Pafudi. I refer to him as Masindi before his accession and *Khosi* Ranwedzi Mphaphuli, or simply Mphaphuli, after he became the ruler. The missionaries recorded Matshekeketsheke as Matseketseke. The "great wife" is the wife whose marriage has been contracted with cattle supplied by the group as a whole (rather than the royal family alone).

which they practised for hunting and warfare. There he already outshone the others in his strength, skill and courage, so that none could compete with him. Because of this, his grandfather loved him very much and gave him preferential treatment, and it really was a special day for the young boy when he was allowed to visit his grandfather at his capital village.[2]

In this description, the missionaries clearly set out to demonstrate that Makwarela was superior to his contemporaries. In doing so, they presumably accepted at face value the oral evidence that they collected from his people. To this day, powerful *mahosi* are frequently portrayed in such terms in oral evidence. The missionaries were probably prepared to accept this version of Makwarela's childhood because it supported their argument that it was his superiority that made him the most likely candidate to lead his people in converting to Christianity.

However, as the account of Makwarela's early life continues, it becomes clear that the missionaries were not prepared to accept that his skills and intelligence were of purely African origin – they introduced the idea that Makwarela learned a great deal from whites.[3] According to this account, Makwarela's grandfather died when he was about twelve years old. Masindi (Ranwedzi) assumed the throne and took the name Mphaphuli. He appointed Makwarela "as the sub-chief of Meloane [Miluwani], giving him Nyamasindi, one of his wives, to cook porridge for him … and to help him to rule".[4]

While ruler of Miluwani, Makwarela "learned to know the first whites". A farmer by the name of Thomas "visited the people frequently, taking a number of wives and living like a native". Ranwedzi Mphaphuli "established relationships with him and gave him a daughter as a wife". He did not stay among the people all the time, and went back to live among the whites from time to time. Although he sometimes took Mphaphuli's daughter with him, she could not stand to be away from her own people for long and "ached to live a kaffir-life". Her husband would then "release her" to go back to her own people. Her nephew, Makwarela, was very fond of her and visited her both when she was living among her own people and among the whites. On these visits, he "learned a great deal from the whites, especially the use of firearms. He also managed to acquire a number of guns for himself".[5]

When he was about eighteen years old, Makwarela's father "gave him the mighty province of Nagabe" to rule:

> Here he built a large capital-village, took many wives and ruled as an independent prince. He depended on his father with the love of a child, while his older brother Tschekalanga [Tshikalange] hated his father out of jealousy.[6]

This introduces the theme of conflict between Makwarela and his brother which pre-dated the arrival of the missionaries. Over time, it would play an extremely important role in influencing the relationship between him and the missionaries:

> One day when Pafudi [Ranwedzi Mphaphuli] was on one of his regular visits to Makoarele [Makwarela], he became sick and could not leave his bed for half a year. A rumour spread that Pafudi had died ... In Bawenda custom the death of a chief is kept secret for a long time. Tschekalanga believed this rumour and thought that Makoarele did not want the death of his father to become known so that he could ensure that he became the ruler. Tschekalanga hurriedly seized hold of the capital village and through complicated trickery sought to win the support of the people for him and turn their hearts away from his brother. However, Pafudi was not dead. For a long time, he was treated by the most famous doctors from all of the neighbouring tribes. The one bled the "Great Lion", the other provided the "Clouds of the Heavens" with an emetic, the third provided yet another treatment for the "Light of the Earth".[b] The sick man continued to deteriorate, until he drove the doctors away.[7]

Both missionary and anthropological literature draw attention to the fact that the death of a *khosi* was usually followed by a succession dispute among two or more of his sons. These conflicts frequently resulted in warfare between the different contending factions.[8] However, in this case, reports about Mphaphuli's death were rumours. The account continues by stating that:

> All of a sudden, he appeared among the people again and kept up the following refrain: "See, see, see, here is Pafudi! He was dead and now he lives! And when he dies three times, he will still live again. You thought that Pafudi was old and had been vanquished by death. But you lied. Yes, he is young. But you will die and Pafudi will be young, even when your children and your children's children have become old. You wanted me dead and made Tschekalanga, the disgraceful, your king and ate my wives, children and cattle. Now, go to him, I want to remain with my son Makoarele."[9]

Makwarela has clearly been presented as the loyal son, deserving to succeed his father when the time comes. With right on his side, he and his father have countered the first serious threat posed by Tshikalange without resorting to the use of arms. As the account continues, Mphaphuli's temperament leads people to fear possible reprisals. In contrast, Makwarela's handling of the

---

b. These were all praise-names of Mphaphuli's (see R. Wessmann, *Philippus Thai*, p. 3).

situation shows great tact and diplomacy and succeeds in achieving a temporary cessation of hostilities by all parties concerned:

> This sudden resurgence of the old [man] led to a great fear throughout the land. Tschekalanga [Tshikalange] fled with his followers and Pafudi and Makoarele entered the capital again. They allowed Tschekalanga to appear before them. After a long acrimonious discussion, Pafudi gathered his people together and gave them the following address: "You held me for dead because I wanted to be dead.[c] My heart grieves me that my people forgot me and my children fought for my kingdom while I was still alive, let me see who has been victorious and won my kingdom." A period of complete silence followed. Eventually, Makoarele said: "I do not fight with my brother, if he also does not hate me." Then, as a sign of peace, the old [man] slaughtered an ox which the two brothers shared as a sign of reconciliation. Tschekalanga received no further punishment. But the disagreement between father and son was only outwardly removed.[10]

Having demonstrated his filial devotion and skills of diplomacy, this account goes on to talk about a number of Makwarela's military campaigns, especially against the "Mabonja [*Mabunyu*], a tribe of the Kaalkaffirs" (Zulu, Swazi or Ndebele raiders). These descriptions reinforce the idea that Makwarela's courage and grasp of military strategy were far greater than that not only of his subjects but also than that of all the other *mahosi* in Vendaland, including his father. In the interpretation of the missionaries, he was indeed an exceptional man among his people and was rapidly making a name for himself as a force to be reckoned with in Vendaland.[11]

According to the continuing account, Makwarela's growing reputation for bravery and his repeated demonstrations of loyalty to Mphaphuli led to his father's sending him as an envoy to the mighty Ndebele king Lobengula, across the Limpopo in about 1874. In so doing, he was attempting to "renew the old friendship which had existed between" Mzilikazi, Lobengula's father and Ratsibi Mphaphuli.[12] Here, Makwarela "was received with all honour and entertained with feasts. He was astonished by much that he had not previously seen", including the "immense armies of cattle" in the royal herd and the large numbers of elephant tusks in the king's possession. "Ten to twelve oxen were slaughtered daily" and the king

> had so many elephant tusks that when their bearers formed a closely-packed chain, they covered fully half a mile.

---

c. In other words: "… I wanted it to appear as if I was dead."

But above all Makoarele was amazed by the whites who lived freely in the lands in subordination to the king and over all the equipment that the same possessed or manufactured, for example, the large, beautiful state carriage of the king, driven by a white coachman, and the beautiful harnesses of the horses. All these things that he saw made a deep impression on the young ruler and awakened in him a longing for similar power and regard. At Lobengulu's court, he also found an English missionary and this urged him to get a missionary for himself and for his own people. He may well have thought that a missionary was just the right man to give him all that he needed to be equal to Lobengulu. With a longing for a missionary, Makoarele returned to his kingdom.[13]

It is clear that the Berlin Missionaries saw this experience as a crucial one in shaping his desire to have the trappings of "European civilisation" and a missionary at his capital.[14] He was soon to be presented with an opportunity to bring this wish to fruition.

HOPES, HOSTILITIES AND POWER

In an effort to test the ground for expansion of mission activity into areas that had as yet to see a missionary, Beuster sent Evangelists Paulus Luvhengo and Johannes Mutshaeni out on a preaching journey from Ha-Tshivhase in November 1875. They were accompanied by David Denga, who acted as their guide. Yet again, it was Africans, rather than a white missionary, who would act as heralds of the new religion. *Khosi* Makwarela Mphaphuli "received them in a very friendly manner and asked them to send him a teacher". Spurred on by this encouragement, Beuster entered into discussions with Makwarela about the possibility of establishing a third station in his lands. The man that he found was not at all what he expected. With his neat western dress and his keen intellect, he could not easily be fitted into any existing stereotype. "Makoarele himself was very obliging and friendly, and Bro. Beuster was astonished to find a more or less decently-clothed man, well-mannered and intelligent, with keen perception, in the middle of the wilds."[15] The *khosi* stated that he was extremely keen to have a "teacher" for his people. He could nevertheless not permit this to happen without the permission of Ranwedzi (Masindi) Mphaphuli, his father and overlord.[16]

Prompted by Makwarela's expressed desire to have a missionary in his area, the first face-to-face meeting between Beuster and Ranwedzi Mphaphuli took place at the *khosi*'s royal capital on 13 December 1875. Two accounts of this meeting were published, both of which drew on Missionary Beuster's diary entry describing what occurred. The first of these was published in the *Missions-Berichte* for 1876. Due to the fact that there was some delay between information being received at headquarters in Germany and its publication, this may in fact be viewed as the contemporaneous account. The second, which could draw on hindsight, was published in *Mitteilungen des Vereins "Heidenfreund"* [which became *Der Bawenda-Freund*] in 1896. Since these two accounts differ very slightly, but in important ways, both should be discussed in some detail. My reading of Mphaphuli's actions and possible intentions at this meeting was influenced by Greg Denning's *Mr Bligh's Bad Language* (1994), his exploration of what he sees as the theatrical nature of the power-play and passion underlying the story of Captain Bligh and the mutiny on the *Bounty*. Denning argues that part of the key to unlock the paradox of why one of the least violent disciplinarians in the British Navy has come to represent the extravagant and violent abuse of power lies in Mr Bligh's "bad language". This term encompasses his vivid, abusive, ungentlemanly language, and un-officerlike conduct, arising largely from his "rage at how distant the wooden world of the *Bounty* was from what he ambitioned it to be".[17] In a similar manner, Ranwedzi Mphaphuli's "bad language" can be deconstructed – his abuse, cursing and swearing, his extremely dramatic and stylised behaviour. This attempts to reveal some of the ways that the missionaries interpreted the performance, some of the message that he can be seen as attempting to convey and some of the ways that this reflected and commented on power, power relations and power-play.

The first account of the meeting with Ranwedzi Mphaphuli states that Beuster was accompanied by Paulus, Johannes and David, the three Christian converts who had visited Makwarela earlier.[18] The second refers only to Johannes.[19] This omission was certainly deliberate. Johannes Mutshaeni was the evangelist whom Beuster came to trust and depend on the most, even writing a tractate about his life.[20] So, it would make sense that his role was emphasised the most. However, much of the more dramatic behaviour of the *khosi* was directed towards Johannes. This focus on Mutshaeni, and the *khosi*'s behaviour towards him, assisted in creating a strong impression that Ranwedzi Mphaphuli was a savage ruler, quick to take offence at the slightest provocation and not entirely in control of his actions. While this is suggested in the first account, explanations given there serve to mitigate this impression of the *khosi*. The later description was carefully crafted to leave no such room for understanding open.

The first account continues by stating that Ranwedzi Mphaphuli

> was an odd person. Beuster and his companions had hardly sat down when ... [he] started shouting at Johannes. At first Brother Beuster did not take much notice of this, and he thought that it was just the way of the old heathen. But he continued scolding Johannes over and over again, becoming more vehement: his scolding became the most vulgar insults. The red eyes of the old man sparkled in a most sinister way, the spittle shot

out of his mouth: he looked like a Satan. Eventually he jumped up, took a stick and lifted his arm to beat Johannes. Johannes warded off the stick. But this just infuriated the king more. "How dare you touch my stick!" With this he lifted his arm again; this time the caning was averted by some court attendants, who sprang between them and begged for mercy. This all happened within a few seconds.[21]

While the information given is basically the same, the more terse style of writing, and the more extreme language, used in the later account gives a much more dramatic picture of the behaviour of the *khosi*:

Hardly had they sat down when ... [he] began to abuse Johannes. His words of abuse became even stronger until they were mostly cursing and swearing. The red eyes of the old man sparkled sinisterly; the spittle shot out of his mouth: he looked like a Satan. Eventually he jumped up, took a stick and careered around with this, although luckily turning the blows away [and not hitting anyone]. And the reason for this fit of rage? By keeping his jacket on, Johannes had not presented himself properly before the king.[22]

Both accounts continue by stating that the missionary felt that he could not tolerate this, and started to leave. The first account has him commenting: "What have you done? You are hitting my child! By doing that you have driven me away!" before walking away. In response to this,

When he had gone, the king and his attendants ran around the house to prevent them from leaving. The king stood in front of the missionary and shouted: "Don't go, *Mynheer*. *Mynheer* must not go! It is all just a prank! You do not know Mpafudi!"[d] His accomplices tried their best to make excuses for the king. With this, Beuster decided to return.[23]

Mphaphuli then engaged in a series of acts which he obviously intended to be read as performances making a point about power, power relations and power-plays. Since (in spite of being related to each other)[e] Mphaphuli and

---

d. Ranwedzi Mphaphuli was well-known as a prankster (S.M. Dzivhani, "The Chiefs of Venḓa", pp. 48–49).
e. The original Mphaphuli and Tshivhase were half-brothers. They, as well as Makhado's forefathers, all came from the Nzhelele valley royal family. Since then, they were also bound by ties of marriage. Each of the two rulers was married to a daughter of the other, making them both father-in-law and son-in-law to each other (*Mitteilungen des Vereins "Heidenfreund"*, V(18), 1887, n.p. [p. 3]). Their sons were also married to each others' daughters. Makwarela, for example, had married one of Tshivhase's daughters in April 1879 (*BMB*, 1879, pp. 411–412).

Tshivhase were old enemies,[24] they were also obviously designed to comment on this. The first account continues by describing that:

> The king ordered food to be brought. Then he played on his *mbila*; when he had done, he got up and pushed it over so that it broke. After this, he sat down and, in his usual way, he started shouting. Beuster said: "King, my ears are hurting when they hear such words." The king answered, annoyed: "May they always remain sore. This is nothing!" He claimed not to be drunk – that was supposed to be a lie. But he had his dagga-pipe brought to him, and with the smoking he began raving again: "Schewasse! Schewasse! [Tshivhase! Tshivhase!] I am coming for you! I will smash you into pieces! Today, this very night, I will set your villages alight!" Then he ordered Beuster to relate all kinds of compliments like these to Schewasse – Beuster politely declined to do so.[25]

In an argument which obviously reflected the fact that Mphaphuli did not trust Beuster because he was Tshivhase's missionary, the first argument then quotes him as saying: "Schewasse kills my children! You are living with him! Why don't you ask him not to do it?"[26]

Both accounts then have Mphaphuli accompanying Beuster out of the capital village and telling him that:

> "You people say that we blacks will burn in fire! Nonsense, do you not see my black skin? This is not burned, it is black, but you are white, you will be burned!"[f] At the same time, the king made all sorts of gymnastic jumps and assumed all sorts of warrior-positions, pouring scorn on the horses of the whites, [and] singing the praises of his axe against these. He would take this in his hand and, with his speedy feet, catch up the fleeing rider and then with his strong arm cut the horse in two under its body. With this, to the delight of his subjects [who had accompanied him], he acted out the movement of chopping and the crashing down of the horse. The capital village already lay some distance behind the travellers, who had strode through a long, thick thorn-forest, the king was still with them; then he wanted to show them his pigs and see his workers.[27]

It was only once he felt that Mphaphuli had calmed down that Beuster was able to broach with him the issue about which he had come. This was the request of his son that he be permitted to have a "teacher" in his lands.

---

f. In other words, a black skin is already black – it cannot be charred any blacker. A white skin can be charred black when it burns.

Mphaphuli would not countenance opening a station at his own capital. He nevertheless gave permission for the missionaries to open a station in the lands of his son: "Between us there is no conflict, you can teach when and where you want to [in his lands]; you can also tell my son that I have nothing against it, if he wants to believe in Jesus."[28]

What the second account omits totally is the explanation offered by Johannes of the *khosi*'s behaviour later when the travellers were alone. This explained his actions in perfectly rational terms. Johannes pointed out that, particularly amongst the three great *mahosi*, there was a continual jockeying for power, status and prestige. On one level, he believed that: "The cause of it was most probably nothing other than proof that Mpafudi had wanted to show what a very big king he was; a king who should receive the necessary respect." Secondly, jackets or coats could be used to conceal weapons. It was customary to remove these in the presence of *mahosi* to show that the visitor or petitioner was unarmed. Johannes himself pointed out that Mphaphuli's "wrath against [him] ... was most probably because he had neglected to take off his coat when he had been granted an audience with the king". Paulus, who was a MoSotho from the Waterberg area, could be excused for this lack of manners as he did not know the customs here. But Johannes should have known the etiquette of the king's court.[29]

Showing Beuster's bias in favour of "his" *khosi*, Tshivhase, the *Missions-Berichte* recorded that "Schewasse does not demand this recognition – everybody knows of him that he is a powerful, legitimate king who does not have to demand respect through swearing". More perceptive was Johannes' comment that:

> As for the insults which are meant for Schewasse, they were just a pretence. If Beuster passed on the messages, it would only result in the two kings re-affirming their friendship and the missionary would be the guilty one – he would be accused of fanning the flames of enmity between the chiefs, like all whites usually do.[30]

With the benefit of hindsight, and a different ideological starting point, it is also clear that Mphaphuli's decision to allow the missionaries to operate in the lands of his son was an extremely shrewd political move – it gave him access to the missionaries without allowing them to encroach into his area of authority. However, such subtleties escaped the missionaries as these did not fit in with their preconceptions about "heathen" rulers. Instead, in 1876, when there was still the remotest possibility that Ranwedzi Mphaphuli would change his attitude to the mission, the rational explanations for his behaviour were still given. By the late 1880s, when it was clear that he would continue to allow a missionary presence but would act to prevent any significant expansion of their activity in his area, he was portrayed as a savage, unstable cannibal king. Explanations of his behaviour were edited out or dropped and the stereotype was further developed to portray him as

> a really cruel man, who took pleasure in a great deal of bloodshed and was often the instigator of battles between his two sons and their followers. He often had the bodies of fallen enemies brought to the capital village, where he defiled them and allowed them to lie unburied in the open country. Out of the bones of the same, he had war pipes [musical instruments] manufactured. From time to time, by his command, at great celebrations, human flesh was cooked together with the meat of oxen. Individual pieces were then placed in the thorn-bushes; from there his people had to take the pieces of flesh with their mouths and eat them, without touching them with their hands.[31]

According to the missionaries, because of the "gruesome events" which took place in this "heathen" capital village, it "was a really dark area". It lay concealed in the "midst of a huge, impenetrable" forest of bushes and thorn-bushes. There were many paths which entered into this but most ended in dead-ends. "Every visitor had to take a guide with him to show him the way." This was a defensive measure and ensured that visitors could not arrive uninvited or unexpectedly in the capital. It also obscured events in the capital from outside eyes. Beyond the consumption of human flesh,

> From time to time, huge dance performances took place in the capital village. Only respected men could dance, that is those who had killed many people in their lives. So one often saw how, to the thudding tones of the large war drum, old men and women turned round in the circle and praised their dark deeds before the chief in song.[32]

Thus, in the missionary descriptions, Ranwedzi Mphaphuli's taking offence at a slight provocation, and his many transgressions – the spittle, the (symbolic) blood in his eyes, the jumping, the verbal abuse – over time, came to be highlighted and read as signs of cruelty, something that may not have been intended by Mphaphuli himself. Yet what he clearly used as a negotiating ploy, the missionaries essentialised. Turning a blind eye to the intricacies of court etiquette which still shone through in the first account, using hearsay against him to better construct Mphaphuli increasingly as "a really cruel man", a warmonger, and, worse still, as a "cannibal" – the quintessential savage ruler – was a deliberate ploy. In the missionary descriptions, the eyes give way to the mouth, reason to emotions and verbal communication to destructive action, until finally the *khosi* is but a grotesque body, devoid of any humanity. On a symbolical level, the missionaries did to Ranwedzi Mphaphuli what they accused him of doing to others.

The published sources, albums and archives of the Berlin Mission contain no traceable photographs of Ranwedzi (Masindi) Mphaphuli. Regular readers of mission society publications would nevertheless have had a mental picture of the kind of person who devoured his fellows. An illustration of a "Cannibal" appearing on the back cover of Merensky's *Die Menschenfresserei in Afrika*, first published in 1895, clearly depicted the kind of skin-clad, muscular and fierce warrior that they could imagine sinking to these depths [see Illustration 24].[33]

Whatever they thought of Ranwedzi Mphaphuli, the missionaries were nevertheless able to act upon the permission that he had given them to open a station in Makwarela's lands. Klaas Koen, the missionary who would found this station, and whose life history was discussed in chapter 2, was already in Vendaland preparing for his task.

MAKWARELA – THE GREAT HOPE

Koen's diary and other mission reports of the first meeting between him and Makwarela on 13 July 1877 state that he received an extremely warm and "merry" welcome from the *khosi* and his people. An ox had been slaughtered in honour of Makwarela's MoSotho brother-in-law, *Kgoši* Magoro, who was visiting at the time. Koen was received "In the royal kitchen, which serves at the same time as the council chamber, next to the fire on which huge pieces of meat were roasting."[34]

The fact that the meeting took place there, rather than in the *khoro*, the usual public space for such meetings, requires comment. On one level, it may be interpreted as a sign of the importance which Makwarela attached to the meeting and the trust which he was exhibiting in his future missionary. This is the interpretation suggested by Koen's account and the various renderings of this in mission publications. However, it is also possible that the apparent sign of trust signified exactly the opposite – that the *khosi* wished to keep the stranger away from his people until he knew more about him. This would also prevent the missionary's strange ideas from contaminating his people. Makwarela's brother-in-law and, presumably, other trusted unnamed attendants and councillors present at the meeting, were safe from corruption and also provided enough protection for the *khosi*, should this prove to be necessary.

Whichever view is more accurate, at this meeting Makwarela held lengthy discussions with Koen, during the course of which they fixed the boundaries of the station. The *khosi* also promised to build the missionary a house in the capital village. Again, it is possible to read this as a sign that he wished to keep an eye on him. Koen was certainly doing this to Makwarela. Based on this meeting, and several which followed, Koen soon developed the following impression of the *khosi*:

> Makoarele [Makwarela] is a half-civilised Mowenda [MuVenda], he goes around neatly dressed in the European manner,

has all sorts of household goods, some [of which] he himself skilfully manufactured, plays [the] concertina, possesses horses and learns to read and write quickly. He is intelligent, quick-witted, skilful and is interested in everything. One can have a far better conversation with him than with any of his people. He does not beg; yet he has many wives and is still buying more.[35]

However, for the missionaries, this "half-civilised" exterior masked a far darker personality:

> That he was nevertheless a raw heathen was attested to by two human heads placed on top of poles. Recently he had attacked a certain chief and killed him, together with his son. The heads were signs of his victory. Kuhn [Koen] argued that this was wrong and pleaded with him for them to be removed.[36]

Modern historians have managed to explain practices such as the display of the severed heads and the destruction of the corpses of enemies in more complex ways. For example, in the context of Shaka and the Zulu kingdom, Carolyn Hamilton has drawn attention to E.V. Walters' argument that Shaka's autocratic and harsh rule – frequently seen as a sign of his madness – can be interpreted differently as "the effective use of terror as a principal means of government".[37] In another intriguing, but at the same time profoundly disturbing, argument, in her study of the Aztecs, Inga Clendinnen has looked at warfare, anthropophagy and the violence of ritual killings as forms of performance art intricately bound to the creation, maintenance and expansion of the state and social existence.[38]

Arising from the nineteenth-century middle-class self-consciousness they were moulded to absorb in their training in the seminary, the early missionaries in Vendaland were unable to exercise these kinds of explanations. It was by attacking, not understanding and explaining, practices such as these that the mission would make advances. The picture of Makwarela's "pleasant" exterior masking a far "darker" hidden core was drawn from Koen's own contemporary writings and from other sources which used these as their primary source. They were not written later with the benefit of hindsight. Against this background, one feels safe in arguing that it reflected a pre-existing stereotype which was refined, rather than dramatically changed, over time. What changed over time was the missionary interpretation of whether or not Makwarela, like Koen, would be able to rise above his background.

In the first years of their sustained interaction with Makwarela, the missionaries believed that this would, indeed, be the case. In discussions with Koen after the missionary had permanently settled in his lands, Makwarela clearly showed his mastery of strategy and diplomacy. The *khosi* stated that he was not yet ready to become a Christian. To do so while many of his subjects remained unconverted would diminish his position as their ruler. He nevertheless had no objection to his people converting. Should they do so, he would have no objection to becoming the Christian King of a Christian people.[39]

As with the picture that the missionaries painted of Makwarela's life before their arrival, their accounts of the early development of Georgenholtz again depicted the *khosi* as an exceptional character – a leader of the people who outshone his subjects, his peers and his superiors in ability and application. In the perception of the missionaries, he clearly continued to strive after acquiring the benefits of "European civilisation", as symbolised by literacy and the manufacture of "well-made European clothing". He was also perceived to be taking the first steps towards converting to Christianity. In contrast, while they sought after the same benefits, his people were not perceived as having the same capacity for application:

> The chief maintained his good opinion of the missionary and aided him whenever he could. He left his people in no doubt that he found it pleasing when many of them went to learn – and himself was the most regular at hearing the preaching and at learning in the school ... With great determination, he also learned to read and write. He also mastered the art of tailoring which, at that time, was unknown to his people ... To those who were enrolled as catechists under the instruction of the missionary, he presented well-made European clothing [which he had made himself] ... Later, when other people were also taught by the missionary, he helped to show them how to cut and sew decent clothes for themselves.[40]

However, the strenuous efforts of Koen were often met with resistance. Despite the enthusiastic support of Makwarela, the spread of Christianity was an uphill task:

> At first, the preaching of the Gospel brought none into line. If the Gospel brought wealth and a life of luxury, all of the Bawenda would have fallen for it. But none of them had the desire to take up the cross ... One day, one man in particular was extremely angry about the sermon and exhorted the others not to move away from the old customs. He frequently stated: "We are the children of Satan and want to remain so." That they listened to this "liar from the beginning" also shows that they often tell the missionary what he wants to hear, but without acting accordingly afterwards.[41]

In spite of these difficulties, by the time of Koen's first Christmas at Georgenholtz, the missionaries felt that there were strong signs that his work was beginning to produce an element of success. It even seemed probable to them that Makwarela himself was ready to convert to Christianity:

> The Word of God ... found others who wanted to be taught [together] with Makoarele and receive baptism. The Lord assisted here by sending signs (Mark 16, 20).[g] Sick people, to whom Kuhn gave homeopathic medicines, were healed. When, in time of a drought against which the rain-makers had no remedies, he prayed for rain, the Lord sent rain. Through this, the missionary won the love and attention of the people from far and wide, and deeply dented the faith in the arts of the *Zauberer*. Makoarele still believed that the *Zauberer* had some power but the power of the Word of God was also clear to him. Kuhn had to visit him in his home in the morning and in the evening, and even in dreams he occupied himself with the question of salvation.[42]

In December 1877, Makwarela related to Koen that, in a dream, he had seen:

> A terribly big fire filled with people in front of me. They were screaming and complaining piteously. On the other side, many people were sitting. All of them were extremely cheerful, praying, reading God's word and singing. I was standing entirely alone. The flames appeared to want to engulf me. I shivered in terrible fear. Then my father, Pafuli [Ranwedzi Mphaphuli], came running, screaming in his fear: "Save my son! Save my son!" Eventually, I discovered a small gap near the fire, fled through this and ran to those praying, pleading with them in my fear: "Help me, help me, in my thirst for knowledge I have merely learned how to read and write, I have often not heard God's word with a heart longing to praise him. Now I seek refuge with you, pray with me." They did this and I awoke. All people that I saw in my dream were blacks.[43]

Makwarela's dream demonstrates the kind of tensions that the presence of the missionaries in his lands had brought to him and to his people. The pressure that Makwarela was under to convert is evidenced by the twice-daily visits that Koen paid to him. His regular attendance at instruction classes and church services would have increased this pressure significantly. As shown by Mphaphuli's comments to Beuster at their first meeting about blacks being "burned in fire", the local people clearly associated the missionaries with their teachings about the fires of hell. Indeed, the missionaries taught that this

---

g. "And they went forth and preached every where, the Lord working with *them*, and confirming the word with signs following. Amen."

was the fate of "heathens" and the godless in general.[44] This remains a recurrent theme in evangelical preaching and tracts to this day.[45]

Moving to the content of the dream itself, not only was Makwarela in fear of damnation but his father was already lost. The consigning of his father to the fires of hell struck at the very root of the religious charter which supported Vhavenda society. The position of the *mahosi* as the religious leaders of their people, the rites and ceremonies attached to their office, the *musanda* language used in royal circles and the patterns of behaviour adopted by subjects in their presence set them apart from ordinary mortals. Moreover, their role as protectors of their communities and final arbiters of the fate of their subjects did not stop with death.[46] Consigning Mphaphuli to the fires of hell thus affected his whole community, not just those of the existing generation but also those of the generations still to come.

From the perspective of the dream, the only solution lay in the wholehearted acceptance of Christianity. Learning the new ways of the whites – as exemplified by reading and writing – was not enough. Makwarela, and his people, would have to leave this past and accept life in Christ and the prayers, support and assistance of those who had already converted. In the view of the missionaries, Koen's successes in treating illness and his successes where the *Zauberer* had failed, reinforced this interpretation. Under such conditions, the dream reveals the great trauma that operation of the Berlin missionaries in his area of authority against a background of increasing white penetration had engendered in *Khosi* Makwarela. The time was not far off when he would have to make far-reaching decisions about his own fate, and the fate of his people.

One is safe in arguing that Makwarela would have had little reason not to at least consider the possibility that his dream should be taken as a serious message from the ancestors or from God. As in other African societies, in local cosmologies dreams have been (and, in many cases, still are) seen as potential messages from supernatural forces or as omens portending good or evil to the dreamer and his or her family or (in the case of *mahosi*) people.[47] Similarly, given Koen's background, he too would have had reason to analyse the content of the dream. In an extremely interesting argument, Elizabeth Elbourne has asserted that in Khoisan spiritual practice, dreams and omens were seen as imparting messages from the supernatural to the natural world. Many converts to Christianity incorporated this idea into their new cosmology, seeing dreams as validating their adoption of the new religion or as a form of direct communication between the dreamer and God or Jesus. Moreover, this was an interpretation which was shared by many Evangelical Christians.[48] Irving Hexham and Karla Poewe have also pointed out that, in general, the Berliners "did not question the reality of dreams and visions in African conversion and Christian life". On the contrary, they saw "such experiences as genuine expressions of the work of the Holy Spirit, and encouraged their converts to report such phenomena".⁴⁹ Thus, even although Koen had become thoroughly "Germanised", there was still room in his theology and in his world-view for taking dreams seriously.⁵⁰ It is also possible that, whether consciously or unconsciously, this may have resonated with various childhood experiences. He certainly took the dream seriously, asking Makwarela if he understood it, arguing that God was using this to "say the same things" that he had "already preached to him". Similarly, Makwarela's "brother Masiti [Masithi] also told him that the dream is very clear, all can see that it is the voice of God that is calling him".ʰ While Makwarela acknowledged that this may have been true, he also allowed for the possibility "that perhaps it was just a dream".⁵¹ It was nevertheless very clear that the dream had "made a deep impression on him".⁵²

The missionaries believed that it was clear that Makwarela "was caught in an inner conflict". This was clear not only from the dream but also by the fact that, at this stage,

> He often acknowledged in conversation that he no longer believed at all in the lying gods of the Bawenda; they [the Vhavenda] had merely been deceived and believed so strongly in these lies because they had been passed down from their great-great grandfathers and were tradition. He had learned enough of God's word to say that they were only fables.

In the interpretation of the missionaries, Makwarela "felt the truth of the Word of God deeply and seriously" but "the fear of diminishing his power and prestige as a chief" and his worries about "his many wives, the number of which he was always increasing, prevented him from seriously moving to convert" to Christianity.⁵⁴ He was also "not completely free from believing in" the "lies" of African religion himself. For example, shortly after telling Koen about his dream, "he told him that the rain doctor of Lowimbi [Luvhimbi] could really make rain". However, in spite of these stumbling-blocks, the dream and the discussions which followed it gave the missionaries a great deal of hope that *Khosi* Makwarela was finally ready to convert to Christianity and become baptised.⁵⁶

These missionary interpretations may also be read in a different light. An alternative explanation could be that Makwarela was in the early stages of

---

h. Masithi was an elder brother of Makwarela's. The missionaries recorded that he had come into contact with Christianity – and been "stimulated" by this – while working as a migrant labourer in the Cape Colony. For a while, Koen had hoped "that he would maybe be the first one of his people to be baptised". However, in the interpretation of the missionaries "the old man [Ranwedzi Mphaphuli] must have noticed this". In order both to tempt him away from Christianity and to make any possible conversion much more difficult, he appointed Masithi as a *gota* and, at the same time, gave him a second wife. The missionaries felt that: "The unfortunate one could not stand up against this temptation as well as the fear of the rage of his very cruel father – he chose the world and seems to be lost for Christendom" (*BMB*, 1878, p. 495).

formulating a strategy which would enable him to attempt to solve the dilemma posed by his liminal position somewhere between "tradition" and the new order held out by the missionaries by bridging the two extremes in his person.

Whether or not Makwarela believed the "truth" that Christianity taught was the only truth, he appears to have realised that abandoning "tradition" and African religion completely would have shaken his society to the core. It would also have been an act of political suicide. It has already been argued that "heathens" often showed considerable "animosity" to those that converted to Christianity.[57] This "animosity" would have been greater in the case of a converted *khosi* than with ordinary commoners. Not only would his father not have accepted his conversion but the overwhelming majority of his people still followed African religion. They would have demanded of him that he rule according to established traditions and beliefs. At best, his conversion would have divided his people; at worst, he would have lost his throne and possibly his life. Moreover, even had he managed to retain power, or a degree of power, his continued rule would have been subject to conditions and constraints imposed by the missionaries.

One solution to this dilemma would be that of taking elements from both traditions and blending them together in a similar way to that which was later to be adopted by African-initiated churches. By the time that the first four adult baptisms took place at Georgenholtz on 27 July 1879, Makwarela apparently wanted both to be baptised and to rule as a "traditional" chief – to blend elements of Christianity with elements of "tradition".[58]

Missionary accounts of these baptisms record that, in spite of the great joy that they brought, Makwarela

> was deeply saddened by these events ... He very much wanted to be baptised also [and had even chosen the name Elias/Elijah as a baptismal name]... However, Klaas Kuhn could not grant him his pleas as he would not leave his many wives and live with only one wife as a Christian. The missionary could make no exception ... [of the rule] for him.[59]

The Berlin Mission had even been unable to accept the more liberal attitude towards baptism held by Allison and the Methodists in Natal.[60] They were even more unable to accept the idea that one could be both a polygamist and a baptised Christian. As a man of his times and his calling, Koen had no choice but to take the stand that he did. Viewed in one way, this refusal to baptise Makwarela must rate as one of the significant missed opportunities for real intercultural exchange in the history of Christian mission in Southern Africa.[61] On the other hand, it may be argued that the missionaries believed that they were in Vendaland to teach and not to learn. They were thus not in a position to perceive their situation of contact with Makwarela as any kind of opportunity for cultural exchange. If one accepts this argument, then there was actually no opportunity to be missed.

However one interprets this, there were also much more immediate effects. In rejecting Makwarela in the name of what he saw as the One and Only Way, Koen brought into the open a tension between the leadership of the mission and the leadership of the people which had previously been hidden beneath the cordiality of their relationship on the surface. He also fomented a tension between him and Makwarela which had not existed previously and which would result in a clearer division between "Christians" and "heathens". In the interpretation of the missionaries,

> There followed difficult times for the young Christians at Georgenholtz. Makoarele took offence that he had not been allowed to be baptised. One should not be surprised that he was hostile to Kuhn; because as a chief he was not used to any dissent. He became a little cooler towards Kuhn; only attending church services infrequently. He nevertheless still claimed to be Kuhn's good friend. Nevertheless, he came more and more under the influence of his mother, who was a bitter enemy of the Gospel. She had become extremely wild when she had heard that her son wanted to become a Christian. On the day of the baptisms, she had said that she wanted to dance at the celebration and then, when Makoarele was also baptised, she would take her own life. Now she was very satisfied that he was for the present remaining with the customs of his father and requested him – not without success – to hinder [the spreading of] the Gospel.[62]

The missionaries argued strongly that, because of the pivotal role that the *khosi* played in the life of his community, this new tension was not restricted to him alone. In their interpretation,

> Many of those who had learned now remained distant because they saw that Makoarele had become half-hearted [about Christianity]. They started to work on Sundays again and all sorts of terrible heathen practices which had been allowed to fall into disuse were again practised.[63]

Because of this atmosphere of tension, the missionaries believed that: "The difference between the Christians and the heathens became increasingly clear." In a vivid statement of what Koen saw as the wild, uncontrolled passions of the "heathens" as opposed to the controlled study, self-improvement and spirituality of his converts, on Sunday 5 October 1879, he wrote:

> Here at the station there is Sunday rest, over there at the heathens there is noise and wild shouting. There, from that kraal, a

woman jumps wildly around to the monotonous music of their drums and pipes [flutes]; she dances and shouts until she can [do so] no longer and is completely exhausted. Then she becomes possessed by spirits and becomes the irrational lute for the expressing of what they see as a higher wisdom.[i] In contrast to this, the converts sit and read. Gathered in groups, they read their Testaments [Bibles] and exercise books, while here and there a spiritual song rings out. What contrast [between] here and there![64]

To Koen's dismay, in January 1880, Makwarela:

Celebrated, in heathen fashion, the festival at which the beer is consecrated. The beer which is brewed first (mokumbi [*mukumbi*][j]) is poured into a big wooden bowl. The chief puts some medicine (made of certain herbs which are first burnt and then ground) into the bowl. Then they all take a long, sharp needle and stab into the beer, and then they kneel around the bowl and drink of the beer. The chief and his mighty ones [councillors] start the ritual; they are followed by the men who during the past year have married widows; then the women who in the same period have lost children; then the rest of the people.[65]

In addition to this, the missionaries reported that the *khosi* "was not satisfied with pulling away from Koen. He already started to keep his people back – yes, he even frightened away those who were already baptised." Twenty-four of the twenty-five people who had requested baptism after the first baptisms at Georgenholtz were intimidated into withdrawing from their classes. Aware of the fact that one of his councillors, Mapatha, was seeking baptism, Makwarela began to send him and others away on special errands on Sundays. He also "presented another candidate with a second wife, in order to keep him away from his faith". On top of this, he "no longer stopped his people from persecuting the Christians".[66] In missionary analysis, "Many heathens cut ties with the believers, hindered them and threatened them in bitter enmity."[67]

In the interpretation of the missionaries, Makwarela was no longer interested in "the Gospel". Instead "he was busy with different plans". Not content to make "himself miserable by sitting idly on the chief's throne," towards the end of the year 1881, he decided to "go and work on the diamond fields, even though he was a chief, and so earn himself an ox-wagon". Commenting

---

i. What is being described here is the *malombo* dance of possession by ancestral spirits, see pp. 182–186.
j. This is the beer usually made from the maroela fruit (*mafula*) . The fruit of the marula tree usually ripens round about late January or early February, long before the maize is reaped in April or May.

on his decision to Koen, he reportedly exclaimed: "Why must I sit here? I am called a chief, but I am nothing. I just sit, drink beer and try to kill time. I want to see the world!"[68]

Hearing "of his son's brain-wave", Ranwedzi Mphaphuli sent a messenger to "report back the exact details, so that he could close that avenue if necessary". Makwarela had just left in the company of fifty of his subjects when the messenger arrived. His mother "knew how to keep the messenger occupied with much good food and other tricks – just long enough to get Makoarele [Makwarela] safely over the border". He and his party reached the diamond fields safely and would later be joined by three hundred more of his subjects.[69]

Some months later, on 2 January 1882, Makwarela returned with a wagon drawn by sixteen oxen. Although he had left many of his party behind to work, he was still accompanied by an impressive retinue on his return. As he drew closer to his capital, "hundreds" of his subjects joined the royal procession, ululating in welcome. Makwarela stopped at the mission station on his way, staying there until the completion of the afternoon service. Only then did he leave "to greet his mother and his wives". The *Missions-Berichte* reported that: "The joy amongst his people at his return was exceptionally great. The old women danced and licked his hands and face."[70] Koen was also extremely pleased to have him back again as the *khosi* "greeted the missionary again as his old friend".[71] In the interpretation of the mission, he at least maintained "an outwardly friendly appearance towards the missionary", protecting him "against the torments of his people who, during the period of his absence, had often become really troublesome".[72]

Other events were also leading to the rebuilding of the friendship between the two men, for:

> At that time there was a great drought in the land. The *Zauberer* tried all their arts to make it rain – but in vain. Then the chief requested the missionary to pray for rain with the Christians. They did this and then, the very next night, came the long-awaited rain. This made a deep impression on the people. However, none converted because of this.[73]

The missionaries argued that it nevertheless did have an effect on Makwarela:

> At night, Makoarele [Makwarela] came to the church service again. Klaas Kuhn [Klaas Koen] preached about the "lost son" so powerfully that it went deep into his heart. However, he wanted to make excuses. He said [that] he wanted to accuse his mother and [his] council for turning him away from the Word of God.[74]

This thawing of relations apparently did not go unnoticed by some of the local notables. On hearing Makwarela say that there was still a possibility that he would be baptised one day, one of Mphaphuli's oldest councillors reportedly said to him:

> Don't talk like this. We all know that one is easily overcome by God's Word if one starts to listen. This is why I don't want to hear any of it. But consider this: you cannot be chief if you are a believer ...[75]

The councillor need nevertheless not have feared. While there would still be many times when friendly relations would prevail between Makwarela and the missionaries, things would never return to the way that they had been in the early days.[76]

With Koen's death in February 1883, Dietrich Baumhöfner "tackled the labour on the soul of the chief", which his predecessor had been forced by his illness to cut back on, "with fresh effort". From the paternalistic perspective of the missionaries, it was clear that, removed from the regular influence of Koen, Makwarela had begun to slip back from the position on the road towards conversion and salvation that he had reached. In so doing, he was again not prepared to stand up to his father and was prepared to use Mphaphuli's hostility as an excuse for his own backsliding. However, the missionaries still held out hope that Baumhöfner would lead him to convert to Christianity:

> First, Makoarele came to him to ask for medicine for one of his wives. Br. Baumhöfner showed him the punishing hand of God in the illness of his wife. Because he had recently taken this wife against Br. Kuhn's objection – he had told him that it was a sin to take more than one wife. By this deed, he had shown the heathens that he did not want to learn. Then he came with many excuses. His father Pafudi had said to him: "You must only dare to learn to read, but when I hear that you have become baptised and have to leave your wives, I will exile you from the lands; then [also] think that you have the children of the greatest in the lands as your wives." About the Sunday labour that he had caused to be performed in his garden the previous day, he willingly said that he would put a stop to this ... When asked for permission for the children of the capital to be given an hour of singing twice a week, he did not do so. But he also did not forbid it. And he visibly took pleasure in the singing of the children and in the great honour shared by him when the young *Mynheer* came to him twice a week, also he heard when Br. Baumhöfner coupled preaching with the singing-hour.[77]

"So Baumhöfner gradually began to touch him." However, with his death in April 1883, missionary hopes for the conversion of Makwarela again receded. For the missionaries, the great worry remained: what would happen to the *khosi*? Revealing the paternalistic importance which they placed on having German-trained missionaries, rather than Native Evangelists, in charge of stations, *Der Bawenda-Freund* recorded that, with the death of Baumhöfner "the congregation in Georgenholtz was orphaned, and also Makoarele was deprived of the direct and regular influence of the Word of God". Instead, they and he had to rely on visits "every now and then" from Br. Beuster.[78] They stated this despite the fact that, subject to the overriding authority of Beuster, leadership of the congregation had been transferred to Franz Maluleke, one of the Native Assistants who had been trained by Koen.[79]

Despite their fears about Makwarela's possible backsliding, the missionaries had to concede that he was "still as well disposed to the mission and to our Franz as he always was".[80] In their opinion, the *khosi*'s strength of character and apparent commitment to conversion was also manifested in other ways. During the time of the station's "abandonment" from April 1883 to July 1887, Dr. Theodor Wangemann, the Director of the Berlin Mission Society from 1865 to 1894, paid his second and final visit to the stations of the Society in South Africa.[k] He also visited Georgenholtz on 11 December 1884 and had a lengthy meeting with Makwarela.[81] In commenting on this meeting, *Der Bawenda-Freund* stated that:

> Dr. Wangemann was so surprised by his intelligence and distinguished appearance that at first he thought that he was a Native Evangelist, rather than a heathen. In this meeting, he showed himself to be very well disposed towards Christianity and was overjoyed when the re-founding of the station was suggested.[82]

However, even in Makwarela's strength, in their paternalism the missionaries saw signs that his commitment was beginning to weaken because of insufficient contact with a white missionary. It would be some time before the missionary spoken about in the meeting with Wangemann could be transferred to the station. In the meantime, Br. Beuster continued to visit him "every now and then". It is clear that Makwarela did not count himself among the saved, or amongst those about to be saved at the time of one of Beuster's visits in the second semester of 1885. As the missionary left, accompanied by

> the festively-attired, singing small congregation, Makoarele said to his heathen crowd: "Hear people, in the days to come, the believers will be with their King Jesus, but we will stand there ashamed; I know all of this because I read God's Word."[83]

---

k. Wangemann visited South Africa in 1866–1867 and 1884–1885.

A relief missionary would come. However, for the missionaries, the question was whether or not this would be in time to save Makwarela. On 28 May 1886, Missionary Reinhold Wessmann arrived at Ha-Tshivhase and began the customary one-year's orientation with Missionary Beuster. It would be just over a year before he and his wife would move to Georgenholtz to re-establish the station on 23 July 1887.[84]

While Wessmann was still at Ha-Tshivhase, as had happened in the past prior to the arrival of the missionaries in Vendaland, the tensions and periodic skirmishes between Tshivhase and Mphaphuli yet again "erupted" into open warfare. For the missionaries, events during this war would confirm their previous unflattering stereotypes of Ranwedzi Mphaphuli. However, despite the fact that Makwarela was an active participant in the fighting, the missionaries did not witness his direct participation in any of the other rituals surrounding warfare. This meant that, while extremely distressed by the violent nature of the conflict, they were able to avoid grappling with the question of whether or not Makwarela had any characteristics in common with his father. It was only later that they would engage issues such as this.

Hostilities broke out in August 1886, when Tshikalange led a night-time raid into *Khosi* Tshivhase's territory "killing two men and two women, and stealing fifteen head of cattle". This prompted a retaliatory raid by Tshivase's forces, unleashing a series of raids and counter-raids.[85] Faced with the escalating conflict, the missionaries attempted to negotiate, if not peace, at least some lessening of the degree of violence. Visiting Mphaphuli's capital village at the beginning of November 1886, Missionaries Beuster and Wessmann (completing his year's orientation at Ha-Tshivhase) witnessed what can be interpreted to be a highly symbolic public ritual performance.

Participation in the most dramatic roles of the ritual was not open to everyone. The central role was played by the *khosi*, ruler of the people and the link between the living and the ancestors. His main assistants were people who had gained respect by their age, and (either directly or implicitly) their courage and their prowess in warfare. It seems that having killed an enemy in warfare was a prerequisite for taking part. At the very least, judging by the age of the participants, one had to have considerable experience of warfare:

> In the meantime, the war drums resounded. The chief and an old, abominable-looking and even more abominably gesticulating woman – who was supposed to have once stoned to death two of the enemy, during a war – these two, together with several old men, danced a wild war-dance. We heard people singing war songs approaching from the distance.[86]

The big war drum which played a central role in the drama is reminiscent of *Ngoma lungundu* (the drum of Mwali), the legendary sacred object, protective force and secret weapon of the VhaSenzi during their migration southwards into the Nzhelele Valley.[87] Since the Mphaphulis traced their origins to this lineage, it is likely that the symbolism was deliberate. In addition, the actions performed with the severed hand of the dead enemy warrior may be interpreted as an allusion to the origins of the name Mphaphuli – "the hacker off of hands" – adopted after the founding ancestor of the group saved himself from being killed in a plot by hacking off the hand of his intended assassin.[88] The purportedly less-concealed symbolism of the actions performed was explained by Beuster:

> The big war-drum immediately resounded and, with our own eyes, we had to see how a wild [savage] warrior jumped about in front of the war-drum. In the one hand he had his weapon and in the other, tied to a long stick, he had the hand of a slain enemy; the hand of the wounded person who had been murdered the previous day. The body itself, tied to stakes, was brought into the court-yard. The big war-drum was dragged to where the body was and wild [savage] dances were performed there. Mpafuli [Mphaphuli] himself, stepped over his conquered [dead] foe and sat down on his chest, while the dancing warriors surrounded him. Then he suddenly shot up, tearing through the yard with enormous leaps; he pointed his bow and arrow in various directions, as a sign that his foes in that direction would quickly meet with the same fate. In all the time that I have been missionary amongst these heathens, I have never before experienced such a horrible, awful sight as this. Who would have thought that such conditions would once again return to here.[89]

The majority of the local people clearly did not share Beuster's revulsion at the events that were taking place. Following normal custom, they offered their visitors food to eat. Mphaphuli and Makwarela were also not too disturbed by Beuster's vociferous vocal objections to what he was witnessing, apparently seeing it as the kind of talk that could be expected from the missionary. However, although Makwarela had played an active role in the fighting, and was present at these acts, he had not played an active role in the ritual. This meant that, for the meanwhile, the missionaries were able to maintain their hopes for, and positive picture of, him.[90]

Freed from such scruples with regard to Ranwedzi Mphaphuli, they were nevertheless able to confirm earlier stereotypes about the *khosi*. The *Missions-Berichte* reported that "Beuster later heard that all sorts of wanton things were done to the body of the dead person in spite of his request." Updating his original diary entry, the published version contained Beuster's addition that:

> It is said that after my departure, Mphaphuli had disfigured and smashed the corpse which I had asked to be buried. He had con-

structed pipes [flutes] from the bones of this victim, which will drive away and destroy the enemy, when they are blown during the war. They had heard that this man who had been killed had been a respected man, an artist in all sorts of iron crafts. Because of this, his body was valuable as it had been attributed with special powers and abilities; an opportunity too good to be missed. Moreover, the witch-doctor, Magoro, is ardently hoping that during a fresh attack, a warrior of royal blood will fall into his hands, so that he can make a piece of clothing for himself from this person's skin; clothing which would protect him from all danger and which would endow him with supernatural powers. In the end he had to return to his home-land, without having fulfilled this wish.[91]

Having failed in his endeavour to talk Mphaphuli and Makwarela into accepting the need for peace, Beuster decided to go to Tshivhase and use accusations that they had levelled against the latter as a starting point for talking about peace. In the missionary's interpretation, Makwarela and Mphaphuli had: "tried to justify the atrocities they had committed by putting the blame for the whole disaster onto Schewasse [Tshivhase] – it was only as a result of Schewasse not sparing the women and children, that they had been driven to killing the wounded of Schewasse's people." So, riding to Tshivhase on 16 November 1886, he used "these accusations to also draw Schewasse's attention to the sins he had committed".

Beuster recorded that Tshivhase

> listened to me without interruption and calmly discussed my counter-proposals, but he reckoned (and I had to silently agree with him) that Mpafuli [Mphaphuli] could truly not reproach him (Schewasse) for any greater atrocities than they themselves had committed. For example, up to now he has never trashed the body of an enemy, be he alive or dead, nor made medicine from his flesh, nor eaten any part of him, as is generally known Mpafuli does.[92]

While Beuster did not specify exactly which exclusions he had requested for women and children, it seems that he also asked Tshivhase that they be excluded from the war altogether and that there be no capture, killing, assault or rape of women and children. He recorded that:

> Schewasse [Tshivhase] did not want to unconditionally grant me my request concerning the women and children. He maintained he could not prevent it. Yet I was convinced that my proposals and pleas had not been totally in vain: he will not totally ignore the words which I tried to impress on his heart and on the

hearts of his two sons. According to my experience, Schewasse usually does more than he promises.[93]

Indeed, despite the fact that his war seems to have been the most serious that the missionaries had witnessed up to that time, Beuster had come to trust direct, and even implied, promises which he received from Tshivhase. His faith also did not go unrewarded. In response to a request from Beuster, Tshivhase had promised to spare any of the mission's outstations which were situated in Mphaphuli's territory. Wangemann recorded that: "The King promised to do so and has kept his word, in spite of all other atrocities which the war brought along with it."[94]

It was against the background of these then-recent tensions that Wessmann and his wife moved in at Georgenholtz. Able to excuse Makwarela for his role in the fighting since he did not seem to have participated in what they saw as the other "atrocities", *Der Bawenda-Freund* noted that: "For the third time, the third missionary at Georgenholtz had the liveliest hopes for Makoarele's conversion."[95]

Describing his early impressions of life in the vicinity of the station, Wessmann wrote of what he saw as the "wild" and "satanic" ways of the "heathens":

> What a turbulent life prevails around Georgenholtz was brought to my attention again this morning. One goes to sleep in the evening with the sound of drums and the wild screaming of the dancing heathens, so we also usually awake again in the early hours of the morning to the inarticulate sounds cast out by an old dagga-smoker in a state of euphoric intoxication ... The sight of such satanic behaviour leads one to acknowledge the force and power of Satan, whereby he blinds and shackles the heathens.[96]

Makwarela was still a "heathen". However, like his predecessors and the wider mission community, Wessmann clearly saw him as being superior not only to his people, just described, but also to other "heathen rulers" as well. He also saw him as still standing on the threshold of conversion and, like his predecessors, saw this conversion as being the key to unlock the floodgates of conversion among the Vhavenda. At about the same time as he described Makwarela's people, Wessmann wrote about the *khosi* himself as follows:

> The visit of a heathen ruler to the home of the mission very seldom excites the same kind of joy as the visit of Makoarele [Makwarela], our ruler ... He does not only go around elegantly dressed but his aristocratic features and his pleasant speech are such that would lead him to be recognised as an educated man in Germany, if his black face did not give away his

> descent. Among the heathens, he is honoured and celebrated as a valiant man and a hero in war. Among our Christians, he is honoured and loved, not only as a ruler but also as a friend and brother. During the visit of other chiefs, it is common for the missionary to be bothered by continuous and great begging, but with Makoarele the opposite is the case, and he does not delight me only, he also regularly serves the members of our congregation with his good deeds and kindness. He stands very close to the Word of God. Also today, he reads with me, and his knowledge of this is not limited. God's spirit has already been working for a long time on his heart, so that he does not only recognise his corruption [sinful nature] but also attempts to comply with the demands of the Word of God. In his lands, he allows Sundays to be observed, and himself provides a good example of this ... Also, blasphemers and mockers [of the Word of God] find no room in his area. If he is won for the Kingdom of God, this will give us a great harvest. With him stands or falls heathendom in these lands. Many only wait for their ruler, Makoarele, to go forward. May many praying hearts at home unite with us to win this one for salvation.[97]

Moreover, in the perception of the mission, Wessmann's admiration for Makwarela was reciprocated by the *khosi*. Not only did he show him honour in various ways, he also relied on him as a source of protection against the Boers:

> On the other hand, the high regard in which Makoarele [Makwarela] held the missionary was shown when, on a four-week journey to Makato [Makhado], he sent back the command that all occurrences that came to light be decided by the missionary and that he had to be consulted. He forbade the common [practice of] the killing of twins and, at the same time, the importation of the brandy brought by Portuguese traders from Delagoa Bay. Makato expended a great deal of effort attempting to move Makoarele into an alliance against the Boers; the first step in this direction was that one had to expel the missionaries. Because the missionaries prepared the ground for the Boers. But Makoarele replied: "Why is it then that the Boers want to grab you by the collar at night when you have still not tolerated a single missionary in your lands?"[98]

In what was becoming a familiar refrain, the Annual Report of the Berlin Mission for 1887 reported that:

> Chief Makoarele [Makwarela] was friendly and obliging towards Brother Wessmann, as he has been to all the missionaries

before. He would certainly have wanted to be baptised, as he has already attained the required realisation of his salvation. But he fears that as a Christian, he would lose the sovereignty over the whole country, after his father Pafudi's [Mphaphuli's] death. One can just painfully regret this half-heartedness. But the assistance which Makoarele [Makwarela] gives ... greatly helps to open the way for the smooth spreading of God's Word.[99]

These extremely positive images of Makwarela are clearly revealed in an illustration titled "In the area of the ruler of the lands" in Wilde's *Schwarz und Weiss* and "Audience with Mpafudi (Makwarela)" in the Northern-Transvaal albums of the Berlin Mission Archives [see Illustration 25].[100] Squatting wearing a top-hat and a jacket with missionaries, Native Evangelists (also squatting) and (apparently) a councillor in attendance, Makwarela looks every bit the "civilised", "aristocratic" and "educated" ruler that we have come to expect from the textual descriptions.[101] However, with extreme irony, what this photograph does not show is that, by the time that it was taken, the Berlin missionaries' picture of Makwarela had changed completely.

MAKWARELA BREAKS FREE

As at the time of Makwarela's dream, the missionaries still did not have any real idea of the kind of complexities of the situation in which the *khosi* had to operate. His interaction with Koen and Baumhöfner over the question of his wives had shown that Makwarela was deeply committed to local ways and had character and power enough (because of his royal position) to withstand what he saw as the unreasonable demands of the Church. Although he at first resented Koen's refusal to baptise him, he re-established ties with the missionary, accepting the situation and moving on. The same applied to his future rule as *khosi*. He knew his duties towards the ancestors and his people as his father's heir. Prepared to embrace change, but cautious about destroying the social fabric, he realised that Christianity on missionary terms would stand in the way of his duties as king.[102] Moreover, if he had any fears for his personal safety should he convert, these would have been very real. It is likely that the case of Khashane Mamatepha provided Makwarela (and other rulers in Vendaland) with a salutary example here. An independent *kgoši* who paid tribute to Queen Modjaji, he was forcibly deposed by her in 1882 as a result of his conversion to Christianity. The Queen seems to have felt that the combination of Khashane and Missionary Fritz Reuter at the Medingen Mission Station in her area provided a threat to her authority. *Kgoši* Mamatepha was martyred for his faith in 1884.[103] It is extremely likely that the case would have known about, and commented on, locally. Not only was there interaction between Tshivenda-speakers and the people of Modjaji through ties of trade and marriage but Missionary Schwellnuss from Tshakhuma acted as mediator between Khashane, Reuter, Modjaji and Albasini.[104] He would presumably have discussed the case with converts and others on his return. These events clearly made a significant impression on Missionary Beuster. Similarly, in 1885, there was at least one case where a Christian convert, Poroa, moved from Ha-Tshivhase to Medingen to escape pressures from his unconverted relatives to abandon his new faith.[105]

Unable to see matters through Makwarela's eyes, just as they thought that things were going so well, the hopes of the missionaries to finally bring Makwarela to conversion were dashed. In their perception, a number of wars, the influence of his father and a lack of frequent contact with Wessmann would gradually strip away Makwarela's veneer of civilisation. Makwarela's "heathen essence" would eventually be starkly revealed in ways that would completely rupture the relationship between him and the missionaries, throw away his chance of salvation and "bring him low". In what they saw as his "return to the darkness of heathenism", he would become little better than, if not as bad as, his father. In the person of Makwarela, the "darkness of the forest" would triumph over the "light of salvation". In missionary analysis, the example set by Koen, and his supreme sacrifice, were to have been in vain.

According to the missionaries, "1889 brought a drastic change".[106] In May of that year, in a revival of previous conflicts between them,[107] Makwarela and his brother Tshikalange became involved in a "bloody struggle" to consolidate their power bases as possible successors to Ranwedzi. The missionaries reported that Mphaphuli himself had been instrumental in engineering the outbreak of this conflict as he was worried about how powerful Tshikalange was becoming. When Tshikalange showed signs of organising to "oust his brother", Mphaphuli encouraged Makwarela to engage his brother on the field of battle.[108]

Makwarela had managed to gain a temporary alliance with *Khosi* Tshivhase, his and his father's old enemy. As a consequence, the war also spread into the latter's lands and dragged the missionaries at Ha-Tshivhase into the conflict.[109] In Beuster's cynical opinion, "Suddenly Tschewasse [Tshivhase] acted as if he was the ally of his erstwhile deadly enemy – most assuredly with the intention of later, when the kingdom had been sufficiently weakened by the war between the two brothers, to attack the kingdom all the more easily".[110] Makhado "also became involved and seized the opportunity provided by the state of war to commit a series of robberies in Tschewasse's area".[111]

At this stage, victory went to Makwarela. On 3 June, Tshikalange and his followers abandoned their capital village and fled across the Luvuvhu River. Beuster reported that:

> Makoarele [Makwarela] and his allies were very happy about this outcome. The warriors rushed into the deserted village and, in a most cruel way, killed whoever had been left behind there

> – namely an old man, a mad woman and two other sick people who had not been able to flee with the others. Then, upon Mpafuli's [Mphaphuli's] order, the capital village was put to fire and burnt down to the ground. Old Mpafuli did not want to enter the village through the usual entrance because he feared the magic potions of his son.[112] They had to break open a new entrance for him through which he entered the village. Anything that could burn outside the village was also thrown into the fire. The new residence, Botshabelo [*Dzhavhelo*] which Tshikalange was in the process of building on a nearby hill – where the chief had, with great trouble and at great expense, almost finished the stone walls of his residence – was destroyed.[1] All the building material, which had in part been made by white people, was thrown into the fire. The whole country of Tschefifi [Tshififi], which was otherwise so crowded with people, was within a few days, transformed into a desolate area.[113]

During the course of the following year, 1890, Makwarela symbolically demonstrated what he saw as his final defeat of his brother by establishing a new capital for himself at the site of Tshikalange's former capital. However, Tshikalange had not yet conceded defeat. During the following year, his forces combined with those of Tshivhase (who had switched sides) to attack Makwarela.[114]

In the opinion of the missionaries, these events served to withdraw Makwarela "from close contact with Brother Wessmann", leading to a situation where

> It still appeared that he was devout and clearly striving for salvation. But, here and there, it could be seen that he was seeking to hinder the wider spread of the Gospel. However, he did not outwardly oppose the missionary as he attached great importance to the fact that the missionary viewed him as a friend and as a patron to Christendom.[115]

More importantly, in contradiction to their attitude towards Makwarela's participation in the earlier fighting against Tshivhase, the missionaries felt that, because of the war with his brother, "in spite of all his Christian understanding", Makwarela had "allowed himself to be pulled back into all sorts of cruelties".[116] They also strongly believed that "these battles served to increas-

---

1. The Tshivenda word for a fortress (a place of refuge or stronghold) is *Dzhavhelo*. Beuster used the Northern Sotho word "Botshabelo". I am sure that Tshikalange would have used the Tshivenda word for his fortress.

ingly shackle the chief to [his] heathen essence".[117] What caused them the gravest concern, however, were not the casualties which the war caused but the way in which victory was sealed in the capital after the return of the warriors. The victory ceremony involved a most dramatic ritual re-enactment of the process of destruction on the bodies of dead enemies, reportedly culminating in acts of anthropophagy, with the *khosi* playing an essential role in it. As Meister of Ha-Tshivhase noted in his diary,

> Monday, 27 July [1891]: We had promised to come [and attend to] the casualties again today. On the way, we heard that bodies of the enemies which had been carried away and the living captives were being taken to the capital of Mpafuli [Ranwedzi Mphaphuli] ... We had no doubt that they would violate the bodies in their extreme heathen manner. But would he not also possibly lift up his hand against the captives? With Mpafuli anything is possible. Therefore we had to go to him. We found everything that had been reported to us [to be] true. Already, the warriors were awaiting the signal to begin with their abominations. I could not resist,[m] I had to express to Makoarele [Makwarela] my great grief that he personally was taking part in such horrors, he that was so close to the Kingdom of God. He excused himself by saying that he would not have carried out these deeds were it not for his father Mpafuli. Mpafuli also promised Br. Beuster that he would do nothing evil to the captives. We did not want to wait at the capital any longer, and witness the horrors. The bodies were already laid out in the *Khoro* [public courtyard] for the Dance of the King, which would be carried out upon their dead bodies while he desecrated them with his spear. Then they were to be cut and torn into pieces, the bones separated out from each other and made into pipes, part of the flesh cooked and eaten, part given to the smiths ... to be put into the smelting oven with the iron-ore to make good iron. We left them and rode away from there.[118]

Bad as things were, they became even worse. The struggle having ended indecisively, a further struggle broke out between the brothers in 1893. This time, Tshivhase again supported Tshikalange. Makwarela was supported by Makhado.[119] During the course of this war, starting on 30 September, Makwarela's warriors reportedly had to undergo an elaborate ritual at the capital before going into the field. Missionary Reinhold Wessmann, stationed at Georgenholtz, claimed to have witnessed it. According to him, "Heathenism again shone through in the chief and came alive in the people". The "really

---

m. In other words, "I had no alternative but to express to Makwarela ..."

heathen festival" was worse than anything he had "experienced before". It lasted for several days, with people "from all sides" attending. There were speeches, incantations, ritual washings, feastings and sacrifices. Wessmann also wrote that "the flesh of human beings [was eaten]". The "heathens" believed that this would "make them strong and invincible and prevent them from being wounded". Having "got rid of his clothes", and with this the trappings of civilisation, "like all his staff", Makwarela "wore only a loin-cloth". He sprinkled his "people, who were also naked, ... with boiling water". Cut-wounds were then "made on their chests and on their backs. These hurt very much after they had been smeared with strong medicine and this made the people restless". Having "grabbed hold of a hot hammer which had been lying in boiling water", Makwarela then "gave everyone a hard hit of the hammer on the chest and on the back. Burning wood was also placed on their feet to prove their loyalty. Strong medicine which was sniffed at, transformed those present into ecstasy". As the ceremony reached its climax, "a thorn tree with three to four inch thorns was erected in the middle of the gathering-place. The inside of the tree was covered with boiled meat so that the bits of meat made it look like a Christmas-tree". All those who had "killed somebody in their lives were told to come forward ... [and] eat the hot meat, which was between the thorns, off the tree. They had to do this using their mouths only, without touching anything with their hands". Overcome by the excitement of the occasion, the "participants rushed forward in a wild hurry. The tree fell over and with this the whole crowd rushed onto the long thorns, which pierced their naked bodies." At the close of the ceremony, the *khosi* danced in front of his people, cheered on by the crowd. When Wessmann later challenged Makwarela on "the futility of the feast", the *khosi* reportedly "laughed and said that the heathens everywhere are laughing at him. They say he has no power. He now wants to show them what he is capable of."[120]

The formulaic rendering of the event clearly shows that Wessmann was relating hearsay, at the very best. Whether he had seen what he described with his own eyes or not did not matter to him, nor did it to the Mission Society and its friends in Europe. For them, what mattered was that the report confirmed their phantasmagoric ideas of savage people.

While Makwarela would continue to allow the mission to operate in his lands, and there were times when he still met with the missionaries, things were never the same again.[121] For the Berliners, Makwarela was about to descend back into "complete heathenism". Henceforth, he was in the same camp as his father, whose actions during the war were described by Wessmann in ways similar to those used to describe the ceremony of the young warriors, yet focusing even more on bodies in action, on smells and sounds. In this context, the gaze disappeared in "frantic" excitement, and with it the personalities of the people involved, reason submerged by passion:

> One Sunday morning, I accompanied a neighbour to the capital
> of the old chief Pafuri [Mphaphuli]. We intended to put in a

good word in favour of the cessation of the war which kept the whole population from their work in the fields, and had interrupted the traffic on the roads. When we spoke to the chief, and had, in consequence of the evil smell emanating from the corpses which were thrown in old maize-holes, changed places with him, suddenly the big war-drum sounded, and a slain enemy was carried within the gate on long poles. Hardly had the chief caught sight of the body than he jumped up, rushed at the corpse like a wild animal, tore it down on the ground, sat on it, and beat it in order to relieve his anger. Soon after the dancers arrived and performed a triumphal war-dance. They consisted of old men and women only; for those alone are entitled to take part in the war-dance who had already killed or poisoned someone. We left the cruel scene without taking leave of the people, who had already gone frantic with excitement; and we returned home without having achieved our object, only hoping that time might remedy this.[122]

It is clear that, at a conscious level, for the missionaries, what marked *Khosi* Makwarela's return to "complete heathenism" was his alleged consumption of war *muti* containing human body parts as one of its ingredients. They did not describe his actions as cannibalism, or him as a cannibal. However, their focus on the consumption of "human flesh" as they called it (German does not differentiate between "flesh" and "meat"), clearly demonstrates that they saw his actions as *Menschenfresserei*, and not as a ritual designed to enhance the prowess and martial spirit of his followers.

For the Berlin Missionaries, cannibalism, which included the consumption of body parts of enemies captured in war, was the supreme symbol of "heathenism" and "savagery", an emblem of all that was strangest, most incomprehensible and horrible in African society. It was inconceivable to them that Christians (people who were fully "civilised" or fully "human") could be cannibals since humankind was created in the image of God and the human body housed the soul. One could sink no lower into "bestiality" than by consuming the image of God and the house of the spirit given by him. Yet, the missionaries took it for granted that, since they were freed from such scruples by their ignorance of the Law of God, "heathens" (read also "savages" or "brutes") could sink to such depths that they could treat the human body as a source of food. In their "blindness" and "superstition" they still had some idea of powers greater than themselves. As such, they could also ingest parts of the human body as sources of power. This, the missionaries believed, was the case not only in Africa but also in other parts of the world such as the South Pacific and, indeed, in the distant "heathen" past of the Germans themselves.[123] In their opinion, in Africa, including South Africa, it was only through the spread of the Gospel, backed up by colonial authority, that cannibalism could be eradicated.[124]

The missionaries clearly had no understanding of the different meanings of "eating", which may range from the purely metaphorical indication of a process of domination, to the very act of incorporating something edible. Nor had they an eye for the spiritual aspects of the ingestion of body parts of an enemy killed in battle in the production and consumption of *muti* which anthropophagy as a ritual practice stands for. In any case, they used the trope and the imagery of cannibalism as the ultimate weapon in their othering of non-Christian Africans, just as the Portuguese had done with the pictures brought back from Brazil by Hans Staden in the mid-sixteenth century and the British did during their wars of colonial aggression in nineteenth-century West Africa.[125]

Surprisingly, against the background of the linguistic work of the Berlin Missionaries, no discussion of the morphology of the term "cannibal" could be traced in mission sources. The Tshivenda dictionary term for cannibal is *Lilema*.[126] However, many people I have spoken to have never heard this term. Instead, in conversation, *lila-vhatu* is usually used. (This was also the term that a Professor in the department of Tshivenda at UNIVEN gave when asked "what is a cannibal in Tshivenda?"[127]) This also refers to "one who takes parts from corpses for medicine".[128] The root is the term "*la*", meaning to eat or enjoy (be the beneficiary of).[129] In Tshivenda, the class 1-noun prefix *mu-* (plural *vha-*), without exception, indicates persons.[130] The class 5-noun prefix *li-* (plural *ma-*) refers to objects ("things"), certain body parts, certain fruits and certain categories of aliens, for example Europeans (*likhuwa*, plural *makhuwa*).[131] Thus, literally translated *lila-vhatu* means "the thing which eats people". In an interesting parallel with the term *Makchema* appearing in Wangemann and Merenksy's tractates, a member of the Mphephu royal family said that the term was *luma vhatu* (singular, *luma muthu*), literally "those who bite".[132] These variations all show that local terms for "cannibalism" dehumanise the perpetrators. Through this, they are condemned and placed beyond the pale of gentile, or "civilised", society.[133] The only exceptions to this rule could lie in acts of anthropophagy where the horror of the act was outweighed by the benefits accruing to society. War *muti* and other rituals surrounding warfare would have been just such an exception.

Missionary interpretation took no account of these subtleties. For them, *Khosi* Makwarela had simply reverted to type. In their opinion, his actions fitted neatly into the paradigm of "cannibalism" as an icon of "heathenism", in other words, "otherness". They believed that he had been exposed to the Law and Grace of God. For him, there was no possibility of claiming ignorance. Just when it seemed that he would accept Christianity, and win salvation for himself and his people, he had plummeted back into the very depths of "heathen darkness". The magnitude of his fall was compounded by the fact that, as a "chief" he had, inevitably, dragged his people down with him. For this, the missionaries believed, God had exacted retribution on him and brought him low.[134]

In May 1894, Wessmann was transferred to Tshakhuma, "leaving Makoarele behind as a heathen".[135] His successor, Carl Gernecke, arrived in October of the same year.[136] In posing the question whether or not "God's Grace will give Br. Gernecke the joy of winning this Great [one] in the lands for the kingdom of Jesus Christ?", *Der Bawenda-Freund* argued that "We dare not ever give up the hope."[137] However, this hope would never be realised.

Hence the missionaries were not surprised when they learned, in 1897, that Makwarela, after suffering great losses in his following due to the combined effects of famine and a lengthy struggle with Tshivhase, had "become a poor, small king" who "sits and ponders revenge". They were convinced:

> He once came close to fully accepting Christianity but, when he was close, he rejected it because he feared losing his chieftainship. Now, because of his heathenism, he has lost his power completely.[138]

Although they prayed to God that he might "win this strong one", Makwarela Mphaphuli never did convert.[139] Ranwedzi passed away in 1901 and Makwarela ascended to his throne. There was no war of succession as Tshikalange had predeceased him at the end of 1896 (possibly having been killed on Makwarela's orders).[140] Despite the fact that the *khosi* no longer had any intention of being baptised himself, Murumo, one of his sons, was among the first group of people to be baptised at New Georgenholtz on 27 June 1909, one and a half years after this station was inaugurated by Ludwig Giesekke and his wife.[141] Old Georgenholtz had been abandoned in 1899.[142] In spite of his alienation from the mission, Makwarela would only allow missionaries from the Berlin Mission to operate in his lands and would not give other "sects", including African-initiated churches, permission to operate there.[143] Makwarela died in April 1928, still a "heathen".[144]

The psychologically minded might speak of a missionary obsession with the violation of human bodies and ask whether this was not echoing their European experience? For one, there is a rich imagery of man-eating-man in European fairy tales such as the tale of Hansel and Gretel, but also in religion, in shipwreck stories and generally in fantasies about the wild. Secondly, in the last third of the nineteenth century, Europe experienced a severe economic depression with the twin processes of urbanisation and industrialisation ever accelerating, uprooting, or "devouring", thousands and thousands of people. Thirdly, innovations in military technology had made wars even more destructive. Henry Dunant had exposed this in his justly famous *Mémoire de Solferino* of 1866, which then led to the foundation of the International Committee of the Red Cross. Europe's hidden darkness is perhaps best revealed through another reference to literature. In Arthur Japin's fictionalised account of the life of Prince Kwasi Boachi of Ashanti, the young royal considers the horror of the Dutch Commissioner van Drunen at sacrifices performed on the royal graves. Japin has Kwasi remarking:

> As a boy, the routine executions were little different to me from the slaughter of goats. Later in life this boyhood insensibility filled me with shame, until I discovered that a man's life counted for just as little in Europe at that time. The wars fought between 1792 and 1815 alone caused the sacrifice of one million five hundred and thirty thousand lives, not counting the loss of life in epidemics spread in the course of these conflicts. Another two hundred thousand souls died in the war between Russia and Turkey, and an equal number in the Polish uprising. At the very time that van Drunen was startled by a few heads lying on his path, tens of thousands of heads were rolling in the Caucasus.[145]

Beyond psychology, we should also look at the historical context of the argument about the situation in Vendaland. Stories about cannibalism are necessarily stories about contact. It thus makes sense to ask whether the "conspicuous anthropophagy" was not a response to colonial expansion, as Gananath Obeyesekere has argued with respect to the South Pacific, and Michael Taussig before him with regard to Amazonia and the Congo Free State in the period of the rubber boom.[146] The Berlin Missionaries, for their part, happened to arrive in the Transvaal at a time when many South African societies were going through a period of severe upheaval. They either suffered from the consequences of earlier wars, or they had to fend off foreign intruders such as the land-grabbing white settlers, or they were involved in wars of succession. Hence the importance of rituals of appropriation, retribution and bonding. And these in turn supplied enough horror stories to those who had an interest to denigrate some people and to frighten others.

Like his father, Ranwedzi Mphaphuli, Makwarela Mphaphuli was attempting to come to terms with the encroaching Boers, the missionaries and internal power-struggles within his society. His father attempted to gain control over the situation by permitting the missionaries to operate in the lands of his son. He would thus have access to them without having to face a direct threat to his authority.

Makwarela attempted to deal with the tensions by forming a close working relationship with the missionaries. It is clear that he found the skill of literacy and the access to western material culture which they brought useful. It also seems that he found the religion that they brought appealing. His strategy underwent changes over time. At first, it seemed likely that he would convert. In time, he realised that conversion would result in the loss of his throne. He then attempted to blend aspects of the new religion with the old. It is clear that, in doing so, he was attempting to retain his power as a ruler.

Over time, and involved in a series of battles for succession with his brother, it became clear to Makwarela that the missionaries would not accept anything but conversion to orthodox Christianity as interpreted by them. His own reading of the alternative possibilities was unacceptable. Had he accepted Christianity on these terms, it is likely that he would have lost the succession struggle with Tshikalange. Even in the unlikely event that he was victorious, he would have lost his power and independence to the missionaries.

Makwarela was trying to operate creatively in a situation of dynamic change. For him, conversion was only one strategy amongst many to deal with encroachment and successionary struggles. The missionaries could not accommodate this. He was to be either a "heathen" or a "Christian", either a savage or a civilised man – there were no shades of grey in between. This static opposition was crucial to their entire world view. To challenge it would be to negate all their work and sacrifice in the area.

At a deeper level, it does not matter whether or not Makwarela Mphaphuli "really" committed an act, or acts, of anthropophagy. Either by doing so, or by allowing the missionaries to believe that he had done so, he was saying that what they believed had no power over him any more. Accepting a position of leadership under, and by the grace of, the white God would, in reality, involve ruling under, and by the grace of, the white missionaries. Instead, Makwarela had reclaimed his throne and the right to rule his people through his birthright and the power of African Religion.

1. *Der Bawenda-Freund*, 14(54), 1896, p. 296; *BMB*, 1880, pp. 211, 413; 1888, p. 532.
2. *Der Bawenda-Freund*, 14(54), 1896, p. 288.
3. This account is reminiscent of the attempts by other authors to explain the ideas adopted by Dingiswayo in restructuring the Mthethwa as having been derived from whites. (See, for example, E.A. Ritter, *Shaka Zulu: The Rise of the Zulu Empire*, London, Longmans Green and Company, 1955, pp. 21–22; J.D. Omer-Cooper, *The Zulu Aftermath*, p. 28. Cf. R. Edgecombe, "The Mfecane or Difaqane", in T. Cameron and S.B. Spies, *A New Illustrated History of South Africa*, p. 116.) I was also surprised to discover that, in his otherwise extremely Venda-nationalistic thesis, Nemudzivhadi raised the possibility that Makhado had learned the principles of military organisation from whites (M.H. Nemudzivhadi, "The attempts by Makhado to revive the Venda kingdom", pp. 22, 50). So, this really looks like a topos.
4. *Der Bawenda-Freund*, 14(54), 1896, pp. 288–289 (quotation, p. 289).
5. *Ibid.* p. 289.
6. *Ibid.*
7. *Ibid.*
8. See, for example, S.M. Dzivhani, "The Chiefs of Venḓa", pp. 37–40, 42, 44–46, 49–50; E. Gottschling, "The Bawenda", pp. 195–221; M.M. Motenda, "History of the Western Venḓa and the Lemba", pp. 54–57, 59–60; E. Mudau, "The Dau of Tshakhuma", pp. 75–76, 78–79; H.A. Stayt, *The Bavenda*, pp. 17, 208–209, 210; and N.J. van Warmelo (ed.), *Contributions towards Venda History*, pp. 6, 12–15, 15–16, 20–22, 24–32, 35–36.
9. *Der Bawenda-Freund*, 14(54), 1896, p. 289.
10. *Ibid.* pp. 289–290.
11. *Ibid.* pp. 290–291.

12. *Ibid.* pp. 291–292. Mzilikazi died in 1868 (J.D. Omer-Cooper, *History of Southern Africa*, Claremont, David Philip, 1987, p. 78).
13. *Der Bawenda-Freund*, 14(54), 1896, p. 292.
14. See, for example, G. Sauberzweig-Schmidt, *Klaas Kuhn*, p. 14.
15. *Der Bawenda-Freund*, 14(54), 1896, p. 292 (quotation); *BMB*, 1876, pp. 397, 400. Note that Makwarela, his dress and Beuster's surprise are expressed in identical terms in both sources.
16. *Mitteilungen des Vereins "Heidenfreund"*, V(18), 1887, n.p. (p. 2); *BMB*, 1876, p. 400.
17. G. Denning, *Mr Bligh's Bad Language*. See especially pp. 57 (quotation), 59–60.
18. *BMB*, 1876, p. 398.
19. *Mitteilungen des Vereins "Heidenfreund"*, V(18), 1887, n.p. (p. 2).
20. C. Beuster, *Johannes Motscheni*. See chapter 2.
21. *BMB*, 1876, p. 398.
22. *Mitteilungen des Vereins "Heidenfreund"*, V(18), 1887, n.p. (p. 2).
23. *BMB*, 1876, p. 399.
24. *Mitteilungen des Vereins "Heidenfreund"*, V(18), 1887, n.p. (pp. 3–4).
25. *BMB*, 1876, p. 399.
26. *Ibid.*
27. *Ibid.*, and *Mitteilungen des Vereins "Heidenfreund"*, V(18), 1887, n.p. (pp. 2–3).
28. *BMB*, 1876, p. 399; *Mitteilungen des Vereins "Heidenfreund"*, V(18), 1887, n.p. (p. 3). Also quoted in *Der Bawenda-Freund*, 14(54), 2 Quartal 1896, p. 292.
29. *BMB*, 1876, p. 400.
30. *Ibid.*
31. R. Wessmann, *Philippus Thai*, pp. 1–2.
32. *Ibid.* p. 2.
33. A. Merensky, *Die Menschenfresserei in Afrika*, back cover. The remarkable resilience of this vignette by the artist C. Roux, and its successive incarnations in various guises, is discussed on p. 149.
34. Tagebuch der Station bei Ha Makoarela (Nicolaus Koen), 13. Juli 1877; *BMB*, 1878, p. 490; G. Sauberzweig-Schmidt, *Klaas Kuhn*, p. 14. Note that Sauberzweig-Schmidt omits any mention of Magoro and erroneously states that the ox had been slaughtered in Koen's honour.
35. *BMB*, 1878, p. 490 (quotation); G. Sauberzweig-Schmidt, *Klaas Kuhn*, p. 14.
36. G. Sauberzweig-Schmidt, *Klaas Kuhn*, p. 14.
37. C. Hamilton, *Terrific Majesty*, p. 18, discussing E.V. Walters, *Terror and Resistance: A Study of Political Violence with Case Studies of Some Primitive African Communities*, New York, Oxford University Press, 1969.
38. I. Clendinnen, *Aztecs: an interpretation*, Cambridge, Cambridge University Press, 1991.
39. *Mitteilungen des Vereins "Heidenfreund"*, V(19), 1887, n.p. (p. 3).
40. *Der Bawenda-Freund*, 14(54), 1896, p. 293; G. Sauberzweig-Schmidt, *Klaas Kuhn*, p. 15.
41. G. Sauberzweig-Schmidt, *Klaas Kuhn*, pp. 15–16. See also *BMB*, 1879, p. 412.
42. G. Sauberzweig-Schmidt, *Klaas Kuhn*, pp. 16–17. See also *Der Bawenda-Freund*, 14(54), 1896, p. 293; *BMB*, 1878, p. 495.
43. Tagebuch der Station bei Ha Makoarela (Nicolaus Koen), 23. Dezember 1877, p. 28, in Berlin Mission Archives, Berlin, Acta der Berliner Missionsgesellschaft betreffend Missionsstationen: Tagebücher der Missionare auf Makoarela (Georgenholtz), Abt. III, Fach 5, No. 16, (I). See also *Der Bawenda-Freund*, VII(27), 1889, p. 86; 14(54), 1896, p. 293; *BMB*, 1878, pp. 495–496; and G. Sauberzweig-Schmidt (a) *Klaas Kuhn*, p. 17 & (b) *Georgenholtz*, p. 8.
44. *BMB*, 1899, p. 249.
45. See, for example, J.R. Gschwend, *Mbilu ya Muthu*, Pretoria, All Nations Gospel Publishers, n.d., p. 28. This tract has been distributed in Vendaland by these publishers since 1936. It is

possible that it was used locally by other missionaries before this. For a discussion of this work, see A. Kirkaldy and A. Wirz, "Picturing the soul", pp. 26–29.
46. See pp. 177–178.
47. H.A. Stayt, *The Bavenda*, p. 362. Cf. J.S. Mbiti, *African Religions and Philosophy*, Second Edition, Oxford, Heinemann International, 1990, numerous references.
48. E. Elbourne (a) "'To Colonize the Mind': Evangelical Missionaries in Britain and the Eastern Cape, 1790–1837", D.Phil. thesis in Modern History, Oxford University, 1991, pp. 124–125 & (b) "Early Khoisan Uses of Missionary Christianity", in H. Bredekamp and R. Ross (eds.), *Missions and Christianity in South African History*, Johannesburg, Witwatersrand University Press, 1995, pp. 76–78.
49. I. Hexham and K. Poewe, "The Spread of Christianity among Whites and Blacks in Transorangia", in R. Elphick and R. Davenport (eds.), *Christianity in South Africa*, p. 132.
50. See p. 104.
51. *Der Bawenda-Freund*, 14(54), 1896, p. 293.
52. G. Sauberzweig-Schmidt, *Klaas Kuhn*, p. 17.
53. *Der Bawenda-Freund*, 14(54), 1896, p. 293. See also *BMB*, 1888, p. 495; G. Sauberzweig-Schmidt, *Klaas Kuhn*, p. 17.
54. *Der Bawenda-Freund*, 14(54), 1896, p. 293.
55. *Ibid*. To varying degrees, all *mahosi* were regarded as having the power to intercede with the ancestors for, or make, rain. However, *Khosi* Luvhimbi was regarded as the greatest rain doctor of all the Vhavenda *mahosi* (*BMB*, 1882, p. 437).
56. *Der Bawenda-Freund*, VII(27), 1889, p. 86; 14(54), 1896, p. 293; *BMB*, 1878, pp. 495–496; and Tagebuch der Station bei Ha Makoarela (Nicolaus Koen), 23. Dezember 1877, p. 29.
57. See p. 59.
58. G. Sauberzweig-Schmidt, *Klaas Kuhn*, p. 21. See also: *Der Bawenda-Freund*, 14(54), 1896, p. 294; *BMB*, 1880, p. 211; *Mitteilungen des Vereins "Heidenfreund"*, V(19), 1887, n.p. (p. 3); and Stationschronik von Georgenholtz, p. 1.
59. G. Sauberzweig-Schmidt, *Klaas Kuhn*, p. 22. See also *BMB*, 1880, p. 211; *Der Bawenda-Freund*, 14(54), 1896, p. 294 and Stationschronik von Georgenholtz, p. 1. For Makwarela's choosing of the name Elias/Elijah at this time (a name he would never use because he was never baptised) see *BMB*, 1890, p. 501. For discussion of the possible symbolic reasons for his choosing this name, see A. Kirkaldy, "Capturing the Soul: Encounters between Berlin Missionaries and Tshivenda-speakers in the Late Nineteenth Century", Ph.D. thesis, University of Cape Town, 2002, p. 447.
60. See p. 62.
61. See H.M Hofmeyr, "Christian Mission and Colonialism in Southern Africa and African Responses: Some case studies", in *Emory International Law Review*, 14(2) (Special Edition), 2000, p. 1056.
62. G. Sauberzweig-Schmidt, *Klaas Kuhn*, p. 23. See also *Der Bawenda-Freund*, 14(54), 1896, p. 294; *BMB*, 1880, p. 211.
63. G. Sauberzweig-Schmidt, *Klaas Kuhn*, p. 23.
64. *BMB*, 1880, p. 414; G. Sauberzweig-Schmidt, *Klaas Kuhn*, p. 24. See Illustration 15.
65. *BMB*, 1880, p. 416.
66. *Der Bawenda-Freund*, 14(54), 1896, p. 294.
67. G. Sauberzweig-Schmidt, *Klaas Kuhn*, p. 23.
68. *BMB*, 1882, p. 436; G. Sauberzweig-Schmidt, *Klaas Kuhn*, p. 24.
69. *BMB*, 1882, p. 436.
70. *Ibid*.
71. G. Sauberzweig-Schmidt, *Klaas Kuhn*, p. 25.
72. *BMB*, 1882, p. 437.
73. G. Sauberzweig-Schmidt, *Klaas Kuhn*, p. 25.

74. Ibid.
75. *BMB*, 1882, p. 437.
76. *Der Bawenda-Freund*, 14(54), 1896, p. 294.
77. *Ibid*. pp. 294–295.
78. *Ibid*. p. 295.
79. Stationschronik von Georgenholtz, p. 1; *BMB*, 1884, p. 223; and G. Sauberzweig-Schmidt, *Klaas Kuhn*, p. 31.
80. *BMB*, 1884, p. 223 (quotation); G. Sauberzweig-Schmidt, *Klaas Kuhn*, p. 31.
81. *Der Bawenda-Freund*, 14(54), 1896, p. 295 (quotation); G. Sauberzweig-Schmidt, *Klaas Kuhn*, p. 31; and Stationschronik von Georgenholtz, p. 1.
82. *Der Bawenda-Freund*, 14(54), 1896, p. 295. See also *BMB*, 1885, p. 76.
83. *Der Bawenda-Freund*, 14(54), 1896, pp. 295–296. See also *BMB*, 1886, p. 413.
84. *Der Bawenda-Freund*, VI(22), 1888, p. 62; VII(26), 1889, pp. 84–85; 14(54), 1896, p. 296; *BMB*, 1887, p. 485; 1888, pp. 223, 530–531; 1889, p. 543; Stationschronik von Georgenholtz, p. 1; and Tagebuch der Station Georgenholtz (Reinholdt Wessmann), 24. Juli 1887.
85. *BMB*, 1887, pp.486–487.
86. Tagebuch der Station Ha Tsevase (Carl Beuster), 13. November 1886, p. 47. See also *BMB*, 1887, p. 487.
87. See p. 18.
88. S.M. Dzivhani, "The Chiefs of Venḓa", pp. 38, 39; N.M.N. Ralushai, "Conflicting Accounts of Venda History", p. 164.
89. Tagebuch der Station Ha Tsevase (Carl Beuster), 13. November 1886, pp. 47–48.
90. *Ibid*. pp. 48–49.
91. *BMB*, 1887, p. 488.
92. Tagebuch der Station Ha Tsevase (Carl Beuster), 16. November 1886, pp. 49–50. See also *BMB*, 1887, p. 489.
93. *Ibid*.
94. *BMB*, 1887, p. 491.
95. *Der Bawenda-Freund*, 14(54), 1896, p. 296.
96. *BMB*, 1888, pp. 531–532.
97. *Der Bawenda-Freund*, 14(54), 1896, p. 296.
98. *Ibid*. pp. 296–297. See also *BMB*, 1888, p. 532–533. For the Delagoa Bay liquor trade, see P. Harries, *Work, Culture and Identity*, pp. 90, 101–103, 108, 152–153, 255 n 131, 256 n 146; C. van Onselen, *Studies in the Social and Economic History of the Witwatersrand 1886–1914*, 1. New Babylon, Johannesburg, Ravan Press, 1982, p. 55.
99. *BMB*, 1887, p. 223. See *BMB*, 1888, p. 534 for a discussion of the land grant.
100. "In the area of the ruler of the lands", in M. Wilde, *Schwarz und Weiss*, p. 73 and "Audienz mit Mpafudi (Mkwarela)"/"Audience with Mpafudi (Makwarela)", in Berlin Mission Archives, Berlin: Album XXIX, Nord-Transvaal 1, Nr. 40.
101. Cf. R. Ross, "The Top-Hat in South African History: The changing significance of an item of material culture", in *Social Dynamics*, 16(1), 1990, pp. 90–100 .
102. For *Gota* Totane's dilemma in this regard, see pp. 43–46, 63–65.
103. *BMB*, 1882, pp. 186, 372–374; 1883; pp. 187, 375–379; 1884, p. 121; 1885, pp. 181–182, 395–396; 1886, pp. 216–217; and 1887, pp. 421–422. See also H.T. Wangemann, *Khashane Mamatepha, Ein Lebensbild aus Nord-Transvaal*, Zweite Auflage, Neue Missionsschriften Nr. 22, Berlin, Buchhandlung der Berliner evangelischen Missionsgesellschaft, 1890.
104. *BMB*, 1883, pp. 376–377.
105. *BMB*, 1886, pp. 420–423.
106. *Der Bawenda-Freund*, 14(54), 1896, p. 287.

107. *Ibid.* pp. 288–290.
108. *Der Bawenda-Freund*, 14(54), 1896, p. 297; *BMB*, 1890, pp. 238, 465, 478–481; and Tagebuch der Station Ha Tsevase (Carl Beuster), 12 Mai. 1889, pp. 50–53; 17 bis 18. Mai 1889, pp. 53–56; 25. Mai 1889, pp. 56–57; 30. Mai 1889, p. 60; 5. Juni 1899, pp. 60–61.
109. *Der Bawenda-Freund*, 8(30), 1890, pp. 97–99; 14(54), 1896, p. 297; *BMB*, 1890, pp. 238–239, 465–481, 484–488; 1891, pp. 460–461; 1892, pp. 271–272, 551–553; and Tagebuch der Station Ha Tsevase (Carl Beuster), 18. Mai 1889, p. 55.
110. *BMB*, 1890, p. 238.
111. *Ibid.* pp. 465–481, 487; *Der Bawenda-Freund*, 14(54), 1896, p. 297.
112. See the discussion of the supernatural protection of villages on p. 221.
113. *BMB*, 1890, p. 481; Tagebuch der Station Ha Tsevase (Carl Beuster), 5. Juni 1889, pp. 60–61.
114. *Der Bawenda-Freund*, 14(54), 1896, p. 297; *BMB*, 1892, pp. 551–553.
115. *Der Bawenda-Freund*, 14(54), 1896, p. 297.
116. *BMB*, 1890, p. 239.
117. *Der Bawenda-Freund*, 14(54), 1896, p. 297.
118. Tagebuch der Johannes Meister vom 1. Juli bis 30. September 1891, Ha Tsevase, in Berlin Mission Archives, Berlin, Acta der Berliner Missionsgesellschaft betreffend Missionsstationen, Tagebücher der Missionare auf der Station Ha Tsevase, 1891–1900, (II), Abt. III, Fach 5, No. 14, entries for 2. 4. & 27. Juli 1891, pp. 5–9 (quotation, 27. Juli 1891, pp. 8–9). See also *Der Bawenda-Freund*, 11(43), 1893, pp. 168–169; *BMB*, 1892, pp. 552–553 (quotation, p. 553).
119. *Der Bawenda-Freund*, 11(42), 1893, pp. 161–162; *BMB*, 1894, pp. 200, 364, 366–367.
120. *Der Bawenda-Freund*, 14(54), 1896, p. 297; *BMB*, 1894, p. 380; and Tagebuch der Station Georgenholtz (Reinholdt Wessmann), 30. September 1893, pp. 38–40.
121. *Der Bawenda-Freund*, 14(54), 1896, pp. 298–299; 15(58), 1897, p. 352; *BMB*, 1894, pp. 201, 368–369; 1896, pp. 112–113, 350; 1897, pp. 90, 112; 1898, pp. 6–8, 11; 1900, pp. 691–692.
122. R. Wesssmann, *The Bawenda of the Spelonken*, pp. 133–134.
123. [Anon.] *Etwas aus der Heidenzeit des deutschen Vaterlandes. Die Bekehrung der Sachsen in der Gegend von Hermansburg*, Neue Missionsschriften Nr. 6, Berlin, Buchhandlung der Berliner evangelischen Missionsgesellschaft, 1890; A. Merensky (a) *Wie die Menschenfresser auf Tongoa Christen wurden*, Missionsschriften für Kinder Nr. 23, Berlin, Buchhandlung der Berliner evangelischen Missionsgesellschaft, n.d. [1895] & (b) *Die Menschenfresserei in Afrika*; and H.T. Wangemann (a) *Die Menschenfresser im Bapediländer* & (b) *Gerettete Menschenfresser in Botshabelo*.
124. See especially A. Merensky, *Die Menschenfresserei in Afrika*, pp. 2–4, 16.
125. A. Kirkaldy and A. Wirz, "Picturing the soul", pp. 41–43.
126. N.J. van Warmelo, *Venda Dictionary*, p. 128.
127. Personal communication, Prof. A.E. Khuba, UNIVEN.
128. N.J. van Warmelo, *Venda Dictionary*, p. 128.
129. Personal communication Dr J.M. Dederen, Department of Anthropology, UNIVEN; N.J. van Warmelo, *Venda Dictionary*, p. 124.
130. N.J. van Warmelo, *Venda Dictionary*, p. 28; D. Ziervogel, P.J. Wentzel and T.N. Makuya, *A Handbook of the Venda Language*, Second Edition, Pretoria, University of South Africa, 1972, p. 12. For example, *munna* = man, plural *vhanna*; *musadzi* = woman, plural *vhaszdzi* and *musidzana* = girl, plural *vhasidzana*.
131. N.J. van Warmelo, *Venda Dictionary*, p. 28; D. Ziervogel, P.J. Wentzel and T.N. Makuya, *A Handbook of the Venda Language*, pp. 18–19. Objects, for example, *l̦iga* = step, plural *maga* and *l̦itavha* = big mountain, plural *matavha*. Body parts, for example, *l̦ila*, the great intestine or colon, plural *mala* and *l̦iṋo* = tooth, plural *maṋo*. Fruits, for example, *l̦ifula* = marula fruit, plural *mafula*.
132. Personal communication, *Vho* Lettie Mphephu-Nengudza; N.J. van Warmelo, *Venda Dictionary*, p. 146.

133. Cf. D.B. Coplan, *In the Time of Cannibals*, p. 1; and especially C. Hamilton, *Terrific Majesty*, pp. 211–212.
134. *Der Bawenda-Freund*, 15(59), 1897, p. 366.
135. Stationschronik von Georgenholtz, p. 2 (126 of file); *Der Bawenda-Freund*, 14(54), 1896, p. 298.
136. Acta der Berliner Missionsgesellschaft betreffend Personalia: Gernecke, Carl and Stationschronik von Georgenholtz, p. 2 (126 of file).
137. *Der Bawenda-Freund*, 14(54), 1896, p. 298.
138. *Der Bawenda-Freund*, 15(59), 1897, pp. 365–366. For discussion of the famine of 1896 to 1897 and its effect on Mphaphuli's area, see p. 24 of this work. For the struggle with Tshivhase, see especially *Der Bawenda-Freund*, 15(57), 1897, p. 345; 15(58), 1897, pp. 352–353; 15(59), 1897, pp. 364–365; and *BMB*, 1897, p. 725; 1898, p. 7.
139. *Der Bawenda-Freund*, 15(59), 1897, p. 366.
140. *BMB*, 1898, p. 7; S.M. Dzivhani, "The Chiefs of Venḓa", p. 50; and H.A. Stayt, *The Bavenda*, p. 17.
141. Stationschronik von Georgenholtz, p. 4 (128 of file). Murumo first joined baptism classes in 1897. Makwarela at first attempted to dissuade him from converting to Christianity but later came to accept this, possibly as he was not a likely successor (*BMB*, 1898, pp. 315, 597).
142. Stationschronik von Georgenholtz, pp. 2–3 (126–127 of file).
143. *Ibid.* p. 25 (149 of file).
144. *Ibid.* p. 37 (161 of file). Note that Dzivhani and Lukhaimane aruge that Makwarela died in 1926 (S.M. Dzivhani, "The Chiefs of Venḓa", p. 50; E.K. Lukhaimane, "A Short History of the Venda", p. 15). Mudau and Stayt argue that he died in 1927, with Mudau giving the date of 25 March (J.R. Mudau, "A Short History of the Mphaphuli Dynasty, 1689–1990", unpublished BA Honours thesis, University of Venda, 1990, p. 33; H.A. Stayt, *The Bavenda*, p. 17).
145. A. Japin, *The Two Hearts of Kwasi Boachi*, translated by Ina Rilke, London, Chatto & Windus, 2000, p. 41.
146. M.J. Taussig, Shamanism, *Colonialism and the Wild Man: A Study of Terror and Healing*, Chicago, Chicago University Press, 1987; G. Obeyesekere, "British Cannibals", pp. 7–32. But consider the qualifications of Peter Geschiere, who has stressed the fact that the trope of cannibalism was used by Africans and Germans alike, albeit with different things in mind. The Maka used it to differentiate between kin and non-kin, the Germans as a marker of savagery (P. Geschiere, "Rubber and Cannibalism: The Germans, the Maka and the Rubberboom in South Cameroon (1900–1914)", unpublished paper presented to the seminar on "Fantasy Spaces – The Power of Images in a Globalizing World", Amsterdam, 27–29 August 1998).

Glossary

Conventicle: The concept of "collegia pietatis", conventicles (small groups or assemblies) of Christians meeting to study the scriptures and devotional literature, was first advanced by the German Protestant reformer Martin Bucer. A century later, Philip Jacob Spener (1635–1705) adopted the idea in an effort to implement the program of reform revolving around Bible study, spiritual exercises, personal piety and increased lay activity that has come to be kown as Pietism. (S.B. Ferguson and D.F. Wright [eds.], *New Dictionary of Theology*, pp. 515–516.)

Gota: See *khosi*.

Khosi: Translating the Tshivenda terms *khosi* (plural, *mahosi* – "kings" or "chiefs") and *gota* (plural, *magota* – "sub-chiefs" or "headman") into English opens a whole debate on the nature of leadership in African societies which I do not want to enter into in this work. After the formation of the Dzata empire, unless in quotation, or directly presenting the views of the missionaries, I avoid using the English terminology.

Khotsi-munene: See *makhadzi*.

Makhadzi: The term refers to a paternal aunt or any other ortho-cousin of the father who is *khaladzi* to him. *Khaladzi* refers to the sister of a male, the brother of a female, and ortho-cousins in the same way (N.J. van Warmelo, *Venda Dictionary*, pp. 99, 168.) In the context of the royal family, as the term is used here, it is also used to represent one of the officials involved in choosing the successor to a *khosi*. According to Vhavenda tradition, the *mahosi* [chiefs] cannot name their successors. At the time of the *khosi*'s passing, his eldest sister from the third house becomes *makhadzi*. In conjunction with the late *khosi*'s elder brother from the second house, the *khotsi-munene*, she chooses the successor within two years of the *mativha o xa* (death of the *khosi*) (C.J. Conerly, "The Surrendering of the Lands", p. xviii). During the *khosi*'s lifetime, the *makhadzi* and the *khotsi-munene* act as his chief advisors. Together with him, they form the top executive structure.

Magaraba: The colloquial Tshivenda name for those working in the mines i.e. working in the towns down South. It seems to have originated from the first workers who went to work on the diamond fields at Kimberley. Those people scratched about in the ground for diamonds. Thus, the Tshivenda word is derived from the Afrikaans word *grawe* – the people who *grawe*/burrow. It also no longer just applies to those burrowing about in the mines, but to all those who work in the cities away from here – at Easter and Christmas the *Magaraba* return home to Venda.

Mudinda (plural, *vhadinda*): henchman, servant, messenger; lad just after the age of puberty.

Mungome: See *traditional healers and specialists*.

Nanga: See *traditional healers and specialists*.

Ritual homicide: See *vhaloi*.

Traditional healers and specialists: The *nanga* (plural, *dzinanga*) came closest to the commonly-held picture of a medicine-man, healer or African Doctor. One of the tools that he used in diagnosing illness was the *thangu* – the so-called "bones" or "divining dice". An exceptionally successful *nanga* was referred to as *dzolokwe*. The term *mungome* (plural, *mingome*), describing a second kind of specialist, was of Tsonga-Shangaan origin and usually indicated a person involved in divination activities, particularly surrounding accusations of *vhuloi*. In addition to the *thangu* and other witch-finding aids such as extendable concertina-like wooden arms which could point out the *muloi*, these specialists frequently used the *ndilo*, or divining bowl, to identify *muloi* [see Illustration 23]. They worked in close co-operation with *dzinanga*. Once the *mungome* had identified the source of evil, he would often direct his clients to a *nanga* for further treatment of the problem. In addition to these, there were other specialists, each with his or her own title, who were concerned with doctoring of the seeds, circumcision, protection of the army, rainmaking, lighting of sacred fires and so on. The *tshifhe* officiated at sacrifices and offerings, led fertility rituals, approached Raluvhimba and acted as intermediaries with the ancestors. The last-mentioned category were often not full-time specialists or "priests" – these functions were often served by homestead or lineage heads, *magota* or *mahosi*. See especially M. Bartels, "Der Würfelzauber südafrikanischer Völker", in *Zeitschrift für Ethnologie*, 35, 1903, pp. 338–379; P.J. Coertze, "Dolosgooiery in Suid-Afrika", in *Annale van die Universiteit van Stellenbosch*, IX, Serie B, Part 2, April 1931, pp. 1–48; E. Giesekke, "Wahrsagerei bei den Venda", in *Zeitschrift für Eingeborenen Sprachen*, XXI(4), 1931, pp. 257–310; J. Loubser, "The Venda Divining Bowl in the Museum", pp. 18–19; A.C.E. Nettleton, "The Traditional Figurative Woodcarving of the Shona and Venda", Ph.D. thesis, University of the Witwatersrand, 1984 (3 Volumes), Volume 1, pp. 304–366; I. Plug, "An Analysis of Witchdoctor Divining Sets", in *Research Natco Museum*, 1(3), 1987, pp. 48–67; H.A. Stayt, *The Bavenda*, especially pp. 31–32, 101–102, 114, 162–165, 207, 220, 246–249, 265–266, 268, 274–302,

307 & 311–314; N.J. van Warmelo (ed.), *Contributions Towards Venda History*, especially pp. 53, 60–61, 62, 68, 70, 154–155, 182 & 197–200; and R. Wessmann, *The Bawenda of the Spelonken*, pp. 84–86 & 90–96.

Tshifhe: See *traditional healers and specialists*.

VhaLemba: The Lemba live among other groups in the Northern Province (particularly the Vhavenda) and in Southern Zimbabwe. An endogamous clan, they migrated into the Northern Province with the VhaSenzi clans and play a major role in the *Ngoma lungundu* founding myth. The men were skilled metal-workers, while their women were famed as potters. Religious and other cultural practices related to endogamy, circumcision rites, animal sacrifice, ritual slaughter and food taboos, as well as their physical features, have led to a lively debate about possible Semitic ancestry. Since the 1990s, genetic evidence has also been brought into the debate, generating a great deal of controversy. Beuster argued (questionably or at least over-simplistically) that the VhaLemba were responsible for introducing the *murnundu* to the Vhavenda. Coupling this with the fact that they came "from beyond the Zambesi [Zambezi]", this led him to conclude "that circumcision has infiltrated into the Black tribes from the Mohammedans rather than from the Jews. The Balemba call themselves 'slams' (in the Cape, the Mohammedans are called *slams*, from the word 'Islam') – in any case, not an African word. As the Arabian traders and slave merchants have already plied their trade north of the Zambezi for hundreds of years, it is not impossible that from them, circumcision has found an outlet into isolated African tribes [*Kafferstämme*]" (*BMB*, 1879, p. 447). Since then, various authors have been divided on the issue of whether or not the Lemba are indeed the descendants of (or the inheritors of a "tradition" rising from cultural contact with) Muslim traders, Black Jews, or developed these beliefs and rites independently. Today, in the Northern Province, Lemba themselves – under the guidance of the Lemba Cultural Association and, until recently, its fervent President, the Late Professor M.E. Mathiva – express the conviction that they are Israelites who migrated to Africa after the Babylonian exile. For me, the question of the "real" origins of the Lemba is not nearly as interesting as the ways that oral history and custom have been used in the construction of identity (see especially G. Buijs, "Black Jews in the Northern Province: a study of ethnic identity in South Africa", in *Ethnic and Racial Studies*, 21(4), July 1998, pp. 661–682).

Vhaloi: Locally, no distinction is made between witches, wizards, warlocks and sorcerers. They are all described as *vhaloi* (singular, *muloi*). Similarly, witchcraft and sorcery are both described as *vhuloi*. During the 1980s and 1990s, the accepted term for ritual homicide was *u via*. However, the verb *via* translates as "to butcher" or "to slaughter". It would appear that, in Tshivenda, there is no generic term for the different kinds of homicide that Westerners lump together under the term "ritual homicide", "ritual murder", "ritual killing" or *muti* murder. I use the term "ritual homicide" as it seems to be the least value-laden. Two government commissions, an HSRC report and a number of academic and popular articles have not adequately explained the hunting of *vhaloi* and the killing of people who had allegedly taken part in ritual homicide in the Venda Bantustan in the 1980s and early 1990s. The field is still open for study. See especially J.M. Dederen, "Book review of *To live in Fear: Witchburning and Medicine Murder in Venda* by A. de V. Minnaar, D. Offringa and C. Payze", in *Social Dynamics: A Journal of the Centre for African Studies, University of Cape Town*, 18(2), December 1992, pp. 95–100; D.H.J. le Roux (sole Commissioner), "Report of the Commission of Enquiry into the Causes of the Unrest in Venda during August 1988 and the Investigation of Ritual Murders"; J. Mihálik and Y. Cassim, "Ritual murder and Witchcraft: A Political Weapon?", in *The South African Law Journal*, Vol. 110, Part 1, February 1993, pp. 127–140; A. de V. Minnaar, D. Offringa and C. Payze, *To Live in Fear: Witchburning and Medicine Murder in Venda*, ASS/BSS–20, Pretoria, Human Sciences Research Council, 1992; M.W. Prinsloo and J.H. du Plessis, "Towenaarmoorde, rituele doding en medisynemoorde in Venda", in *Tydskrif vir die Suid-Afrikaanse Reg/Journal of South African Law*, 4, 1988, pp. 617–624; and N.V. Ralushai (Chairperson), "Report of the Commission of Inquiry into Witchcraft, Violence and Ritual Murders", 1995/1996. Far more effective work has been done for the neighbouring Lebowa Bantustan. See especially I.A. Niehaus (a) "Witch-Hunting and Political Legitimacy: Continuity and Change in Green Valley, Lebowa, 1930–91", in *Africa*, 63(4), 1993, pp. 498–530 & (b) "Witchcraft, Power and Politics: An Ethnographic Study of the South African Lowveld", Ph.D. thesis, University of the Witwatersrand, 1997; and I.A. Niehaus with E. Mohlala and K. Shokane, *Witchcraft, Power and Politics: Exploring the Occult in the South African Lowveld*, Anthropology, Culture and Society series, Cape Town, David Philip and London, Pluto Press, 2001.

Zauberei: This German word can be translated as magic, conjuring, witchcraft and sorcery. The missionaries used it to refer to witchcraft beliefs, the activities of traditional healers and diviners and Vhavenda beliefs in the supernatural in general. Sometimes they also described beliefs of this nature as *Aberglaube* [superstition]. Similarly, the word *Zauberer* [also *Zauberer* in plural] may be translated as magician, sorcerer, wizard or conjurer. The missionaries used it to refer to all categories of traditional healers and witch-finders and, less frequently, to those who were accused by others of practising witchcraft.

Bibliography

UNPUBLISHED SOURCES
(a) Berlin Mission Archives, Berlin

(i) Acta der Berliner Missionsgesellschaft betreffend Missionsstationen:

Georgenholtz: NT von 1877 bis 1899; AUFB. FRIST a; ABGEL. III, 5, 16; Bd. 1

Tagebücher der Missionare auf Makoarela (Georgenholtz), Abt. III, Fach 5, No. 16, (I).

Georgenholtz: NT von 1901 bis 1970; AUFB. FRIST a; ABGEL. III, 5, 16; Bd. 2–4.

Acta der Gesellschaft zur Beförderung der evangelischen Missionen unter den Heiden zu Berlin betreffend die Missions-Station Georgenholtz, Band II, Abt. 3, Fach 5, Nr. 16, Angefangen 1901, Beendigt 1933.

Georgenholtz: NT von 1906 bis 1962; AUFB. FRIST a; ABGEL. IV, 2E, 13; Bd. 1.

Acta der Berliner Missionsgesellschaft betreffend Missions-Station Georgenholtz, Abt. IV, Fach IIE, Nr. 13, Stations Synodalakte Band I von 1906 bis 1962.

Ha Tschewasse [Ha Tshivhase / Beuster]: NT von 1872 bis 1900; AUFB. FRIST a; ABGEL. III, 5, 14; Bd. 1 & 2.

Acta: Tagebücher der Missionare auf der Station Ga Sebase, 1872–1891, (I), Abt. III, Fach 5, No. 14.

Acta: Tagebücher der Missionare auf der Station Ha Tsevase, 1891–1900, (II), Abt. III, Fach 5, No. 14.

Acta: Tagebücher der Missionare auf der Station Ha Tsevase, 1892, (II), Abt. III, Fach 5, No. 14 [Envelope].

Ha Tschewasse [Ha Tshivhase / Beuster]: NT von 1900 bis 1959; AUFB. FRIST a; ABGEL. III, 5, 14; Bd. 3–5.

Acta der Gesellschaft zur Beförderung der evangelischen Missionen unter den Heiden zu Berlin betreffend die Missions-Station Ha-Tschewasse, 1900–1903, Abt. 3, Fach 5, Nr. 14, 1900–1926 (Band III).

Ha Tschewasse [Ha Tshivhase / Beuster]: NT von 1908 bis 1956; AUFB. FRIST a; ABGEL. IV, 2E, 11; Bd. 1.

Acta der Berliner Missionsgesellschaft betreffend Missions-Station Tsewasse, Abt. IV, Fach IIE, Nr. 11, Angefangen 1908 Beendigt 1956, Band 1.

Tschakuma [Tshakhuma]: NT von 1907 bis 1965; AUFB. FRIST a; ABGEL. IV, 2E, 12; Bd. 1 & 2.

Acta der Missionare auf Tsakoma (Ga Matzebandela), I, 1874–1892, Abt. III, Fach 5, No. 15. [According to the classificatory sytems used by the archives, and the labels on boxes, this should actually be filed in the next box. It would appear that it was placed in this box because of its size. I have followed its actual placement in making the bibliographical entry.]

Tschakuma [Tshakhuma]: NT von 1874 bis 1899; AUFB. FRIST a; ABGEL. III, 5, 15; Bd. 1&2.

Tagebücher Tsakoma, 1892–1899, Abt. III, Fach 5, No. 15.

Halbjahrsberichte der Station Tsakoma, 1887–1889, III, 5, 15.

Tschakuma [Tshakhuma]: NT von 1900 bis 1966; AUFB. FRIST a; ABGEL. III, 5, 15; Bd. 3–5.

Acta der Gesellschaft zur Beförderung der evangelischen Missionen unter den Heiden zu Berlin betreffend die Missions-Station Tshakoma, Band III, Abt. 3, Fach 5, Nr. 15, Angefangen 1900, Beendigt 1926.

(ii) Acta der Berliner Missionsgesellschaft betreffend Personalia:

Baumhöfner, Dietrich, Abt. II, Fach 3, Nr. 9, 1875–1883.

Beuster, Carl, Abt. II, Fach 3, Nr. 14, 1865–1902.

Endemann, Christian, Abt. II, Fach IIIG, Nr. 8, Angefangen 1891, Beendigt 1976.

Gernecke, Carl, Abt. II, Fach 3, No. 28, 1856–1948.

Giesekke, Ludwig, Abt. II, Fach IG, Nr. 2a, Angefangen 1898, Beendigt 1955.

Gottschling, Ernst, Abt. II, Fach 3, No. 27, Band 1, 1877–1956. Abt. II, Fach 3G, No. 27, Band 2, Angefangen 1913, Beendigt 1952.

Klatt, Carl Otto, Abt. II, Fach 3K, No. 42, 1891–1943.

Koen, Klaas, Abt. II, Fach 3K, No. 7, 1876–1883.

Meister, Johann, Abt. II, Fach 3, No. 6, 1884–1892.

Schwellnus, Erdmann, Abt. II, Fach 3, No. 25, n.d.

Sonntag, Christoph, Abt. II, Fach 3, No. 13, 1878–1952.

Stech, Carl, Abt. II, Fach 3, No. 1, 1866–1911 (Bd. 1). Acta betreffend die Disciplinare-Untersuchung gegen dem Missionar Carl Stech, 1892, Abt. II, Fach 3, No. 1 (Bd. 2).

Stork, Hellmuth, Abt. II, Fach St3, Nr. 8, Angefangen 1926, Beendigt 19–.

Wessmann, Reinhold, Abt. II, Fach 3W, No. 16, 1880–1907.

Westphal, Gotthardt, Abt.II, Fach II20, Nr. 5A, Angefangen 1902, Beendigt 1929.

(b) Government commissions, Republic of Venda and Northern Province

Le Roux, D.J.H. (sole Commissioner) "Report of the Commission of Enquiry into the Causes of the Unrest in Venda during August 1988 and the Investigation of Ritual Murders".

Ralushai, N.V. (Chairperson) "Report of the Commission of Inquiry into Witchcraft, Violence and Ritual Murders", Member of the Executive Council for Safety and Security, 1995/1996.

(c) Photographic collections

(i) Berlin Mission Archives, Berlin, Album XXIX – Nord-Transvaal 1:
"Die Helfer in Tschakoma"/"The Helpers [Native Evangelists] at Tschakoma [Tshakhuma]", Nr. 27.

"Tschikonatanz in Ngovela bei Ha Tschewase"/"Tshikona Dance at Ngovela, near Ha Tshivhase", Nr. 35 [15188].

"Audienz mit Mpafudi (Makwarela"/"Audience with Mpafudi (Makwarela)", Nr. 40.

"Flussübergang in Bowenda"/"Crossing a river in Bowenda", Nr. 59 [15197].

(ii) Berlin Mission Archives, Berlin: Album, Vendaland von Missionar G. Westphal, Nr. 8529:
"Die Dorfschneider von Beuster"/"The Village-Tailor of Beuster", Nr. 8530.

"Eine 'Thondo' Mauer"/"A 'Thondo' Wall" , Nr. 8541.

"Aussenstation Ha Begwa – Darbietung der Braut (Hackenstiel) durch die Makadzi (Hauptfrau der Sippe) für einen verstorbenen Jüngling, dem man noch keine Braut gesucht hatte."/"Out-Station Ha Begwa: Offering the bride (hoe-handle) by the Makadzi (head-woman of the extended family) for a deceased young man, because he had not yet looked for a bride", Nr. 8616.

"Miryam mit dem kleinen Nathanael auf dem Rücken kocht für die Erbauer der Kapelle von Alt-Georgenholtz."/"Miryam with the young Nathanael on her back cooks for the builder of the chapel of Old-Georgenholtz.", Nr. 8620.

[No Title] Warrior, Nr. 8632.

(iii) Berlin Mission Archives, Berlin: Unlabelled file, Gertrudsburg:
"Gertrudsburg 1926 – Konfirmanden, Pfingsten 1925"/"Gertrudsburg, 1926, Candidates for Confirmation, Pentecost, 1925", Nr. 1134.

(iv) Märkishes Museum, Berlin
Map Collection: "Plan von Berlin", Blatt IA, 1894–1903, N63/3437R [Friedrichshein].
Photographic Collection: "Georgenkirche" [Max Missmann], 1904, no number.
Photographic Collection: "Georgenkircheplatz 8–9", no date, N65/556V.
Photographic Collection: "Landsberger Tor & Strasse" [Max Missmann], 1906, N67/138V.
Post-Card Collection: No title ["Greifswalderstrasse mit Bartholomäus-Kirche, 1910" on face], N61/3885V.

(v) South African Museum, Cape Town:
[No Title] *Ndilo* (Divining bowl), photographed by Lindsay Cooper, Collections Manager, Human Sciences.

(vi) Collection of Dr Ulrich van der Heyden, Seminar für Afrika-wissenschaften, Prenzlauer Promenade 149–152, 13189 Berlin:
"Tanzende Heiden"/"Dancing Heathens" (originally published in T. Wangemann *Geschichte der Berliner Missionsgesellschaft in Südafrika*, Berlin, Evangelisches Missionshaus, 1877).

(d) Personal communications

Personal communications from: Dr J. Becher, Afrika Seminar, Humboldt Universität zu Berlin; Dr J.M. Dederen, Department of Anthropology; Dr W.F. Malunga, Department of History; Rev. M. Moremi, Department of Religious Studies; Dr N. Musehane & Prof. E.A. Khuba, Department of Tshivenda, University of Venda; Dr W. de Villiers, General Practitioner, Makhado/Louis Trichardt; Mr M. Goldblatt, Johannesburg-based photographer and Ms L. Nengudza-Mphephu, sister of the late *Khosi* P.R. Mphephu.

PUBLISHED SOURCES
a) Official publications [Southern Africa]
Bureau for Economic Research: Co-operation and Development and the Institute for Development Studies, Rand Afrikaans University, *The Independent Venda*, Pretoria, Benso, 1979.

Republic of Venda (a) *Venda Land Of Legend, Visitors' Map*, Sibasa, Venda Tourism, n.d.

(b) *Venḓa Travelogue*, Sibasa, Department of Information and Broadcasting, n.d.

Van Warmelo, N.J. (ed.) (a) *Contributions Towards Venda History, Religion and Tribal Ritual*, Union of South Africa, Department of Native Affairs, Ethnological Publications, Volume III, Pretoria, Government Printer, 1932.

(b) *The Copper Miners of Musina and the Early History of the Zoutpansberg*, Union Of South Africa, Department of Native Affairs, Ethnological Publications, Vol. VIII, Pretoria, Government Printer, 1940.

Van Warmelo, N.J. in collaboration with W.M.D. Phophi (a) *Venda Law: Part 2, Married life*, Ethnological Publications No. 23, Pretoria, Government Printer, 1948.

(b) *Venda Law: Part 4, Inheritance*, Ethnological Publications No. 23, Pretoria, Government Printer, 1949.

B) Berlin Mission Society

(i) Annual Reports

Berliner Missions-Berichte, Nr. 12 u 13, 1870 [Jahresbericht 1869], pp. 177–272 bis Juni 1900 [Jahresbericht 1899], pp. 257–440.

Siebenundsiebzigster Jahresbericht der Gesellschaft zur Beförderung der evangelischen Missionen unter den Heiden zu Berlin für das Jahr 1900, Berlin, Verlag der Berliner Missionsgesellschaft, 1901 [160 pp.].

Achtundsiebzigster Jahresbericht der Gesellschaft zur Beförderung der evangelischen Missionen unter den Heiden zu Berlin für das Jahr 1901, Berlin, Verlag der Berliner Missionsgesellschaft, 1902 [160 pp.].

Berliner Missions-Berichte, Juni 1903 [Jahresbericht 1902], pp. 177–400.

[No cover, bound in *Berliner Missions-Berichte* 1904 Volume] Jahresbericht 1903 [288 pp.] to [No cover, bound in *Berliner Missions-Berichte* 1909 Volume] Jahresbericht 1908 [184 pp.].

Sechsundachtzigster Jahresbericht der Berliner Missionsgesellschaft für das Jahr 1909, Ausgegeben Mai 1910, Berlin, Georgenkirchstrasse 70, 1910 [216 pp.] bis *Neunundachtzigster Jahresbericht der Berliner Missionsgesellschaft für das Jahr 1912*, Ausgegeben Mai 1913, Berlin, Georgenkirchstrasse 70, 1913 [224 pp.].

[No cover, bound in *Berliner Missions-Berichte* 1914 Volume] Jahresbericht 1913 [232 pp.].

Einundneunzigster Jahresbericht der Berliner Missionsgesellschaft für das Jahr 1914, Juni 1915, Berlin, Georgenkirchestrasse 70, 1915 [32 pp.].

(ii) Reports and News-Magazines

Der Bawenda-Freund, Nr. 20, 1. Januar 1888, VI. Jahrgang to Nr. 1, Januar 1920 [Continuation of *Mitteilungen des Vereins "Heidenfreund"*.]

Berliner Missionsberichte (*Missions-Berichte* from 1868), Nr. 3, März 1848; Nr. 10, Oktober 1850 und Nr. 1, 1860 bis Nr. 9, September 1915.

Missions-Berichte der Gesellschaft zur Beförderung der Evangelischen Mission unter den Heiden zu Berlin für das Jahr 1833, Berlin, Der Gesellschaft, 1833.

Der Missions-Freund: Ein Volksblatt, die Liebe zur Mission im deutschen Volke zu wecken und zu erhalten, XXXI. Jahrgang, 1876 bis XXXII. Jahrgang, 1877 und XLVII. Jahrgang, 1892.

Mission und Pfarramt: Herausgegeben im Auftrage der Berliner Missionsgesellschaft vom Missionsinspektor M. Wilde, 1. Jahrgang, 1908 bis 5. Jahrgang 1912.

Mission und Unterricht: Missionspädagogische Handreichung der Berliner Missionsgesellschaft, 24. Jahrgang, 1936, Heft 1 bis Heft 3.

Mitteilungen des "Heidenfreund", Nr. 16, 1. April 1887, V. Jahrgang bis Nr. 19, 1. Oktober 1887, V. Jahrgang [Continued as *Der Bawenda-Freund*].

(iii) Instructional Material and Regulations

Wangemann, H.T. (a) *Motive und Erläuterungen zu der Missions-Ordnung der Berliner Gesellschaft zur Beförderung der Evangelischen Missionen unter den Heiden*, Berlin, Selbstverlag des Evangel. Missionshauses, Friedenstrasse 6, 1882.

(b) *Unterrichtsordnung des Berliner Missionsseminars*, Berlin, Verlag des Evangelischen Missionshauses, 1882.

(iv) Tractates – Dornen und Ähren vom Missionsfelde

Sauberzweig-Schmidt, G. *Klaas Kuhn, ein Missionar aus den Hottentotten*, Vierte Auflage, Dornen und Ähren vom Missionsfelde Nr. V, Berlin, Buchhandlung der Berliner evangelischen Missions-Gesellschaft, n.d.

(v) Tractates – Berliner Missionstraktate, Neue Folge

Wangemann, H.T. (a) *Die Menschenfresser im Bapediländer*, Berliner Missions-Traktate, Neue Folge, Nr. V, Dritte Auflage, Berlin, Selbstverlag des Missionhauses, 1883. [1. Auflage, 1871, 2. Auflage, 1876.]

(b) *Gerettete Menschenfresser in Botshabelo*, Berliner Missions-Traktate, Neue Folge, Nr. VI, Dritte Auflage, Berlin, Selbstverlag des Missionhauses, 1883. [1. Auflage, 1871.]

(vi) Tractates – Neue Missionsschriften

[Anon.] *Etwas aus der Heidenzeit des deutschen Vaterlandes. Die Bekehrung der Sachsen in der Gegend von Hermannsburg*, Neue Missionsschriften Nr. 6, Berlin, Buchhandlung der Berliner evangelischen Missionsgesellschaft, 1890.

[Anon.] *Dietrich Baumhöfner, ein Missionar aus dem Ravensburger Land*, Neue Missionsschriften Nr. 18, Berlin, Buchhandlung der Berliner evangelischen Missionsgesellschaft, 1890.

Beuster, C. *Johannes Motscheni. Ein Lebensbild aus der Missionsarbeit in Nord-Transvaal*, Neue Missionsschriften Nr. 26, Berlin, Buchhandlung der Berliner evangelischen Missiongesellschaft, 1890. [Zweite Auflage, 1897.]

Sauberzweig-Schmidt, G. (a) *Ha Schewasse, eine Hütte Gottes unter den Bawenda*, Zweite Auflage, Neue Missionsschriften Nr. 32, Berlin, Buchhandlung der Berliner evangelischen Missionsgesellschaft, n.d. [1896]. [Erste Auflage, 1890.]

(b) *Georgenholtz im Lande der Bawenda*, Neue Missionsschriften Nr. 33, Berlin, Buchhandlung der Berliner evangelischen Missions-Gesellschaft, 1891. [Zweite Auflage, 1891; Dritte Auflage, 1896.]

Wangemann, H.T. *Khashane Mamatepha, Ein Lebensbild aus Nord-Transvaal*, Zweite Auflage, Neue Missionsschriften Nr. 22, Berlin, Buchhandlung der Berliner evangelischen Missionsgesellschaft, 1890. [Erste Auflage, 1888 (?); Dritte Auflage, 1893.]

Wessmann, R. *Der Häuptling August Makhahane, ein Lebensbild aus der Bawenda-Mission*, Berlin, Buchhandlung der Berliner evangelischen Missionsgesellschaft, 1892. [Zweite Auflage, 1897, Dritte Auflage, 1903.]

(vii) Tractates – Neue Missionsschriften [Neue Folge]

Heimbach, P. *Neu-Georgenholtz im Wenda-Lande*, Neue Missionsschriften [Neue Folge] Nr. 25, Berlin, Berliner Missiongesellschaft, n.d. [1909].

(viii) Tractates – Missionsschriften für Kinder

Merensky, A. (a) *Wie die Menschenfresser auf Tongoa Christen wurden*, Missionsschriften für Kinder Nr. 23, Berlin, Buchhandlung der Berliner evangelischen Missionsgesellschaft, n.d. [1895].

(b) *Die Menschenfresserei in Afrika*, Missionsschriften für Kinder Nr. 25, Berlin, Buchhandlung der Berliner evangelischen Missions-gesellschaft, n.d. [1895].

Wessmann, R. *Philippus Thai, ein Treuer Nationalhelfer im Bawendalande*, Missionsschriften für Kinder Nr. 46, Berlin, Buchhandlung der Berliner evangelischen Missionsgesellschaft, n.d. [1902].

(ix) Other Booklets published by the Berliner Missionsgesellschaft:

[Anon.] *75th Anniversary of the Berlin Mission Station Tshivhase*, 8 November, 1872–1947, Pamphlet distributed for the celebrations, No Publisher [Berlin Mission Society], n.d. [1947].

Bodenstein, R. *Die Schriftenreihen der Berliner Missionsgesellschaft*, Berlin, Berliner Missionswerk Bibliothek, 1996.

Bressani, M.I. [Comp.] *Im Dienst der Mission: Ein Gedenkbüchlein der Berliner Missionsgesellschaft*, Berlin, Berliner Missionsgesellschaft, 1963.

(c) Dictionaries and Lexicons

De Kock, W.J. (ed.in chief) *Dictionary of South African Biography*, Volume I, Cape Town, Published for the National Council for Social Research, Department of Higher Education by Nasionale Boekhandel Beperk, 1968.

Ferguson, S.B. and Wright, D.F. (eds.) *New Dictionary of Theology*, Leicester and Illinois, Inter-Varsity Press, 1988.

Krüger, D.W. (ed. in chief) and Beyers, C.J. *Dictionary of South African Biography*, Volume III, Cape Town, Published for the Human Sciences Research Council by Tafelberg Uitgewers Ltd., 1977.

Meyer, H.J. (ed.) *Neues Konversations-Lexikon*, 15 Bände, Zweite Auflage, Hildburghausen, 1869.

Van Warmelo, N.J. *Venda Dictionary: Tshivenda–English*, Pretoria, J.L. van Schaik, 1989.

(d) Books

Agar-Hamilton, J.A.I. *The Native Policy of the Voortrekkers: An essay in the history of the interior of South Africa – 1836–1858*, Cape Town, Maskew Miller, 1928.

Ambrosini, R. *Conrad's Fiction as Critical Discourse*, Cambridge, Cambridge University Press, 1991.

Appiah, K.L. and Gates, H.L. (eds.) *Identities,* Chicago, Chicago University Press, 1995.

Arens, W. *The Man-eating Myth: Anthropology and Anthropophagy*, Oxford, Oxford University Press, 1979.

Bender, B. (ed.) *Landscape: Politics and Perspectives*, Oxford, Berg, 1993.

Berkhof, L. *The History of Christian Doctrines*, Edinburgh, The Banner of Truth Trust, 1969.

Boeyens, J.C.A. *Die konflik tussen die Venda en die Blankes in Transvaal, 1864–1869*, Archives Year Book for South African History, Pretoria, Government Printer, 1990. Part I.

Bonner, P. *Kings, Commoners and Concessionaires: The evolution and dissolution of the nineteenth-century Swazi state*, Johannesburg, Ravan Press, 1983.

Bosch, D.J. *Transforming Mission: Paradigm Shifts in Theology of Mission*, New York, Orbis Books, 1991.

Brantlinger, P. *Rule of Darkness: British Literature and Imperialism, 1830–1914*, Ithaca Cornell University Press, 1988.

Bredekamp, H. and Ross, R. (eds.) *Missions and Christianity in South African History*, Johannesburg, Witwatersrand University Press, 1995.

Burke, E.E. (ed.) *The Journals of Carl Mauch: His travels in the Transvaal and Rhodesia 1869–1872*, Transcribed from the original by Mrs. E. Bernhard and translated by F.O. Bernhard, Salisbury, National Archives of Rhodesia, 1969.

Cameron, T. and Spies, S.B. (eds.) *A New Illustrated History of South Africa*, Second Edition, Johannesburg, Southern Book Publishers and Cape Town, Human & Rosseau, 1991.

Carruthers, E.J. *Game Protection in the Transvaal, 1846 to 1926*, Archives Year Book For South African History, Pretoria, Government Printer, 1995.

Ching-Liang Low, G. *White Skins/Black Masks: Representation and Colonialism*, London, Routledge, 1996.

Clendinnen, I. *Aztecs: an interpretation*, Cambridge, Cambridge University Press, 1991.

Comaroff, J.L. and Comaroff, J. (a) *Of Revelation and Revolution: Christianity, Colonialism and Consciousness in South Africa*, Volume One, Chicago, University of Chicago Press, 1991.

(b) *Of Revelation and Revolution: The Dialectics of Modernity on a South African Frontier*, Volume Two, Chicago, University of Chicago Press, 1997.

Conrad, J. *Heart of Darkness*, Harmondsworth, Penguin Books, 1995.

Coombes, A.E. *Reinventing Africa: Museums, Material Culture and Popular Imagination*, New Haven and London, Yale University Press, 1994.

Cooper, F. and Stoler, A.L. (eds.) *Tensions of Empire: colonial cultures in a bourgeois world*, Berkeley, Los Angeles and London, University of California Press, 1997.

Coplan, D.B. *In the Time of Cannibals: The Word Music of South Africa's Basotho Migrants*, Johannesburg, Witwatersrand University Press, 1994.

Courtine, Jean-Jaques and Haroche, C. *Histoire du visage, XVIe – début XIXe siècle*, Paris, Rivage/Histoire, 1988.

De Kock, L. *Civilising Barbarians: Missionary Narrative and African Textual Response in Nineteenth-Century South Africa*, Johannesburg, Witwatersrand University Press, 1996.

Delius, P. *The Land Belongs To Us: The Pedi Polity, the Boers and the British in the Nineteenth Century Transvaal*, Johannesburg, Ravan Press, 1983.

Denning, G. *Mr Bligh's Bad Language: Passion, Power and Theatre on the Bounty*, Cambridge and New York, Canto (Cambridge University Press), 1994.

De Vaal, J.B. *Die Rol van João Albasini in die Geskiedenis van die Transvaal*, Argiefjaarboek vir Suid-Afrikaanse Geskiedenis, Pretoria, Staatsdrukker, 1953, Deel I.

Dicke, B.H. *The Bush Speaks, Border Life in the Old Transvaal*, Second Edition, Pietermaritzburg, Shuter & Shooter, 1937.

Eldredge, E.A. and Morton, F. (eds.) *Slavery in South Africa: Captive Labour on the Dutch Frontier*, Boulder, San Fransisco and Oxford, Westview Press and Pietermaritzburg, University of Natal Press, 1994.

Ellenberger, F. *History of the Basuto: Ancient and Modern*, London, Caxton, 1912.

Elphick, R. and Davenport, R. (eds.) *Christianity in South Africa: A Political, Social & Cultural History*, Oxford, James Currey and Cape Town, David Philip, 1997.

Feustel, J. *Spaziergänge in Frederichshain*, Berlinsche Reminiszenzen No. 64, Berlin, Haude & Spener, 1994.

Finley, G. *Landscapes of Memory: Turner as Illustrator to Scott*, Berkeley, University of California Press, 1980.

Flygare, J. *De Zoutpansbergen en de Bawenda Natie*, Pretoria, The State Library Reprints, No. 86, 1979 (originally published at Pretoria, De Volksstem Drukkerij, 1899).

Geary, C.M. *Images from Bamum. German Colonial Photography at the Court of King Njoya, Cameroon, West Africa, 1902–1915*, Washington DC, Smithsonian Institution Press, 1988.

Gluckman, M. *Custom and Conflict in Africa*, Oxford, Basil Blackwell, 1973.

Gründler, W. *Geschichte der Bawenda-Mission in Nord-Transvaal*, Berlin, Buchhandlung der Berliner evangelischen Missionsgesellschaft, n.d. [1897].

Gschwend, J.R. *Mbilu ya Muthu*, Pretoria, All Nations Gospel Publishers, n.d.

Hall, M. *The Changing Past: Farmers, Kings and Traders in Southern Africa, 200–1860*, Cape Town, David Philip, 1987.

Hamilton, C. (ed.) *The Mfecane Aftermath: Reconstructive Debates in Southern African History*, Johannesburg, Witwatersrand University Press and Pietermaritzburg, University of Natal Press, 1995.

Hamilton, C. *Terrific Majesty: The Powers of Shaka Zulu and the Limits of Historical Invention*, Cape Town, David Philip, 1998.

Hammond-Tooke, W.D. (ed.) *The Bantu-Speaking Peoples of Southern Africa*, Second Edition, London, Routledge and Kegan Paul, 1974.

Harries, P. *Work, Culture and Identity: Migrant Labourers in Mozambique and South Africa, c. 1860–1910*, Social History of Africa Series, Portsmouth, Heinemann, Johannesburg, Witwatersrand University Press and London, James Currey, 1994.

Harris, M. (a) *Cannibals and Kings: The Origins of Cultures*, Glasgow, Fontana/Collins, 1978.

(b) *Cultural Materialism: The Struggle for a Science of Culture*, New York, Vintage Books, 1980.

Henige, D. and McCaskie, T.C. (eds.) *West African Economic and Social History. Studies in memoriam of Marion Johnson*, Madison, University of Wisconsin Press, 1990.

Hofmeyr, S. *Twintig Jaren in Zoutpansberg. Een Verhaal van Twintig Jarigen Arbeit onder de Heidenen in de Transvaal door den Eerw. Stéfanus Hofmeyr*, Kaapstad, J.H. Rose & Co., 1890.

Japin, A. *The Two Hearts of Kwasi Boachi*, translated by Ina Rilke, London, Chatto & Windus, 2000.

Johnson Barker, B., Maclay, G and Steyn, A. *Off the Beaten Track: Selected Day Drives in Southern Africa*, Cape Town, AA The Motorist Publications, 1996.

Kantorowicz, E.H. *The King's Two Bodies: A Study in Medieval Political Theology*, Princeton, Princeton University Press, 1957.

Kennedy, R.F. (comp.) (a) *Catalogue of Prints in the Africana Museum and in books in the Strange Collection of Africana in the Johannesburg Public Library up to 1870,* Volume One: A–K, Johannesburg, Africana Museum, 1975.

(b) *Catalogue of Prints in the Africana Museum and in books in the Strange Collection of Africana in the Johannesburg Public Library up to 1870,* Volume Two: L–Z and Index, Johannesburg, Africana Museum, 1976.

Kritzinger, J.J., Meiring, P.G.I. and Saayman, W.A. *On being Witness*, Halfway House, Orion Publishers, 1994.

Lamar, H. and Thompson, L. *The Frontier in History: North America and Southern Africa Compared*, New Haven, Yale University Press, 1981.

Le Breton, D. *Des Visages. Essai d'anthropologie*, Paris, Éditions A.M. Métaillié, 1992.

Lehmann, H. (a) *150 Jahre Berliner Mission*, Stuttgart, Ev.-Luth. Mission Erlangen, 1974.

(b) *Zur Zeit und zur Unzeit: Geschichte der Berliner Mission, 1918–1972* (Drei Bände), Berlin, Berliner Missionswerk, 1989.

Lewis, I.M. *Ecstatic Religion: An Anthropological Study of Spirit Possession and Shamanism*, Harmondsworth, Penguin Books, 1971.

Mackenzie, R. *David Livingstone: The Truth behind the Legend*, Chinhoyi, Fig Tree Publications Zimbabwe, Fourth Edition, 1997.

Magubane, P. *Vanishing Cultures*, Cape Town, Struik, 1998.

Mair, L. *An Introduction to Social Anthropology*, Second Edition, Oxford, Clarendon Press, 1972.

Maree, W.L. *Lig in die Soutpansberg: Die Sendingwerk van die Nederduitse Gereformeerde Kerk in Noord-Transvaal, 1863–1963*, Pretoria, Sinodale Sendingskommissies van die Nederduitse Gereformeerde Kerk, 1962.

Marks, S. and Atmore, A. (eds.) *Economy and Society in Pre-Industrial South Africa*, London, Longmans, 1980.

Marks, S. and Rathbone, R. (eds.) *Industrialisation and Social Change in South Africa: African class formation, culture and consciousness 1870–1930*, London and New York, Longmans, 1982.

Marwick, M. (ed.) *Witchcraft & Sorcery*, Harmondsworth, Penguin Books, 1970.

Matsebula, J.S.M. *A History of Swaziland*, Third Edition, Cape Town, Longman, 1988.

Maylam, P. *A History of the African People of South Africa: from the Early Iron Age to the 1970s*, Cape Town, David Philip, 1986.

Mbiti, J.S. *African Religions and Philosophy*, Second Edition, Oxford, Heinemann International, 1990.

Minnaar, A. de V., Offringa, D. and Payze, C. *To Live in Fear: Witchburning and Medicine Murder in Venda*, ASS/BSS–20, Pretoria, Human Sciences Research Council, 1992.

Möller-Malan, D. *The Chair of the Ramabulanas*, South Africa, Central News Agency Ltd., 1953.

Morphy, H. *Ancestral Connections: Art and an Aboriginal System of Knowledge*, Chicago, Chicago University Press. 1991.

Moser, S. *Ancestral Images. The Iconography of Human origins*, Stroud, Sutton Publishing, 1998.

Niehaus, I.A. with Mohlala, E. and Shokane, K. *Witchcraft, Power and Politics: Exploring the Occult in the South African Lowveld*, Anthropology, Culture and Society series, Cape Town, David Philip and London, Pluto Press, 2001.

Omer-Cooper, J.D. (a) *The Zulu Aftermath: A Nineteenth-Century Revolution in Bantu Africa*, London, Longman, 1966.

(b) *History of Southern Africa*, Claremont, David Philip, 1987.

Oosthuizen, G.C. and Hexham, I. (eds.) *Afro-Christian Religion at the grassroots in Southern Africa*, African Studies, Volume 19, Lewiston, Edwin Mellen Press, 1991.

Parfitt, T. *Journey to the Vanished City: the search for a lost tribe of Israel*, London, Phoenix (Orion Books), 1997.

Pratt, M.L. *Imperial Eyes: Travel Writing and Transculturation*, London, Routledge, 1992.

Radcliffe-Brown, A.R. and Forde, D. *African Systems of Kinship and Marriage*, London, International African Institute, Oxford University Press, 1950.

Richter, D.J. *Geschichte der Berliner Missionsgesellschaft, 1824–1924*, Berlin, Buchhandlung der Berliner ev. Missionsgesellschaft, 1924.

Ritter, E.A. *Shaka Zulu: The Rise of the Zulu Empire*, London, Longmans Green and Company, 1955.

Saunders, C. (ed.) *Reader's Digest Illustrated History of South Africa: The Real Story*, Cape Town, Reader's Digest Association, 1988.

Stayt, H.A. *The Bavenda*, London, Oxford University Press, 1931.

Street, B.V. *The Savage in Literature: Representations of 'primitive' society in English fiction, 1858–1920*, London, Routledge & Kegan Paul, 1975.

Sundkler, B.G.M. *Bantu Prophets in South Africa*, Second Edition, London, Oxford University Press, 1961.

Sundkler, B. and Steed, C. *A History of the Church in Africa*, Cambridge, Cambridge University Press, 2000.

Surplus People Project. *Forced Removals in South Africa, Vol. 5: The Transvaal*, Cape Town and Pietermaritzburg, Surplus People Project, 1983.

Sutton, P. *Dreamings: the Art of Aboriginal Australia*, Asia Society Galleries, New York, George Braziller, 1988.

Taussig, M.J. *Shamanism, Colonialism and the Wild Man: A Study of Terror and Healing*, Chicago, Chicago University Press, 1987.

Tempelhoff, J.W.N. *Townspeople of the Soutpansberg: A Centenary History*, Louis Trichardt, Greater Louis Trichardt Transitional Local Council, 1999.

Vail, L. (ed.) *The Creation of Tribalism in Southern Africa*, London, James Currey, 1989.

Van der Heyden, U. and Becher, J. (eds.) *Mission und Moderne. Beiträge zur Geschichte der christlichen Missionen in Afrika anläßlich der*

Jahrestagung der VAD und des 12. Afrikanistentages vom 3–6 Oktober 1996 in Berlin, Köln, Rüdiger Köppe Verlag, 1998.

Van der Merwe, D.W. (a) *Die geskiedenis van die Berlynse Sendinggenootskap in Transvaal, 1860–1900*, Argiefjaarboek vir Suid-Afrikaanse Geskiedenis, Pretoria, Staatsdrukker, 1984, Deel I.

(b) *Die Berlynse Sendinggenootskap en Kerkstigting in Transvaal, 1904–1962*, Argiefjaarboek vir Suid-Afrikaanse Geskiedenis, Pretoria, Staatsdrukker, 1987, Deel II.

Van Onselen, C. *Studies in the Social and Economic History of the Witwatersrand 1886–1914*, 1. *New Babylon*, Johannesburg, Ravan Press, 1982.

Wangemann, T. *Geschichte der Berliner Missionsgesellschaft in Südafrika*, Berlin, Evangelisches Missionshaus, 1877.

Warneck, D.G. (a) *Abriss einer Geschichte der protestantischen Missionen von der Reformation bis auf die Gegenwart. Ein Beitrag zur neueren Kirchengeschichte*, Siebente Auflage, Berlin, Verlag von Martin Warneck, 1901.

(b) *Outline of a History of Protestant Missions from the Reformation to the Present Time: A contribution to Modern Church History*, Authorised translation from the Seventh German Edition [see above], Edinburgh and London, Oliphant Anderson & Ferrier, 1901.

Watt, I. (a) *Conrad in the Nineteenth Century*, London, Chatto and Windus, 1980.

(b) *Essays on Conrad*, Cambridge, Cambridge University Press, 2000.

Wessmann, R. *The Bawenda of the Spelonken (Transvaal): A contribution towards the psychology and folk-lore of African peoples*, translated from the German original text by L. Weinthal, London, 'The African World' Ltd., 1908.

White, A. *Joseph Conrad and the Adventure Tradition: Constructing and deconstructing the imperial subject*, Cambridge, Cambridge University Press, 1993.

White, L. *Speaking with vampires: rumor and history in colonial Africa*, Berkeley, Los Angeles and London, University of California Press, 2000.

Wilde, M. *Schwarz und Weiss: Bilder von einer Reise durch das Arbeitsgebiet der Berliner Mission in Südafrika von M. Wilde, Missionsinspektor*, Berlin, Buchhandlung der Berliner evangelischen Missionsgesellschaft, 1913.

Wilson, M. and Thompson, L. (eds.) *The Oxford History of South Africa, Volume I. South Africa to 1870*, London, Oxford University Press, 1969.

Wright, M. *German Missions in Tanganyika 1891–1941: Lutherans and Moravians in the Southern Highlands*, Oxford, Clarendon Press, 1971.

Ziervogel, D., Wentzel, P.J. and Makuya, T.N. *A Handbook of the Venda Language*, Second Edition, Pretoria, University of South Africa, 1972.

(e) Articles

Anderson, A. and Pillay, G. "The Segregated Spirit: The Pentecostals", in R. Elphick and R. Davenport (eds.), *Christianity in South Africa*, pp. 227–241.

[Anon.] "Das Missionshospital der Mission Romande in Elim", in *Mitteilungen des Berliner Vereins für Ärtzliche Mission und seiner Zweigvereine*, Nr. 2, Berlin, März 1910, pp. 49–56; Nr. 3, Mai 1910, pp. 73–83 and Nr. 4, Juli 1910, pp. 101–107.

Bartels, M. "Der Würfelzauber südafrikanischer Völker", in *Zeitschrift für Ethnologie*, Vol. 35, 1903, pp. 338–379.

Bender, B. "Introduction: Landscape – Meaning and Action", in B. Bender (ed.), *Landscape: Politics and Perspectives*, pp. 1–17.

Boeyens, J. (a) "Louis Tregardt en die Opvolgingstryd tussen Ramabulana en Ramavhoya", in *South African Historical Journal/Suid-Afrikaanse Historiese Joernaal*, 23 (1990), pp. 41–53.

(b) "'Zwart ivoor': Inboekelinge in Zoutpansberg, 1848–1869", in *South African Historical Journal/Suid-Afrikaanse Historiese Joernaal*, 24 (1991), pp. 31–66.

(c) "'Black Ivory': The Indenture System and Slavery in Soutpansberg, 1848–1869" (revised, English version of "Zwart ivoor"), in E.A. Eldredge and F. Morton (eds.), *Slavery in South Africa*, 1994, pp. 187–217.

Brantlinger, P. "Victorians and Africans: The Genealogy of the Myth of the Dark Continent", in *Critical Inquiry*, Vol. 12, No. 1, Autumn 1985, pp. 166–203.

Buijs, G. "Black Jews in the Northern Province: a study of ethnic identity in South Africa", in *Ethnic and Racial Studies*, Vol. 21, No. 4, July 1998, pp. 661–682.

Cobbing, J. "The Mfecane as Alibi: Thoughts on Dithakong and Mbolompo", in *Journal of African History*, 29, 1988, pp. 487–519.

Coertze, P.J. "Dolosgooiery in Suid-Afrika", in *Annale van die Universiteit van Stellenbosch*, Vol. IX, Serie B, Part 2, April 1931, pp. 1–48.

Comaroff, J.L. "Images of Empire, Contents of Conscience: Models of Colonial Domination in South Africa", in F. Cooper and A.L. Stoler (eds.), *Tensions of empire*, pp. 163–197.

Cosgrove, D. "Landscapes and Myths, Gods and Humans", in B. Bender (ed.), *Landscape: Politics and Perspectives*, pp. 281–305.

Dederen, J.M. "Book review of *To live in Fear: Witchburning and Medicine Murder in Venda* by A. de V. Minnaar, D. Offringa and C. Payze", in *Social Dynamics: A Journal of the Centre for African Studies, University of Cape Town*, Vol. 18, No. 2, December 1992, pp. 95–100.

Delius, P. "Migrant Labour and the Pedi, 1840–80", in S. Marks and A. Atmore (eds.), *Economy and Society in Pre-Industrial South Africa*, pp. 293–312.

Dornan, S.S. "Some Beliefs and Ceremonies connected with the Birth and Death of Twins among the South African Natives", in *South African Journal of Science*, Vol. XXIX, October 1932, pp. 690–700.

Du Plessis, H. "Die Territoriale Organisasie van die Venda", in *African Studies*, Vol. 4, No. 3, September 1955, pp. 122–127.

Dzivhani, S.M. "The Chiefs of Venḓa", in N.J. van Warmelo (ed.), *The Copper Miners of Musina*, pp. 33–50.

Edgecombe, R. "The Mfecane or Difaqane", in T. Cameron and S.B. Spies (eds.), *A New Illustrated History of South Africa*, pp. 115–126.

Elbourne, E. "Early Khoisan Uses of Missionary Christianity", in H. Bredekamp and R. Ross (eds.), *Missions and Christianity in South African History*, pp. 65–95.

Eldredge, E. "Delagoa Bay and the Hinterland in the Early Nineteenth Century: Politics, Trade, Slaves and Slave Raiding", in E.A. Eldredge and F. Morton (eds.), *Slavery in South Africa*, pp. 127–165.

Elphick, R. "Africans and the Christian Campaign in Southern Africa", in H. Lamar and L. Thompson (eds.), *The Frontier in History*, pp. 270–307.

Fischer, G. "Die Bawenda, ein neues Bild in der Mission", in *Der Missions-Freund: Ein Volksblatt, die Liebe zur Mission im deutschen Volke zu wecken und zu erhalten*, XXXII. Jahrgang, No. 4, 1877, pp. 49–64.

Frobenius, L. "Die Waremba, Träger einer fossilen Kultur", in *Zeitschrift für Ethnologie*, Vol. 70, 1938, pp. 159–175 (article first written in 1929).

Geary, C.M. (a) "Photographs as Materials for African History: Some Methodological Considerations, in *History in Africa*, 13 (1986), pp. 89–116.

(b) "Impressions of the African Past: Interpreting Ethnographic Photographs from Cameroon", in *Visual Anthropology*, 3/2–2 (1990), pp. 289–315.

(c) "Missionary Photography. Private and Public Readings", in *African Arts*, 24/4 (1991), pp. 48–59, 98–100.

Giesekke, E.D. (a) "Der Eisenindustrie der Bawenda", in *Die Brücke*, 7, July 1930, pp. 5–9.

(b) "Wahrsagerei bei den Venda", in *Zeitschrift für Eingeborenen Sprachen*, Vol. XXI, No. 4, 1931, pp. 257–310. [Note that the second initial does not appear here.]

Gottschling, E. "The Bawenda, A sketch of their history and customs", in *Addresses and Papers read at the Joint Meeting of the British and South African Associations for the Advancement of Science held in South Africa, 1905*, Volume III, Johannesburg, South African Association for the Advancement of Science, 1905, pp. 195–221.

Grant, W. "Magato and his Tribe", in *Journal of the Royal Anthropological Institute*, Vol. 35, London, 1905, pp. 266–270.

Hammond-Tooke, W.D. "World-view II: A System of Action", in W.D. Hammond-Tooke (ed.), *The Bantu-Speaking Peoples of Southern Africa*, pp. 344–363.

Hampson, R. "Introduction", in J. Conrad, *Heart of Darkness*, pp. ix–xliv.

Hanisch, E.O.M. "Legends, Oral Traditions and Archaeology: A look at early Venda history", in *Luvhone*, Department of Education and Culture, Venda, Vol. 3, No. 4., April 1994, pp. 68–76.

Harries, P. (a) "Exclusion, Classification and Internal Colonialism: The Emergence of Ethnicity Among the Tsonga-Speakers of South Africa", in L. Vail (ed.), *The Creation of Tribalism in Southern Africa*, pp. 82–117.

(b) "Through the Eyes of the Beholder: H.A. Junod and the Notion of Primitive", in *Social Dynamics*, Vol. 19, No. 1, June 1993, pp. 1–10.

Hayes, S. "The African Independent Churches: Judgement through terminology?", in *Missionalia*, Vol. 20, No. 2, August 1992, pp. 139–146. [See also *Missionalia* Homepage.]

Heese, H. "Diakonie en Digitalisering: Sendingrekords en geskiedenis in die 21ste eeu", in *Historia: Journal of the South African Historical Association*, Vol. 43. No. 2, November 1988, pp. 24–39.

Hendrickx, B. "The Ancient Origin of the Lemba (Mwenye): A critical overview of existing theories", in *Journal of Oriental and African Studies*, (Athens) Vol. 3, 1991, pp. 172–193.

Hexham, I. and Poewe, K. "The Spread of Christianity among Whites and Blacks in Transorangia", in R. Elphick and R. Davenport (eds.), *Christianity in South Africa*, pp. 121–134.

Heydenrych, D.H. "The Boer Republics, 1852–1881", in T. Cameron and S.B. Spies (eds.), *A New Illustrated History of South Africa*, pp. 143–179.

Hoffmann, C. "Die Sünde der Welt im Heidentum", in *Mission und Unterricht: Missionspädagogische Handreichung der Berliner Missionsgesellschaft*, 24. Jahrgang, 1936, Heft 1, p. 26.

Hofmeyr, H.M. "Christian Mission and Colonialism in Southern Africa and African Responses: Some case studies", in *Emory International Law Review*, Vol. 14, No. 2 (Special Edition), 2000, pp. 1029–1088.

Huffman, T.N. (a) "The Rise and Fall of Zimbabwe", in *Journal of African History*, Vol. XIII, No. 3, 1973, pp. 353–366.

(b) "Snakes and birds: expressive space at Great Zimbabwe", in *African Studies*, 40(2), 1981, pp. 131–150.

(c) "Archeology and the ethnohistory of the African Iron Age", in *Annual Review of Anthropology*, 11, 1982, pp. 133–150.

(d) "Broederstroom and the Central Cattle Pattern", in *South African Journal of Science*, Vol. 89, 1993, pp. 220–226.

Huffman, T.N. and Hanisch, E.O.M. "Settlement Hierarchies in the Northern Transvaal: Zimbabwe Ruins and Venda History", *African Studies Journal*, Vol. 46, No. 1, 1987, pp. 79–116.

Jaques, Alexandre "Les coutumes funéraires des meurt dans l'eau", in *Bulletin de la Mission Suisse Romande*, Vol. XXXVI, No. 475, March – April 1927, pp. 256–258.

Jaques, Auguste "Craintes de guerre", in *Bulletin Missionnaire des Églises Libres de la Suisse Romande*, Vol. 6, No. 73, August 1887, pp. 280–282.

Jenkins. P. "In the Eye of the Beholder: An Exercise in the Interpretation of Two photographs Taken in Cameroon Early in This Century", in D. Henige and T.C. McCaskie (eds.), *West African Economic and Social History. Studies in memoriam of Marion Johnson*, pp. 93–103.

Junod, H.A. (a) "The Balemba of the Zoutpansberg (Transvaal)", in *Folk-Lore: A Quarterly Review of Myth, Tradition, Institution and Custom*, Vol. 19, No. 3, London, 1908, pp. 276–287.

(b) "Some Features of the Religion of the Ba-Venda", in *South African Journal of Science*, Vol. 17, 1920, pp. 207–220.

Khuba, A.E. "The Significance of the Musanda Language in Venda", in *Luvhone*, Department of Education and Culture, Venda, Vol. 3, No. 4, April 1994, pp. 29–31.

Kimble, J. "Labour migration in Basutoland, c.1870–1885", in S. Marks and R. Rathbone (eds.) *Industrialisation and Social Change in South Africa*, pp. 119–141.

Kirkaldy, A. (a) "Makoarele's return to 'the darkness of heathenism': Khosi Makwarela and the Berlin Missionaries", in U. van der Heyden and J. Becher (eds.), *Mission und Moderne Beiträge zur Geschichte der christlichen Missionen in Afrika anläßlich der Jahrestagung der VAD und des 12. Afrikanistentages vom 3–6. Oktober 1996 in Berlin*, pp. 121–142.

(b) "'Dark Forests and Dark Hearts': Berlin Missionary Constructions of Vendaland, c.1870–1900", in *Psychology Bulletin*, Vol. 9, No. 2, December 1999, pp. 75–105.

(c) "The Darkness within the Light: Berlin missionaries and the Landscape of Vendaland, c. 1870–1900", in *Historia*, 48(1), May 2003, pp. 169–202.

Kirkaldy, A. and Wirz, A. (a) "Picturing the soul: missionary encounters in late 19th and early 20th century South Africa", in *Working Papers on African Societies*, Nr. 44, Berlin, Das Arabische Buch, 2000.

(b) "Writing the soul in light: missionary encounters in late nineteenth-century Vendaland, Blouberg and beyond", *SHS Monograph Series*, Vol. 1, No. 1, Thohoyandou, School of Human Sciences, University of Venda for Science and Technology, October 2000.

Kügler, S. "Landscape as Memory: The Mapping of process and its Representation in a Melanesian Society", in B. Bender (ed.), *Landscape: Politics and Perspectives*, pp. 85–106.

Le Roux, M. "African 'Jews' for Jesus: A preliminary investigation into the Semitic origins and missionary initiatives of some Lemba communities in southern Africa", in *Missionalia*, Vol. 24, No. 4, December 1997, pp. 493–510. [See also *Missionalia* Homepage.]

Lestrade, G.P. (a) "Some notes on the political Organisation of the Venda Speaking Tribes", in *Africa: Journal of the International Institute of African Languages and Cultures*, Vol. III, No. 3, July 1930, pp. 306–322. [Also appears in N.J. van Warmelo (ed.), *Contributions towards Venda History, Religion and Tribal Ritual*, pp. I–XI.]

(b) "Some Notes on the Ethnic History of the Vhavenda and their Rhodesian Affinities", in N.J. van Warmelo (ed.), *Contributions towards Venda History, Religion and Tribal Ritual*, pp. XX–XXVIII. [Reprinted from *South African Journal of Science*, Vol. XXIV, pp. 486–495.]

Liesegang, G. "New light on Venda traditions: Mahumane's account of 1730", in *History in Africa*, 4, 1977, pp. 163–181.

Loubser, J. "The Venda Divining Bowl in the Museum", in *National Museum News*, No. 36, April 1989, pp. 18–19.

Maggs, T. "The Early History of the Black People in South Africa", in T. Cameron and S.B. Spies (eds.), *A New Illustrated History of South Africa*, pp. 37–43.

Marks, S. and Atmore, A. "Introduction", in S. Marks and A. Atmore (eds.), *Economy and Society*, pp. 1–43.

Mauss, M. "Les techniques du corps", in *Journal de psychologie normale et pathologique*, Vol. 32, 1935, pp. 271–293.

Mayer, P. "Witches", Inaugural Lecture, Rhodes University, 1954, in M. Marwick (ed.), *Witchcraft & Sorcery*, pp. 45–64.

McDonald, D. "Vendaland", in *The Blythswood Review: A South African Journal of Religious, Social and Economic Work*, Vol. X, No. 110, February 1933, pp. 12–13, No. 111, March 1933, p. 28 and No. 112, April 1933, pp. 28–29.

Mihálik, J. and Cassim, Y. "Ritual murder and Witchcraft: A Political Weapon?", in *The South African Law Journal*, Vol. 110, Part 1, February 1993, pp. 127–140.

Miller, S.M. and Tempelhoff, J.W.N. "Die romantiek van 'n grensterrein", in *Fauna and Flora*, Transvaalse Direktoraat Natuur- en Omgewingsbewaring, No. 47, 1990, pp. 32–39.

Mitchell, T. "The world as exhibition", in *Comparative Studies in Society and History*, 31, 1989, pp. 217–236.

Morphy, H. (a) "From dull to brilliant: the aesthetics of spiritual power among the Yolngu", in *Man* (N.S.), 24 (1), 1989, pp. 21–41.

(b) "Colonialism, History and the Construction of Place: The Politics of Landscape in Northern Australia", in B. Bender (ed.), *Landscape: Politics and Perspectives*, pp. 205–243.

Motenda, M.M. "History of the Western Venḓa and of the Lemba", in N.J. van Warmelo (ed.), *The Copper Miners of Musina*, pp. 51–70.

Mudau, E. (a) "Ngoma lungundu and the early invaders of Venḓa", in N.J. van Warmelo (ed.), *The Copper Miners of Musina*, pp. 10–32.

(b) "The Dau of Tshakhuma", in N.J. van Warmelo (ed.), *The Copper Miners of Musina*, pp. 71–80.

Niehaus, I.A. "Witch-Hunting and Political Legitimacy: Continuity and Change in Green Valley, Lebowa, 1930–91", in *Africa*, Vol. 63, No. 4, 1993, pp. 498–530.

Norden, L. "Die Heilige Tamboere van Tshiendeolo", in *Die Huisgenoot*, 6 November 1942, pp. 7–8.

Obeyesekere, G. "'British Cannibals': Contemplation of an Event in the Death and Resurrection of James Cook, Explorer", in K.A. Appiah and H.L. Gates (eds.), *Identities*, pp. 7–32.

Pauw, B.A. "The Influence of Christianity", in W.D. Hammond-Tooke (ed.) *The Bantu-Speaking Peoples of Southern Africa*, pp. 415–440.

Plug, I. "An Analysis of Witchdoctor Divining Sets", in *Research Natco Museum*, Vol. 1, No. 3, 1987, pp. 48–67.

Pretorius, H. and Jafta, L. "'A Branch Springs Out': African Initiated Churches", in R. Elphick and R. Davenport (eds.), *Christianity in South Africa*, pp. 211–226.

Prinsloo, M.W. and Du Plessis, J.H. "Towenaarmoorde, rituele doding en medisynemoorde in Venda", in *Tydskrif vir die Suid-Afrikaanse Reg/ Journal of South African Law*, 4, 1988, pp. 617–624.

Ross, R. "The Top-Hat in South African History: The changing significance of an item of material culture", in *Social Dynamics*, Vol. 16, No. 1, 1990, pp. 90–100.

S[ampson], P.J. "'Fertilising the Corn': Being a true story of the weird and terrible Bawenda special rite of 'Mokuku wa mabeli' whereby the seed corn is made fertile and brings forth abundant crops", in *The Nongqai*, 12, January 1921, pp. 18–19.

Schlömann, [H.D.]. "Die Malepa in Transvaal", in *Zeitschrift für Ethnologie*, Vol. 26, 1894, pp. 64–70.

Schoene, S. "Zwillingskinder! Von Heidenelend und Christenglück in Südafrika", in *Der Missions-Freund*, 88. Jahrgang, 1936, pp. 68–70.

Schwellnus, T. "Die Valemba", in *Mission und Pfarramt: Herausgegeben im Auftrage der Berliner Missionsgesellschaft vom Missionsinspektor M. Wilde*, 5. Jahrgang 1912, pp. 116–120.

Smith, J. "People Eaters", in *Granta*, 52, Winter 1995, *Food: The Vital Stuff*, pp. 69–84.

Speicht, W.L. "Human Sacrifice in South Africa", in *The Nongqai*, 26, February 1935, pp. 152; 164.

Stayt, H.A. "Notes on the Balemba: An Arabic-Bantu tribe living among the BaVenda and other Bantu tribes in the Northern Transvaal and Southern Rhodesia", in *Journal of the Royal Anthropological Institute*, Vol. 61, 1931, pp. 231–238.

Stoler, A.L. and Cooper, F. "Between Metropole and Colony: Rethinking a Research agenda, in F. Cooper and A.L. Stoler (eds.), *Tensions of Empire*, pp. 1–56.

Tempelhoff, J. and Nemudzivhadi, H. "Riding the storm of change: Makhado, Venda and the South African Republic (1864–1895)", in *New Contree* (Department of History, University of the North West), No. 45 (September 1999), pp. 101–116.

Thomas, J. "The Politics of Vision and the Archaeologies of Landscape", in B. Bender (ed.), *Landscape: Politics and Perspectives*, pp. 19–48.

Thompson, L. "Co-operation and Conflict: The High Veld", in M. Wilson and L. Thompson (eds.), *The Oxford History of South Africa, Volume I. South Africa to 1870*, pp. 391–446.

Thompson, L.C. "The Ba-Lemba of Southern Rhodesia", in *NADA: Southern Rhodesia Native Affairs Department Annual*, 19, 1942, pp. 72–86.

Turrell, R. "Kimberley: labour and compounds, 1871–1888, in S. Marks and R. Rathbone (eds.), *Industrialisation and Social Change in South Africa*, pp. 45–76.

Van der Heyden, U. (a) "The Fighting Tradition of the Venda People", in *Sechaba*: *Official Organ of the African National Congress of South Africa*, January 1986, pp. 8–12.

(b) "The Archives and Library of the Berlin Mission Society", in *History in Africa: A Journal of Method*, Vol. 23, 1996, pp. 411–427.

Van der Merwe, D.W. "Niklaas Theunissen Koen, 1852–1883, Lewensskets van 'n pioniersendeling onder die Bawenda", in *Kleio*, Deel IX, 1&2, Junie 1977, pp. 22–30.

Van Warmelo, N.J. (a) "Courts and Court Speech in Venda", in *African Studies*, Vol. 30, No. 3–4, 1971, pp. 355–370.

(b) "Volksgebruike van die Venda", in *South African Railways and Harbours Magazine*, Vol. 25, No. 7, July 1931, pp. 998–1000.

Vilakazi, A.L. "Magic and Seperatist or Independent Churches", in G.C. Oosthuizen and I. Hexham (eds.), *Afro-Christian Religion at the grass-roots in Southern Africa*, pp. 164–170.

Wagner, R. "Zoutpansberg: the dynamics of a hunting frontier, 1848–67", in S. Marks and A. Atmore (eds.), *Economy and Society in Pre-Industrial South Africa*, pp. 313–349.

White, L. "Cars out of place: vampires, technology and labour in East and Central Africa", in F. Cooper and A.L. Stoler (eds.), *Tensions of Empire*, pp. 436–460.

Wright, J. "Political Transformations in the Thukela-Mzimkhulu Region in the Late Eighteenth and Early Nineteenth Centuries", in C. Hamilton (ed.), *The Mfecane Aftermath: Reconstructive Debates in Southern African History*, pp. 163–181.

f) Newspapers and magazines

Balic, S. "Change brings muti murders", in *New African*, No. 272, May 1990, pp. 32–33.

De Vaal, J.B. "Yster vir Assegaai se Lem", in *Die Brandwag*, 14 June 1946, pp. 12–13, 56.

Klein, H. "Die Wit Opperhoof Van die Sjangaans", in *Die Brandwag*, 8 July 1938, pp. 8, 9, 43.

Koch, E. and Ritchken, E. "The political economy of witchcraft", in *Weekly Mail*, 23–29 March 1990, pp. 10–11.

The Star, 26 February 2001.

Electronic media and the internet

i) General

Blacking, John. *Venda Girls' Initiation Schools*, Electronic Edition, designed and edited by Suzel Ana Reily and Lev Weinstock, Produced by the Department of Social Anthropology, The Queen's University of

Belfast, co-ordinated by Michael Fischer and David Zeitlyn, March 1998 at http://era.anthropology.ac.uk:

(a) "The Initiation Cycle: vhusha, tshikanda and Domba", at http://era.anthropology.ac.uk/Era_R...aGirls/Introduction/I_GIS_Text.html, accessed 29 September 2000.

(b) "Vhusha", at http://era.anthropology.ac.uk/Era_R...ra/VendaGirls/Vhusha/V_Opening.html, accessed 29 September 2000.

(c) "Tshikanda", at http://era.anthropology.ac.uk/Era_R...VendaGirls/Tshikanda/T_Opening. html (and following links), accessed 29 September 2000.

(d) "The Drama of Thovhela and Tshishonge", at http://era.anthropology.ac.uk/Era_R...a/VendaGirls/Tshikanda/T_Text2. html (and following links), accessed 29 September 2000.

(e) "Domba", at http://era.anthropology.ac.uk/Era_R...Girls/Domba.School/D_00_Opening.html, accessed 21 September 2000.

Buchhorn, Richard *A Taste for Chinese*, (first appeared in *the Skeptic* Vol. 14, No. 1), at http://www.skeptics.com.au/journal/canib-chinese.htm, accessed 15 February 1999.

Fog, Agner *Cultural selection* © 1996, chapter 8: Sociology of deviance, at http://announce.com/agner/cultsel/chap8.html, accessed 25 November 1997.

Giblett, Rod "Cities and Swamp Settling: decolonizing wetlands", in Michèle Drouart (ed.) *Postcolonial Fictions*, SPAN: Journal of the South Pacific Association for Commonwealth Literature and Language Studies Number 36 (1993), electronic edition at http://humpc61.murdoc.edu.au/cntinuum/litserv/SPAN/36/giblett. html, accessed 10 February 1999.

(ii) **Missionalia** *(the Journal of the South African Missiological Society)* **Homepage**

Hayes, Stephen (a) *The African Independent Churches: Judgement through terminology?*, at http://www.geocities.com/ missionalia/aic-stud.htm, accessed 16 October 2000. [See also Articles.]

(b) *Christian Reponses to Witchcraft and Sorcery*, November 1995, at http://www.geocities.com/missionalia/witch1.htm, accessed 16 October 2000.

Le Roux, Magda *African "Jews" for Jesus: A preliminary investigation into the Semitic origins and missionary initiatives of some Lemba communities in southern Africa*, at http://www.geocities.com/missionalia/jews4j1.htm, accessed 16 October 2000. [See also Articles.]

Pakendorf, Gunther "For there is no power but of God": *The Berlin Mission and the Challenges of Colonial South Africa*, at http://www.geocities.com/missionalia/germiss1.htm, accessed 16 October 2000.

Theses, papers, manuscripts and assignments

Albasini III, J. "João Albasini, 1813–1888", pamphlet produced by the Albasini family and printed by Leach Printers, Louis Trichardt, no date (1988?).

Cobbing, J. "Grasping the Nettle: The Slave Trade and the Early Zulu", unpublished paper privately circulated by the author, September 1990.

Conerly, C.J. "The Surrendering of the Lands in the Northern Transvaal of Mahosi Davhana, Makhado, Mphephu and Sinthumule", B.A. Honours thesis, University of Cape Town, 1990.

Dederen, J.M. "Venda for the inquisitive tourist", Tourist Workshop, Department of Anthropology, University of Venda, 1986.

Dreyer, M. "'Welche Gleichgültigkeit! Welch Widerstand!' – Elim Hospital 1899–1906", student seminar paper, University of Basel, 1999.

Elbourne, E. "'To Colonize the Mind': Evangelical Missionaries in Britain and the Eastern Cape, 1790–1837", D.Phil. thesis in Modern History, Oxford University, 1991.

Fish, W.S. "Cows and Kraals: The Early Iron Age, Nandoni and interaction", unpublished paper presented at the international conference "From the Zoutpansberg to the Sea" held at the University of Venda, 16–18 September 1995.

Geschiere, P. "Rubber and Cannibalism: The Germans, the Maka and the Rubberboom in South Cameroon (1900–1914)", unpublished paper presented to the seminar on "Fantasy Spaces – The Power of Images in a Globalizing World", Amsterdam, 27–29 August 1998.

Giesekke, H. "The History of Erdmann Schwellnus in Venda", typed with written comments by family members added, n.d.

Khuba, A.E. "The significance of the Musanda language in Venda: a diglossia", Ph.D. dissertation, Pretoria, University of South Africa, 1993.

Kirkaldy, A. (a) "Makoarele's return to 'the darkness of heathenism': *Khosi* Makwarela and the Berlin Missionaries in Vendaland, C. 1876–1897", unpublished paper presented to the Second CSSALL Interdisciplinary Conference, University of Durban-Westville, 26 September 1997.

(b) "'Digging in the Archives': *Khosi* Masindi Mphaphuli, *Khosi* Makwarela Mphaphuli and the Berlin Missionaries in Vendaland, c.1876–1897", unpublished paper presented to the Biennial Conference of the South African Association of Archaeologists, Thohoyandou, 6 July 1998.

(c) "Capturing the Soul: Encounters between Berlin Missionaries and Tshivenda-speakers in the Late Nineteenth Century", Ph.D. thesis, University of Cape Town, 2002.

Lukhaimane, E.K. "A short history of the Venda", unpublished manuscript held in the Special Collections section of the University of Venda Library, n.d.

Malunga, W.F. "A Century of Dutch Reformed Church Missionary Enterprise in the Soutpansberg Area – the story of Kranspoort", M.A. thesis, University of the North, 31 January 1986.

Meintjes, S.M. (a) "Law and Authority on a Nineteenth Century Mission Station in Natal", University of the Witwatersrand, History Workshop Conference, Class Community and Conflict: Local Perspectives, February 1994. [Note that the second initial is absent here.]

(b) "Edendale 1850–1906: A Case Study of Rural Transformation and Class Formation in an African Mission in Natal", Ph.D. thesis, School of Oriental and African Studies, University of London, 1988.

Mminele, S.P.P. "The Berlin Lutheran Missionary Enterprise at Botshabelo, 1865–1955: An Historical-Educational Study", Master of Education thesis, University of the North, 1983.

Mudau, J.R. "A Short History of the Mphaphuli Dynasty, 1689–1990", B.A. Honours thesis, University of Venda, 1990.

Nemadodzi, M.P. "Main themes in the history of Venda over the past twenty-five years", unpublished History 300 Assignment, University of Venda, 10 June 1991.

Nemudzivhadi, M.H. "The attempts by Makhado to revive the Venda kingdom 1864–1895", Ph.D. thesis, Potchefstroom University for Christian National Higher Education, Vaal Triangle Campus, 1998.

Nettleton, A.C.E. "The Traditional Figurative Woodcarving of the Shona and Venda", Ph.D. thesis, University of the Witwatersrand, 1984 (3 Volumes).

Niehaus, I.A. "Witchcraft, Power and Politics: An Ethnographic Study of the South African Lowveld", Ph.D. thesis, University of the Witwatersrand, 1997.

Ralushai, N.M.N. (a) "Conflicting Accounts of Venda History with Particular Reference to the Role of Mutupo in Social Organization", Ph.D. thesis, Queen's University of Belfast, 1977.

(b) "A Preliminary Report on the Early History of Thulamela Archaeological Site", Unpublished report, Kruger National Park/ Thulamela Project, n.d. (1997). [Note that his initials here appear as N.V.]

Thavhiwa, T.N. "Elim Hospital: Pure, Medical and political Administration, 1899–1997", B.A. Honours thesis, University of Venda, 1998.

Van der Merwe, D.W. "Van Paternalisme tot Selfbeskikking: Die Berlynse Sendinggenootskap en Kerkstigting in Transvaal, 1904–1962, D.Litt. et

Phil. thesis, University of South Africa, 1980. [Subsequently published as *Die Berlynse Sendinggenootskap en Kerkstigting in Transvaal, 1904–1962*, Argiefjaarboek vir Suid-Afrikaanse Geskiedenis, Pretoria, Staatsdrukker, 1987, Deel II.]

Van Ryneveld, T.A. "Remembering Albasini", M.A. thesis, University of Cape Town, 1998.

INDEX

African Initiated Churches, 189, 255
African Religion, 11, 12, 187, 254, 255, 275
Albasini, João, 22, 130, 191, 198, 267
Allison, James, 41, 42, 43, 47, 51, 62, 255
Amalienstein, 91
Amoebic dysentery, 59
ancestors, 13, 16, 45, 137, 176, 178, 179, 180, 181, 183, 188, 189, 205, 212, 220, 239, 253, 261, 266, 282
ancestral copper rings, 179
ancestral iron rings, 179, 181
ancestral spears, 179, 181
ancestral spirits, 172, 175, 180, 223, 257
Anhalt-Schmidt, 100
anthropophagy, 208, 234, 269, 272, 274, 275. *See also* cannibalism
apprentices, 22, 88
baboons, 48, 125
badgers, 50
BaLobedu, 37
bananas, 125, 127, 145, 150
baobabs, 151
Bartholomäuskirche, 102
Basotho, 27, 126, 130, 204, 224, 225, 226
BaTlokwa, 20
Baumbach, 26, 47, 52, 53, 54, 56
Baumhöfner, Dietrich, 87, 91, 108, 109, 111, 134, 231, 259, 260, 266
beads, 152, 159
beer, 44, 95, 126, 151, 161, 171, 174, 176, 177, 257, 258
Belingwe Province, 168
Berthoud, Paul, 74
Bethanien, 82
Bethel, 82
Beuster (Brache), Elisabeth, 84
Beuster (Koboldt, born Oberländer), Emma, 70, 84, 216
Beuster, Carl, 26, 27, 37, 38, 39, 40, 43, 44, 46, 49, 50, 51, 54, 55, 56, 57, 59, 60, 61, 62, 63, 64, 65, 66, 67, 68, 69, 70, 71, 72, 73, 74, 84, 85, 86, 87, 88, 89, 90, 91, 94, 104, 105, 106, 108, 110, 111, 130, 131, 132, 133, 134, 135, 137, 150, 151, 152, 153, 155, 168, 169, 170, 171, 172, 173, 179, 180, 181, 182, 183, 184, 187, 188, 189, 190, 191, 192, 193, 198, 206, 207, 208, 210, 211, 213, 214, 215, 216, 217, 218, 222, 226, 227, 228, 231, 243, 244, 245, 246, 247, 252, 260, 261, 262, 263, 264, 267, 268, 269, 283
Beyer, 26, 27, 43, 47, 52, 53, 54, 55, 58, 60, 63, 123, 124, 125, 126, 127, 169, 175

Bibles, 46, 57, 84, 92, 148, 168, 257, 281
birds, 48, 125
blankets, 155, 159
Blauberg, 26, 43, 47, 55, 57, 58, 59, 60, 85, 86, 127, 128, 169
Blouberg, 18, 19, 123
Boachi, Kwasi, 273
bodies, 13, 151, 152, 156, 158, 174, 177, 178, 203, 221, 226, 228, 234, 248, 269, 270, 273
body, 13, 14, 52, 57, 62, 67, 72, 73, 80, 100, 108, 111, 134, 152, 154, 155, 156, 157, 170, 171, 175, 182, 184, 185, 197, 199, 203, 221, 222, 223, 228, 232, 246, 248, 262, 263, 271, 272
Boers, 15, 20, 22, 23, 24, 25, 30, 37, 38, 39, 40, 41, 42, 48, 49, 50, 55, 69, 132, 188, 227, 265, 274
books, 11, 55, 68, 95, 111, 131, 257. *See also* Bibles
Botshabelo, 27, 84, 85, 86, 87, 90, 91, 105, 131, 231, 232, 234, 268
buffalos, 126, 192
bulls, 190, 219, 220
Buys brothers, 19, 20
Buys people, 25, 46
Buys, Coenraad, 19, 20
Buys, Gabriël, 20
Buys, Michael, 20
cannibalism, 149, 203, 222, 223, 224, 225, 226, 227, 228, 229, 230, 231, 232, 233, 234, 248, 249, 263, 270, 271, 272, 274. *See also* anthropophagy
Cape Colony, 11, 19, 21, 37, 41, 82, 90, 91, 100, 103, 254
Cape Town, 82, 91, 284, 293
cattle, 16, 20, 38, 40, 44, 48, 124, 129, 135, 138, 150, 152, 176, 180, 181, 191, 192, 194, 197, 206, 221, 225, 226, 239, 241, 242
chickens, 101
children, 19, 23, 43, 44, 45, 46, 56, 59, 61, 66, 85, 86, 87, 90, 91, 100, 101, 102, 103, 106, 109, 110, 132, 134, 138, 157, 158, 159, 160, 161, 162, 180, 188, 189, 190, 192, 193, 208, 214, 215, 216, 217, 218, 221, 230, 231, 234, 241, 242, 246, 251, 257, 259, 263
China, 82
cholera, 58
Christianenburg, 56, 86, 91
Christianity, 11, 14, 29, 37, 39, 43, 44, 46, 52, 59, 62, 63, 64, 65, 67, 70, 71, 72, 92, 106, 134, 139, 140, 149, 152, 189,

198, 203, 210, 227, 231, 232, 239, 240, 251, 252, 253, 254, 255, 256, 259, 260, 266, 272, 273, 275
Christians, 11, 13, 37, 43, 47, 50, 51, 52, 53, 54, 59, 61, 62, 63, 64, 65, 66, 67, 68, 72, 79, 88, 95, 97, 101, 105, 106, 107, 111, 112, 152, 155, 157, 161, 163, 167, 189, 191, 206, 215, 217, 218, 232, 253, 256, 257, 258, 265, 271, 281
Chuniespoort River, 124
circumcision, 13, 50, 59, 156, 167, 203, 204, 205, 206, 207, 208, 209, 210, 282, 283
class, 12, 83, 92, 99, 121, 250
cloth, 108, 155, 185, 194, 224
clothing, 13, 55, 56, 57, 69, 100, 108, 111, 133, 146, 147, 148, 150, 151, 152, 154, 155, 156, 157, 158, 159, 160, 161, 162, 163, 174, 185, 187, 192, 208, 219, 225, 243, 249, 251, 263, 264, 270
coffee, 105, 154
commando, 22
conventicle, 11, 37, 43, 47, 52, 68
conversion, 13, 37, 40, 45, 51, 80, 81, 83, 87, 88, 100, 105, 150, 167, 174, 198, 203, 213, 232, 239, 253, 254, 255, 259, 260, 264, 266, 267, 274, 275
converts, 11, 13, 14, 28, 29, 30, 37, 38, 43, 47, 52, 59, 62, 67, 71, 94, 95, 98, 104, 106, 134, 146, 154, 156, 161, 163, 205, 209, 210, 219, 224, 233, 239, 244, 253, 256, 257, 267
copper, 16
councillors, 67, 69, 96, 137, 172, 195, 198, 205, 212, 249, 257, 259, 266
cremation, 176, 182
crocodiles, 136, 147
culture, 12, 17, 102, 104, 137, 139, 145, 147, 153, 155, 183, 198, 207, 239, 274
curriculum, 92, 210
dagga, 246, 264
dancing, 54, 105, 149, 151, 158, 159, 182, 183, 184, 185, 204, 207, 257, 262, 264
Daniel, 170, 198
dark forests, 13, 139, 150, 163
dark hearts, 13, 139, 150
darkness, 12, 14, 48, 55, 99, 122, 125, 126, 131, 139, 140, 146, 147, 149, 150, 151, 167, 176, 179, 198, 223, 267, 272, 273
dassies, 50
Davhana, 98
Delagoa Bay, 18, 265
Denga, David, 11, 47, 48, 49, 50, 52, 70, 71, 72, 73, 74, 75, 215, 222, 223, 243

Dhlo Dhlo, 18
diamond fields, 41, 194, 257, 258, 281
Difaqane, 230. *See also Mfecane*
divine, 40, 170, 176, 178, 191
divine kingship, 176, 177, 178
domba, 159, 171, 210
Dombu, Jeremiah, 95
Dorpsrivier, 123
dreams, 252, 253, 254, 266
dresses, 162, 163
drought, 24, 155, 252, 258
Dunant, Henry, 273
Dutch, 18, 22, 25, 26, 46, 53, 55, 59, 90, 92, 100, 149, 214, 274
Dzata, 16, 18, 19, 178, 281
dzinanga, 65, 184, 185, 186, 187, 188, 189, 190, 197. *See also mingome*, witch-doctors, *Zauberdoktoren* and *Zauberer*
Early Iron Age, 16, 296
East Africa, 82, 90
elephants, 21, 242
Elijah, 255
Elim, 30, 134, 227
Ellenberger, D. Fred., 225, 226, 228, 231
Emmaus, 82
Englishmen, 23, 41
environment, 12, 13, 103, 122, 128, 130, 132, 134, 137, 139, 140, 150, 151, 153, 160, 163, 196, 225
Eucalyptus, 133
eyes, 41, 43, 56, 99, 104, 110, 111, 122, 123, 124, 128, 135, 138, 148, 151, 156, 157, 162, 174, 175, 178, 192, 195, 196, 213, 224, 244, 245, 248, 262, 267, 270
Famadi, 182
famine, 24, 28, 108, 182, 273
feasting, 54
fever, 12, 25, 84, 88, 90, 105, 106, 107, 108, 130, 131, 132, 133, 134
Fisher, Christine, 85
Flygare, Johannes, 28
forests, 55, 122, 123, 125, 126, 127, 129, 133, 136, 137, 139, 145, 147, 148, 149, 150, 151, 171, 172, 173, 174, 185, 192, 246, 248, 267
Franke, Therese, 90
Franz, 215, 216
Friedrichshain, 103
Fuzane, David, 214, 215
gardens, 24, 48, 72, 123, 127, 150, 151, 155
gaze, 13, 147, 156, 157, 162, 163, 175, 270

INDEX

Georgenholtz, 27, 28, 29, 87, 89, 90, 91, 95, 102, 104, 105, 106, 108, 110, 134, 136, 138, 139, 150, 161, 170, 176, 180, 183, 184, 187, 191, 193, 196, 198, 204, 206, 211, 239, 251, 255, 256, 257, 260, 261, 264, 269, 273
Gerlachshoop, 82
Gernecke, Carl, 90, 134, 273
Gertrudsburg, 30, 87, 91, 162
Giesekke family, 134
Giesekke, Ludwig, 273
goats, 60, 61, 124, 138, 176, 183, 187, 274
God's gardens, 13, 139, 150, 163
Goedewensch, 21
Gondo, 71
gone native, 99
Gottschling, Ernst, 91, 171, 176, 198, 212, 224
grain, 155, 245
Great Zimbabwe, 17
Grita, 95
Gründler, 198
Grützner, Heinrich, 21, 26, 27, 59, 103, 128, 129, 130
Gunhuvkuvhu, 171
guns, 21, 22, 23, 39, 41, 42, 48, 50, 51, 52, 128, 139, 147, 190, 204, 240
Gutu, 90
Haarlem, 100
Haggard, H. Rider, 225
half-civilised, 155, 249, 250
Hanglip, 124
harvest, 180, 182, 192, 221, 222, 265
Harz Mountains, 124, 129
hats, 146, 162, 163
Ha-Tshivhase, 13, 27, 28, 29, 57, 59, 66, 68, 69, 70, 71, 74, 84, 85, 86, 87, 88, 89, 90, 91, 94, 106, 128, 130, 134, 135, 137, 150, 188, 189, 193, 199, 206, 207, 211, 214, 217, 231, 243, 261, 267, 269
Heart of Darkness, 12, 94, 99
heathens and heathenism, 13, 43, 48, 51, 54, 62, 67, 68, 71, 73, 81, 85, 87, 88, 98, 100, 101, 102, 104, 106, 107, 111, 121, 127, 132, 134, 135, 139, 147, 148, 149, 150, 155, 156, 157, 158, 159, 160, 161, 167, 169, 184, 188, 191, 193, 196, 197, 198, 205, 206, 209, 211, 213, 214, 217, 218, 222, 223, 232, 244, 247, 248, 250, 253, 256, 257, 259, 260, 262, 264, 265, 267, 269, 270, 271, 273, 275
Heese, Daniel, 90
Heese, Paul, 90
Heese, Paula, Bertha, 90
hell, 61, 252, 253
Herbertsdale, 91
hippopotami, 136
hoes, 93, 151, 182, 206, 207, 222
Hofmeyr, Stéfanus, 25
Holtz, Georg, 104
Holy Forests, 171, 172, 173, 174, 180, 182, 198
horses, 39, 42, 54, 85, 123, 135, 193, 194, 196, 243, 246, 250
housing, 56, 70, 71, 74, 86, 104, 105, 106, 123, 124, 127, 128, 133, 138, 152, 154, 155, 156, 159, 160, 162, 173, 174, 212, 219, 223, 249
human fat, 226, 228, 231
human flesh, 158, 207, 208, 222, 225, 226, 227, 228, 231, 232, 233, 234, 248, 263, 269, 270, 271
human skin, 221, 263
hunting, 16, 19, 20, 21, 22, 23, 37, 39, 48, 49, 225, 226, 240, 284
hyenas, 139
hymns, 46, 111
inboekelinge, 22, 37, 38, 48, 59. See also apprentices
iron, 14, 16, 104, 138, 154, 222, 223, 263, 269
Isaiah, 65, 66
ivory, 21, 194
Jaques, Auguste, 227, 228
Jensen, Rasmus, 96, 98
Johanna, 95
Johannesburg, 90, 91, 161, 233
Joseph, 58, 59, 60
Junod, Henri-Alexandre, 99
K2, 16
Karanga, 48, 49, 168, 170, 184
Khoisan, 27, 82, 94, 100, 101, 102, 112
khoro, 96, 179, 186, 249
khotsi-munene, 26, 182, 205, 281
Khuswane, 170
Kimberley, 41, 281
Klatt (Auerbach), Helene, 91
Klatt, Otto, 87, 91, 96
Knopneusen, 20, 132, 198, 205, 208
Koboldt, Heinrich, 70, 84, 216
Koboldt, Maria, 70, 84
Koen (Bröse), Maria, 102, 103, 105, 106
Koen, Gerhard August Peter, 106
Koen, Hedwig, 106
Koen, Klaas, 12, 27, 56, 83, 84, 87, 88, 94, 100, 101, 102, 103, 104, 105, 106, 107, 108, 109, 110, 111, 112, 134, 136,

138, 150, 151, 157, 180, 183, 184, 187, 193, 204, 206, 211, 231, 249, 250, 251, 252, 253, 254, 255, 256, 257, 258, 259, 260, 266, 267
Koen, Piet, 100, 101
Köhler, Bruno, 26, 84
Kokwane, 170
Kranskop, 70, 84
Krausc, Oswald, 85, 96, 97, 98
Kreuzburg, 90
Kruger National Park, 17
Kruger, Paul, 22, 23
Kühl, Robert, 84
Kurulen, 30
labia minora, 13, 203, 210
labour, 20, 24, 37, 38, 40, 41, 49, 50, 67, 87, 93, 129, 130, 151, 152, 153, 163, 222, 259
Ladysmith, 91, 134
Laingsburg, 91
Lake Fundudzi, 171
Lalumbe, Asaf, 161
Lalumbe, Mashudu, 161
Lalumbe, Miryam, 161
Lalumbe, Nathanael (Nathaniel), 105, 106, 161
Lalumbe, Nathanael (Nathaniel) Jr., 161
Lambane, 71, 176, 182
Landesdoktorei, 187
landscape, 12, 25, 26, 112, 121, 122, 124, 125, 126, 128, 130, 131, 134, 135, 137, 140, 158
Lekgalekgale, 57, 58
Lemba, 198, 204, 208, 283
Lembethu, 17
leopards, 126, 138, 139, 192, 197
light, 12, 40, 42, 99, 101, 122, 124, 131, 139, 140, 146, 147, 149, 150, 151, 175, 182, 196, 198, 206, 213, 223, 227, 232, 233, 254, 265, 267
Limpopo, 15, 16, 17, 18, 25, 151, 242
lions, 39, 62, 137, 138, 139
Lobengula, 242
loin-cloths, 55, 57, 147, 270
losha, 177, 212
Lottering, 25
Luvhengo, Paulus, 70, 71, 215, 243, 244
Luvhimbi, 254
Luvuvhu River, 15, 23, 267
Lwamondo, 19, 55, 205, 224, 225, 228, 245
Mabunyu, 242
Madima, Johannes, 90, 172
Madzhie, 20, 23, 26

Madzivhandila, 19, 27, 172, 173, 190, 205, 209, 210
Magdalena, 95, 96
Magoro, 249, 263
magota, 16, 19, 30, 171, 179, 207, 209, 211, 281, 282
mahosi, 13, 15, 16, 18, 19, 23, 24, 25, 26, 30, 67, 135, 136, 170, 171, 174, 176, 177, 178, 179, 182, 186, 197, 203, 204, 205, 210, 211, 217, 219, 221, 239, 240, 242, 247, 253, 281, 282
Mahumane, 18
maine a tshele, 185
maize, 55, 109, 123, 124, 126, 151, 152, 155, 161, 257, 271
Makapanspoort, 57, 124
Makgabêng, 26, 124, 128
Makhado, 15, 19, 23, 24, 25, 26, 27, 30, 49, 52, 53, 54, 123, 125, 126, 136, 169, 198, 204, 205, 209, 245, 249, 265, 267, 269
Makhado/Louis Trichardt, 20, 25, 30
Makhahane, 17
malaria, 19, 22, 23, 30, 59, 74, 91, 122, 130, 131, 132, 133, 134, 188
Malokông, 84
malombo, 167, 182, 183, 184, 185, 186, 198, 257
Maluleke, Franz, 110, 260
Mamatepha, Khashane, 266
Maneledzi, 171
Mangale, 188, 190
Mankopane, 57
Maphophe, 245
Maphuphe, 19, 205
Mapungubwe, 17
Marabastad, 23
Margaretha, 96
Martha, 96
Marula, 125
Mashau, 204
Mashonaland, 82, 90
Masia, 98
matangwa, 204
Matlala, 58, 59, 84, 85, 124, 131, 173
Matsheke, 170, 198
Matshema, 17
Mauch, Carl, 224, 225
Maune, 124
Mavhungo, 109
Mawewe, 21
Mbedzi, 17, 171, 182
mbila, 246
McKidd, Alexander, 25

INDEX 315

meadows, 122, 125, 129, 150
Medingen, 266
Meister, Johann, 88, 89, 90, 91, 231, 269
men, 22, 37, 42, 43, 51, 54, 55, 58, 61, 89, 96, 97, 129, 147, 148, 151, 155, 157, 159, 160, 162, 175, 181, 184, 186, 187, 190, 203, 204, 206, 207, 209, 210, 212, 213, 226, 230, 248, 249, 257, 258, 261, 271, 283
Merensky, Alexander, 22, 26, 132, 149, 231, 233, 234, 249
Methodist, 41, 62
Mfecane, 226, 230, 231
Mianzwi, 17
miasma, 132, 133
milayo, 204, 207
Miluwani, 239, 240
mingome, 189, 190, 192, 195, 196, 282.
  See also *dzinanga*, witch-doctors, *Zauberdoktoren and Zauberer*
Moafé, Maria, 95
Modimolle, 84
Modjaji, 266
mofula, 172
Mohlomi, 225, 226
Moletshe, 124
Moloko, 17
monkeys, 125
Moshoeshoe, 226
Mossel Bay, 91
Mount Belingwe, 168
Mountain Kaffirs, 224
mountains, 17, 18, 19, 20, 23, 24, 25, 38, 53, 54, 58, 104, 122, 123, 124, 125, 126, 127, 129, 130, 132, 133, 134, 135, 147, 150, 169, 170, 193, 231, 245
Mozambique, 21, 22
Mp'hôme, 87, 94
Mphaphuli, 14, 19, 23, 24, 49, 71, 73, 199, 205, 235, 240, 245, 262, 264
Mphaphuli, Makwarela, 14, 27, 48, 67, 71, 89, 95, 104, 105, 106, 108, 109, 111, 155, 183, 187, 191, 195, 196, 197, 198, 206, 210, 218, 239, 240, 241, 242, 243, 244, 245, 249, 250, 251, 252, 253, 254, 255, 256, 257, 258, 259, 260, 261, 263, 264, 265, 266, 267, 268, 269, 270, 271, 272, 273, 274, 275
Mphaphuli, Masithi, 254
Mphaphuli, Matshekeketsheke, 195, 196, 239, 256, 258
Mphaphuli, Murumo, 273
Mphaphuli, Ranwedzi, 14, 19, 27, 109, 187, 206, 215, 218, 227, 228, 239, 240, 241, 242, 243, 244, 245, 246, 247, 248, 249, 252, 253, 254, 258, 259, 261, 262, 263, 266, 267, 268, 269, 270, 273, 274
Mphaphuli, Ratsibi, 239, 242
Mphaphuli, Tshikalange, 218, 240, 241, 242, 267, 268, 269, 273, 275
Mphephu, 15, 19, 23, 25, 30, 161, 205, 272
Mubvumela Mountain, 168, 169, 171
Muhali-muhulu, 168
mungome, 188, 282
Murray, Charles, 26
murundu, 13, 203, 204, 205, 206, 207, 208, 209, 210, 211
muruthu, 195
Mutakolwe, 17
Mutale, 17
Mutale River, 17
muti, 177, 219, 223, 271, 272, 284
Mutle, 26, 84, 124
Mutshaeni, Johanna (Mufanatsho), 46, 47
Mutshaeni, Johannes, 11, 37, 38, 39, 40, 41, 42, 43, 44, 46, 47, 48, 49, 50, 52, 55, 56, 57, 59, 61, 63, 65, 67, 68, 69, 70, 71, 72, 73, 74, 75, 137, 154, 172, 210, 214, 215, 222, 223, 243, 244
Mutshindudi River, 137, 172, 198
mutupo, 194
Mwali, 168, 171, 261
Mwali (Mwari), 18
Mzila, 21
Mzilikazi, 242
Nagabe, 240
naked, 100, 124, 137, 147, 148, 157, 187, 208, 211, 270
Nako, 132
nanga, 282
Natal, 11, 21, 37, 40, 41, 44, 47, 50, 51, 56, 59, 60, 62, 63, 66, 68, 82, 86, 87, 90, 91, 105, 129, 134, 155, 213, 214, 255
Native Assistants, 53, 68, 72, 75, 89, 106, 132, 136, 215, 218, 260. See also Native Evangelists
Native Evangelists, 162, 260, 266. See also Native Assistants
Ndebele, 27, 130, 242
ndilo, 194, 282
Ndjabane, 227, 228, 229
Neitz, Johannes, 90
Nethathe, 172
Netshaulu, 71
Netshiendeulu, 17
Netshitongani, 172

Ngoma Lungundu, 18, 283
Ngona, 171, 182
Ngovela, 159
Njamande, 219
Nyai, 17
Nzhelele, 18, 19, 137, 170, 245, 261
Olifants River, 18, 124
Oorlamstaal, 59
opgaaf, 20
oxen, 48, 50, 56, 57, 176, 180, 190, 208, 225, 242, 248, 249, 258
palms, 125, 148, 149, 150, 192
paternalism, 93, 94, 95, 260
Paulus, 109, 110, 247
Pedi, 15, 20, 37, 51, 52, 82, 224, 231, 232
penis, 161
People of the Book, 43, 61, 65, 74
petite-bourgeois, 12
Phiphidi, 137, 171
Pietermaritzburg, 41, 56, 57
Pietersburg (Polokwane), 23, 90, 91
Pietism, 80, 83, 281
pigs, 126, 139, 246
pioneers of culture, 13, 139
polygyny, 38, 40, 44, 59, 60, 62, 63, 65
Poroa, 198, 267
Port Elizabeth, 37, 85
Portuguese, 19, 150, 265, 272
Potgieter, Hendrik Andries, 20
praise-names, 128, 174, 175, 177, 241
prayers, 39, 253
Prietsch, 100, 101, 102, 109
rain, 105, 123, 130, 132, 135, 152, 190, 222, 252, 254, 258
Raknopa, Paulus, 191
Raluvhimba, 168, 169, 170, 178, 282
Ramabulana, 19, 20, 205
Ramavhoya, 20
Rammba, Dorka (Rambau, Dorkus?), 98
Ranwedzi Mphaphuli, 240
Ravele, 19
reading, 26, 42, 43, 46, 57, 65, 67, 145, 195, 231, 234, 245, 248, 249, 250, 251, 252, 254, 257, 259, 260, 271
Reuter, Friedrich, 96, 97, 98
Reuter, Fritz, 266, 267
ritual homicide, 14, 203, 219, 221, 250, 284
ritual homicide – burial of subjects with rulers, 193, 219
rivers, 15, 17, 18, 99, 105, 122, 125, 126, 129, 130, 131, 132, 133, 135, 136, 137, 145, 146, 147, 150, 173, 181, 204, 207, 210, 211, 219

Riversdale, 90, 91
roads, 38, 52, 67, 68, 70, 124, 127, 145, 150, 152, 187, 220, 221, 259, 271
royal mortuary rites, 171, 176, 182, 193, 219, 220
Ruth, 95
sacred, 127, 136, 169, 171, 176, 177, 179, 212, 220, 221, 261, 282
sacred (supernatural) lion, 172
sacred bulls, 180, 181
sacred cattle, 179
sacred cows, 180
sacred goats, 179
sacred river pools, 182
sacred rivers, 176
sacred snakes, 176
sacred stones, 176, 179, 181
Salmonellosis, 59
salt, 16, 20, 21, 25, 152
Samuel, 52, 53, 54, 104, 124, 126, 127
Satan, 13, 67, 88, 99, 138, 167, 168, 190, 197, 213, 245, 251, 264
Schoemansdal, 20, 21, 22, 23, 24, 25, 38, 49, 123, 159
Schroda, 16
Schwellnus (Manz), Dorothea, 86, 87, 155
Schwellnus, Erdmann, 27, 65, 73, 83, 84, 86, 89, 103, 104, 108, 111, 125, 138, 145, 146, 149, 154, 172, 173, 190, 206, 209, 231
Schwellnus, Theodor, 96
Sekhukhune, 26, 84, 124, 232
Sekwati, 232
semen, 161
sermons, 42, 59, 68
Sesotho, 17, 227
severed hands, 262
severed heads, 250
sewing, 151, 155, 251
sexual harassment, 95
Shaka, 18, 179, 250
sheep, 124
Shona, 17
Singo, 15, 17, 18, 19, 137, 171, 178, 182, 205
skin, 100, 103, 108, 151, 156, 163, 219, 239, 246, 249
skins, 57, 139, 154, 192
skulls, 221
skuts, 21
smallpox, 30, 41, 72, 73, 74, 132, 222, 223
snakes, 12, 138, 197
snuff, 49, 175, 177, 210

Solomon, 11, 37, 42, 43, 46, 47, 52, 53, 54, 57, 58, 59, 60, 61, 62, 63, 65, 66, 85, 136
Sonntag, Christoph, 98
sorghum, 123, 126
Sotho, 15, 17, 25, 26, 37, 46, 53, 57, 58, 70, 86, 87, 127, 204, 207, 247, 249, 268
Soutpansberg, 17, 20, 26, 49, 123, 150. *See also* Zoutpansberg
Spelonken, 123, 157, 159, 162, 283
Stech, Carl, 12, 26, 27, 54, 55, 56, 57, 58, 59, 60, 62, 63, 84, 85, 94, 112, 130, 131, 134, 231
Steelpoort River, 51
Stoffel, 215, 216, 218
strangulation, 20, 46, 176, 220, 232
succession disputes, 18, 20, 241
Sudeten Mountains, 124, 129
suits, 162, 163
supernatural defences of villages, 67, 220, 221, 268
superstition, 13, 54, 135, 149, 167, 176, 187, 193, 197, 227, 228, 271, 284
Swazi, 132, 242
tailoring, 155, 161, 251
thangu, 66, 188, 190, 193, 194, 282
Tharant, 127
Thathe Vondo, 172
Thavhatsinde, 171, 182
Thengwe, 151, 176
Thoho-ya-Ndou, 19
thondo, 13, 167, 203, 204, 206, 211, 212, 213
thorns, 270
Thovhela, 18, 170
Thula Mela, 17
Thutloane, 84, 86
tigers, 126, 137, 139, 192, 197
Timotheus, 97
tobacco, 49
Totane (also known as Piet), 11, 37, 41, 42, 43, 44, 45, 46, 61, 63, 64, 65, 66, 67, 68, 213
trade, 16, 17, 21, 23, 41, 152, 154, 188, 234, 267, 283
traders, 16, 19, 23, 125, 155, 265, 283
Trechardt (Trichardt), Louis, 20
trees, 74, 101, 103, 123, 125, 127, 129, 130, 131, 133, 145, 148, 150, 151, 160, 162, 168, 172, 173, 188, 209
Tropenkollered, 99
trousers, 146, 155, 161, 174, 185
Trümpelmann, 26
tsetse, 50

Tshakhuma, 19, 27, 28, 29, 47, 55, 70, 86, 89, 91, 95, 97, 103, 104, 107, 136, 138, 150, 154, 155, 162, 172, 190, 209, 267, 273
Tshaluvhimbi, 17
Tshamaano, 176
Tshamatangwi, 204
Tshiendeulu, 18
Tshififi, 268
Tshiheni, 38, 41
tshikanda, 171, 210
Tshikaranga, 185
tshikona, 159
tshikumo, 220
Tshikundu, 138
Tshikwarakwara, 104
tshilombo, 184, 185
Tshilonge, 171
Tshimange, August, 191
Tshitaka tsha Makoleni, 17
Tshitungulu, 173
Tshivenda, 15, 16, 17, 27, 53, 57, 58, 68, 84, 86, 127, 128, 160, 172, 182, 185, 204, 224, 266, 268, 272, 281, 284
Tshivhase, 19, 23, 24, 26, 27, 37, 38, 43, 44, 47, 52, 53, 54, 55, 62, 63, 65, 66, 67, 69, 70, 85, 89, 123, 125, 126, 127, 128, 129, 130, 133, 135, 137, 169, 172, 174, 176, 189, 192, 193, 205, 206, 207, 209, 210, 211, 214, 215, 216, 217, 219, 245, 246, 247, 261, 263, 264, 267, 268, 269, 273
Tshivhase, Luvhengo, 209
Tsonga-Shangaan, 15, 20, 21, 22, 23, 25, 37, 154, 208, 219, 282
Tswana, 17, 53, 57, 127
twins, 13, 45, 156, 203, 213, 214, 215, 216, 217, 218, 219, 265
u pembela, 177, 178, 181
vagina, 160, 161
Valdezia, 30, 74
van der Goltz, Maria, 94
van Warmelo, N.J. (Rev.), 24
Vendaland, 28, 29
Verdun, 17
vhaloi, 189, 190, 191, 192, 193, 194, 196, 233, 282, 283. *See also* Zauberer
VhaMbedzi, 168
Vhangona, 17
VhaSenzi, 168, 261, 283
vhukunda ha mulenzhe, 161
vhukunda tshotshane, 161
vhusha, 13, 203, 210, 211
vhutuka, 13, 203, 204, 211

von Kröcher, Frau, 102
Voortrekkers, 20
wages, 12, 38
waistcoats, 146, 147, 185
Wangemann, Hermann Theodor, 68, 79, 103, 104, 105, 107, 131, 149, 155, 159, 198, 231, 232, 233, 234, 260, 264, 272
war, 15, 19, 21, 23, 24, 25, 49, 150, 152, 156, 158, 205, 207, 212, 221, 227, 229, 248, 261, 262, 263, 264, 265, 267, 268, 269, 270, 271, 272, 273, 274
warfare, 24, 156, 158, 221, 222, 227, 240, 241, 250, 261, 272
warriors, 20, 149, 158, 160, 177, 212, 227, 246, 249, 262, 263, 267, 269, 270
Waterberg, 23, 41, 70, 87, 90, 215, 216, 247
Wedepohl, Johannes, 90
Wessmann, Reinhold, 12, 84, 89, 94, 95, 96, 97, 98, 99, 100, 112, 134, 139, 157, 158, 159, 170, 174, 175, 177, 179, 181, 182, 193, 194, 195, 196, 197, 198, 213, 221, 231, 261, 264, 265, 267, 268, 269, 270, 273
Westphal, Gotthardt, 158, 160, 161
wild-man, 137
witchcraft, 45, 60, 190, 198, 221, 229, 283, 284
witch-doctors, 69, 192, 193, 194, 196, 197, 263. See also dzinanga, mingome, Zauberdoktoren and Zauberer
women, 22, 23, 56, 66, 85, 95, 97, 98, 107, 128, 151, 155, 157, 158, 159, 162, 174, 177, 182, 184, 186, 190, 194, 203, 204, 207, 208, 210, 211, 230, 248, 257, 258, 263, 271, 283
Xikundu, 23
Zauberdoktoren, 192, 194, 199. See also dzinanga, mingome, witch-doctors and Zauberer
Zauberei, 60, 135, 186, 284
Zauberer, 72, 167, 187, 190, 193, 196, 252, 253, 258, 284. See also dzinanga, mingome, vhaloi, witch-doctors and Zauberdoktoren
Zimbabwe, 17, 18, 48, 90, 168, 283
Zoutpansberg, 21, 23, 24, 26, 125, 132, 162, 191, 219, 224. See also Soutpansberg
Zulu, 26, 41, 82, 125, 179, 226, 242, 250
zwidudwane, 137, 171